supervision
in the hospitality industry

supervision
in the hospitality industry

FOURTH EDITION

Jack E. Miller

John R. Walker

Karen Eich Drummond

 JOHN WILEY & SONS, INC.

Published by John Wiley & Sons, Inc., Hoboken, New Jersey
Published simultaneously in Canada.

For general information on our other products and services or for technical support, please contact our
Customer Care Department within the United States at (800) 762-2974, outside the United States at (317)
572-3993 or fax (317) 572-4002.

Wiley also publishes its books in a variety of electronic formats. Some content that appears in print may not
be available in electronic books.

Library of Congress Cataloging-in-Publication Data:
Miller, Jack E., 1930–
   Supervision in the hospitality industry / Jack Miller, John Walker,
Karen Drummond.—4th ed.
      p. cm.
   ISBN 0-471-39689-3
   1. Hospitality industry—Personnel management.   I. Walker, John R.,
1944– II. Drummond, Karen Eich. III. Title.
   TX911.3.P4 M55 2001
   647.94′068′3—dc21

Printed in the United States of America.

10   9   8   7   6   5   4   3   2   1

∾ dedication

To the late Jack Miller. Also to the students and professors of the many colleges and universities using this book.

❧ contents

✬ chapter 3

Workplace Diversity   52

✬ chapter 4

Communicating Effectively   69

∾ chapter 5

Creating a Positive Work Climate   103

❧ chapter 6

Developing Job Expectations   139

❧ chapter 7

Recruiting and Selecting Applicants 170

❧ chapter 8

Employee Training and Development 218

∾ chapter 9

Evaluating Performance   256

❧ chapter 10

Discipline and the Marginal Employee 287

❧ chapter 11

Planning, Organizing, and Controlling 331

∾ chapter 12

Decision Making and Problem Solving   366

∾ chapter 13

Delegating   396

∾ chapter 14

Additional Supervisory Topics 420

⚋ preface

Ask any hospitality manager what their greatest challenge is, and they will probably reply, "finding and keeping employees." For many recent college graduates, supervision is an added challenge because they may be promoted quickly because of their degree and hourly work experience, but often they have no supervisory experience.

This book is a primer to the management of people in the hospitality industry. It is about supervising the people who cook, serve, tend bar, check guests in and out, carry bags, clean rooms, mop floors—the people on whom the success or failure of every enterprise depends. It is a book about first-line supervision, written especially for the beginning manager, for the new supervisor promoted from an hourly job, and for students planning a career in the hospitality field. But even experienced managers will find it full of useful ideas and insights for dealing with people productively.

This book was written to fill a definite need. Here is an industry heavily dependent on its human resources but plagued with people problems—its demands, its people, its pace, its long hours, the typical attitudes and habits of managers and workers, and the special problems of time pressure, of the unpredictable, of everything happening at once.

This book is still unique in focusing directly on the first-line hospitality supervisor and applying the wisdom of management theory and experience to the hard realities of the hospitality industry in down-to-earth terms. It is practical, concrete, results-oriented. The spotlight is on the real setting and everyday problems. Principles of good people management are presented in terms of how they apply on the job.

Our primary objective is still to provide the reader with a basic understanding of the supervisor's role and responsibilities, a basic yet comprehensive knowledge about the different elements of the supervisor's job, and a basic awareness and appreciation of the skills, attitudes, and abilities needed to manage people successfully. A firm grasp of these three basics can provide a solid foundation for increasing skills and knowledge on the job and ultimately for achieving success through people at any level of management.

Yet basics are not necessarily simple. We do not give the reader sets of rules; we discuss the concepts, theories, and principles behind good supervisory practice in order to give depth to understanding. We define terms clearly and explain them fully; we show how they apply, using examples and incidents from the industry. In sum, we have written this book to be read, understood, absorbed, and put to work— a how-to book that provides the understanding necessary to adapt, to take off from, to use in one's own circumstances in one's own way.

If you are a student, you will find here not only what you need to make it through the course, but also the realities you will meet in your first supervisory job. Even more important, you can gain the knowledge and insight that will help you to grow as a supervisor, to develop the skills and personal qualities you need, and to work out your own management style. We suggest you begin by assuming that you are a supervisor. Apply the discussions to your own situation, real or imagined. Use the incidents, discussion questions, and case studies as springboards for your own opinions and conclusions and your own creative ideas for solving problems and getting results. Take time now to master basic principles and think things through, because you won't have much time later.

If you are a professor, we hope that you will find this book not only satisfying in content but also easy to use and appealing to students. It assumes no specific knowledge other than a general familiarity with a hospitality, foodservice, or lodging operation. It can be used at any course level in a hospitality or culinary arts program after the first semester or the first year. It is also suitable for seminars and continuing education courses and makes a good supplementary text for courses with an academic, theoretical approach.

If you are in management, you will find this book helpful in developing your supervisory personnel, especially those who have been promoted from hourly positions or are first-time supervisors from outside the industry. The material is solid, the scene familiar, and the presentation clear and easy to follow. It will help your supervisors to understand and develop the skills and abilities in dealing with hourly employees. It will help you to bring supervisors to the level of productivity and the manner of performance that you want in your organization. In developing supervisors as the key people in your operations, you will help your enterprise become more profitable and to serve its guests well.

Since the first edition of *Supervision in the Hospitality Industry* was published in 1985, the authors have been committed to focusing directly on the first-line hospitality supervisor and applying the wisdom of management theory and experience to the hospitality workplace in down-to-earth terms. This new fourth edition is no exception in being a practical, how-to book written for hospitality students or the new supervisor promoted from an hourly job.

New to This Edition

This fourth edition is designed to help supervisors meet the challenges and demands of the new millennium, to be leaders, to possess excellent human relations skills, to be highly productive, and to be flexible. New to this edition:

Each chapter has been modified, revised and updated

Industry examples and sidebars have been added throughout the text

The diversity and leadership chapters have been significantly amended

A new section on substance abuse has been added to Chapter 14

New artwork and photographs have been added throughout the text

Profiles of supervisors have been added to the text

"Check your knowledge" questions have been added every few pages as a student learning aid

Features

The text is carefully structured for teaching and learning. It is organized in logical teaching units, but the sequence can be changed to fit your needs. Following are the pedagogical features found within each chapter:

At the beginning of each chapter, an *Overview* section lists the chapter's major headings to help the student see what topics will be covered and their relationship to each other.

The chapter openings help to structure assignments and set learning goals by describing a supervisory situation and listing the chapter objectives.

New photographs enliven the text, and diagrams, flow charts, and sample materials provide focal points for discussion.

Profiles allow professionals in the industry to give their perspective on human resource and supervisory issues.

"Check Your Knowledge" questions are spaced throughout the chapters for students to review important topics and concepts.

Key Points summarize the important concepts in the chapter.

Key terms are boldfaced in the text, reemphasized in the end of chapter list *Key Terms,* and assembled in the *Glossary* for reference and review.

The *Review Questions* and *Activities and Applications* can be used to test knowledge, spark interest, bring out opposing views and different approaches, and involve students in typical supervisory problems and situations.

Supplementary Materials

An *Instructor's Manual* (ISBN 0-471-20775-6) to accompany the textbook is available to qualified adopters upon request from the publisher. It contains various materials designed to assist in the classroom.

The National Restaurant Association (NRA) Educational Foundation, in consultation with the author, has developed a *Student Workbook* for its ProMgmt. certificate program. The workbook contains exercises and a study outline for each chapter, and a practice test of 80 multiple-choice questions. This practice test will assist students in preparation for the certificate examination.

In addition, an *Instructor's Guide* (ISBN 0-471-31170-7) is available to qualified adopters to complement and highlight the information in the textbook and Student Workbook.

Acknowledgments

The authors greatly acknowledge the following reviewers, who provided feedback and insight: Robert A. Palmer and William B. Martin, California State Polytechnic University, Pomona; Brenda Hodgins, Red Deer College; Leslie Bilderback and Dina Altieri, Southern California School of Culinary Arts; and James Zielinksi, College of DuPage.

Special thanks to Sodexho, for allowing us to use a selection of photos from their library to enhance the text. We are grateful to Simone Trafford and Josielyn Teves for their invaluable assistance in various aspects of manuscript preparation. Thanks also to the industry reviewers and supervisors who allowed us to profile them. We are grateful to La Jolla Beach and Tennis Club for kindly allowing photos to be taken.

Wishing you a successful course and career!

supervision

in the hospitality industry

~ chapter 1

The Supervisor as Manager

overview

The Supervisor's Role

Obligations and Responsibilities of a Supervisor

Functions of Management

Theories of People Management

Managerial Skills

On Restaurant Row in one city, one family restaurant has had 12 different busboys in two months. In the restaurant next door, the food is superb one week and terrible the next. The bar on the corner cannot find a decent bartender, much less keep one. Across the street, one restaurant had a near-riot in the kitchen resulting from an argument between the cooking staff and servers. The Italian restaurant two doors down is losing customers steadily because its service is so poor. But the oldest restaurant on the block is packing them in night after night, with staff who have been there for years.

Across town, students at the local community college would rather eat at the local fast-food restaurants than in the school's cafeteria, where the pizza and burgers leave much to be desired. On the outskirts of the city, students at the state university rave about the quality of the food and the tremendous choices they have. Many of the students look for jobs working for the university foodservice.

In many of the city's hotels, the employee turnover rate is fantastically high. Every seven days we turn 250,000 employees in this industry. We don't have a

1

"labor" crisis. We have a turnover crisis.[1] Service is poor and guests complain, but then that's just part of the game, isn't it? Yet several hotels in town have few staffing problems and happy guests.

Throughout the city a common cry in the hospitality industry is that you just can't get good people these days. People don't work hard the way they used to, they don't do what you expect them to, they come late and leave early or don't show up at all, they are sullen and rude, they don't always speak English; the complaints go on and on. The rotten help you get today must cause all the problems.

Is this true? If it is true, what about those establishments where things run smoothly? Can it be that the way in which the workers are managed has something to do with the presence or absence of problems? You bet it does! And that is what this book is all about. In this chapter we explore the management aspect of the supervisor's job. It will help you to:

∾ Describe the primary role of a supervisor in the hospitality industry.

∾ Explain the different levels of supervision, and identify first-line supervisors on an organizational chart.

∾ Define the terms *authority* and *responsibility.*

∾ Explain the difference between exempt and nonexempt employees.

∾ Outline the supervisor's obligations and responsibilities to owners, customers, and employees.

∾ Describe briefly the important functions of management.

∾ Explain the challenge of applying common management theories in the hospitality work environment.

∾ Compare and contrast the major theories of people management as they relate to hospitality employees.

∾ List examples of technical, human, and conceptual skills used by hospitality supervisors.

The Supervisor's Role

In the hospitality industry almost everything depends on the physical labor of many hourly (or nonmanagerial) workers: people who cook, serve tables, mix drinks, wash dishes, check guests in and out, clean rooms, carry bags, mop floors. Few industries are as dependent for success on the performance of hourly workers. These employees make the products and they serve the customers—or drive them away.

How well these workers produce and serve depends largely on how well they are managed. If they are not managed well, the product or the service suffers and the establishment is in trouble. It is the people who supervise these workers who hold the keys to the success of the operation.

[1]Jim Sullivan, "People, performance, and profits, Lebhar-Friedman, Inc.," *Nation's Restaurant News,* November 8, 1999, Monday section.

A **supervisor** is any person who manages people who make products and/or perform services. A supervisor is responsible for the output of the people supervised—for the quality and quantity of the products and services. A supervisor is also responsible for meeting the needs of employees and can ensure the production of goods and services only by motivating and stimulating employees to do their jobs properly. Today's employees are different than they were 10 to 20 years ago; they no longer give their allegiance to the supervisor automatically in exchange for a paycheck. Instead, they give their supervisor the right to lead them. Usually, a supervisor is the manager of a unit or department of an enterprise and is responsible for the work of that unit or department. In large enterprises there are many levels of supervision, with the people at the top responsible for the work of the managers who report to them, who in turn are responsible for the performance of those they supervise, and so on, down to the **first-line supervisor** who manages the **hourly workers.** First-line supervisors and unit managers are the primary focus of this book.

Figures 1.1 and 1.2 show typical **organizational charts** for a large hotel and a large restaurant. An organizational chart shows the relationship among and within departments. **Line functions** (associates directly involved in producing goods and services) and staff functions (the advisers) are spelled out. The human resources (or personnel) and training departments are examples of staff who advise line departments, such as the food and beverage department, on matters including hiring, disciplining, and training employees.

Using the organization chart, you can also see the various levels of management, with authority and responsibility handed down from the top, level by level. **Authority** can be defined as the right and power to make the necessary decisions and take the necessary actions to get the job done. **Responsibility** refers to the obligation that a person has to carry out certain duties and activities. First-line supervisors represent the lowest level of authority and responsibility, and hourly workers report to them.

Many supervisors—station cooks, for example—also do some of the work of their departments alongside the workers they supervise. Thus they are typically in close daily contact with the people they supervise and may even at times be working at the same tasks. They are seldom isolated in a remote office but are right in the middle of the action. They are known as **working supervisors.**

> No one is more responsible for a business's success than the manager. It takes a lot of savvy to manage a bar or restaurant well, and not just anyone can pull it off. There are some qualities that make up the all-pro manager. For example, all-pro managers not only have a working knowledge of the business they operate but also possess a sound grasp of business in general. A good manager knows his or her market, knows the competition and what they are doing, and responds accordingly. Other all-pro manager traits include a desire to lead, maturity/stability, a good money sense, possession of street smarts, and legal knowledge.

Each supervisor's job is probably described in terms of a job title and the scope of the work required rather than in terms of the people to be supervised. A sous chef, for example, is responsible for all kitchen production. An assistant housekeeper in a hotel is responsible for getting the guests' rooms made up. A food and nutrition supervisor in a hospital may be responsible for serving patient meals. A restaurant manager or a unit manager in a food chain is responsible for the entire operation. Thus the focus is placed on the work rather than on the workers. But since the work is done by people, *supervision is the major part of the job.*

As a supervisor, you depend for your own success on the work of others, and you will be measured by their output and their performance. *You will be successful*

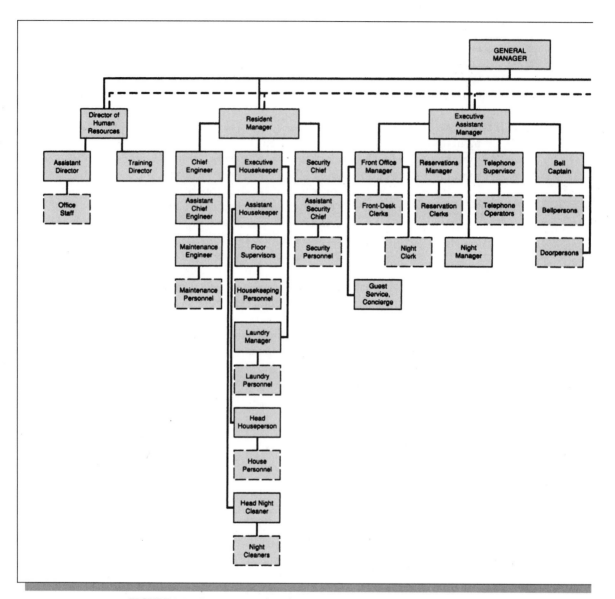

FIGURE 1.1   Organization chart for a large hotel. Boxes with dashed lines indicate hourly workers. Dashed reporting lines indicate staff (advisory) positions.

FIGURE 1.1 *(Continued)*

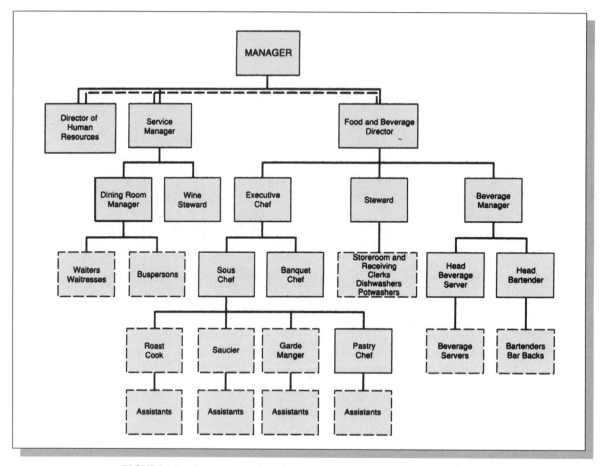

FIGURE 1.2   Organization chart for a large restaurant. Boxes with dashed lines indicate hourly workers. Dashed reporting lines indicate staff (advisory) positions.

in your own job only to the degree that your workers allow you to be, and this will depend on how to manage them. This will become clearer as you explore this book.

Obligations and Responsibilities of a Supervisor

When you begin to supervise the work of other people, you cross a line that separates you from the hourly workers—you step over to the management side. In any work situation there are two points of view: the hourly workers' point of view and management's point of view. The line between them is clearcut; there are no fuzzy edges, no shades of gray. When you become a supervisor, your responsibilities are

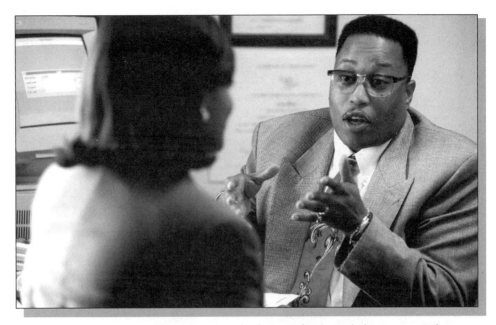

Other organizational terms with which you need to become familiar include *exempt employees* and *nonexempt employees*. Hourly employees are considered **nonexempt employees** because they are *not* exempt from federal and state wage and hour laws. In other words, they are covered by these laws and are therefore guaranteed a minimum wage and overtime pay after working 40 hours in a workweek. Supervisors are considered **exempt employees;** they are not covered by the wage and hour laws and therefore do not earn overtime pay when certain conditions are met: when they spend 50 percent or more of their time managing, when they supervise two or more employees, and under federal law when they are paid $1000 or more per month (or more if the state imposes a higher standard). (Courtesy of Sodexho)

management responsibilities, and you cannot carry them out successfully unless you maintain a manager's point of view.

The Supervisor in the Middle

As a hospitality supervisor, you have obligations to the owners, the customers, and the people you supervise, which puts you right in the middle of the action (Figure 1.3). To your employees, you represent management: authority, direction, discipline, time off, more money, and advancement. To the owners and your superiors in management, you are the link with the workers and the work to be done; you represent productivity, food cost, labor cost, quality control, and customer service; you also represent your people and their needs and desires. To the customers, your output and your employees represent the enterprise; if the food is good, it's a good restaurant; if the doorperson and the desk clerk and the server in the coffee shop provide high-quality service, it's a good hotel. No matter how modest your area of responsibility, it is a tough assignment.

Many new supervisors are promoted from hourly jobs and suddenly find themselves supervising people with whom they have worked side by side for years. You

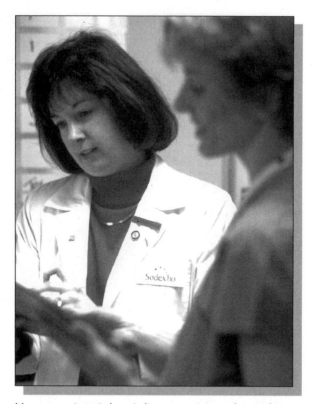

Many supervisors in hospitality enterprises work countless hours of overtime, and it is not at all uncommon for some hourly workers, such as bartenders and serving personnel, to take home more pay than that received by their supervisors, when tips and overtime pay are added to their hourly wages. (Courtesy of Sodexho)

worked together, drank beer together, griped about the company together, conspired together to keep from working too hard. Now you find yourself on the other side of that line between management and workers. Now you may be carrying out policies you used to complain about. You may have to work your entire crew on Christmas Day. You may have to discipline your best friend.

It is lonely on that side of the line, and *the temptation is great to slip back to your buddies,* to the old attitudes, the old point of view. We call this **boomerang management**—going back to where you came from—and it doesn't work. You've got to maintain a manager's point of view; you've got to stay in charge. There is no compromise. You can empathize with your workers; you can listen and understand. But your decisions must be made from management's point of view. Your employer expects it, and your people expect it. If you try to manage from your workers' point of view, they will take advantage of you. They really want you to manage.

Now, let's look in more depth at the supervisor's obligations to the big three: owners, customers, and employees.

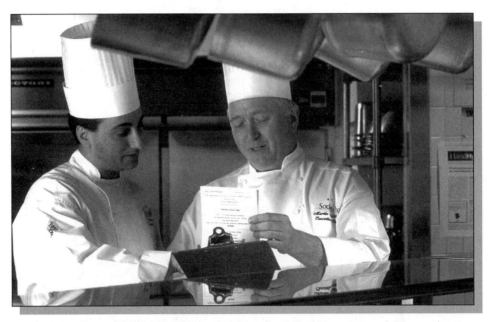

When you become a supervisor, your responsibilities are management responsibilities, and you cannot carry them out successfully unless you maintain a manager's point of view. (Courtesy of Sodexho)

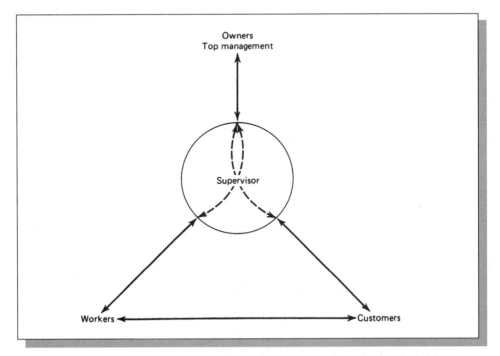

FIGURE 1.3 The supervisor: right in the middle of everything and everybody—the link between top management and the workers and customers.

Obligations to Owners

Your primary obligation to the owners is to make their enterprise profitable. They have taken the risk of investing their money, and they expect a reasonable return on that investment. The major part of your responsibility to them is to run your part of their business to produce that return. That is what they are interested in; that is what they have hired you to do.

They also want you to run things *their way*. If they tell you how they want it done, you have an obligation to do it that way, even though you see better ways to do it. They are paying you to do it their way, and you have an obligation to do anything they require that is morally and legally correct.

Suppose that the owners have a system for everything. They don't want you to change anything; they want you to oversee their system. Suppose you don't agree with it. Suppose you think they don't put enough French fries on each plate; you think the customer should have more and so does the customer. Do you add a few fries to each order? No! You leave the system as it is and you oversee it—you see that your people follow it.

Suppose you see a better way of doing something. You don't take it upon yourself to make a change. You go back to the owner or to your supervisor and you explain your idea and why it would be better. The two of you must agree on what changes, if any, you are going to make.

Suppose the people who hire you don't tell you how they want things done. This happens all too often in the restaurant business; they hire you and put you to work without telling you what to do. They may have definite expectations of you, but they do not verbalize at least 50 percent of what they ought to; they expect you to know what they want. You must find these things out for yourself—ask questions, get things straight. What are the guidelines and procedures? What authority do you have? Where, if anywhere, do you have a free hand? Since you must manage, as they want you to manage, it is your obligation to find out what they want and be sensitive to their expectations. Because of your daily interactions with customers and employees, you also have an obligation to communicate their desires to the owners.

Suppose that you are hired to run a hospital kitchen. Although there may be no profit involved, your obligation to follow the system is absolute, because the health of the patients is at stake. Patient health is the purpose of the hospital, and food is a basic element in patient care. Every recipe must be followed to the letter and to the quarter ounce. Every grain of salt is important. Every sanitation procedure is critical. You must not change a thing without having the authority to do so.

Obligations to Customers

Your second obligation as a supervisor is to the customers. They are the reason a hotel or restaurant exists, and they are the source of its profits. They come to your enterprise by choice. If they are treated well, they may continue to come. If they are not, you will probably never see them again. The importance of customer service seems obvious, yet poor service is all too common, and it is one of the big reasons for failure in the hospitality industry. Most of the people who never come back are responding to poor service or to the fact that an hourly employee was insensitive to their needs.

Consider the following scenario. You are a customer arriving at a hotel after a long and tiring trip, and you tell the desk clerk you have a reservation. She runs your name through her computer and says, "No, you don't have a reservation." How do you feel? You are frustrated and angry because you know you made a reservation. "Well," you ask, "do you have any rooms?" "Yes," she says, "we have rooms, but you don't have a reservation." Now you are not only frustrated and angry but you are beginning to feel rejected. "Well," you say, "may I have a room?" She lets you *(lets you)* have a room. As you start off with your bags, fluffing, she says, as though to a bad child, "But you *didn't* have a reservation!" Will you stay at that hotel again? Not if you can help it.

That desk clerk obviously had not been trained by her supervisor in customer relations. *Furthermore, chances are good that she picked up her attitude and behavior from the supervisor.* It is very easy, when your mind is on a million other things, to blame the customers for being demanding and unreasonable, and you often feel that if it weren't for the customers, you could get twice as much work done in half the time. You forget that if it weren't for the customers, you would have no work to do. As a manager you must fulfill their needs and desires, and that also means training your people to assume this obligation. Never forget that your employee is a direct reflection of *you.*

In a hotel or restaurant, customers usually encounter only hourly workers. Hotel guests see the desk clerk, the bellperson, the server in the restaurant, and the housekeeper, who is sure to be cleaning their room when they get back after breakfast. Restaurant patrons see the host or hostess, servers, and perhaps a bartender or cashier. These hourly workers represent you, they represent the management, and they convey the image of the entire establishment. As a supervisor you have an obligation to these customers to see that your workers are delivering on the promises of product and service that you offer—giving the guests what they came for. And you should be visible in person—customers like to feel that the manager cares, and your workers work better when you are present and involved in the action.

In a hospital or nursing facility kitchen, you have an obligation to the patients to see that they get the kind of food the doctor ordered and that it is not only nourishing and germ-free but that it looks good and tastes good. The food cannot help the patients recover if they don't eat it.

For many people in hospitals, food may be the most important part of their day. They lie in bed with nothing to do, and breakfast, lunch, and dinner become major events. You have an obligation to those patients to speed their recovery by giving your best effort to making their meals a pleasure.

As a supervisor in a school cafeteria, you have an obligation to the students. As a supervisor in a U.S. Army or Navy kitchen, you have an obligation to your country. Wherever you work, you have an obligation to the consumer of the product your workers prepare and to the user of the services your people provide.

Obligations to Employees

Your third obligation as a supervisor is to the people you supervise. It is up to you to provide these employees with an environment in which they can be productive

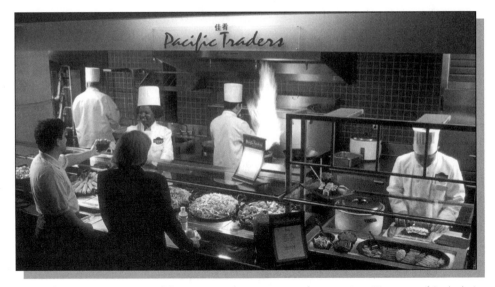

The work environment is one of the most important aspects of supervision. (Courtesy of Sodexho)

for you. This is something *you* need, because you are directly dependent on them to make you successful. You certainly can't do all the work yourself.

The most important value for most employees is the way the boss treats them. They want to be recognized as individuals, listened to, told clearly what the boss expects of them and why. If they are going to be really productive for you, they want a climate of acceptance, of approval, of open communication, of fairness, of belonging. With most workers today, the old hard-line authoritarian approach simply does not work. You owe it to your workers and to yourself to create a work climate that makes them willing to give you their best.

A poor **work climate** can cause high labor turnover, low productivity, and poor quality control and can ultimately result in fewer customers—problems that are all too common in restaurants, hotels, and hospitals. It is easy for employers to blame these problems on "the kind of workers we have today" and to look at these workers as a cross they have to bear. There is an element of truth here: It *is* difficult to get people who will do a good job day after day after day in repetitive jobs—washing pots in a hot kitchen, handling heavy luggage, busing dirty dishes, mopping the same dirty floors, making the same beds, cleaning the same toilets, walking the same empty corridors all night as a security guard.

The fact is, though, that two enterprises hiring from the same labor pool can get radically different results according to the work climate their supervisors create. You can see this in multiunit operations: There is always one unit that is consistently better than the others—one that is cleaner, has a better food cost, has a better labor cost, and has more satisfied customers. It is always the manager who makes this difference, and usually this manager has created a climate in which the workers will give their best.

So Who's Number One?

There's an expression in the hospitality industry that goes like this: "If you [the manager] take care of the employees, the employees will take care of the customers, and the profits will take care of themselves." As a supervisor, your number one concern is your employees. You need to be committed to serving the employees who serve the customer, because the way you treat your employees will be reflected in how they treat the customer. When you treat employees the way you want them to treat customers (with consideration, respect, and so on), employees then tend to provide high-quality service. This keeps customers happy and increases the chances of return visits, meaning more business and more money spent. This in turn helps build profits and keeps the owners happy. Studies involving various companies show that those who value their employees highly (by providing training, rewards, and so on) have higher customer satisfaction and profitability.

Check Your Knowledge

1. What is the primary role of a supervisor?
2. Briefly discuss the obligations that a supervisor has to his or her employees.

Functions of Management

Are first-line supervisors really managers? Yes, indeed. A **manager** is a person who directs and controls an assigned segment of the work in an enterprise. Although supervisors often do not have the title *manager,* although midlevel managers and top executives in large enterprises may not regard them as part of the management team, supervisors have crossed that line from the workers' side to the management side, and they perform the functions of management in their area of control. So we need to examine the functions of management.

The Theory

Books on management theory usually list four or five functions and up to 20 major activities that a manager performs. Here are some of the more important ones:

- ∾ **Planning:** looking ahead to chart goals and the best courses of future action; involves, for example, determining who, what, why, when, where, and how work will be done
- ∾ **Organizing:** putting together the money, personnel, equipment, materials, and methods for maximum efficiency to meet an enterprise's goals, such as developing employee work teams
- ∾ **Staffing:** determining personnel needs and recruiting, evaluating, selecting, hiring, orienting, training, and scheduling employees

∾ **Leading:** interacting and guiding employees about getting certain goals and plans accomplished; involves many skills, such as communicating, motivating, delegating, instructing, supporting, developing, and mentoring employees

∾ **Controlling and evaluating:** monitoring and evaluating results in terms of goals and standards previously agreed upon, such as performance and quality standards, and taking corrective action when necessary to stay on course

∾ **Coordinating:** meshing the work of individuals, work teams, and departments to produce a smoothly running operation

∾ **Problem solving and decision making:** using a logical process to identify causes of and solutions to problems or to make decisions

∾ **Representing:** representing the organization to customers and other people outside the enterprise

And so on.

Does this list seem remote and unreal to you? It does to many people who run hotels and foodservice operations, and there is nothing like management experience to upset management theory. A busboy quits, the dishmachine breaks down, two waitresses are fighting in the dining room, the health inspector walks in, an official from the liquor control board is coming at 2:00 this afternoon, and someone rushes up and tells you there's a fire in the kitchen. How does management theory help you at a moment like this?

The Reality

There is nothing wrong with management theory; it can be useful, even in a crisis. The problem is how to apply it. In the circus we call the hospitality industry, nothing comes in neat and tidy packages. Managers seldom have control over the shape of their day. *The situation changes every 20 to 48 seconds,* and the unexpected usually happens. In a foodservice operation you are manufacturing, selling, and delivering a product, all within minutes. In a hotel you may have 5,000 customers one day and 50 the next. You deal with your superiors, you deal with your subordinates, and you deal with your customers, all coming at you from different directions. Salespeople, deliveries, inspectors, customer complaints, and applicants for jobs interrupt you. You are likely to have only a few seconds available when you make many important decisions.

In such circumstances managers usually react to situations rather than acting on them according to a preconceived plan plotted out in the quiet of an office. Managing becomes the ability to adjust actions and decisions to given situations according to the demands of those situations. It is a *flex style of management,* calling upon theory, experience, and talent. It is a skill that cannot be taught but has to be developed in supervised experience on the job. It means doing what will be most effective in terms of the three elements involved: *the situation, your workers, and yourself.* It means developing techniques and applying principles of management in ways that work for you.

The fact is that most textbooks on management were written to be read by MBA students headed for middle-management jobs in large corporations, and they do not often address the problems of the small individual enterprise, the supervisor of hourly workers, and the nitty-gritty of managing production and service. They also don't always address the art of managing people. According to a survey by the Center for Creative Leadership, a research firm in Greensboro, North Carolina, poor interpersonal skills represent the single biggest reason that managers fail. Managers who fail are often poor listeners, can't stimulate their employees, don't give and take criticism well, and avoid conflict. Managers need to learn how to manage people, just as you do, through supervised experience on the job. They must learn how to convert classroom theories into practical applications that are accepted by the people they supervise. No one can teach you; it is theory, then practice, then experience.

As a flex-style manager reacting to constantly changing situations, your on-the-spot decisions and actions are going to be far better if you too can draw on sound principles of management theory and the accumulated experience of successful managers. In this book we introduce you to those principles and theories that can help you to work out your own answers as a supervisor in a hotel or foodservice setting. They can provide a background of knowledge, thoughts, and ideas that will give you confidence and a sense of direction as you meet and solve the same problems that other managers before you have met and solved.

Theories of People Management

The development of management as an organized body of knowledge and theory is a product of the last hundred years. It was an inevitable outgrowth of the Industrial Revolution and the appearance of large enterprises needing skilled managers and new methods of running a business.

Scientific Management

One of the earliest developments affecting the management of people was the **scientific management** movement appearing around 1900 and stemming from the work of Frederick Taylor. Taylor's goal was to increase productivity in factories by applying a scientific approach to human performance on the job. Using carefully developed time-and-motion studies, he analyzed each element of each production task and by eliminating all wasted motions, arrived at the "one best way" to perform the task. In the same way he established a "fair day's work," which was the amount of work a competent worker could do in one workday using the one best way.

The system Taylor developed had four essential features:

1. Standardization of work procedures, tools, and conditions of work through design of work methods by specialists

2. Careful selection of competent people, thorough training in the prescribed methods, and elimination of those who could not or would not conform

3. Complete and constant overseeing of the work, with total obedience from the workers

4. Incentive pay for meeting the fair day's work standard—the worker's share of the increased productivity

Taylor believed that his system would revolutionize labor–management relations and would produce "intimate, friendly cooperation between management and men" because both would benefit from increased productivity. Instead, his methods caused a great deal of strife between labor and management. Workers who once planned much of their own work and carried it out with a craftsman's pride were now forced into monotonous and repetitive tasks performed in complete obedience to others. Taylor believed that higher wages—"what they want most"—would make up for having to produce more and losing their say about how they did their work. But his own workers, with whom he was very friendly, did everything they could to make his system fail, including breaking their machines. The craft unions of that day fought Taylor's system bitterly, and relations between management and labor deteriorated. Productivity, however, increased by leaps and bounds, since fewer workers could do more work.

Another innovator, Frank Gilbreth, carried forward the search for the one best way of performing tasks, or **work simplification.** Using ingenious time-and-motion study techniques, he developed ways of simplifying tasks that often doubled or tripled what a worker could do. His methods and principles had a great impact in foodservice kitchens, where work simplification techniques have been explored extensively and widely adopted.

Taylor's innovations began a revolution in management's approach to production. His theories and methods were widely adopted (although the idea that the worker should share in the benefits of increased productivity seldom went along with the rest of the system). A whole new field of industrial engineering developed in which efficiency experts took over the planning of the work. In this process the workers came to be regarded as just another element of the production process, often an adjunct to the machine. Their job was to follow the rules, and the supervisors saw to it that they did, and this became the prevailing philosophy of people management.

Everything is systematized, and the worker is simply taught to run the machines, follow the rules, and speak given phrases. When the bell rings, the worker turns the hamburgers on the grill. To make a pancake, the worker hits the batter dispenser one time. There is no room for deviation.

Such standardization has many benefits to the enterprise. It maintains product consistency from one unit to the next. It allows the use of unskilled labor and makes training quick, simple, and inexpensive. It is well suited to short-term workers on their first jobs. But such complete standardization may not work so well in other settings or for other types of workers. When there is no room for deviation, there is no opportunity for originality, no relief from monotony. Enterprises less completely geared to high turnover may have problems with training and morale.

You can also see scientific management at work in the standardized recipe, the standardized greeting, the standardized hotel registration procedures, and the

In the foodservice industry you can see the influence of scientific management in some fast-food chains. (Courtesy of Sodexho)

standardized making of a hospital bed. But scientific management as a whole is practiced in restaurants and hotels far less than it could be. We have the methods and techniques, but we seldom use them. We may have standardized recipes, but except in baking, many cooks never look at them. We may standardize procedures, but we seldom enforce them. We hire in panic and in crisis; we take the first warm body that presents itself and put it to work. We use the magic apron training method: We give the new employee an apron and say "Go." We assume that anyone knows how to do some of our entry-level jobs. We hang on to inefficient workers because we are afraid that the next ones we hire will be even worse. As for overseeing their work, who has time to do that?

Probably the very nature of the hotel and food businesses makes them unsuitable for totally scientific management. Still, there are important elements of the method that can be used to increase productivity, achieve consistent results, make customers happy and patients well, increase profit, and make a manager's life much easier, all without making workers into human machines.

Human Relations Theory

In the 1930s and 1940s, another theory of people management appeared that of the **human relations** school. This was an outgrowth of studies made at the Hawthorne plant of Western Electric Company. Researchers testing the effects on productivity of changes in working conditions came up with a baffling series of results that could not be explained in the old scientific management terms. During a prolonged series of experiments with rest periods, for example, the productivity of the small test group rose steadily whether the rest time was moved up or down or was eliminated altogether. Furthermore, workers in the test group were out sick far less often than the large group of regular workers, and the test group worked without supervision. It became obvious that the rise in productivity was the result of something new, not the economic factor of a paycheck or the scientific factors of working conditions or close supervision.

Elton Mayo, the Harvard professor who conducted the experiments, concluded that a social factor, the sense of belonging to a work group, was responsible. Other people had other theories to explain the increased productivity: the interested attention of the researchers, the absence of authoritarian supervision, participation in the planning and analysis of the experiments. People are still theorizing about what human relations theory can do for you. We explore this in later chapters.

Total Quality Management

Total quality management (TQM) is a participative process that empowers all levels of employees to work in groups to establish guest service expectations and determine the best way of meeting or exceeding those expectations. TQM is a continuous improvement process that works best when supervisors and managers are good leaders. A successful company will employ leader-managers who create a stimulating work environment in which guests and employees become an integral part of the mission by participating in goal and objective setting.

Installing TQM is exciting because once everyone becomes involved, there is no way of stopping the creative ways in which employees solve guest-related problems and improve service. Other benefits include cost reductions, increased guest and employee satisfaction, and ultimately, profit.

Participative management was the real meaning of the Hawthorne experiments, but everyone agrees that the experiments shifted the focus of personnel management to the people being managed. Now enter the human relations theorists, who stressed the importance of concern for workers as individuals and as members of the work group. "Make your employees happy and you will have good workers," they said. "Listen to your people, call them by name, remember their birthdays, help them with their problems." This was the era of the company picnic, the company newspaper, the company bowling team, the company Boy Scout troop. Human relations practitioners flourished especially in the 1940s, during World War

II and after, and many of their theories are still at work, maintaining a healthy focus on the importance of the individual.

But happiness, it turns out, does not necessarily make people productive. You can have happy workers who are not producing a thing: There is more to productivity than that. Yet we do need nearly everything the human relations theorists emphasized. Supervisors do need to know their workers, to treat them as individuals, to communicate and listen, to provide a pleasant working environment, and to encourage a sense of belonging. But we need still more. It isn't happiness that will make your workers produce; it is your own ability to lead your people. Some of the human relations techniques, such as listening and communicating and treating people as individuals, can make you a better leader, and this is the biggest thing that human relations theory can do for you. We explore this in later chapters.

Participative Management

Building on the new interest in the worker, a trend toward **participative management** developed in the 1960s and 1970s. In a participative system, workers participate in the decisions that concern them. They do not necessarily make the decisions; this is not democratic management by majority vote. The manager still leads and usually makes the final decision, but he or she discusses plans and procedures and policies with the work groups who must carry them out, and considers their input in making final decisions. In taking part in such discussions, workers come to share the concerns and objectives of management and are more likely to feel committed to the action and to being responsible for the results.

Participative management as a total system is probably not suited to the typical foodservice or lodging enterprise. Nevertheless, certain of its elements can work very well. Discussing the work with your people, getting their ideas, and exchanging information can establish a work climate and group processes in which everybody shares responsibility to get results. You might call it *management by communication*.

Humanistic Management

What is likely to work best in the hotel and foodservice industries is selective borrowing from all three systems of management: scientific, human relations, and participative. We need to apply many of the principles of scientific management: We need standardized recipes, we need to train workers in the best ways to perform tasks, and we need systems for controlling quality, quantity, and cost. But one thing we do not need from scientific management is its view of the worker as no more than a production tool. Here we can adapt many features of the human relations approach. If we treat workers as individuals with their own needs and desires and motivations, we can do a much better job of leading them and we are far more likely to increase productivity overall. From participative management we can reap the advantages of open communication and commitment to common goals, so that we are all working together. The successful manager will blend all three systems, deliberately or instinctively, according to the needs of the situation, the workers, and his or her personal style of leadership. We call this **humanistic management.**

∾ profile

LAURA HORETSKI

Courtesy of Laura Horetski

I was asked what leadership means to me as the front office manager of a major hotel chain. When you look at the definition of a leader, it states, "one who leads or guides." And we've all heard the phrase "lead by example." I don't think that is enough. There are at least seven qualities of leadership that I can think of that make a good leader.

A good leader is someone who is not afraid to get his or her hands dirty. Someone who will do the same job, duty, or task alongside subordinates, peers, and supervisors, while keeping a positive attitude. This helps build and gain respect. Besides, how else can you expect someone to do the job you ask him or her to do if you do not know how or are not willing to do it yourself?

A person who listens, not just hears. Pay complete attention to what the person is saying. Look them in the eyes, acknowledge them and don't interrupt. Ask questions of clarification, reiterate what they are saying, and ask the person if you understand them correctly. But listening doesn't stop there. You need to follow through on the conversation and do what you said you would do. Build integrity and trust.

Make good business decisions but show compassion when needed. The bottom line is the bottom line. You don't have to be cruel to accomplish tough results. Be honest, state the facts, ask for suggestions, and make the best decision. A lot of times things look good on paper but don't really work in reality. Sometimes those who are on the front lines and performing the job everyday give the best answers. Not only do you get the answer you may be looking for, you also build confidence and develop future managers and supervisors.

Like Frederick Taylor 100 years ago and all the theorists since, today's supervisor is concerned with productivity: getting people to do their jobs in the best way, getting the work done on time and done well. This is an age-old problem: When Pope John XXIII was asked how many people worked for him, he answered "About half of them." It is sad but human that many people will do as little work as possible unless they see some reason to do better. Often they see no reason.

This is where leadership comes in: the supervisor interacting with the workers. Look at it as a new form of ROI, not *return on investment* but *return on individuals*. As a supervisor you will succeed only to the degree that each person under you produces; you are judged on the performance, the productivity, and the efficiency of others. The only means for your success is a return on each person who works for you. As a leader you can give them reasons to do better. Use your I's: imagination, ideas, initiative, improvement, interaction, innovation, and—why not?—inspiration. It is the personal interaction between supervisor and worker that will turn the trick.

Treat others fairly, including yourself. Favoritism has no place at work. Is it hard not to solely rely on those who are the strongest? Absolutely. But as a leader it's your job to encourage and improve your subperformers. Favoritism also provides an impartial playing field for everyone. Learn to delegate to improve teamwork and lighten the load for everybody.

Learning never stops. I try to learn something new every day, sometimes without even seeking it out. You also need to be open to learning from subordinates, peers, and supervisors. There is no one person who has all the answers. The workforce is always changing in every aspect and you need to be able to adapt. It's important to stay fresh and current. Think outside the box; there's usually more than one way to accomplish a goal. If the way you tried doesn't work, you've learned, and it's what you take from the experience that's important.

Develop those under you. The fastest way to move up is to train someone to take your job. This is one of the best ways to show leadership. Too often, people are afraid of "losing their jobs" because someone else knows how to do their job. This is not the case. This frees up time for you to develop your skills in another position you are interested in, while developing your successor.

Finally, you need to be able to admit that you've made mistakes. As I said earlier, no one person has all the answers. You're going to stumble, trip, and even fall. But those who are honest and admit their failures will gain the respect of others and will learn the most. There's a saying "No question is a dumb question." I say, "No mistake is a mistake."

I have had many teachers throughout my career and I have taken pieces of their leadership style along with me. You are never done learning how to lead. Each circumstance has its own manner in how to approach it. Above all else, a good leader is fair and ever changing.

Above all, have fun!

Managerial Skills

Management at any level is an art, not a science providing exact answers to problems. It is an art that can be learned, although no one can really teach you. You do not have to be born with certain talents or personality traits. In fact, studies of outstanding top executives have failed to identify a common set of traits that add up to successful leadership, and experts have concluded that successful leadership is a matter of individual style. There are, however, certain **managerial skills** essential to success at any level of management: **technical skill, human skill,** and **conceptual skill.** At lower levels of management, technical and human skills are most important because managers here are concerned with the products and the people making them. Conceptual skill is necessary, too, but not to the same degree. In top-management positions in large corporations,

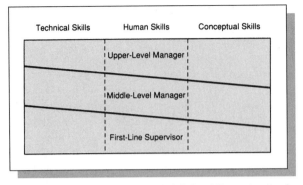

FIGURE 1.4 Use of managerial skills by different levels of management.

conceptual skill is all-important, and the other skills come into play less often (see Figure 1.4).[2]

All these skills can be developed through exercise, through study and practice, through observation and awareness of one self and others. We will look at them as they apply to supervisors in foodservice and hospitality enterprises. Then we add to the list of skills a fourth essential for managerial success: some personal qualities that will enable you to survive and prosper.

Technical Skills

The kind of technical skill useful to you as a supervisor is the ability to do the tasks of the people you supervise. You may not have their proficiency—you may not be able to make a soufflé or operate a hotel telephone system—but you should know what these tasks involve and in a general way know how they are carried out. You need such knowledge to select and train people, plan and schedule the work in your department, and take action in an emergency. Most important, your technical skills give you credibility with your workers. They will be more ready to accept and respect you when they know that you have some competence in the work you supervise.

If you have been an hourly worker, you may already have the technical skills you need. Many supervisors pick up these skills from their workers on the job. In large organizations some supervisors are required to go through the same skills training as the workers.

Human Skills

The skill of handling people successfully is really the core of the supervisor's job. Such skill has several ingredients and it is not achieved overnight.

First in importance is *your attitude toward the people who work for you.* You must be able to perceive and accept them as human beings. If you don't—if you think of them as cogs in the wheels of production, or if you look down on them be-

---

[2]The three-skill approach to effective management was developed by Robert L. Katz in "Skills of an effective administrator," *Harvard Business Review,* January–February 1955, reprinted and updated September–October 1974.

cause you are the boss and they scrub floors for a living—they will not work well for you or they will simply leave. *They will not let you succeed.*

A second ingredient of human skills is *sensitivity,* the ability to perceive each person's needs, perceptions, values, and personal quirks so that you can work with each one in the most productive way. You need to be aware that José still has trouble with English, and that Rita will cry for days if you speak sharply to her but Charlie won't do anything at all unless you almost yell. You need to realize that when Jim comes in looking like thunder and not saying a word, he's mad about something and you had better find a way to defuse him before you turn him loose among the customers. You need to be able to sense when a problem is building by noticing subtle differences in employee behavior.

A third ingredient is *self-awareness.* Have you any idea how you come across to your workers? You need to be aware of your own behavior as it appears to others. For example, in your concern for quality, you may always be pointing out to people things they are doing wrong. They probably experience this as criticism and see you as a negative person who is always finding fault. If you become aware of your habits and their reactions, you can change your manner of correcting them and balance it out with praise for things well done.

You also need to be aware of your own perceptions, needs, values, and personal quirks and how they affect your dealings with your workers. When you and they

You need to establish person-to-person relations with individual workers. Call them by name; get to know them as people—their families, their hobbies, and so on. They must be able to accept you as a human being, too, so they can look you in the eye and not be afraid of you. They will listen better to your instructions, and they will do better work if you act like a person as well as a boss. (Courtesy of Sodexho)

perceive things differently, you will have trouble communicating. When you and they have different needs and values in a work situation, you may be working at cross-purposes. To take a small example, say that you don't smoke and that while you are talking to Alice over lunch, you put your cracker wrappers and sugar papers in the ashtray. Alice, who smokes steadily whenever she can, doesn't say anything to you because you are her boss, but she is so frustrated and preoccupied with what to do with her ashes and cigarette butt that she cannot concentrate on what you are saying. If you are aware of what is going on, you can put your paper trash somewhere else.

Human skills come with practice. You have to practice treating people as individuals, sharpening your awareness of others and of yourself, figuring out what human qualities and behaviors are causing problems and how these problems can be solved. This is another instance in which the flex style of management figures: responding to your people, yourself, and the situation. It is a continual challenge because no two human situations are ever exactly alike. The ultimate human skill is putting it all together to create an atmosphere in which your people feel secure, free, and open with you and are willing to give you their best work.

Conceptual Skills

Conceptual skills require the ability to see the whole picture and the relationship of each part to the whole. The skill comes in using that ability on the job. You may need to arrange the work of each part of your operation so that it runs smoothly with the other parts—so that the kitchen and the dining room run in harmony, for example. Or you may need to coordinate the work of your department with what goes on in another part of the enterprise. For example, in a hotel the desk clerk must originate a daily report to the housekeeper showing what rooms must be cleaned, so that the housekeeper can tell the cleaning associates to draw their supplies and clean and make up the rooms. When they have made up the rooms, they have to report back to the housekeeping department so that the rooms can be inspected and okayed, and then the housekeeping department has to issue a report back to the desk clerk that the rooms are ready for occupancy. If you are the front office manager, you must be able to see this process as a whole even though the front desk cares only about the end of it—are those rooms ready? You must understand how the front desk fits into a revolving process that affects not only housekeeping and cleaning personnel but laundry, supplies, storage, and so on, and how important that first routine report of the desk clerk is to the whole process, to everyone involved, to customer service, and to the success of the enterprise.

In departments where everyone is doing the same tasks, conceptual skill is seldom called on, but the more complicated the supervisor's responsibilities, the greater the need for conceptual skill. A restaurant manager, for example, has a great deal of use for conceptual ability since he or she is responsible for both the front and the back of the house as well as the business end of the operation.

Consider what happened to this new restaurant manager. Things got very busy one night, and a waitress came up to him and said, "We can't get the tables bused." "Don't worry about it," he said, and he began to bus tables. Another waitress came to him and said, "We can't get the food out of the kitchen quick enough to serve the people." "Don't worry about it," he said, "I'll go back there and help them cook the food." While he was cooking, another waitress came in and said, "We can't get the dishes washed to reset the tables." "Don't worry about it, I'll wash the dishes," he said. While he was washing the dishes, another waitress came in and said, "We can't get the tables bused." And so it went: the tables, the food, the dishes, the tables, the food. . . . At this point the owner came in and said, "What the *hell* are you doing?" "I'm washing the dishes, I'm busing the tables, I'm cooking the food, and before I leave tonight I'm gonna empty the garbage," said the manager with pride. *"Look at this place!"* the owner shouted. "I hired you to manage, not to bus tables and cook and wash dishes!"

That manager had not been able to see the situation as a whole, to move people about, to balance them out where they were needed most: to *manage*. He had boomeranged back to doing the work himself because it was easier than managing, more familiar than dealing with the whole picture. Supervisors who are promoted from hourly positions often have this problem. When they finally learn to look at the whole picture and *deal with* the whole picture, they have truly attained the management point of view.

Check Your Knowledge

1. Define the following terms: *scientific management; humanistic management.*

Personal Skills and Qualities

In addition to managing others, *supervisors must be able to manage themselves.* This, too, is a skill that can be developed through awareness and practice. It means doing your best no matter what you have to cope with, putting your best foot forward and your best side out, keeping your cool. It means setting a good example; it means self-discipline. You cannot direct others effectively if you cannot handle yourself. It also means having self-control and supporting your own supervisor even when you personally disagree with a decision or action.

Managing yourself also means thinking positively. According to Manz, two different patterns of thinking are opportunity thinking and obstacle thinking. When faced with a challenging situation, **opportunity thinkers** concentrate on constructive ways of dealing with the circumstances, whereas **obstacle thinkers** focus on why the situation is impossible and retreat. Let's say that you are a supervisor and your evening dishwasher calls in sick. If you are an opportunity thinker, you'll look at the work schedule to see who else may be able to fill in and take steps to contact them. If you are an obstacle thinker, you'll think there's nothing you can do except ask the staff to switch to disposable dishes, even though you know it costs a lot more and the food doesn't look as good. Work on being an opportunity thinker, and if you make mistakes, learn from them and don't make yourself miserable. Everyone makes mistakes, even the people at the top of the organization chart. Guilt and worry will wear you down; self-acceptance and self-confidence will increase your energy.

Your own moods will affect your workers, too; they can run right through your whole department. Your employees watch you more carefully than you think; they can tell if your day is going fine or if you just had a frustrating meeting with your boss. When you get right down to it, your employees need a boss with a consistently positive outlook and attitude on the job.

You need to build a good, *strong self-image*. You have obligations to yourself as well as to others. Give yourself credit when you are right; face your mistakes when you are wrong and correct them for the future. You need to know yourself well, including your strengths and weaknesses, to work out your personal goals and values as they apply to your job, to know where you stand and where you are going.

In addition to having faith in your own ability to reach goals, you need to *believe that employees will perform effectively* when given a reasonable chance. You need to realize that you are also responsible for developing your employees through techniques such as coaching and counseling.

Another pair of useful personal qualities are *flexibility* and *creativity*. No hospitality manager can survive for long without flexibility, the ability to respond effectively to constantly changing situations and problems, to adapt theory to the reality of the moment, to think creatively because there are no pat answers. You must be able to respond to changes in the industry, too; yesterday's solutions will not solve tomorrow's problems. These again are skills that you can learn and practice; you do not have to be born with them.

Finally, being a supervisor requires *high energy levels and the ability to work under great pressure*. The time pressure in the hospitality field is unlike that in many other businesses; the meals must be served in a timely fashion; the rooms have to be ready in time for the next guest; the diabetic hospital patient needs his snacks at 2:00 P.M. and 8:00 P.M., period. Much stamina is needed to deal with these pressures.

You need to make a conscious and deliberate decision to be a manager. Here are three questions you must answer:

1. *Do you really want it?* Is there something about being a manager in this hospitality business (or wherever you are) that provides the responsibility, the challenge, and the fulfillment you want from the work you do?

2. *What is the cost?* Without tips or overtime pay, you'll probably make less money than some of your workers do. The hours are long, you'll work on weekends when everyone else is playing, the responsibility is unremitting, and the frustration level is high. You are squarely in the middle of all the hassle: Your employer is telling you, "I want a lower food cost, I want a lower labor cost, and I want this place cleaned up." Your workers are saying, "I can't be here Friday night, that's not my job, get somebody else to do it, I want more money." The customers are saying, "The food is cold, your service is slow, and your prices are too high." And your family is saying, "You're never home, we never get to go out together, you don't have time to help us with our homework, what do you mean fix you a cheese sandwich after you've been down there with all that food all day?" You work with people all day long, and yet it is a lonely job.

3. *Is it worth the cost?* Is the work itself satisfying and fulfilling? Will you learn and grow as a professional and as a person? Are you on the path you want to be on? Do you want to be a manager enough to pay the price?

If your answer is yes, then pay the price—pay it willingly and without complaint, pay it gladly. This may be the most important quality of all—to have the maturity to decide what you want and accept the tough parts with grace and humor; or to see it clearly, weigh it carefully, and decide you are not going that way after all.

∾ key points

1. A supervisor is any person who manages people making products or performing services. A supervisor is responsible for the quality and quantity of the products and services and for meeting the needs of employees. Only by motivating and stimulating the employees to do their jobs properly will high-quality products and services be produced.

2. Using an organization chart, you can see line and staff functions as well as how authority and responsibility are handed down from the top level of management to the first-line supervisors.

3. As a supervisor, you depend for your own success on the work of others, and you will be measured by their output and their performance. You will be successful in your own job only to the degree that your workers allow you to be, and this will depend on how you manage them.

4. As a hospitality supervisor, you have obligations to the owners, customers, and employees. To your employees, you represent management. To the owners and your bosses, you are the link with the workers and the work to be done; you represent productivity, cost control, quality control, and customer service. You also represent your people and their needs and desires. To the customers, your output and your employees represent the company.

5. As a supervisor, you've got to maintain the management point of view. You can't go back to where you came from (boomerang management).

6. As a supervisor, if you take care of the employees, the employees will take care of the customers, and the profits will take care of themselves. Your principal concern is your employees.

7. Some of the most important management activities you will be involved in are planning, organizing, staffing, leading, controlling or evaluating, coordinating, problem solving and decision making, and representing.

8. Managing is the ability to adjust actions and decisions to given situations—it is a flex style of management, calling upon theory, experience, and talent. It is a skill that cannot be taught but has to be developed on the job.

9. The successful manager will blend principles of scientific management, human relations, and participative management, according to the needs of the situation and the employees, into a style referred to as humanistic management.

10. For success, managers need technical skills, human skills, conceptual skills, and certain personal skills.

❧ key terms

authority	obstacle thinkers
boomerang management	opportunity thinkers
conceptual skill	organizational chart
controlling	organizing
coordinating	participative management
decision making	planning
evaluating	problem solving
exempt employees	representing
first-line supervisor	responsibility
hourly workers	scientific management
humanistic management	staff functions
human relations	staffing
human skill	supervisor
leading	technical skill
line functions	total quality management
manager	work climate
managerial skills	working supervisor
nonexempt employees	work simplification

❧ review questions

Answer each question in complete sentences. Read each question carefully and make sure that you answer all parts of the question. Organize your answer using more than one paragraph when appropriate.

1. In one paragraph, describe what a supervisor does. Is a supervisor a manager? Why or why not?

2. Are supervisors exempt or nonexempt employees? What is the difference between the two categories?

3. Describe and explain the necessary change in point of view when an hourly worker becomes a supervisor.

4. Briefly describe a supervisor's responsibilities to owners, customers, and employees. Who should be the most important, and why?

5. Give an on-the-job example of each of the management functions discussed.

6. Compare and contrast the principles of scientific management, human relations theory, and participative management. What elements of each school of thought are appropriate in the hospitality industry?

7. What types of human skills does a supervisor need? Why does a supervisor need human skills?

8. Give three examples of personal skills and qualities supervisors need.

❧ activities and applications

1. Discussion Questions

- Do you think it is true that "you just can't get good people these days"? If so, why can't you? If it isn't true, why do so many managers believe that it is?
- Why can't a supervisor manage workers successfully from a worker's point of view?
- Which three human skills do you consider most important in supervising people at work? Why?
- Can you think of a situation in which a supervisor is given responsibility for seeing that a certain job gets done but has no authority to see it through?
- Why is the supervisor called a *linking pin*?
- What problems does boomerang management cause?
- Do you agree that a supervisor's principal priority should be his or her employees? Why or why not?
- What should be the priority of the hourly employees? Why?

2. Organizational Charts

Bring in organizational charts from various hospitality operations. Working in small groups, identify the number of management levels, the titles of all first-line supervisors, the titles of hourly employees, and any staff functions.

3. Management Functions

Mrs. R. is a dining room manager in a white tablecloth restaurant. Each of her activities described here are examples of management functions. Identify each management function or functions.

- **A.** Mrs. R. writes out the work schedule for her employees for the next two-week rotation.
- **B.** It is brought to Mrs. R's attention that a server has been late enough times to possibly be disciplined. Mrs. R. reviews the records and sits down with the server for a talk.
- **C.** Every day, Mrs. R. observes the dining room to see how her employees are performing.
- **D.** Every day, Mrs. R. greets and chats with many of the restaurant's customers.
- **E.** Mrs. R. works out the next year's budget for her area.
- **F.** Mrs. R. talks with the chef about improving communications between the kitchen and the dining room.
- **G.** Mrs. R. holds a training session for all servers.
- **H.** At the end of the shift, Mrs. R. totals up sales and compares the figure to projections.
- **I.** Two servers want to switch shifts. Mrs. R. decides that they can do so.
- **J.** Mrs. R. is made aware of a problem between the bussers and the servers. Mrs. R. starts to gather information about it.

4. Brainstorming

Brainstorm examples of technical, human, and conceptual skills, and also the personal skills and qualities needed by hospitality supervisors.

5. Case Study: The Good-Guy Supervisor

Three weeks ago Bernie was promoted from assistant manager to manager of the employee cafeteria at City Hospital. It was a big move up for him, but he had always been a conscientious, hardworking, and loyal employee, and he felt that his promotion was well deserved. He knows the operation backward and forward, having worked both in the kitchen and on the line, and he has always been well liked by his fellow workers, so he figured he would have no problems in the new job. When he took the job, Bernie promised himself that he would never forget how it felt to be a worker and be ordered around, always being told what you're doing wrong, like Debra, the manager before him, used to do. Everyone hated her. He was determined to do things differently and not be such an all-fired drill sergeant. He'd be friendly, relaxed, and helpful, and people would do their best for him in return.

But things are not going quite the way he thought they would. Several of the line servers have become very careless about clean uniforms and wearing hairnets, and one of them, Esther, has come in late several times and he has had to fill in for her on the line. He finally spoke to her about it, but when she told him her problems with her husband, who brings her to work, he could see how it kept happening and he felt sorry for her. But it is worrying him.

A couple of other things are worrying him, too. Erma, who makes the salads, does not always have them ready on time, and yesterday the lettuce was gritty and several people complained. This morning Bernie helped her wash it, which made her mad, and he couldn't understand that. Dan, the head cook and a good friend of Bernie's saw the whole thing and laughed at his reaction. "Wise up, Bernie," he said, "you're never gonna make it this way." And he lit a cigarette right in front of Bernie after he took the chicken out of the oven.

QUESTIONS

1. What did Dan mean?
2. Why was Erma mad?
3. What should Bernie do about Esther? About Erma? About Dan and the smoking, which is strictly against the rules?
4. Why isn't Bernie able to maintain performance standards?
5. If you were Bernie's supervisor, what advice would you have given him before he started on the job? What would you say to him now?
6. Do you think that Bernie's supervisor is in any way to blame for Bernie's predicament?
7. What is Bernie doing when he takes Esther's place on the line and helps Erma wash the lettuce?
8. What is the fundamental principle of supervision involved in Bernie's case?

chapter 2

The Supervisor as Leader

overview

You and Your People

The Nature of Leadership

Choosing a Leadership Style

The idea that a supervisor must be a leader comes as a surprise to people who have never thought about it before. The term *leader* is likely to be associated with politics or religious movements or guerrilla-warfare situations in which people voluntarily become followers of the person who achieves command. Although it is not necessarily true, it is generally assumed that the one who is followed is a "born leader" whose influence is based at least partly on charisma or personal magnetism.

In a work situation, the supervisor is in command by virtue of being placed there by the company and its superiors. In the hospitality industry the term *supervisor* refers to a manager at a lower organizational level who supervises entry-level or other employees who themselves do not have supervisory responsibilities. The workers are expected to do what the boss tells them to do—that's just part of the job, right?

But if employees simply do what they are told, why is labor turnover so high, productivity so low, and absenteeism so prevalent? Why is there conflict between labor and management? The truth of the matter is that the boss is in charge of the workers, but that does not guarantee that the workers will put all of their efforts into the job. This is where leadership comes in.

In this chapter we explore the kinds of interactions between a supervisor and his workers that relate to the building of leadership in work situations. It will help you to:

∾ Identify typical hourly jobs in foodservice and lodging establishments.

∾ Outline the demographics of the labor pool typically hired for hourly jobs in the hospitality industry.

∾ Explain the concept of leadership on the job.

∾ Compare and contrast the concepts of formal authority and real authority.

∾ Describe and give examples of four leadership styles—autocratic, bureaucratic, democratic, and laissez-faire.

∾ Compare and contrast Theory X and Theory Y management styles.

You and Your People

More than one out of every eight Americans now working have worked in a Mc-Donald's since the first one opened over 40 years ago in California. It seems an incredible statistic, but keep in mind that 8 percent of American employees work in foodservice, and many young people find their first job in foodservice or a hotel. You may already have worked in a hospitality operation yourself.

The hospitality industry is composed of 70 percent part-time, short-term people. They are "only working here until"—until they get out of high school, until they get out of college, until they have enough money to buy a car, or until an opening comes up someplace else. It is not uncommon to hear a young hourly employee say, "I'll keep this job until I can get a real job," for what they often mean is that they plan to switch from an hourly to a salaried position.

The Jobs and the Workers

Hotels and restaurants are dependent on large numbers of people to fill low-wage entry-level jobs that have little interest and no perceived future. Washing pots, busing tables, dishing out the same food every day from the same steam table, lifting heavy bags, mopping dirty floors, cleaning rest rooms, straightening up messy rooms left by unheeding customers every single day can become very tiresome. Workers take these jobs either because no special skill, ability, or experience is required, or because nothing else is available.

Some of these people consider the work demeaning. Even though they are doing demanding work that is absolutely essential to the operation, management often looks down on them. They are frequently taken for granted, ignored, or spoken to only when reprimanded. Given the nature of the work and the attitudes of management and sometimes of other workers, it is no wonder that turnover is high.

Another level of hourly worker is the skilled or semiskilled: the front desk clerk, the cashier, the bartender, the cook, the waiter and waitress. These jobs are more appealing, the money is better, and there is sometimes a chance for advancement. Yet here, too, you often find temporary workers—students, moonlighters, people who cannot find anything in their own fields—people working there *until.*

Many employers assume that their employee will not stay long, and most of them do not. According to a National Restaurant Association's Restaurant Industry Operations Report, the turnover rate for hourly workers in full-service operations is 100 percent. That means that your typical full-service restaurant will lose every one of its hourly employees during one year and have to fill every position. (A study by the Educational Foundation of the National Restaurant Association asked 857 ex-foodservice workers to explain why they left their jobs. The most frequently cited reasons were more money, a better work schedule, and more enjoyable work.)

There is really no valid stereotype of today's hospitality worker. The industry employs people of all ages and backgrounds. In fact, an already diverse workplace is becoming more diverse than ever. This is due in part to the fact that new workers entering the workforce are overwhelmingly non-Caucasian ethnic minorities, immigrants, and women.

Approximately half of the foodservice workforce, as well as a big presence in hotels, are employees from 18 to 34 years old, a group referred to as **Generation X.** X'ers will work hard, but they will also make certain demands. They want to do work that they consider worthwhile as well as work they enjoy doing. The employees want their supervisors to let them be more involved by listening to them and by allowing them to participate in decision making. Not surprisingly, employees do not want supervisors to bark orders in a militant fashion, they want training and expect management to invest time and money in their training and development.

> Everyone knows that hanging onto the right people is really hard. In fact, most emerging businesses say that this is their greatest challenge. And instead of wondering where all of the employees have gone, shouldn't we ask where all the good leaders have gone?
>
> *Source:* "Labor crisis or lapse in leadership?" *Restaurant Hospitality,* Vol. 83, No. 7, p. 58. July 1999.

At least 50 percent of both foodservice and hotel workers are women. There are more women working now than ever before and they are not necessarily satisfied with traditional women's jobs. There are many female bartenders, cooks, and chefs, as well as many other management positions now filled by women.

The fastest-growing ethnic groups in the United States are Hispanics, people of Asian origin, and African-Americans, so it is not surprising to see many of these people in hospitality jobs. Did you know that Hispanics have been the biggest minority in foodservice since 1993? Did you also know that one out of six foodservice workers speaks a language other than English at home? We discuss diversity of the hospitality workforce in more detail in Chapter 3.

As we noted in Chapter 1, many of today's workers tend to have a higher expectation level and a lower frustration tolerance than workers of past generations. They expect more out of a job than just a paycheck. Most are not tied by need to jobs they don't like; in good times, hospitality jobs are usually plentiful, and unemployment insurance tides workers over during a move from one job to another. Availability of jobs, of course, varies with economic conditions and from one area to another. But even needing that paycheck does not guarantee that a person will work well on the job. That is why it is necessary to have supervisors and managers.

Approximately half of the foodservice workforce, as well as a big presence in hotels, are employees from 18 to 34 years old, a group referred to as **Generation X.** (Courtesy of Sodexho)

The Nature of Leadership

You are going to be a **leader.** Now, you may wonder, "What is a leader, and how is it any different from being a manager?" These are good questions. As a part of the management staff, one is expected to produce goods and services by working with people and using resources such as equipment and employees. That is what being a manager or supervisor is all about. As discussed in Chapter 1, an important managerial function is to be a leader. A leader can be defined as someone who guides or influences the actions of his or her employees to reach certain goals. A leader is a person whom people follow voluntarily. What you, as a supervisor, must do is to direct the work of your people in a way that causes them to do it voluntarily. You don't have to be a born leader, you don't have to be magnetic or charismatic; you have to get people to work for you willingly and to the best of their ability. That is what **leadership** is all about.

Although it is true that many leadership skills are innate and that not all managers make great leaders, it is also true that most managers will benefit from leadership training. Moreover, natural leaders will flourish in an environment that supports their growth and development. Therefore, activities surrounding leadership development are worth the time and expense. Traditional characteristics of leadership development are[1]:

[1]"Labor crisis or lapse in leadership?" *Restaurant Hospitality,* Vol. 83, No. 7, July 1999, p. 58.

1. We spend millions of dollars teaching managers technical skill and administrative functions.
2. Managers' "numbers" are the primary benchmark for evaluating their successes and failures.
3. Management training programs are more focused on short-term skills than on long-term development processes.

You need to break out of this limited training "box" if you want to develop leaders who can help your businesses grow. There are seven steps to establishing a foundation for leadership development:

1. Commit to investing the time, resources, and money needed to create a culture that supports leadership development.
2. Identify and communicate the differences between management skills and leadership abilities within the organization.
3. Develop quantifiable measurables that support leadership skills. These include percentage of retention, percentage of promotables, and percentage of cross-trained team members.
4. Make leadership skills a focus of management training. These include communication skills (written, verbal, nonverbal, and listening), team-building skills (teamwork, coaching, and feedback), proactive planning skills (transitioning from managing shifts to managing businesses), and interpersonal skills (motivation, delegation, decision making, and problem solving).
5. Implement ongoing programs that focus on leadership skills, such as managing multiple priorities, creating change, and presentation skills.
6. Know that in the right culture, leaders can be found at entry level.
7. Recognize, reward, and celebrate leaders for their passion, dedication, and results.

In theory, you have authority over your people because you have **formal authority,** or the right to command, given to you by the organization. You are the boss and you have the **power,** the ability to command. You control the hiring, firing, raises, rewards, discipline, and punishment. In all reality, your authority is anything but absolute. **Real authority** is conferred on your subordinates, and you have to earn the right to lead them. It is possible for you to be the **formal leader** of your work group as well as have someone else who is the **informal leader** actually calling the shots.

The relationship between you and your people is a fluid one, subject to many subtle currents and cross-currents between them and you. If they do not willingly accept your authority, they have many ways of withholding success. They can stay home from work, come in late, drag out the work into overtime, produce inferior products, drive your customers away with rudeness and poor service, break the rules, refuse to do what you tell them to, create crises, and punish you by walking off the job and leaving you in the lurch. Laying down the law, the typical method of control in hospitality operations, does not necessarily maintain authority; on the contrary, it usually creates a negative, nonproductive environment.

What it all adds up to is that your job as a supervisor is to direct and oversee a group of transients who are often untrained, all of who are different from each other, and many of whom would rather be working somewhere else. You are dependent on them to do the work for which you are responsible. You will succeed only to the degree that they permit you to succeed. It is your job to get the workers to do their best for the enterprise, for the customers, and for you. How can one do this?

As a distinguished leadership expert noted, "managers are people who do things right, and leaders are people who do the right things." Think about that for a moment. In other words, managers are involved in being efficient and in mastering routines, whereas leaders are involved in being effective and turning goals into reality. As a supervisor and leader, your job is to **do the right things right,** to be both efficient and effective. An effective supervisor in the hospitality industry is one whom, first, knows and understands basic principles of management, and second, applies them to managing all the resource operations.

In the hospitality industry we use a technique referred to as **MBWA,** *management by wandering around,* spending a significant part of your day talking to your employees, your guests, and your peers. As you are walking around and talking to these various people, you should be performing three vital roles discussed in this book: listening, coaching, and troubleshooting.

Check Your Knowledge

1. What is a leader?
2. What is the difference between formal and informal authority?

Choosing a Leadership Style

The term *leadership style* refers to your pattern of interacting with your subordinates: how you direct and control the work of others, and how you get them to produce the goods and services for which you are responsible. It includes not only your manner of giving instructions, but the methods and techniques you use to motivate your workers and to assure that your instructions are carried out.

Leadership Styles

There are several different forms of **leadership style:** autocratic, bureaucratic, democratic, and laissez-faire being the most popular styles today. Before choosing a style of leadership, one must identify the pros and cons of each and then decide if it will be the most effective style in the hospitality industry.

Autocratic leadership style can be identified with the early, classical approach to management. A supervisor practicing an autocratic style is likely to make decisions without input from staff, to give orders without explanation or defense, and to expect the orders to be obeyed. When this style of leadership is used, employees become dependent on supervisors for instructions. The wants and needs of the employees come second to those of the organization and the supervisor.

In bureaucratic leadership style, a supervisor manages "by the book." The leader relies on the property's rules, regulations, and procedures for decisions that he makes. To the employees, their leader appears to be a "police officer." This style is appropriate when the employees can be permitted no discretion in the decisions to be made.

Democratic (also called *participative*) leadership style is almost the reverse of the autocratic style discussed previously. A democratic supervisor wants to share decision-making responsibility. They want to consult with the group members and to solicit their participation in making decisions and resolving problems that affect the employees. The employer strongly considers the opinions of employees and seeks their thoughts and suggestions. All employees are informed about all matters that concern them. One could compare a democratic supervisor to a coach who is leading his or her team.

Laissez-faire (also called *free-rein*) leadership style refers to a hands-off approach in which the supervisor actually does as little leading as possible. In effect, the laissez-faire supervisor delegates all authority and power to the employees. The supervisor relies on the employees to establish goals, make decisions, and solve problems. At best, the laissez-faire style has limited application to the hospitality industry.

The Old-Style Boss

In the hospitality industry, the traditional method of dealing with hourly workers has generally been some variation of the command–obey method combined with **carrot-and-stick techniques** of **reward and punishment.** The motivators relied upon to produce the work are money (the carrot) and fear (the stick)—fear of punishment, fear of losing the money by being fired. All too often, the manner of direction is to lay down the law in definite terms, such as cursing, shouting, and threatening as necessary to arouse the proper degree of fear to motivate the worker.

People who practice this **autocratic method** of managing employees believe that it's the only method that employees will understand. Perhaps that is the way the supervisor was raised, or perhaps it is the only method the supervisor has ever seen in action. In any case, it expresses their view of the people involved that "workers these days are no good."

Some workers are simply bad workers. However, cursing, shouting, and threatening seldom helps them improve. Many workers do respond to a command-obey style of direction, but those workers often come from authoritarian backgrounds and have never known anything else. This style is traditional and military; the style of dictatorship in countries from which some immigrants come. However, for your average American employee, it does not work. It may be enough to keep people on the job but not working to their full capacity.

When coupled with a negative view of the worker, this style of direction and control is far more likely to increase problems than to lessen them, and to backfire by breeding resentment, low morale, and adversary relationships. In extreme cases, the boss and the company become the bad guys, the enemy, and workers give as little as possible and take as much as they can. In response, close supervision and tight control are required to see that nobody gets away with anything. In this type of atmosphere, customer service suffers and patrons go somewhere else.

We are also learning more about what causes workers to work productively, including many of the things we have been talking about, such as positive work climate, person-to-person relations, and other people-oriented methods and techniques. At this point, let us look at some current theories of leadership and see how—or whether—they can be applied in hotel and foodservice settings. These theories emerged in the 1950s and 1960s, following the discovery that making workers happy does not necessarily make them productive. The theories are based on what behavioral scientists, psychologists, and sociologists tell us about human behavior. They explore what causes people to work productively and how this knowledge can be used in managing employees.

Theory X and Theory Y

In the late 1950s, Douglas McGregor of the MIT School of Industrial Management advanced the thesis that business organizations based their management of workers on assumptions about people that were wrong and were actually counterproductive. He described these faulty assumptions about the average human being as **Theory X**[2]:

1. They have an inborn dislike of work and will avoid it as much as possible.
2. They must be "coerced, controlled, directed, threatened with punishment" to get the work done.
3. They prefer to be led, avoid responsibility, lack ambition, and want security above all else.

McGregor argues: "These characteristics are not inborn." He believed people behaved this way on the job because they were treated as though these things were true. In fact, he stated, "this is a narrow and unproductive view of human beings," and he proposed **Theory Y**[3]:

1. Work is as natural as play or rest; people do not dislike it inherently.
2. Control and the threat of punishment are not the only means of getting people to do their jobs. They will work of their own accord toward objectives to which they feel committed.
3. People become committed to objectives that will fulfill inner personal needs, such as self-respect, independence, achievement, recognition, status, and growth.
4. Under the right conditions, people learn not only to accept responsibility, but also to seek it. Lack of ambition, avoidance of responsibility, and the desire for security are not innate human characteristics.

[2]For a more detailed explanation of Theory X please refer to: Douglas McGregor. *The Human Side of Enterprise.* McGraw-Hill, 1960.
[3]Ibid.

5. Capacity for applying imagination, ingenuity, and creativity to solving on-the-job problems is "widely, not narrowly, distributed in the population."

6. The modern industrial organization uses only a portion of the intellectual potential of the average human being.

Thus, if work could fulfill both the goals of the enterprise and the needs of the workers, they would be self-motivated to produce, and consequently, coercion and the threat of punishment would be unnecessary.

Theory X fits the old-style hospitality manager to a T, and it is safe to say that this pattern of thinking is still common in many other industries as well. However, behavioral science theory and management practice have both moved in the direction of Theory Y. Theory Y is a revised view of human nature with emphasis on using the full range of workers' talents, needs, and aspirations to meet the goals of the enterprise.

A popular way of moving toward a Theory Y style of people management is to involve one's workers in certain aspects of management, such as problem solving and decision making. Usually, such involvement is carried out in a group setting: meetings of the workers for the specific purpose of securing their input. The degree of involvement the boss allows or seeks can vary from merely keeping the workers informed of things that affect their work to delegating decision making entirely to the group.

The participative management style, mentioned in Chapter 1, results when workers have a high degree of involvement in such management concerns as planning and decision making. Enthusiasts of a participatory style of leadership believe that the greater the degree of worker participation, the better the decisions and the more likely they are to be carried out. However, others point out that the degree of participation that is appropriate for a given work group will depend on the type of work, the people involved, the nature of the problem, the skill and sensitivity of the leader, and the pressures of time—the situational leadership approach, to be discussed shortly. The degree to which the boss involves the workers may also vary from time to time, depending on circumstances. You are not going to make a group decision when a drunk is making a scene in the dining room or when a fire alarm is going off on the seventh floor.

Situational Leadership

In the **situational leadership** model developed by Kenneth Blanchard and Paul Hersey, leadership behaviors are sorted into two categories: directive behavior and supportive behavior. *Directive behavior* means telling an employee exactly what you want done, as well as when, where, and how to do it. The focus is to get a job done, and it is best used when employees are learning a new aspect of their jobs. *Supportive behavior* is meant to show caring and support to your employees by praising, encouraging, listening to their ideas, involving them in decision making, and helping them reach their own solutions. This method is best used when an employee lacks commitment to do a job.

By combining directive and supportive behaviors, Hersey and Blanchard came up with four possible leadership styles for different conditions. When an employee

∾ profile

JIM SULLIVAN

Courtesy of Jim Sullivan

I like what I do. Every year I arrange dozens and dozens of service and sales-building seminars for successful companies around the world. I also help overhaul and re-design manager and server training manuals and programs for a variety of success-ful chains and independent restaurants. And in doing so, I get to assimilate a wide variety of best practices relating to customer service, employee retention, same-store-sales building, cost controls, and creative management. I also see subtle pat-terns, trends, and evolutions occurring in hospitality management theory and prac-tice. In case you hadn't noticed, a sea change of behavior is in full swing right now. I'd like to outline and possibly debunk nine customer service myths that used to hold water in our industry and now are losing value as operating principles. Do you agree or disagree with the following points and counterpoints? The way you think about each one may provide a road map for your operation's success in the looming new century.

No. 1: "The customer comes first." Really? Today you need good employees more than they need you. As Wally Doolin, chief executive of TGI Friday's parent, Carlson Restaurants Worldwide, pointed out at the recent Multi-Unit Foodservice Operators confab: "Our employees are our first market." Amen. So, instead of rank-ing relationships between customers and employees, we should focus on establish-ing equity instead. In other words, never treat a customer better than you do an em-ployee. Service, like charity, begins at home, and if you're not investing in serving your team as well as you serve your customers, you're headed for trouble, pure and simple.

No. 2: "A satisfied customer comes back." Customer "satisfaction" is meaning-less. Customer loyalty is priceless. People don't want to be "satisfied" as customers. Heck, Kmart can "satisfy" customers, for crying out loud. They want fun, flair, and memorable experiences. A satisfied customer doesn't necessarily ever come back. As the noted New York restaurateur Danny Meyer says, "Give your guests what they remember and give them something new each time they visit."

No. 3: "We've got to focus on the competition." That's right. But what you may not realize is that your competition is the customer, not other restaurants. So stop looking across the street and focus on the face above the tabletop or at the counter.

No. 4: "Comment cards and 'secret' shoppers accurately measure service." Mea-suring customer satisfaction in your restaurant merely by tallying mystery-shopper scores and comment cards is like judging chili by counting the beans. Measure what matters: Same-store sales increases, higher customer traffic, and lower employee turnover are just as important—if not more so. Mystery shopping is effective, but only if it measures the good as well as the bad and the "shoppers" are people with hos-pitality experience who know the subtleties to look for. Focus on creating internal quality for your staff first, and they will build a happy customer. A happy customer buys more.

No. 5: "People are our most important asset." That old adage is wrong. The right people are your most important asset. The right people are not "warm bodies." The right people are those servers, cooks, hostesses, or managers who exhibit the desired team and customer service behavior you want, as a natural extension of their character and attitude, regardless of any control or incentive system. Hire the personality; train the skills. Where do you find them? See No. 6.

No. 6: "There's a labor crisis." According to the National Restaurant Association and the Bureau of Labor Statistics, every seven days we turn over 250,000 employees in this industry. Yikes. But where do they go? Is it to other industries or other restaurants? Get straight on this: We don't have a "labor" crisis. We've got a turnover crisis. So the tough question you have to ask yourself about your operation is not, "Are there enough people available to work?" but rather, "Are there enough people available to work who want to work for us?" Make your operation a fun, reputable, and caring place to work.

No. 7: "Invest first in building the brand." Sorry, I disagree. Invest first in people, second in brand, third in bricks and mortar. Mike Snyder, president of Red Robin International Inc., summed it up this way. He said, "Give me a Weber [barbecue] and a tent in a parking lot along with the best service-oriented people who take care of the customer and each other, and I'll beat the off the restaurant with the multimillion-dollar physical plant every shift."

No. 8: "Information is power." Know the difference between "information" and "communication." Those two words often are used interchangeably but in fact mean two different things. Information is "giving out"; communication is "getting through." Training is your secret weapon, but I suspect that much of your training informs more than it communicates. Besides, the belief that information is power leads managers to hoard it, not share it, and that's backward thinking. Sharing information not only enlightens but also shares the burden of leadership and engages the creativity and solutions of the entire team.

No. 9: "We need new ideas to progress." Why do companies always want new ideas? I'll tell you why: Because "new ideas" are easy. That's right. The hard part is letting go of ideas that worked for you two years ago and are now out of date. So before you and your team brainstorm dozens of new ideas that get listed on flip charts, give everyone a warm fuzzy feeling and that never are implemented, allow me to suggest a different angle. The newest and most innovative thing you can do for your business may be to master the "basics" that everyone knows and no one executes consistently. I'm referring to caring behavior, service with flair, and employee appreciation. Because, unlike Nehru jackets and the Backstreet Boys, the basics of great service never go out of style.

In summary, remember that there is no silver bullet for guaranteeing great service and a great team. Maybe Darrell Rolph, chief executive of Carlos O'Kelly's, says it best: "Keep it fresh, keep it focused, and remember to say thank you."

has much commitment or enthusiasm but little competence to do a job, a **directing style** is needed; this is high on directive and low on supportive behaviors. Suppose that you have a new employee full of enthusiasm who knows little about how to do the job. A directing style is appropriate: You train the new employee by giving multiple instructions, you make the decisions, you solve the problems, and you closely supervise. Enthusiastic beginners need this direction. A directing style is also appropriate when a decision has to be made quickly and there is some risk involved, such as when there is a fire and you need to get your employees out of danger.

As new employees get into their jobs, they often lose some of their initial excitement when they realize that the job is more difficult or not as interesting as they originally envisioned. This is the time to use a **coaching style,** with lots of directive behaviors to continue to build skills and supportive behaviors to build commitment. In addition to providing much direct supervision, you provide support. You listen, you encourage, you praise, you ask for input and ideas, and you consult with the employee.

As employees become technically competent on the job, their commitment frequently wavers between enthusiasm and uncertainty. In a situation like this, the use of a **supporting style** that is high on supportive behaviors and low on directive behaviors is required. If an employee shows both commitment and competence, a **delegating style** is suitable. A delegating style of leadership is low on directive and supportive behaviors because you are turning over responsibility for day-to-day decision making to the employee doing the job. These employees don't need much direction, and they provide much of their own support.

Using this view of situational leadership, you need to assess the competence and commitment level of your employee in relation to the task at hand before choosing an appropriate leadership style (Table 2.1). As a supervisor, your goal should be to build your employees' competence and commitment levels to the point where you are using less time-consuming styles, such as supporting and delegating, and getting quality results.

TABLE 2.1   ⚘   **Situational Leadership**

When an Employee Demonstrates:	*Use:*
Low competence, high commitment	Directing leadership: high directive, low supportive
Some competence, low commitment	Coaching leadership: high directive, high supportive
High competence, variable commitment	Supporting leadership: low directive, high supportive
High competence, high commitment	Delegating leadership: low directive, low supportive

Adapted from Kenneth Blanchard, Patricia Zigarmi, and Drea Zigarmi, *Leadership and the One Minute Manager.* New York: William Morrow, 1985.

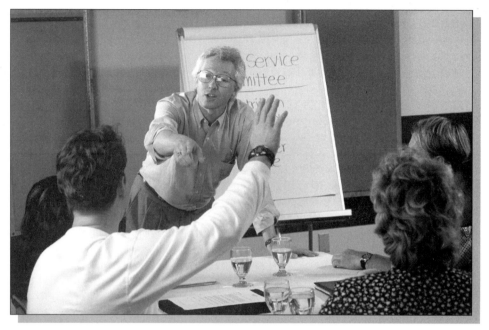

Transactional leaders motivate workers by appealing to their self-interest. (Courtesy of Sodexho)

Transformational Leadership

Bums, a prominent leadership researcher, proposed that leadership is a process that is either transactional or transformational in nature.[4] **Transactional leaders** motivate workers by appealing to their self-interest. In other words, workers do their jobs and give their compliance in return for rewards such as pay and status. Transactional leaders stress communication of job assignments, work standards, goals, and so on, in order to maintain the status quo.

On the other side of the fence are informational leaders. Instead of using rewards and incentives to motivate employees, **transformational leaders** do the following.

1. Communicate with and inspire workers about the mission and objectives of the company.
2. Provide workers with meaningful, interesting, and challenging jobs.
3. Act as a coach and mentor to support, develop, and empower workers.
4. Lead by example.

By appealing to workers' higher-order needs, transformational leaders gain much loyalty that is especially useful in times of change.

[4]Transactional and transformational leadership are discussed in depth by Bums (1978), Bass (1985), and Seltzer and Bass (1990).

Developing Your Own Style

Applying theory to reality is going to be something you work out for yourself. No one can teach you. Since even the theorists disagree among themselves, the choice is wide open. But don't throw it all out; a lot of what the behavioral scientists are saying can be very useful to you. There does seem to be general agreement, supported by research and experience, that the assumptions Theory X makes about people are, at best, unproductive and at worst counterproductive, if not downright destructive. However, an authoritarian style of leadership can be effective and even necessary in many situations, and there is actually no reason why it cannot be combined with a high concern for the workers and achieve good results.

As for Theory Y, probably two-thirds of the workforce has the potential for a Theory Y type of motivation—that is, working to satisfy such inner needs as self-respect, achievement, independence, responsibility, status, and growth. The problem with applying this theory in the hospitality industry is really not the workers. It is the nature of the work, the number of variables you have to deal with (including high worker turnover), the unpredictability of the situation, the tradition of authoritarian carrot–stick management, and the pressures of time. The pace and pattern of the typical day do not leave much room for group activity or for planning and implementing changes in work patterns to provide such motivation. Furthermore, your own supervisor or your company's policies may not give you the freedom to make changes. In conclusion, Theory Y does not always work for everyone.

However, it is remarkable what is possible when an imaginative and determined manager sets out to utilize this type of motivation and develop this type of commitment. We will have a lot more to say about motivation in Chapter 5.

> Success in life is measured by what we have overcome to be what we are and by what we have accomplished. How we are is more important than what position we have.

The best style of leadership, for you, is whatever works best in terms of these three basics: your own personality, the workers you supervise, and the situations you face. It should be a situational type of leadership, just as your management style must be a flex style that reacts to situations as they arise.

You may give an order to Peter, but say "please" to Paul. You may stop a fight in the kitchen with a quick command when waitress Margie and waiter Charley keep picking up each other's orders, and then later you may spend a good hour with the two of them helping them reach an agreement to stop their running battle. You may see responsibilities you could delegate to Evelyn or John. You may see opportunities to bring workers in on solving work problems, or you may solve them yourself because of time pressures or because the problems are not appropriate for group discussion.

You can borrow elements and techniques of Theory Y without erecting a whole system of participative management. If something does not work for all three of you—yourself, the workers, the situation—don't do it.

What you need most in finding what works best is *awareness:* awareness of yourself and the feelings, desires, biases, abilities, power, and influence you bring to a situation; awareness of the special needs and traits of your various workers and awareness of the situation, the big picture, so you can recognize what is needed, conceptual skills and human skills.

The best style of leadership is to be yourself. Trying to copy someone else's style usually does not work—the situation is different, you are different, the shoe does not fit.

Being a Winner!

The Winner—is always part of the answer.

The Loser—is always part of the problem.

The Winner—always has a program.

The Loser—always has an excuse.

The Winner—says "Let me do that for you."

The Loser—says, "That's not my job."

The Winner—sees an answer for every problem.

The Loser—sees a problem for every answer.

The Winner—sees a green near every sand trap.

The Loser—sees two or three sand traps near every green.

The Winner—says, "It may be difficult but it's possible."

The Loser—says, "It may be possible, but it's too difficult."

BE A WINNER

∾ key points

1. Hotels and restaurants depend on large numbers of people to fill entry-level low-wage jobs that have little interest and no perceived future.

2. Turnover in the hospitality field is generally high. For example, your typical full-service restaurant will lose every one of its hourly employees during one year and have to fill every position.

3. There is really no valid stereotype of today's hospitality workers. The industry employs people of all ages and backgrounds. As a matter of fact, an already diverse workplace is becoming more diverse than ever. The hospitality industry employs many young people, many women, and many members of minority groups.

4. Being a leader means guiding or influencing the actions of your employees to reach certain goals. A leader is a person who people follow voluntarily.

5. As a supervisor, you have been given the formal authority to oversee your employees. Your subordinates confer real authority, and you have to earn the right to lead them.

6. As a supervisor and leader, your job is to do the right things right.

7. Leadership style refers to your pattern of interacting with your subordinates, how you direct and control the work of others, and how you get them to produce the goods and services for which you are responsible.

8. The old-style boss uses an autocratic method of managing employees that relies on the motivators of money or fear.

9. According to McGregor, the autocratic style is typical of Theory X bosses. Theory Y bosses believe that workers will work of their own accord toward objectives to which they feel committed.

10. In situational leadership, the leadership style is adapted to the uniqueness of each situation. The four primary styles of leading are directing, coaching, supporting, and delegating.

11. Transactional leaders appeal to workers' self-interest. Transformational leaders appeal to workers' higher-order needs.

12. Employers and employees must develop mutual respect for success.

&cue; key terms

autocratic method	leadership style
carrot-and-stick technique	MBWA
coaching style	power
delegating style	real authority
directing style	reward and punishment
do the right things right	situational leadership
formal authority	supporting style
formal leader	Theory X
Generation X	Theory Y
informal leader	transactional leader
leader	transformational leader
leadership	

&cue; review questions

Answer each question in complete sentences. Read each question carefully and make sure that you answer all parts of the question. Organize your answer using more than one paragraph when appropriate.

1. Identify typical hourly jobs in foodservice and lodging establishments. Include both skilled and unskilled jobs.
2. If a restaurant's turnover rate is 100 percent, what does that mean?
3. Define *leader* and *leadership*.
4. What is meant by "do the right things right"?
5. Compare and contrast the concepts of formal and real authority.
6. Why does a fear-and-punishment approach to supervision usually create a negative, nonproductive environment?
7. In two sentences, describe the essence of each of the following leadership styles: autocratic, Theory X, Theory Y, situational leadership, and transformational leadership.

&cue; activities and applications

1. **Discussion Questions**
   - Why do you think turnover is high in hotels and restaurants? If you resigned from a hospitality job, what were your reasons? What could be done by management to reduce turnover?

- Why might it be difficult to supervise workers in minimum-wage or low-wage hospitality jobs that require no special skills? What kinds of problems might arise? What can be done to solve these problems or avoid them?
- Which view of people is more accurate: Theory X or Y? Give examples from your own work experience to support your view.
- Under what circumstances might you need to be an autocratic leader?
- Describe situations in which each of the four styles of situational leadership would be appropriate.

3. Leadership Assessment

Using Figure 2.1, assess your leadership abilities.

4. L-E-A-D-E-R Activity

Using the letters in the word *leader,* think of a leader's qualities and actions that make him or her a good leader and fit as many as possible into L-E-A-D-E-R. For example, L—lends a hand; E—ethical; A—aware; D— . . . , and so on.

5. Case Study: Firm, Fair, and Open?

Cree has just been hired as the dining room supervisor on the noon shift in the coffee shop of a large hotel. She came from a similar job in a much smaller hotel, but she feels confident that she can handle the larger setting and the larger staff. Because she is eager to start things off right, she asks all the servers to stay for 10 minutes at the end of the shift so that she can say a few words to everyone.

She begins by describing her background and experience and then proceeds to her philosophy of management. "I expect a lot of my people," she says. "I want your best work, and I hope you want it, too, for your own sake. You will not find me easy, but you will find me fair and open with you, and I hope you will feel free to come to me with suggestions or problems. I can't solve them all, but I will do my best for you." She smiles and looks at each one in turn.

"Now, the first thing I want to do," she continues, "is to introduce a system of rotating your stations so that everyone gets a turn at the busiest tables and the best tips and the shortest distance to the kitchen. I've posted the assignments on the bulletin board, and you will start off that way tomorrow and keep these stations for a week. I will be making some other changes, too, but let's take things one at a time."

"Are there any questions or comments?" Cree pauses for three seconds and then says, "I am very particular about being on time, about uniforms and grooming, and about prompt and courteous customer service. I advise you all to start off tomorrow on the right foot and we'll all be much happier during these hours we work together. See you tomorrow at 10:25."

QUESTIONS

1. What kind of impression do you think that Cree is making on the workers?
2. What are the good points in her presentation?
3. What mistakes do you think she is making?
4. Why did nobody ask questions or make comments?
5. From this first impression, what would you say is her management style?

Directions: Answer each question realistically using the following scale.

1 — I do this seldom or never.
2 — I do this occasionally.
3 — I do this always or most of the time.

If your total points are:

175–210   You are an excellent leader.

120–175   You are probably new to leadership and trying hard. Work on the areas where you rated yourself a "1."

Below 120   You need to improve in many areas.

Personal Qualities

SELF-CONFIDENT

_____   1. I believe in myself.

CONSISTENT/COMMITTED

_____   2. I stay focused on the vision.

_____   3. I keep my word.

UPBEAT/POSITIVE

_____   4. I am a positive thinker.

_____   5. I am an optimist — my glass is half-full.

HONEST/OPEN

_____   6. I am up-front and honest with others.

_____   7. I do not get defensive in conversation.

INTEGRITY

_____   8. I honor my commitments and promises.

FUNNY

_____   9. I use my sense of humor.

_____   10. I love to laugh at myself.

RISK-TAKING

_____   11. I take calculated risks when appropriate.

_____   12. I let myself and others make mistakes.

CREATIVE/DIVERGENT & ABSTRACT THINKER

_____   13. I encourage and try to look at things in new and different ways.

INTELLIGENT/COMPETENT

_____   14. I am knowledgeable and competent in my field.

_____   15. I can make the complex simple.

_____   16. I am a life long learner.

WIN/WIN ORIENTATION

_____   17. In interactions with others, I want everyone to be a winner.

ETHICAL

_____   18. I maintain ethical standards.

ORGANIZED

_____   19. My work and paperwork is well-organized.

FIGURE 2.1   Leadership assessment tool. Adapted from Kenneth Blanchard, Patricia Zigarmi, and Drea Zigarmi, *Leadership and the One Minute Manager.* New York: William Morrow and Company, 1985.

LOOKS TO FUTURE

_____ 20. I keep an eye and ear directed to trends in my industry.

_____ 21. I try to innovate.

CONGRUENT

_____ 22. I walk the talk.

FLEXIBLE

_____ 23. I keep an open mind.

_____ 24. I can change my mind and change my plans when appropriate.

Vision

VISION

_____ 25. I let my company's vision be my guide.

PERSONAL VISION

_____ 26. I write and revise my personal mission statement yearly.

Managing Relationships

SUPPORTING

_____ 27. I seek first to understand, then to be understood.

_____ 28. I genuinely show acceptance and positive regard toward staff.

_____ 29. I refrain from rudeness and treat others diplomatically and politely.

_____ 30. I maintain the self-respect of all individuals.

_____ 31. I have an open-door policy.

DEVELOPING/MENTORING

_____ 32. I believe developing and mentoring others is part and parcel of being a professional, and that this will enhance, not detract, from my career.

_____ 33. I actively develop and act as a mentor.

EMPOWERING

_____ 34. I actively empower staff to do their jobs in the manner they want as long as it supports our mission.

RECOGNIZING & REWARDING

_____ 35. I use a variety of techniques to recognize and reward staff for their achievements and contributions.

_____ 36. I provide fair, specific, and timely recognition and rewards.

_____ 37. I recognize and reward more people than just the top performers.

_____ 38. I use recognition and rewards that are desirable to the recipients.

MANAGING CONFLICT & CHANGE

_____ 39. I see conflict as an opportunity to grow.

_____ 40. I mediate conflicts and encourage constructive resolution of conflicts.

_____ 41. I work on building and maintaining cooperative staff relationships.

_____ 42. I realize that people generally don't resist change, but they do resist being changed.

TEAMBUILDING

_____ 43. I understand the teambuilding process.

_____ 44. I model teambuilding skills.

_____ 45. I help form and monitor teams.

FIGURE 2.1 *(Continued)*

NETWORKING

_____ 46. I actively network with people both within and outside of the industry.

_____ 47. I keep in touch with members of my network.

_____ 48. I am good at remembering names.

Managing the Work

PLANNING

_____ 49. After considering input, I help establish clear priorities and goals for our unit/department.

_____ 50. Unit/department policies and procedures are spelled out.

_____ 51. Budgets are devised yearly and compared to monthly reports.

ORGANIZING

_____ 52. The work of my unit/department runs efficiently.

DECISION MAKING

_____ 53. I do much information gathering and get much input before making decisions.

_____ 54. I build commitment for my decisions.

_____ 55. I develop creative solutions.

PROBLEM SOLVING

_____ 56. I identify problems and take responsibility for them.

_____ 57. I use the problem-solving process including trying creative solutions.

_____ 58. I don't ignore problem behaviors and I deal effectively and quickly with them.

CLARIFYING ROLES & OBJECTIVES

_____ 59. My employees know what is expected of them.

INFORMING

_____ 60. I interact with and inform my colleagues.

_____ 61. I keep my supervisor informed about what I am doing.

_____ 62. I prepare meeting agendas for all meetings I conduct.

_____ 63. I keep staff informed about policies, procedures, and all changes.

MONITORING

_____ 64. I monitor the performance of staff.

_____ 65. I meet regularly with staff.

_____ 66. I periodically walk around to talk with employees and guests.

_____ 67. I attend monthly meetings of the local hospitality owners/operators.

MANAGING TIME

_____ 68. I set daily priorities and do first things first.

_____ 69. I set time aside every day for physical exercise.

DELEGATING

_____ 70. I delegate appropriate tasks.

FIGURE 2.1 _(Continued)_

6. Do you think that people will feel free to come to her with suggestions and problems?
7. Do you think that she will set a good example?
8. Is she fair in her demands?
9. Do you think that her people will "start off on the right foot" as she suggests?
10. Do you think that she sees herself clearly? Is she aware of her impact on others?

∾ chapter 3

Workplace Diversity

overview

∾ As a hospitality supervisor, you will be supervising people from cultures quite different from your own. A "standard" approach to supervision, which does not consider each employee's cultural background, will often create communication barriers. Culturally appropriate communication strategies are needed. But what exactly is culture? Our **culture** is defined as our values, which are manifested in the way we behave, speak, think, dress, our religious beliefs, the music we like, the way we interact, and the food we eat. Culture strongly influences behavior.

Failure to understand and respect the diverse cultural backgrounds of your employees, and the differences among them, can result in misunderstandings, tension, poor performance, poor employee morale, and higher rates of absenteeism and turnover. On the other hand, when differences are respected, the working environment is richer, much more fun, and even more interesting. Employee satisfaction and performance improve because of this. Diversity in the workplace is a given. Whether you decide to recognize it and build on it is a personal choice.

In this chapter we help you to:

∾ Define the term *diversity*.

∾ Explain the difference between a cultural tendency and a stereotype, and outline the cultural tendencies associated with several minority populations in the U.S.

∽ Describe steps that increase positive cross-cultural communication skills.

∽ List guidelines for managing diversity issues positively.

What Is Diversity?

Up until the late 1980s, white males made up the majority of the U.S. workforce. Now this group represents less than 50 percent of the workforce. Many of the new workers entering the labor force are minorities, such as Hispanics, Latinos, Asians, and many immigrants. The reasons behind these trends include a young, growing minority population and a continuing high rate of immigration.

Understanding and embracing diversity is of critical importance in today's increasingly multicultural and diverse society. The term **diversity** is used often when discussing people of different cultures. *Diversity* refers to the following cultural as well as physical dimensions which separate and distinguish us both as individuals and as groups.[1]

- Culture
- Ethnic group
- Race
- Religion
- Language
- Age
- Gender
- Physical abilities and qualities
- Sexual orientation

These dimensions seem to have the most significant impact in the workplace, so we refer to them as the **primary dimensions of diversity** (Figure 3.1). Other dimensions that are changeable, but have less significance, include occupation and work experience, education, income, and marital status. These are referred to as the **secondary dimensions of diversity.**

Culture, ethnic group, and race are related terms. *Culture* is a learned behavior consisting of a unique set of beliefs, values, attitudes, habits, customs, traditions, and other forms of behavior. Culture influences the way that people behave. Cultural behavior varies from culture to culture.[2] Culture refers to the behaviors, beliefs, and characteristic of a particular group, such as an ethnic group. *Ethnic groups* share a common and distinctive culture, including elements such as religion and language. *Race* refers to a group of people related by common descent.

The population of the United States is becoming more multicultural, and diverse, every day. Almost one in four Americans has African, Asian, Hispanic, or Native American ancestry. It is estimated that by 2020, the number will rise to almost one in three, and by 2050, the number will be almost one in two. The fastest-growing segments of the U.S. population are minority groups.

[1]M. Loden and J. B. Rosener, *Workforce America! Managing Employee Diversity as a Vital Resource.* Homewood, IL: Business One Irwin, 1991.

[2]John Walker, *Introduction to Hospitality,* 2nd ed. Upper Saddle River, NJ: Prentice Hall, 1999, pp. 429–430.

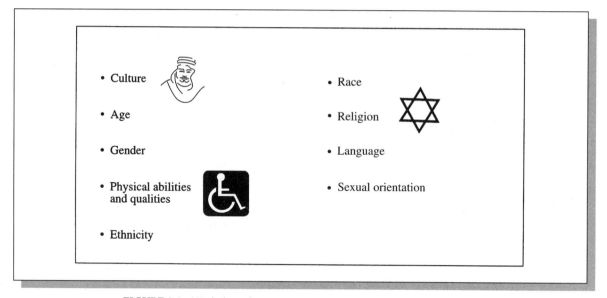

FIGURE 3.1 Workplace diversity.

As the United States becomes more diverse, so does the workplace. Companies today practice diversity cosmetically; "it is like buying insurance for the future."[3] The hospitality workplace employs a particularly diverse group of employees. A restaurant's staff often resembles a miniature United Nations, with employees from all around the globe. According to the U.S. Department of Labor, twelve percent of foodservice employees are foreignborn, compared to 8 percent in other occupations. Foodservice also employs many more Hispanics and African-Americans than other industries. In fact, Hispanics have been the largest minority in foodservice for almost a decade.

In the hospitality workforce it is vital that multicultural management recognizes cultural differences among employees, and allows and encourages them. It is important to have cross-cultural awareness and to respect the cultures of others. In today's hospitality industry understanding and harmonizing with other cultures is necessary for all employees in order to avoid misunderstandings. By allowing and encouraging variation, blends of people from all different kinds of backgrounds are able to learn from one another and grow in aspects of the workplace.[4]

Diverse Voices

Members of each group to be discussed here often share certain values, attitudes, and perspectives. Of course, not all members of the group share these tendencies, but many will. When you say that Asian-Americans have a tendency to be polite, be

[3]S. Hume, "Two-way street," *Restaurants and Institutions,* Vol. 109, No. 34, pp. 57–62, December 15, 1999.
[4]Walker, *Introduction to Hospitality.*

Diversity in the workplace is on the increase. (Courtesy of Sodexho)

aware that you are referring to a tendency, not a stereotype. Cultural tendencies need to be distinguished from cultural stereotypes. A **stereotype** is when one attributes tendencies of some individuals in a group to all individuals of that group. Stereotypes are inflexible; they lie at the heart of prejudice. They prevent one from being able to think about people as individuals. For example, the view that immigrants don't want to speak English is a stereotype. That may be true of some immigrants, but certainly is not true for most or all immigrants.

African-Americans are the largest minority group in the United States. One distinguishing characteristic that sets them apart from other minorities is that most African-Americans have been born in North America; indeed, many families have had a long history in the United States.

Some of the cultural tendencies of African-Americans include respect for family, religion, and community and an expressive, emotional, direct, and candid manner of speaking. Being an African-American person in the workplace means that any number of barriers may be set up against you. At work, African-Americans often complain that they are either oversupervised or undersupervised and that it takes them a lot longer to prove that they can do their jobs. In addition, supervisors often misinterpret their direct and expressive communication style.[5]

In the African-American culture, the people are concerned with their future. Whether recruiting for restaurant- or corporate-level positions, concerns are the same for most African-Americans. They want to know if they will be able to build a

[5]R. Blank and S. Slipp, *Voices of Diversity: Real People Talk about Problems and Solutions in a Workplace Where Everyone is Not Alike.* New York: AMACON, 1994.

∾ profile

GERRY FERNANDEZ

Courtesy of Gerry Fernandez

Gerry Fernandez began working as a cook at Royal's Healthside Restaurant in Rutland, Vermont. Ernest Royal, owner of the restaurant and a noted New England restaurateur, was the first African-American board member of the National Restaurant Association. Royal had experienced considerable racism, and in his honor, Gerry Fernandez conceived the Multi-Cultural Foodservice and Hospitality Alliance (MFHA). The MFHA is dedicated to promoting diversity within the foodservice industry.

Since his first position as cook at Royal's, Gerry has a successful career beginning with an associate degree in culinary arts, followed by terms as sous chef, manager, and general manager of various New England restaurants.

In 1995, Gerry moved to General Mills as a technical service specialist in foodservice research and development. He provided support and training as well as sales marketing and product development teams. Additionally, he evaluated current new competitor products; conducted recipe development, concept testing, tolerance testing, photo shots, and product presentations.

Gerry is currently a national account manager of foodservice sales with General Mills, where he is on leave to be president of MFHA. In a recent interview Fernandez spoke about the vision of the MFHA organization and its intended impact on foodservice operations worldwide.

How does diversity affect foodservice in general? Comprehensive diversity issues exist in many large companies, and they are asking foodservice operators, "Where do you stand?" It is coming, whether or not you like it. Diversity is not simply a social agenda issue; it is a bottom-line issue. When people talk about diversity, they think about inclusion of more women and more people of color. They tend to think only about the soft issues, the green issues. Diversity really is a green discussion more

stable career or if the efforts they are putting in will have little outcome. It is important for organizations to demonstrate that African-Americans can be successful. The greater the number of African-Americans who are successful in an organization, the more other people will believe that they, too, have the chance to be successful.[6]

Hispanics are a very diverse group, with roots in Mexico, Puerto Rico, Cuba, El Salvador, the Dominican Republic, and other Latin American countries. Hispanics may be white, Indian, black, or a mixture of any of these groups. The Latino population in the United States tends to be young. Latinos suffer from an identity problem: Many people assume that a Latino in Miami must be Cuban or that a Latino in New York City must be Puerto Rican. Although many Cubans are in Miami, and

[6]P. King, "Diversity at work: African Americans," *Nation's Restaurant News*, Vol. 33, No. 21, May 24, 1999.

than it is any other color. MFHA is striving to make this an economic discussion rather than a social discussion.

What is the object of MFHA? To be the solutions bridge for multiculturalism in the foodservice industry so that operators can leverage diversity as a positive influence on the bottom line. We think of multicultural diversity as a way to improve the food-service business in all aspects: human resources, marketing, training, community relations, and so on. We are the multicultural Yellow Pages for the industry. We are solution focused: a connector of people to issues and people to information.

What does MFHA offer operators? This is a place to start the diversity process. If operators are looking for opportunities, recipes, programs, or qualified diversity experts, they can call on us. Whether you are an on-site operator—self-op or contract managed—there is a concern regarding bids for city, state, and federal contracts. These potential clients are inquiring directly as to what percentage of your business purchases are from women and minority-owned businesses. Companies are realizing that they need a way to address this issue. We offer a context in which such issues can be explored constructively.

What kind of services does MFHA have available? We help identify qualified women and minority-owned business operators who can do business with the big boys. Additionally, MFHA can provide in-house solutions in the form of awareness and skills training, recruiting and retention, marketing, purchasing, and referral services.

How is MFHA evolving? The last three years have been internally focused as we have developed the infrastructure. Now we are focused externally on our members. We will be able to provide more research and, through focus groups and bench marking, help operators by training in ways to be more strategic in their diversity effort and to recruit better talent. It's not about one company or one ethnic segment, it's about our industry as a whole reaching out and recruiting from and to every segment of the population.

Source: Diane Ridge, "Diversity runs deep," *Food Management,* Vol. 35, No. 7, pp. 48–52, July 2000. Last update March 21, 2001.

many Puerto Ricans are in New York City, Latinos come from many countries. Spanish is a common bond among many Latinos, but Latinos speak various dialects of Spanish. A common bond among many Latinos is an emphasis on family.

A common complaint among Hispanic workers is that supervisors have low expectations of them. Many also want their supervisors to be more than just the boss but also something of a personal friend. The workplace to them is almost like an extension of the family.[7]

Asian-Americans are also a very diverse group. Over 60 percent of the world's population lives in Asia. The six largest Asian groups in the United States are the Chinese, Filipinos, Japanese, Indians, Koreans, and Vietnamese. Although Asian-Americans

[7]Ibid.

come from many different lands and speak a wide variety of languages, many share such cultural traits as working hard, being very loyal to family, respecting authority, being sensitive to others' opinions, and being reluctant to complain or confront.

Like anyone else, Asian-Americans are offended when others assume that they are either Japanese or Chinese when their country of origin is other than Japan or China. At work, Asian-Americans may feel taken advantage of when supervisors know they will not complain if given a lot of work to do.

Developing Cross-Cultural Interaction

A Company Culture

"We define the diversity process as quality of life enhancement in the workplace," says Joe Machicote, director of relations' developments, Compass Group. "While many people cite diversity as a race and gender issue, we see those as only a small piece of that puzzle." According to Machicote, Compass Group began a vigorous diversity process in January 1999, and the company has moved (not literally) at lightning speed to identify employee needs and to develop a company-wide initiative dedicated to embracing diversity. Through cultural audits of employees and management, Compass has developed a diversity philosophy called Charged for Change. "If we charge our people up with dignity, opportunity, equity, and respect—the top four needs outlined by our employees—they'll take care of our customers and our customers. . . . That's the very, very, basic overview of what our process is

Diversity in itself is not a challenge but, in fact, an opportunity. It is an opportunity for us to build diverse teams; diverse knowledge perspective and experiences can solve business problems and create value for our shareholders and customers. The second prong in the initiative is moving beyond awareness training and moving toward diversity skills training, which helps to enhance the skills of managers and supervisors in communication across lines of difference. This enhances the ability to recognize and respond to the needs of our diverse customers. Every successful business needs to practice sensitivity to diversity as well as to our diverse makeup.

By developing cross-cultural interaction skills, you will be better equipped to do your job and to motivate diverse employees to accomplish company goals. But don't think you will be able to develop these skills overnight or, for that matter, even over a few months. By considering the major steps listed in Table 3.1, you will better appreciate that this process is complex (not easy or quick to master), personal (not a mechanical process that anyone can do), and involves much change.[8] The effective supervisor is aware that employees come from different cultural backgrounds, learns about how their cultures differ, and works with employees without passing judgment about their cultures.

Shifting demographics make practicing diversity more than just a politically correct idea in the hospitality industry. Diversity is anything that makes people different from each other, such as gender, race, ethnicity, income, religion, and disabilities. Foodservice has welcomed minorities for a long time, and minorities make up the largest percentage of workers in the foodservice industry. For supervisors in the hospitality industry it is important to encourage minority talent. By promoting a variety of people into positions of

[8]Reva T. Frankle and Anita Yanochik Owen, *Nutrition in the Community: The Art of Delivering Services.* Mosby, St. Louis, MO, 1993, p. 42.

power a supervisor can help promote minorities in advancement in the foodservice industry. There are great benefits from having a multicultural boardroom. More and more companies are putting diversity into practice. If you want employees to share new ideas and knowledge, make them feel valued for who they are. Create an organization where all types of people are able to work well together. In an industry reliant on labor, diversity is fast becoming an economic necessity.[9]

Increasing Personal Awareness

Without realizing it, it is possible to become **culture bound,** meaning that you believe that your culture and value system are the best, the one and only. You think your way of talking; perceiving, thinking, valuing, and behaving are normal and right. For example, when you hear someone talking with an accent, you are likely to think how strange it sounds, or even how wrong or abnormal it is. How many of us realize that each of us has an accent, which probably sounds strange to those of different backgrounds?

The first step in developing your cross-cultural skills is to examine how your own culture has influenced who you are. Consider, for example, how your culture has influenced your attitudes toward the following.

- Education
- Work
- Family
- Self-sufficiency
- Money
- Authority
- Expression of emotion

An activity at the end of this chapter will help you look more deeply at your own cultural attitudes and compare them to others.

Learning about Other Cultures

After becoming more aware of your own culture, the next step is to learn various facts of other cultures. As a supervisor, it is crucial to see other cultures as objectively as possible and not pass judgment. By learning about another culture, it is hoped that you will be better able to understand people from that culture, as well as to be understood better in turn. Some aspects of another culture that are interesting to learn include verbal and nonverbal language differences, values (see Table 3.2), customs, work habits, and attitudes toward work.

A danger in learning about any culture is that the information may be overgeneralized, thereby promoting stereotypes. It is important to keep in mind that regardless of cultural background, a

aimed at doing." Machicote stresses that the company's diversity process is just that—a process, not a program. "When you say 'program' it implies something that's going to end, whereas a process is something that will grow with us," he explains. What helps to derive the Compass process is a diversity council made up of 25 people from across all the sectors of Compass employees located across the country, all with different dimensions of diversity: age, socioeconomic, sexual orientation, race, and ethnicity, from line servers to corporate heads. "When I was young, my mom told me it's like cleaning up a neighborhood block," says Machicote. "The way to clean up the block is to sweep in front of your own house. You have to start small"—that is, if you can call a company with 60,000 employees small.

Source: Diane Ridge, "Diversity runs deep," *Food Management,* Vol. 35, No. 7, pp. 48–52, July 2000.

[9]R. Allen, "Diversity at work: the changing faces in foodservice," *Nation's Restaurant News,* Vol. 33, No. 21, pp. 203–210, May 24, 1999.

TABLE 3.1   ∾   **Developing Cross-Cultural
Interaction Skills**

1. Increase personal awareness.
2. Learn about other cultures.
3. Recognize and practice cross-cultural interaction
   skills.
4. Maintain awareness, knowledge, and skills.

person is still an individual and needs to be treated as someone with a unique personality, wants, and needs.

You can learn about other cultures in various ways: reading about them in books and magazines, attending cultural fairs and festivals, and interacting with individuals from other cultures. By learning about other cultures and interacting with people of varying backgrounds, you can work on valuing your differences as well as uncovering and overcoming any of your own fears, stereotypes, and prejudices.

Recognizing and Practicing Cross-Cultural Interaction Skills

A person's nationality, culture, race, and gender affect how he or she communicates. However, communication between people of different cultures can often be difficult when neither person is familiar with the other's style of communicating. Three

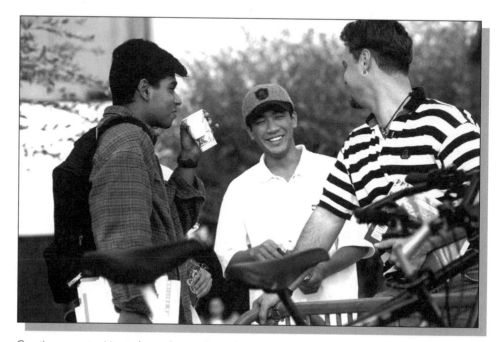

Creating opportunities to learn about other cultures is helpful in creating cultural harmony.
(Courtesy of Sodexho)

TABLE 3.2 ∾ **Cultural Values**

Values Associated with Countries Outside the U.S.	Values Associated with the U.S.
Fate	Personal control over the environment
Tradition	Change
Human interaction dominates	Time dominates
Hierarchy/rank/status	Human equality
Group welfare	Individualism/privacy
Birthright inheritance	Self-help
Cooperation	Competition
Past orientation	Future orientation
"Being" orientation	Action/goal/work orientation
Formality	Informality
Indirectness/ritual/"face"	Directness/openness/honesty
Idealism/theory	Practicality/efficiency
Spiritualism/detachment	Materialism

specific problem areas that supervisors must takes steps to overcome are (1) the tendency not to listen carefully or pay attention to what others are saying, (2) speaking or addressing others in ways that alienate them or make them feel uncomfortable, and (3) using or falling back on inappropriate stereotypes to communicate with people from other cultures. To be an effective supervisor in a culturally diverse workforce, you must be able to recognize the different ways that people communicate, be sensitive to your own employees' cultural values, and adapt your own supervisory style accordingly.

Cultures use language in different ways. For example, people in North America and Australia rely heavily on language to get their point across. As such, they are very precise in the spoken and written words they use. However, in many Asian and Middle Eastern cultures, the language someone uses is only one component of the message the person wants to get across. Listeners must also pay attention to the "context" of the communication, including body language, the physical setting, and past relationships, all of which add meaning to what is being said.

The use of personal space is another important culture difference. If you step into someone's personal space, they will often step back, in order to maintain their space. People from Latin America, Africa, the Middle East, and South America prefer to communicate at much closer distances than would seem comfortable for people from Canada or the United States. Asians, by contrast, sometimes prefer even more personal space. As a supervisor, if an employee steps into your personal space and you step back, your action may be seen as being aloof or not wanting to talk. To adjust to situations when talking with someone, stay put and let the other person stand where he or she is comfortable.

Eye contact and facial expressions are two other nonverbal communication techniques that vary among cultures. Whereas in North America it is common to maintain good eye contact and employ facial cues such as nodding the head when listening to someone speak, not all cultures share those practices. In many Asian and African cultures, people will make greater eye contact when speaking, but when listening, make infrequent eye contact. They also do not use facial expressions when listening to others. These nonverbal communication differences may lead to misunderstanding. A supervisor may wrongly misinterpret that an employee who does not make eye contact or nod in response is simply not listening or doesn't care, when that isn't the case.

Cultural differences also affect other areas of communication, such as the rate at which people speak, the volume, speech inflections, and the use of pauses and silence when speaking. It is common in Europe and North America to speak whenever there is silence in a conversation, and to speak loudly. This is not always the case in other cultures. In Asian cultures, silence is as much a part of conversation as speaking is, and they will want to continue speaking about the topic at hand after the silence. Silence is also often used as a sign of politeness and respect for elders in other cultures rather than a lack of desire to keep talking. Whereas a North American's loud speech in many Asian countries is often interpreted as being aggressive or even angry, an Asian's soft-spoken voice in the United States might be seen as a sign of weakness or shyness.

A final communication difference is the tendency in Europe and the United States to be direct in conversation and get to the point. In many other cultures, this practice is considered impolite and rude. To an Asian-American, being direct might be interpreted as being insensitive to the feelings of others. Native Americans, Asian-Americans, and some Hispanic-Americans value respect and harmony and will use indirect, not direct, speaking methods to achieve those ends.

As a supervisor, you should be sensitive to your employees' cultural values and understand their different communication styles. Always be open for feedback when communicating. Feedback can tell you how you are perceived by others as well as how well you are getting your point across. Table 3.3 summarizes communication style differences among various groups. As you look at the table, you should also keep in mind that it is only natural that people from other cultures speak with a different tone of voice, rhythm, and pace. Finally, as a supervisor, you can also focus on core values that transcend cultural boundaries by creating a workplace where all employees feel valued, safe, and respected.

Check Your Knowledge

1. Describe the process of developing cross-cultural interaction skills.
2. Define *culture bound.*

New York Foodservice Director Celebrates Diversity

Tom Monetti, foodservice director at Mount Sinai–NYU Medical Center in New York City has lived in Manhattan the better part of 30 years, has seen firsthand the ebb and flow of ethnic peoples, and has adopted a new and unique way to cater to their tastes. "We've adapted the 'festival' idea to showcase different ethnic foods to our customers, something New Yorkers have done for many years," says Monetti. He's referring to the colorful ethnic celebration street festivals that are held periodically on the streets of New York. "Depending on the neighborhood, you can find people celebrating May Day, Chinese New Year, African-American History Month, Columbus Day, St. Patrick's Day, Feast of Three Kings—you name it. There is always something going on!" Yet no matter which particular ethnic food theme they're promoting on a given day, "for our diverse foodservice customers, graphics and signage have become very important. They tell the customer what you really are and that you're there for them no matter who they are," says Monetti.

Source: Diane Ridge, "Diversity runs deep," *Food Management,* Vol. 35, No. 7, pp. 48–52, July 2000.

TABLE 3.3 ∾ **Communication Style Differences**

Native Americans	Asian-Americans/ Hispanics	Whites	Blacks
1. Speak softly/slower	1. Speak softly	1. Speak loud/fast to control listener	1. Speak with affect
2. Indirect gaze when listening or speaking	2. Avoidance of eye contact when listening or speaking to high-status persons	2. Greater eye contact when listening	2. Direct eye contact (prolonged) when speaking, but less when listening
3. Interject less/seldom offer encouraging communication	3. Similar rules	3. Head nods, nonverbal markers	3. Interrupt (turn taking) when able
4. Delayed auditory (silence)	4. Mild delay	4. Quick responding	4. Quicker responding
5. Manner of expression low-keyed, indirect	5. Low-keyed, indirect	5. Objective, task oriented	5. Affective, emotional, interpersonal

Source: D. W. Sue and D. Sue, *Counseling the Culturally Diverse: Theory & Practice,* 4th ed. New York: Wiley, 2003. Reprinted with permission.

Managing Diversity Issues Positively

Use the following list of tips and suggestions to help you manage diversity issues positively.

General Guidelines

∾ Get to know your employees, what they like about their job, what they do not like, where they are from, what holidays they celebrate. Listen to their opinions. Help to meet their needs.

∾ Treat your employees equitably but not uniformly. Do not treat everyone the same when, after all, they are all different. Of course, there must be some consistency to what you do, but as long as you apply the same set of goals and values to each situation, you can treat each employee individually and consistently.

∾ Watch for any signs of harassment, such as employees telling jokes that make fun of a person's cultural background, race, sexual preference, religion, and so on. Know your company's policies on harassment.

∾ Foster a work climate of mutual respect.

∾ Encourage the contributions of diverse employees at meetings, in conversations, in training. Recognize their valuable contributions. Also, allow differences to be discussed rather than suppressed.

Gender Issues

☙ Make sure that you are not showing favoritism to males or females, by, for instance, granting time off more readily or allowing certain employees to come in late or leave early.

☙ Show the same amount of respect and listen actively to both genders.

☙ Know your company's policy on sexual harassment and take seriously any charge of misconduct.

Cultural Issues

☙ Learn some of the foreign language phrases that are used by your employees. It shows respect for the employees who speak that language and improves communication.

☙ Find out how your employees want to be addressed in their own language and how to pronounce their names correctly. Avoid using slang names such as "Honey," "Sweetheart," "Dear," "Fella," and so on. They are disrespectful and annoying.

☙ Give rewards that are meaningful and appropriate for different groups of employees.

☙ When an employee is having trouble with English, you need to speak more slowly, use simple words, avoid slang words and expressions, and check periodically the employee's understanding of what you have said. Make it clear that you want employees to tell you when they do not understand or do not know.

☙ Be cautious about the use and interpretation of gestures. Gestures such as thumbs up are by no means universal. For example, in the United States, a customer may gesture "one" to a server in a restaurant by putting up an index finger. In some European countries, this gesture means "two." If you are not sure what someone's gesture means, ask for the meaning.

☙ Avoid touching employees.

Religious Issues

☙ Be consistent in allowing time off for religious reasons.

Age Issues

☙ Both the young and the old sometimes feel that they do not get the respect they deserve. They need to know what is going on in the department and how well they are doing their jobs, just like anyone else. Make them feel like part of the team.

☙ Young workers want to do work they consider worthwhile and to have fun doing it. They want their supervisors to listen to them, to let them participate in decision making. Not surprisingly, they do not want supervisors to bark orders military-style. They like to have time and money invested into their training and development.

☙ Do not have higher expectations of older adults than of their peers, and don't patronize them.

Planting Roots of Acceptance

Planning a diverse menu is one way of starting to address the diversity issue. But diversity is more than simply eating different kinds of ethnic foods. As the face of our country becomes many faces made up of a myriad of colors and cultures, the ability to communicate effectively becomes key in both interpersonal and business situations. Perhaps the best way is to begin the learning process of diversity at a young, impressionable age. And the younger you can educate kids about the positive aspects of diversity the better. The Energy Zone program's mission is to expand students' knowledge of different cultures and their foods, to enhance employees' sensitivity to the multicultural student population and to strengthen the role of foodservices as a partner in the school community. And as the ethnic student population continues to grow, expansion of the international menu series is critical. All of us in the community have a responsibility to enhance our understanding of the foods and cultures of our students and team members.

Source: Diane Ridge, "Diversity runs deep," *Food Management,* Vol. 35, No. 7, pp. 48–52, July 2000.

Differently Abled Issues. About 43 million Americans have a physical disability. At work, people with disabilities often feel that supervisors do not see beyond their disabilities and do not think they are capable. Co-workers may seem to patronize them and, because of embarrassment, may avoid speaking directly to them.

∾ Look at the differently abled employee as a whole person with likes, dislikes, hobbies, and so on, and encourage the employee's co-workers to do so.
∾ Speak directly to the differently abled employee.
∾ Hiring of handicapped workers does have a positive effect on the economy.
∾ Disabled workers are good for the community and for employers.
∾ The hospitality industry has a responsibility to provide job opportunities for all.
∾ Differently abled workers are not the most productive, but they show up to work every day, and are great with other staff and with customers.

Even with great cross-cultural interaction skills, you will occasionally do something that offends an employee. When this happens, do the commonsense thing: Apologize sincerely.

∾ key points

1. Failure to understand and respect the differences, or the diversity, of your employees can result in misunderstandings, tension, poor performance, poor employee morale, and higher rates of employee absenteeism and turnover. On the other hand, when differences are respected, the working environment is richer, more fun, more interesting, and employee satisfaction and performance improve.
2. Diversity in your workplace is a given; whether you decide to understand it and build on it is a choice.
3. Diversity refers to the following cultural and physical dimensions that separate and distinguish us as individuals and groups: culture, age, gender, physical abilities and qualities, ethnicity, race, religion, language, and sexual preference. These dimensions, which we cannot change, seem to have the most significant impact in the workplace, so we refer to them as the primary dimensions of diversity.
4. Other dimensions that are changeable, but have less significance, include occupation and work experience, education, income, and marital status. These are referred to as the secondary dimensions of diversity.

5. The hospitality workplace is very diverse. Some of the diverse voices include African-Americans, Hispanics, Asian-Americans, and people with disabilities.

6. Steps to develop cross-cultural interaction skills are:
   a. Increasing personal awareness
   b. Learning about other cultures
   c. Recognizing and practicing cross-cultural interaction skills
   d. Maintaining awareness, knowledge, and skills

7. The chapter lists tips that can be used to manage diversity issues positively.

∾ key terms

culture   primary dimensions of diversity
culture bound   secondary dimensions of diversity
diversity   stereotype

∾ review questions

Answer each question in complete sentences. Read each question carefully and make sure that you answer all parts of the question. Organize your answer using more than one paragraph when appropriate.

1. Compare and contrast culture and diversity.

2. List the primary and secondary dimensions of diversity. Which are changeable?

3. Describe group tendencies of African-Americans, Hispanics, and Asian-Americans. How is a group tendency different from a stereotype?

4. What complaints might the three groups listed in question 3 have that are related to diversity issues?

5. Describe the process of developing cross-cultural interaction skills.

6. Give two tips for managing each of these diversity issues: gender, culture, religion, age, and differently abled.

∾ activities and applications

1. **Discussion Questions**
   • Have you ever been discriminated against in the workplace, or observed when someone else was discriminated against? Describe what happened and how it could have been handled better.

- Do you know a supervisor/manager who handles diverse employees skillfully? If so, what skills does he or she have?
- What are some family traditions that are important in your family? After those of several families have been discussed, look for similarities and differences.
- What are some foods and dishes native to your culture?

2. Group Activity: First Impressions

In groups of two (or four) students, each student writes down two adjectives (positive or negative) that come to mind for each of these groups: New Yorkers, Californians, Latinos, lesbians, whites, Asian-Americans, women, teenagers, elderly, men, Catholics, African-Americans, and disabled. Discuss your reactions with the group using the following discussion questions.

- Were there any groups you know so little about that you felt uncomfortable writing about them?
- Were any of your adjectives used because you had limited personal experience?
- Were any of your adjectives reflective of stereotypes?
- Do you think the way you described certain groups would affect how you would communicate with them?
- How quick are we to prejudge others when we know little about them?

3. Group Activity: The Cultural You

In groups of two, each student should first write down his or her attitudes toward each of the following:

Money	Expression of emotions
Time	Religion
Education	Authority
Family	Independence
Work	Children
Competition	Use of alcohol

Next, discuss your attitudes with your partner. Identify to what extent your culture has influenced your attitudes.

4. Case Study: Culture Clash

As the new head of housekeeping, Nancy, a white middle-aged woman, oversees a staff of predominantly African-Americans. She is not sure that she is getting her messages through to the African-Americans because they do not look her in the eye when she gives directions. They also do not nod their heads or say "Hmm," as her former staff members would, so she is starting to wonder if they are really listening. To solve this problem, Nancy decides to spend a half-hour each day supervising the employees directly.

One week later, she comes to the conclusion that just about everyone is doing the job the way they should, but she hears from another department head, who is black, that housekeepers are grumbling about being watched over. Later that day, one of the housekeepers complains in a very emotional way, and Nancy isn't sure what to do.

QUESTIONS

1. What did Nancy do right?
2. What did Nancy do wrong?
3. In what ways was Nancy insensitive to cultural differences?
4. What should Nancy do now? How can she learn more about the African-American culture to help her to do her job better?

~ chapter 4

Communicating Effectively

~ We human beings communicate all day every day. We spend over 70 percent of our waking hours sending or receiving messages: speaking, listening, writing, reading, pushing keys on computers, watching the television screen. Since we communicate so much, we ought to be pretty good at it. But we're not. There are probably as many opportunities to be misunderstood as there are people with whom we communicate. Different people interpret what you say in different ways, and not necessarily in the way that you meant, and you do the same with what they say to you. Many of the problems we have on the job—and in our personal lives, too—involve some type of communication failure.

No one has yet found a theory or method or set of communications principles guaranteed to be 100 percent effective. Experts know a lot about why people fail in communicating, and they can explain the ingredients for success, but there is no formula that will work everywhere, every time, for everybody. Nevertheless, understanding how communication takes place, why it fails, and what can be done to improve it will increase enormously the chances for success.

As a supervisor in a hospitality enterprise, you will be communicating constantly. You will be both a sender and a receiver of messages, and both roles will be very important. You must understand what comes down to you from the top so that you can carry out your supervisor's instructions and the policies of the company. You must communicate clearly with other supervisors to coordinate your work with theirs. You must communicate effectively with customers. Most important of all, you must communicate successfully with the people you supervise so you will have the power to get things done. You cannot manage effectively if you cannot communicate effectively.

In this chapter we examine the communication process and its central role in managing people at work. It will help you to:

∾ List and describe various types of communication.

∾ Diagram the communication process and analyze common breakdowns at each step in the process.

∾ Explain how effective communication skills are important to success as a hospitality supervisor.

∾ Describe personal characteristics that affect communication skills.

∾ List examples of non-verbal communication.

∾ Discuss common obstacles to good communication and recommend tactics to avoid them.

∾ Compare and contrast effective and ineffective listening practices.

∾ Illustrate the use of effective communication skills in directing employees.

∾ Outline common pitfalls of business writing and list guidelines for avoiding them.

∾ List guidelines for effective business meetings.

Good Communications and Their Importance

Communications is the general term that sums up the sending and receiving of messages. According to Tubbs and Moss, it is the "process of creating a meaning between two or more people." It may take many forms.[1]

Types of Communication

A communication may be a word-of-mouth message such as a verbal instruction given on the job or an announcement at a meeting. Or it may be a written communication: a letter, a memo, a production sheet, a housekeeper's report, or a recipe.

A message may go from one person to another, as when the sous chef tells the soup cook what soups to prepare for lunch; when the housekeeper tells a maid what

[1]S. L. Tubbs and S. Moss, *Human Communication*, 7th ed. New York: McGraw-Hill, 1994.

rooms she is to make up; or when one person says to another, "It's nice to have you back, we missed you." This is known as **interpersonal communication.**

A message may go down the corporate ladder from the president of the company to the general manager to the food and beverage director to the executive chef to the sous chef to the station cooks to the cooks' helpers. Such a message is likely to be a policy directive or some other matter affecting the organization as a whole. This is an example of **organizational communication.**

This type of message is likely to be reworded at each level, and there is little chance that much of the original meaning will survive the journey. One study of 100 companies showed that workers at the bottom of a five-rung ladder typically received only 20 percent of the information coming down from the top. The chances of messages going up the ladder from workers to top management are even less likely, unless it is bad news.

When messages move freely back and forth from one person to another, or up the ladder as well as down, we say that we have good **two-way communication** or **open communication.** Such communication contributes to a positive work climate and high productivity.

In addition to interpersonal communication and organizational communication, there are other forms of communication that a supervisor may be involved in.

1. **Interviewing** is often defined as a conversation with a purpose. Supervisors use interviewing skills not only to screen job applicants but also to get needed information from workers and their own supervisors.

2. In **small-group communication,** three or more group members communicate in order to influence one another. Meetings are examples of small-group communication.

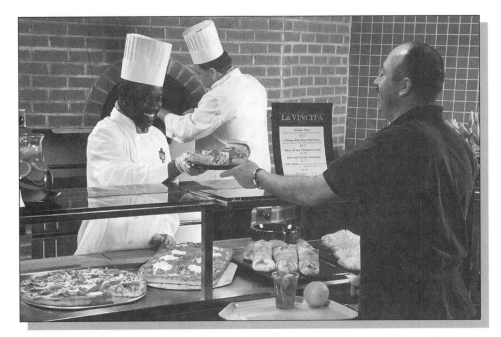

A communication is an interaction between a sender and a receiver. (Courtesy of Sodexho)

3. **Mass communication** refers to messages sent out to many people through newspapers, magazines, books, radio, television, and other media. Hospitality organizations often use mass communication to advertise for customers as well as job applicants. A restaurant newsletter is another example.

Although each context is different, they all have in common the process of creating a meaning between two or more people.

The Communication Process

A communication is an interaction between a sender and a receiver. In a successful communication, the sender directs a clear message to someone and the receiver gets the message accurately. It sounds simple enough. The problems lie in the words *clear* and *accurately*.

Let us take the process apart a little bit, using Figure 4.1. The sender has something to tell someone—an idea in his mind that he needs to communicate. The sender knows what he means to say to the receiver, but he cannot transmit his meaning to her directly by mental telepathy. Therefore, he puts his meaning into words (symbols of his meaning) and sends the message by speaking the words to her or writing out the message. That is his part of this communication—conceiving the idea, expressing it, and sending it.

The receiver receives the message by hearing or reading the words, the symbols of the sender's meaning. She must translate or interpret the words in order to understand what the sender meant. Does she translate the words to mean what he intended them to mean? Does she then understand the message that was in the sender's mind before he put it into words? Receiving, translating, and understanding are her part of this communication.

These six processes happen almost simultaneously in spoken messages, but it is useful to break the process down because something can go wrong in any one of the six steps. From the beginning the message is influenced by the sender's personality, background, education, emotions, attitudes toward the receiver, and so on. This in turn affects the sender's choice of symbols, how his meaning is expressed in these symbols, and whether he adds nonverbal symbols such as gestures and tone of

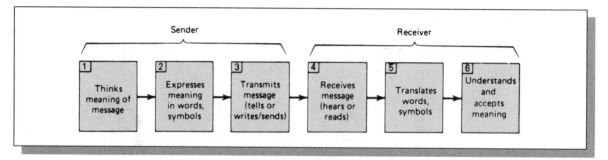

FIGURE 4.1 Six elements of a successful communication.

voice. How he sends the message—whether he speaks or writes it, and when, and where—may affect its impact—how the receiver receives it or even whether she receives it. How the receiver translates the symbols, both verbal and nonverbal, will be affected in turn by her personality, emotions, and attitude toward the sender and so will her final understanding and acceptance of his meaning. We explore all this in detail shortly.

You can see that there are opportunities all along the way for things to be left out, misstated, missent, or misinterpreted. Sometimes, messages are not sent or received at all. The sender forgets or is afraid to send the message; the receiver does not hear or read or register it.

Often, people think they have communicated when in fact they have not. The sender may think the receiver has understood. The receiver may think so, too, when in fact this hasn't happened.

Check Your Knowledge

1. What is considered to be good communication? Why is it important?
2. Explain why communication is important for supervisors.

> This illusion was commonly expressed on bumper stickers and desk plaques a few years ago:
>
> I know you believe you understand
> what you think I said,
> but I am not sure you realize
> that what you heard is not
> what I meant.

When you see how complicated good communications really are and how easily they can go wrong, you may wonder how we ever get messages through. Yet nothing is more important to a supervisor both as a sender and as a receiver of messages.

Why Communication Is So Important

Most supervisors probably think of themselves as senders rather than receivers, and most of the time they are; they spend the best part of their time at it. They direct the work of their subordinates; that is their major function as a manager. They give instructions and assign tasks: who will do this, who will do that, how they will do it, when it must be done. They provide information that their people need to do their jobs: how many people are guaranteed for this banquet, who is on duty, who is off, what room the banquet is in. They train people—communicate to them how to do the work their job requires. They give feedback on how well or how poorly people are doing. They recruit and interview and hire and fire. They discipline; they tell workers what they are doing wrong and how to do it right and what will happen if they don't shape up. Good supervisors also talk to their people informally to build working relationships, a positive climate, and a sense of belonging.

All these kinds of messages are vital to the success of your department. It is essential to send your messages clearly and explicitly to make sure that the meaning gets through. Only if your messages are understood and accepted and acted upon can you get things done.

Messages that are garbled or misinterpreted or stalled along the way can make all kinds of trouble. They can waste time and labor and materials. They can cause crises, gaps in service, poor performance, and higher costs. Whenever they make something go wrong, they cause frustration and usually hard feelings on both sides. If poor communication is habitual on the supervisor's part, it can build lingering resentment and antagonism and cause low morale and high employee turnover.

Not every supervisor realizes the importance of the other half of the communication process, the receiving of messages. Listening is probably the most neglected of communication skills. Moreover, in the hospitality industry, it is often hard to find time to listen. Yet it is very important to take that listening time with two kinds of people: the workers you supervise and the customers you serve. Your workers hold your success in their hands. Your customers hold the success of the enterprise in theirs.

The people you supervise want you to listen for many reasons. They want to give you their ideas and information. They want you to do something about a problem. They want to vent their anger and frustration. They want you to listen just for the sake of hearing them because they are human beings and they need to relate to people.

It is very easy to put aside these reasons for listening as being irrelevant to the job you are trying to do. You may think that you don't need people's ideas—they don't know anything you don't know. You certainly don't need their problems, their anger, their frustrations; and you don't have time to listen just for the sake of listening.

But the truth is that you really do need all these things. You need their ideas and their information because you may learn something new and valuable. You need to

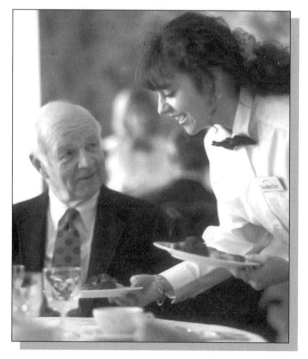

Listening to guests is critical in any organization. (Courtesy of Sodexho)

deal with the problems, the anger, and the frustrations even when you think you can't do anything about them, because the listening itself does a lot about them. You need to listen for listening's sake because you need the good human relations that it builds. And you need to keep the door open all the time for upward communication, to build that positive work climate you must have to lead effectively.

Listening to guests is important for similar reasons. Usually, they want to talk to you because they are complaining about something—the steak is tough, the pizza is cold. You don't want to hear about it and you offer to get them another one. But wait! Maybe you have not received the message correctly. They really want to tell you how angry and disappointed they are and how they deserve better treatment, *and they want you to listen.* Certainly, they do not want another tough steak or another cold pizza. The amazing thing is that if you do hear them out with a sympathetic ear, nine times out of 10 you will defuse their anger. Eventually, you can get them to suggest what they would like you to do about it—provide a tender steak, a hot pizza, or something entirely different—and you will have made a friend for your restaurant.

Obstacles to Good Communication

We mentioned earlier the many problems in getting the sender's meaning through to the receiver. Figure 4.2 illustrates the most common barriers to good communication and shows how they can influence the message on its journey. In the next few pages we discuss these problems in detail.

How the Communicators Affect the Message

Both sender and receiver can obscure or distort messages without being aware of it. In Figure 4.2, the two stages labeled 1 and 4 list various personal characteristics that can affect communication, especially if these characteristics are different for the sender and receiver. Differences in *background, education, past experience,* and *intelligence* can often cause communication difficulties. Big words, long sentences, and formal delivery may not get through to a school dropout or a person of limited background or intelligence. Today's slang may not reach someone older than you. Kitchen jargon may not be intelligible to a new employee. As a sender of messages, you need to adjust to such differences. You must be aware of where you are and where the other person is so that you can make your messages understandable to that person.

People also differ in *attitudes, opinions,* and *values,* and these differences can inhibit communication or garble messages. You may like to swear and tell off-color jokes as an informal and comfortable way of communicating, but some of your people may find such speech obscure, offensive, and shocking and may therefore miss your message entirely. Something that is important to you may mean nothing to your workers if it does not affect them. You care a lot about food costs and waste, but you have trouble getting that message through to your kitchen staff because they don't care—it's not their money going into the garbage can.

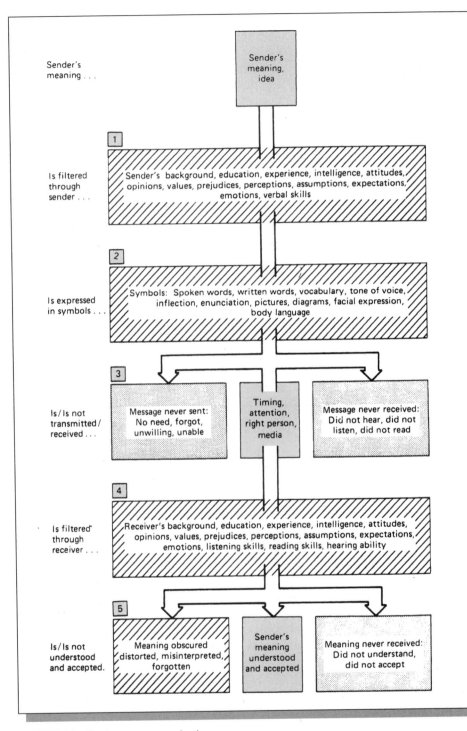

FIGURE 4.2 Barriers to communication.

Prejudices can distort communication; this includes not only biases of the usual kind against women or ethnic groups but some intangible thing from your past that makes you sure that all men with beards or all tall women who wear thick glasses are not to be trusted. Prejudice can turn up in the words you choose in communicating or in your tone of voice, or it can make you leave something out of the message or forget to send it at all. If you let prejudice creep into something you say, it is likely to stir up anger and cause the message to be misinterpreted or rejected.

Sender and receiver may have different *perceptions* about the subject of a communication. Nobody can perceive reality directly; it is conveyed to us through our five senses, and its meaning is filtered through our minds and our emotions. Since we are all different, we do not always agree on what reality is. We do not see and hear things the same way. We do not agree on big and small, mild and hot, loud and soft, sooner and later. How many is several? How much is a lot? What does "season to taste" mean?

Everyone perceives things selectively and subjectively. If you are trying to calm down a couple of people who are having a fight, you will get two entirely different versions of the incident because each perceives and experiences it in his or her own way. They are not lying; they are telling you the truth as they see it.

As you give your people instructions and information, they all see and hear you subjectively, and they all tend to magnify what is pleasing to them in what you are saying and to play down what they do not want to hear or know about. Many times your message will be exaggerated out of all proportion to the point where you would not recognize what you said if they repeated it back to you.

Often, the sender and receiver of an instruction do not have the same perception of its importance. The supervisor may say, "Will you get this done for me?" and the worker may reply, "Yes, I will," and the supervisor may mean by noon today, whereas the worker is thinking in terms of the day after tomorrow or next week. They are focusing differently; each perceives things according to his or her own needs of the moment.

Assumptions and *expectations* distort communications. We assume that our listeners know what we are talking about, but sometimes they don't, and the entire message goes over their heads. We assume that our message has been received and we are angry with people when they don't do what we tell them to do.

One supervisor told a cook, "Cook the chicken." What he meant was to cook the usual number of portions for a Thursday night dinner, and he assumed the cook would prepare about 20 pounds of chicken. In the cook's mind the message registered, "Cook all the chicken that was delivered today." When the supervisor found 150 pounds of chicken ready for service at 5 o'clock, the predictable heated conversation ensued: "Why in the name . . . ?" "But you didn't say that!" "Well, you should have *known!*"

When we make assumptions, we often jump to conclusions. If you see a bellperson sitting with his or her feet propped on a table and eyes closed, you assume that the bellperson is goofing off. If you see the director of marketing in the same pose, you assume that he or she is thinking. Your conclusions may be wrong; you do not know in either case what is really going on.

Often, we think we know what people are going to say, so that is what we hear, even when someone says something entirely different. Sometimes we even finish their sentences for them. Often in listening we extend the speaker's meaning far beyond what was said, and we answer inappropriately, as when the customer says, "My steak is tough," and you say, "I'll get you another one," and what the customer really wants is your attention to his or her feelings.

We make many assumptions about how people think and feel, what interests them, and what they value. If you assume that all people are lazy, are interested only in their paychecks, and have to be ordered around to get any work out of them (Theory X), you have probably closed the door to all meaningful communication and you will never find out what they are truly capable of.

One of the biggest troublemakers in communicating is the *emotions* of the people who are sending and receiving the messages. If you say something in anger, it is the anger that comes across, not the message, no matter what words you use. It always triggers emotions in the receiver: anger, hate, and fear. The message is buried under the emotions, and the emotions become the message. The receiver is likely to hear things that were not said, and the sender is likely to say things that were not intended. Communication becomes hopelessly snarled.

Sometimes underlying emotions color all communications between the supervisor and the people supervised. If there is contempt and suspicion on the part of the supervisor, there will be hatred, anger, and fear among the workers. The communications climate is thoroughly polluted, and messages are taken in the wrong way, or are rearranged according to suspected hidden motives, or are totally rejected. *The only healthy climate for communication is an atmosphere of trust.* If your people do not trust you, they will not be receptive to anything you have to say. Only if they trust you will they receive your messages willingly, understand them correctly, carry out your instructions, and feel free to send you messages of their own.

The *verbal skills* of the sender will have a lot to do with the clarity of messages sent. Some people have the knack of saying things clearly and simply; others leave things out, or choose the wrong words, or tangle up the thought in long, strung-out sentences. Sometimes they mumble or speak too softly, or they write illegibly, and the receiver is not interested enough to ask the sender to translate or is afraid to ask.

On the receiving end, accurate reception depends in part on the *listening* or *reading skills* or sometimes even the *hearing ability* of the receiver. People who cannot read or hear and people who do not listen are not going to get the message.

How Symbols Can Obscure the Meaning

Since we can't transmit messages directly by telepathy, we use various **symbols** to express our meaning (Figure 4.2, stage 2). Usually, the symbols are words, either spoken or written. Sometimes we use abbreviations (symbols of symbols). Sometimes we use pictures: diagrams showing how to operate equipment, posters dramatizing safety messages, movies or filmstrips demonstrating techniques or procedures. Graffiti in appropriate places are often used to send anonymous messages of anger or contempt. International symbols such as those in Figure 4.3 are used for instant recognition by anyone speaking any language.

The trouble with words is that they are often misinterpreted. Many words have several meanings. The 500 most often used words have an average of 28 different meanings apiece; the word *round* has 73 meanings. Many words and the abbrevia-

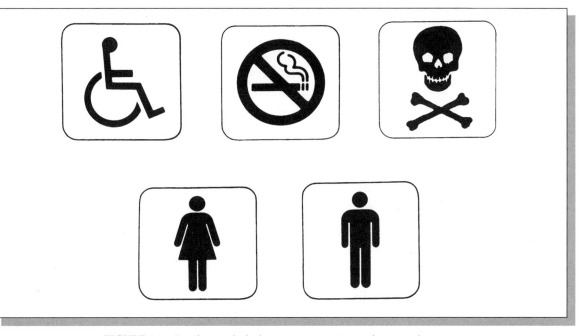

FIGURE 4.3   Familiar symbols that convey meaning without words.

tions are unfamiliar to inexperienced workers. Many words and phrases are vague (*they, that stuff, things, the other part,* and so on). Many words mean different things to people from different backgrounds. Slang expressions from yesterday may mean nothing to the teenager of today. You have to choose words that will carry your meaning to the people you want the message to reach.

If you have workers who do not speak English, you will have to speak in their language or use sign language, gestures, or pictures. Such situations require the sender of the message to watch carefully for signs of the receiver's comprehension. Actually, this is a good idea in all oral communication.

Written words have the advantage that you can read them over to see if they express your meaning clearly. On the other hand, you have no feedback from the receiver unless you ask for a reply.

People also communicate without using words; this is generally referred to as **nonverbal communication.** They can deliberately use signs, gestures, and **body language** to convey specific meanings. Nodding one's head indicates, "I agree with you" or "I hear you." A smile says "I want to be friendly" and invites a return smile. Amorous glances extend invitations. Shaking one's fist means, "I'm dead serious and don't you dare provoke me any further." A listener pays as much, if not more, attention to nonverbal as to verbal communication.

People also convey feelings and attitudes unconsciously, through facial expression, tone of voice, intonation, gestures, and body language. Receivers often perceive them almost intuitively rather than consciously and respond with feelings and attitudes of their own. Figure 4.4 shows some typical bodily expressions of attitude, and emotions.

FIGURE 4.4 Body language: (*a*) accepting, ready to take action (leaning forward on edge of chair, arms open, legs and feet uncrossed); (*b*) open (open hands, palms up, open coat) versus defensive, resisting, rejecting (closed coat, crossed arms and legs, leaning backward); (*c*) nervous, anxious, uptight, holding in emotions (crossed arms, fists clenched or hands gripping arms, locked ankles); (*d*) frustrated, angry, explosive (leaning far forward, head thrust forward, hands spread on table); (*e*) threatening (shaking fist).

Sometimes nonverbal messages run counter to the sender's words, and a mixed message is sent out. A speaker may tell new employees the company has their welfare at heart while frowning and shaking a fist at them about the rules they must follow (Figure 4.4e). Usually, the action speaks louder than words in mixed message, especially if the nonverbal message is a negative one. The receiver responds to the attitude or the emotion expressed nonverbally rather than to the spoken words.

Problems in Sending the Message

The simple mechanics of sending a message can often stop it in its tracks (Figure 4.2, stage 3). If you send it at the wrong time, to the wrong people, by the wrong means, it may never reach its destination.

Timing is important. For a message to get through, you have to consider the receiver's situation. The wrong time may be too soon or too late or a time when the receiver cannot receive it or cannot do anything in response to it.

If you send it too soon, it may not sink in or it may be forgotten. If you send it too late, there is no time for action. The sales manager, for example, must be able to tell the chef and beverage manager about the convention in time for them to order the food and liquor and hire the extra help and alert the station cooks.

Some people are more receptive at certain times of day. Their body clocks run fast in the morning and slow at night or the other way around. Give an early bird messages in the morning and a night person messages at night.

Sometimes the message is not received because you do not have the receiver's attention. There is no point in telling people anything when they are right in the middle of something else. A switchboard operator is not going to hear his boss tell him to postpone his lunch hour when he is handling 17 calls at once. A bartender is not going to remember what her boss said right after she dropped a jug of wine on her big toe and broke both the toe and the bottle.

To get a message through, you need to send it to the *right person*. Give it to the person directly; do not ask someone else to relay it. The "right person" always means everyone concerned. Leaving someone out can fail in two ways: He or she does not get the message and therefore does not carry out the instruction, and he or she then feels left out, put down, unimportant, neglected. Don't let yourself be embarrassed by an employee saying "No one told me."

To get a message through, you must choose the *right means of sending it.*

∾ If you announce it in a meeting, a few people will hear it correctly. Some people will hear it but will not understand it. Some people will hear you say something you did not say. Some people will not hear it at all.

∾ If you send the message in a memo, a few people will read it correctly, some will not understand it, some will misread it, some will read it two weeks later, some will not read it at all, and some will not even get the memo.

∾ If you post it on the bulletin board, no one will read it. Some people won't even know that you have a bulletin board.

∾ If you tell people individually, you may get your message through to most people. But some of them will be angry because they were the last to know.

You can't win. Your best shot is to tell each person individually, one to one, which is how most communication takes place at this level in this industry. Most hospitality and foodservice people are better at seeing and hearing than they are at reading, and individual contact reinforces the impact of the message.

Sometimes, messages are *never sent at all.* Sometimes, supervisors assume that communication is not needed. They assume that people know things: If they bused tables in another restaurant, they don't need to be told how to do it in my restaurant. They don't need to be told how to put paper napkins in napkin dispensers—even a 5-year-old can do that—but on the other hand, it is their fault when customers can't get the napkins out.

There are other reasons why messages do not get sent. Sometimes the sender simply forgets to send the message. Sometimes he or she is unwilling, unable, or afraid to send the message because of the way the receiver might react. Supervisors who are uneasy in their relationships with their people may avoid telling them things they know people will not like, even though the people need to know. This does no one any good. A supervisor may be unwilling to send a message when he doesn't want people to know as much as he does. In other words, he feels threatened. At other times, a supervisor may not send a message because he isn't really sure of the message himself. Sometimes, people do not communicate with the boss because they are unable, unwilling, or afraid or because they think the boss will not pay any attention. This also does no one any good.

Problems in Receiving the Meaning

When the receiver hears or reads a message (Figure 4.2, stage 5), there may still be problems in understanding or accepting it. The meaning may be obscured by the way it is phrased or by something left out, assumptions, and so on. Sometimes the wrong message comes through; sometimes it is meaningless; sometimes nothing comes through at all.

Sometimes the receiver is preoccupied with something else or may not be interested enough to listen carefully. If you want people to listen actively and open themselves to receiving a message, there has to be something in it for them. It may be information necessary to doing their job, or it may relate to changes that affect them. It does not have to be pleasant; it just has to be important to them. If they think it does not affect them, they will not pay attention, or they will half listen and then forget.

Sometimes a message or the way it is delivered will trigger emotions that make it unacceptable, and people will either tune it out or will react negatively. If a supervisor talks down to them, or talks over their heads, or makes threatening or scornful remarks, or speaks in a condescending tone of voice, or tells them to do something they do not consider part of their job, they are not going to accept the message as it was intended. They will misinterpret the instructions inadvertently or on purpose, or they may find other ways to withhold good performance sometimes out of hostility, sometimes out of inertia. If people do not like the way they are being treated, it is quite literally hard for them to do a good job.

Removing Obstacles to Communication

To summarize, let's list the many ways of removing obstacles to communication that have been mentioned in this section.

1. Build a climate of trust and respect in which communication is encouraged and messages are communicated with respect. Communicate to employees the way you would like them to communicate to you.

2. Send your messages clearly and explicitly, use language the receiver can understand, don't assume that the receiver knows anything, and take into account the receiver's ability to hear, read, and listen.

3. Send your message at the best time, and make sure that you have the receiver's attention.

4. Send your message to the right person(s): in other words, to everyone concerned.

5. Choose the best means of sending your message.

6. Check that your message has been understood, accepted, and acted upon.

7. Listen, listen, listen. This is discussed in detail next.

8. Be as objective as possible when communicating. Don't let any of your own stereotypes or prejudices shape what you say or how you send your message.

9. Avoid using slang names such as "Honey," "Babe," "Sweetheart," 'Dear, "Guy," "Fella." They are disrespectful and annoying. Also, don't tell jokes that poke fun at anybody.

10. Never communicate with someone when you are angry. Cool off first.

Check Your Knowledge

1. List three obstacles when communicating. Explain each one briefly.

2. Why do symbols obscure the meaning of messages?

Listening

If you want your people to listen to you, listen to them. If you want to be able to size them up, to figure out who has potential and who is a bad apple, listen to them. If you want loyal, willing, cooperative workers, listen to them. If you want to minimize conflict and complaints and to solve people problems, listen, and listen well. **Listening** means paying complete attention to what people have to say, hearing them out. It is the second half of the communication process: the most neglected half and sometimes the most important. It is a learnable management skill.

What can your people say that is worth listening to? They can keep you in touch with what is going on throughout your operation. They can tell you what customers think. They can suggest ways to make the work easier, improve the product, reduce costs. They can clue you in on trouble that is brewing.

They want you to hear their problems and complaints. And what if you cannot solve them? Never mind; they still want you to listen. This may be the most significant listening you do.

Bad Listening Practices

Anyone as busy as a supervisor in a hospitality enterprise is going to have trouble listening. Your mind is on a million other things, and you go off on tangents instead of paying attention to the person trying to talk to you. And *going off on tangents* is the first bad listening practice. You must give the speaker your full attention.

It is hard to do this. You can think four times as fast as a person can talk. People talk at 100 to 125 words a minute and think at 500 words a minute, so you have three-fourths of your listening time for your mind to wander. You may be preoccupied with other things: the convention coming in next week, the new furniture that has not arrived, the tray carts that don't keep the food hot all the way to the last patient at the end of the corridor. You may not really be interested in what the speaker is saying, or it may concern a touchy subject you would rather avoid, so you tune out. You may be distracted by your phone, your beeper, your unopened mail, or some unconscious habit of the speaker, such as pulling his beard or curling the ends of her hair around her fingers. Or maybe the speaker is following you around to talk to you while you do a dozen other things.

> When you are off on a tangent or uninterested or tuned out or distracted or preoccupied, it is quite apparent to the person who is trying to talk to you. Even if you fake attention and put in the listening time, that person will know you have not really been there. The talk will dwindle and stop and the speaker will give up, feeling frustrated, put down, rejected. And you will have lost a chance to learn something, to solve a problem, to make someone feel like a valuable person instead of a nobody, to build a positive work climate.

Another bad listening practice is to *react emotionally* to what is being said. If someone says something against your favorite person or cherished belief or political conviction, it is very easy to get excited and start planning what you will say to show him or her how wrong they are. That is the end of the listening. They may, in fact, go on to modify their statement or to present evidence for what they are saying, but you will not hear it. You are too busy framing your reply. You may even interrupt and cut the communication short with an emotion-laden outburst and start arguing. The effect is to cheat yourself out of the remainder of the message and to antagonize the person who was talking to you, especially if you misinterpret the message. It is essential to hear the speaker out before you make a judgment and reply.

Sometimes there are words that hook your emotions and make you lose your composure, such as "baby" or "gal" or "dear" to a woman or "boy" or "buddy" to a man, or some of the more vivid four-letter words to some people. Once your emotions flood forth, you can no longer listen and the speaker can no longer speak to you. Chances are that the emotional cloud will also hang over future communications, inhibiting them and fogging the messages back and forth.

You have to stay calm and collected. Maybe the speaker was deliberately trying to goad you. If so, the speaker has won and has found a vulnerable spot or word that can be used again. On the other hand, if the speaker used the fateful word without meaning anything by it, he or she will become embarrassed and defensive and will not try to communicate with you again.

If certain words raise your temperature to the boiling point, try to find some way to word-proof yourself. It makes no sense to let a couple of words interfere with communication between you and your people.

Still another bad listening practice is to *cut off the flow of the message*. Certain kinds of responses on your part will simply shut the door before the speaker has finished what he or she needed to say.

Suppose that one of your people is upset about a personal problem concerning a co-worker. One way of shutting the door is to tell the person what to do. You may do this by giving orders, threatening consequences, preaching—"You ought to do this; you should have done that"—asserting your power and authority as the boss. Such negative responses not only end the conversation but arouse resentment and anger. They are bad for communication, bad for the work climate, and bad for the person's self-respect.

Other ways of telling people what to do may seem positive on the surface: giving advice, giving your opinion, and trying to argue them into accepting it. You may think you are being helpful, but you are really encouraging dependency along with feelings of inadequacy and inferiority. When you solve people's problems for them, you may be plagued with their problems from then on. If they reject your solution, they may resent you for having tried to argue them into something.

Probing, interrogating, or analyzing their motives only complicates your relationship to them. This is not what they came to you for; they do not want to expose their inner selves. They do not want you to see through them, and they resent your intrusion. Besides, your analysis may be wrong, and they may feel that you are accusing them unjustly. Even though they came to you with the problem, they may end up feeling that it is none of your business. They may find your probing scary and threatening, and from then on they worry about working for you when you know so much about them—or think that you do.

Still other ways of responding will also close the door and end the discussion—for example, blaming the person for having the problem in the first place or calling the person stupid or worse for getting into the predicament. Whatever the truth of the matter, this type of response solves nothing and only arouses negative feelings: anger and resentment toward you plus feelings of self-doubt and self-reproach.

Responses at the opposite extreme, although not so destructive, may still close the door on the communication and the problem. You may try to sympathize, console, and reassure the person in an effort to make the feelings go away, or you may belittle the problem by refusing to take either the problem or the feelings seriously. Neither response works. The problem and the feelings are just as big as ever, and you have in effect told that person you don't want to hear any more about it.

What about cheering this person up with something positive, such as saying what a good job he or she is doing? It may improve the climate momentarily, but it will not solve anything unless it is related to the problem and *unless it is true*. If the worker knows it isn't true—and who knows this better than the worker?—your praise only raises doubts about your sincerity and increases the distance between you.

All these ways of responding to a worker who is communicating a problem are ways of refusing to listen any more. They are different ways of saying, "Go away, that's all I want to hear." The employee stops talking to you, and the problem goes unsolved. Table 4.1 lists these and other roadblocks to listening.

How to Listen

Good listening does not come easily to most busy people in charge of getting things done. You have to learn to listen, and you have to make a conscious and deliberate effort to discard all of the bad listening practices you may have been using. Here are five principles of good listening, along with a few techniques for putting them into practice.

1. *Give the other person your undivided attention.* You set aside everything you are doing and thinking and you concentrate on what that person is saying. You don't answer your phone, you don't open your mail, you don't look at your watch, and you don't let other people interrupt. You don't make that person follow you around while you are tending to something else. You take whatever time is necessary, and you take seriously the person's need to talk. You keep your mind on the message and you don't go off on mental tangents. You look the person in the eye with an interested but noncommittal expression on your face.

2. *Hear the person out.* You don't stop the flow; you don't tell the person what to do, or comment or argue or console or in any way take the conversation away from the person talking. You keep the door open: "I'd like to hear more. Tell me why you feel this way." In this way you acknowledge their right to talk to you and let them know you really want them to.

You encourage. At appropriate times you grunt ("unnh," "ummmm," "uh-huh"), you say "Oh" and "Yes," and you nod your head. This lets the person know you really are tuned in and you really are listening. And you really do listen.

This type of listening is known as **active listening.** It is most appropriate when a person is upset about something or has a complaint or a problem. It takes concentrated effort on your part. You suspend all your own reactions, you make no judgments or evaluations, and you do your best to understand how things look from the speaker's point of view and especially, how he or she feels about them. The purpose of active listening is to find the ultimate solution to the problem.

TABLE 4.1   ∾   Roadblocks to Listening

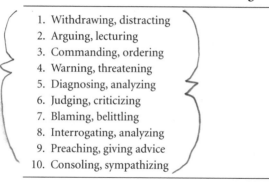

1. Withdrawing, distracting
2. Arguing, lecturing
3. Commanding, ordering
4. Warning, threatening
5. Diagnosing, analyzing
6. Judging, criticizing
7. Blaming, belittling
8. Interrogating, analyzing
9. Preaching, giving advice
10. Consoling, sympathizing

You can raise the level of active but neutral listening by mirroring the speaker's words. When the speaker says, "I don't think you're being fair to me," you say, "You don't think I'm being fair to you." You can go further and paraphrase: "You feel I'm giving you more than your share of the work." You can take the process still further by mirroring the speaker's feelings as well as the words: "You feel I'm being unfair, and it's really making you angry, isn't it?" These techniques, as well as others described in Table 4.2, used sensitively, will move the flow along until the speaker has said everything that he or she wants to say. Only then do you respond from your point of view as supervisor.

3. *Look for the real message.* It may not be "Solve my problem"; it may just be "Hey, I need to talk to someone who understands." Or there may be a message underneath

TABLE 4.2 ∽ **Techniques Listeners Can Use to Increase Understanding**

Technique	*Objective*
1. Acknowledgment *Examples:* "Uh-huh . . ." "Ummm . . ." "I see." "I understand." "Let's look at and discuss your last comment."	To show interest, to encourage an employee to keep talking
2. Clarifying questions *Examples:* "What exactly do you mean by . . . ?" "Will you explain what you mean by . . . ?" "What I understand you to say is . . . , is that right?"	To clarify and/or confirm a message
3. Mirroring statements *Examples:* "You feel it was unfair that Jimmy got Friday off instead of you." "You think someone else should help you in the dishroom." "You think you're being treated differently than the other people you work with."	To keep the speaker talking
4. Summarizing check *Examples:* "Let's hold on for a moment and review what we have discussed so far . . ." "These seem to be the key points you've expressed to me . . ." "To summarize, the key ideas as I hear them are . . ."	To pull together important points in order to confirm understanding, review progress, and possibly lead to more discussion

the verbal message. Often, the first spurt of speech is not the real problem but a way of avoiding something that is difficult to talk about. Look for nonverbal cues: tone of voice, anxious facial expression, clenched fists, body tension. If the speaker is still tense and anxious when he or she stops talking, you probably have not heard the real problem yet. Wait for it; open the door for it; use active listening techniques. But remember that interrogating and analyzing are turnoffs, not invitations to go on.

4. *Keep your emotions out of the communication.* You stay cool and calm; you don't let your own feelings interfere with the listening. You let remarks pass that you are tempted to respond to; you keep your emotions in check and concentrate on the message. You remain inwardly calm all the time this person is talking, and you do not get sidetracked planning a hard-hitting reply. You concentrate on listening and staying neutral so that you can get the message and so this person can vent his or her emotions and clear the air, and maybe you can help keep your own emotions down by looking for the message behind the message that is causing this person to make such remarks to you. You don't let this person grab you with loaded words; you don't react. You get the message straight and clear, and *then,* when the flow stops, you can respond appropriately.

5. *Maintain your role.* You can listen to personal problems, but you do not try to solve them; you do not get involved. You do not boomerang back over that line between manager and worker to help a buddy out. You do not let yourself be maneuvered into relaxing company policies or making promises you cannot keep. You stay in your role as manager; you accept the message with understanding and empathy, but you do not take on anything that is not your responsibility.

If the problem is job-related and within your sphere of authority, and if you have listened successfully, you and the worker can talk about it calmly. Suppose, for example, that the real problem turns out to be something that makes this person—let us call him John—furious at you, and he has been seething about it for weeks. Listening successfully means that you are able to keep your own emotions out of it even though he ends up screaming at you and calling you choice names, and that you manage to refrain from making judgments and jumping to conclusions and telling him off. Because you listen, John unloads his emotions and begins to simmer down, and when you don't get mad or shut him up he begins to appreciate that you are not using your position of power against him, and pretty soon he comes around to seeing that he has exaggerated a few things and is sorry about some remarks. Now you and John can begin to explore the causes of the problem and perhaps come up with a solution.

To demonstrate to the person that you have been paying close attention, try pausing before giving a response. When you pause, you convey that you have been giving careful consideration to his or her words. Pausing always helps you to hear more clearly what the other person has said. Asking questions is a way to prove that you have concern for the situation at hand. It is important that you ask questions to help you gain clarification. Think about asking open-ended questions such as "What do you mean?" People will often rephrase their words so that you can better understand them. Questions such as "how," "when," "what," "why," "where," and "who" will prove to be useful. Asking questions will help employees to expand their thoughts and also help you to gain a better understanding of what they want.[2]

[2]Brian Tracy, "Effective communication," *Executive Excellence,* Vol. 15, No. 10, October 1998.

Of course, it doesn't always work. But if you stay in the boss's role and use a positive, person-to-person leadership approach, you have a chance of turning listening into two-way communication that works. Here are the principles of good listening:

1. Give the other person your undivided attention.
2. Hear the person out: "A good listener listens [95 percent] of the time."[3]
3. Look for the real message.
4. Keep your emotions out of the communication so that you receive a clear message.[4]
5. Maintain your role.

This kind of listening is not a skill you can develop overnight. Like everything else about leadership, it takes understanding and awareness and practice and maybe supervised training on the job. It is not common in our industry; there is too little time and too much to do, and we have other traditional ways of dealing with people. But it has tremendous potential for solving people problems if you can learn how to put it to work.

Companies that have trained their supervisory personnel in active listening techniques have found them extraordinarily effective. One manufacturing company that was losing money and suffering labor problems brought in a psychologist to train all its foremen in an intensive two-week course in listening. The investment paid off—grievances declined by 90 percent, and the company began making money again.

Many industries today are paying a great deal of attention to what workers have to say about their work and are finding it very profitable. In our time-pressured industry it is easy to think we do not have time for listening. But often it does not take long to receive a message. What it does take is an *attitude of openness*. A few minutes—a few seconds even—of total attention can pay off in countless ways.

Check Your Knowledge

1. Explain the problems in receiving the meaning in good communication.
2. What is listening? Why is it important?
3. Discuss briefly the principles of how to listen.

Directing People at Work

Effective communication leads to effective management: It gives you the power to get things done. One of your major functions as a supervisor is **directing:** assigning tasks, giving instructions, telling people how to do things, and guiding and controlling performance. If you can give your people direction in a way that will get them

[3]Personal conversation with Rick Nargi, January 14, 2001.
[4]Todd Gunderson, "Listen and learn," *Restaurant Hospitality,* Vol. 83, No. 3, p 26, 1999.

∾ profile

MEL BAGABAC

Courtesy of Mel Bagabac

As the housekeeping supervisor with Shangri-La Hotel, I need to be a leader who inspires others, is approachable, and a good listener—"by listening you connect with their hearts." I need to be a role model using a "do as I say" approach, like being at work on time. I also need to be tough when necessary and enforce regulations. Aspiring to be a great supervisor entails being a teacher and mentor. I need to show and tell my employees how to do everything and follow up to see how well they have done. Constant positive reinforcement and mentoring helps create a harmonious working environment.

to do things as you want them done, you will be an effective communicator and an effective manager.

Your effectiveness as a communicator depends on several positive things that you can do to avoid the many obstacles to good communication. The most important are to send clear messages, to get people to accept your messages, and to make a positive impact. Let us look at each of these in detail.

Sending Clear Messages

A clear message is one that is *specific, explicit, and complete.* It tells everything the other person needs to know: the who, what, when, where, how, and why of the information to be given or the task to be done. Most of the communicating you do in directing your people will be giving instructions and information on the job. It will be very informal, and it will likely be one of those 48-second contacts that make up your day. It will be in the middle of a kitchen, or on the front desk, or out in front of the hotel or the country club, or it will be in the storeroom or the bar or the laundry or wherever the person you need to talk to is working. It will probably be a fragment of conversation, and it may take place under severe time pressure, so it will be very easy to run into all the common obstacles to good communication. But brief as it is, and however difficult the circumstances are, you need to give each person the *entire message.*

"Cook the chicken" is not an entire message. "Cook 30 dinner portions of fried chicken to be ready at 5 P.M." is specific and complete. It makes no assumptions, takes nothing for granted. It tells all. Say it clearly and distinctly, or write it down clearly and distinctly. Or do both. It takes only 25 of your 48 seconds.

A clear message is also one that is *understandable* and *meaningful* to the person to whom it is sent. It must be phrased in terms that *that person* can understand. It must be delivered on *that person's* level. It must be meaningful within *that person's* experience.

It is important for me to set my priorities, concentrating on getting the job done. I also seek a healthy relationship with my employees. "It doesn't matter how much you know—it matters how much you care for your employees."

I'm at work by 7.30 A.M. reviewing the VIP requirements for the day; checking the house count—arrivals, departures, and stayovers; checking the staffing schedule to ensure adequate coverage for the anticipated workload and allocating sections to the housekeepers. At 8 A.M. we have the morning briefing and room allocations. The rest of the day is taken up with spot-checking rooms, training associates, and ensuring that all VIP requests are met. Taking care of guests and employees puts me in the middle of pleasing both—a situation that requires tact and diplomacy.

Making messages understandable and meaningful requires awareness on your part. It takes awareness of the other person's background and experience and ability to comprehend, awareness of your own assumptions about this person and how he or she regards you, awareness of your tone of voice and choice of words and how you come across to other people. It means deliberately adapting your message to your audience. It means knowing your people and knowing yourself.

Getting Your Messages Accepted

Of the six steps of communicating (see Figure 4.1 to refresh your memory), you as the sender control only three. The other three are up to the receiver. How can you influence that person to come through on the other three steps: to receive and understand and accept your message?

The first essential here is *trust*. If your people trust you, they will have a built-in attitude of acceptance, of willingness to do as you say and do a good job for you. If they do not trust you, the message probably will not come through to them clearly. Their opinion of you or their feelings about you are likely to distort facts and meaning and are also likely to lessen their desire to carry out your instructions.

Building trust takes time. Meantime, in dealing with someone you know does not trust you, you should do your best to maintain a pleasant atmosphere and a calm and confident manner. Be extra careful to send clear, simple, and very explicit messages and to explain why the task or information is important. Then follow up to make sure that the person in question is carrying out the task correctly.

A second essential for acceptance is *the interest of the receiver* in the message: People have to see what's in it for them. Make sure that they understand what your messages have to do with their work, as well as how and why the information or instructions affect them. Perhaps something of value for them is involved: better tips, more satisfaction in the work itself. Or perhaps it is something less pleasant, yet something they must adjust to. Whatever it is, people will pay careful attention to anything affecting them. Look at your messages from their point of view and emphasize whatever is important to them.

A third essential for acceptance is that your instructions must be reasonable. The task to be done must be possible to do within the time allowed. It must be within the ability of the person you are asking to do it and within the scope of the job as the employee sees it. It must be legally and morally correct and compatible with the needs of both the person and the organization. If you violate any of these criteria, the worker is likely to balk openly or to do the task grudgingly or leave it unfinished to prove that it is impossible.

When instructions that seem unreasonable to a worker seem perfectly reasonable to you, you need to discuss them—find out why they seem impossible and explain how and why it really is possible to do what you want done. It may be that your communication was poor the first time.

Making a Positive Impact

If you want people to get your messages clearly and do willingly what you want them to do, your messages must have a positive impact. People must *feel like complying*. They must not be put off by the way you have delivered your messages.

Many supervisors make the mistake of talking to their people from a position of power, authority, or status. In effect, they are commanding, "You'd better hear what I say because I am your boss, and what I say is important because I say it is, and you'd better pay attention and you'd better do what I tell you to do."

In this top-down type of communication there is no sense of the receiver as another human being, no chance for question and feedback. The boss has lost sight of the fact that communication is an *interaction* between two people and that the receiver really controls its success or failure. A message delivered in a condescending, contemptuous, or commanding manner and tone of voice can only have a negative impact. The receiver will not complete the communication in the way the sender wants. The more authoritarian and insistent this type of message is, the more negative the impact and the more negative people's reactions will be.

In every instance where you are directing people, you must remember to think, "How are the people I am talking to going to hear me, and how will they feel about it?" Your purpose as a manager, as a supervisor, is not to impress them but to get across the message that you want to give them. So put yourself on their level and talk to them person to person.

The situation affects your style of communication. Sometimes, in pressure situations, it is all too easy to let your emotions take over and to yell and scream orders when the food is not going out fast enough or customers are waiting and the tables are not being cleared. Unfortunately, yelling and screaming sometimes stops the action entirely. Remember that emotion takes over the message: People react to the emotion rather than the instruction, and anger and fear drive out good listening and good sense. In a real emergency a sharp, controlled command may be appropriate, but never one expressing anger, fear, or loss of control.

Giving Instructions

Here is a detailed set of directions for giving instructions or orders. Not every step will apply to every kind of instruction or every circumstance, but it is a good standard you can adapt to your own needs. There are five steps.

The first step is to *plan*. You plan *what* it is that you are going to say (the who, what, how, when, where, and why of the task), *whom* you will say it to, *when* you will give the instruction, *where* you will give it, and *how* (orally or in writing or both, with maybe additional materials such as diagrams, recipes, or a manual of procedures).

Generally, an oral order is best suited to simple tasks, to things that people have done a hundred times before, to filling in details, to explaining or amplifying written orders, to helping someone or showing somebody how to do a task (show and tell). It is also appropriate to something requiring immediate action, such as an emergency, or to instances where a written order is not likely to be read or understood. As mentioned earlier, most people in the hospitality business are not great readers; there is nearly always a time pressure; and communication tends to be oral, for better or worse, and with all its attendant risks.

Oral instructions risk most of the common obstacles to good communication: assuming knowledge and understanding, mumbling your words or talking too fast, using unfamiliar words, leaving out important details, telling people too many different things at once, telling them things when they are not paying attention, taking the risk of telling them something important and having them forget it. Another cause of difficulty is giving orders to someone who is also getting orders from someone else. Everybody tells the busperson what to do, and everyone wants it done right now. Still another problem with oral instructions arises when you give them as commands and people react negatively.

Written instructions are best when precise figures or a lot of detail is involved, such as specifications, lists of rooms to be made up, recipes, production sheets, specific needs. You might need 150 salad plates and 250 dessert plates in the banquet kitchen by 4 o'clock, and you would write this order out for the dishwashers so that there will be no chance of mistake. It is best to use written instructions when the details of the task are very important, when mistakes will be costly and there is no margin for error, when strict accountability is required, when you are dealing with a slow or forgetful or hostile person with a poor track record, or when you are repeating orders from above or are enforcing company policy.

Written instructions should be short, complete, clearly written or typed, and clearly stated in simple words. You should write them with the reader in mind, and you should read your message over to be sure that it includes everything and says it clearly.

Written instructions are not appropriate when time is short, when immediate action is called for, or when it is likely that people will not read them or will not grasp the meaning. They can cause problems when they are not written clearly, when they are incomplete, or when they are too long or too complicated. Or complicated, or when they are poorly organized (such as a recipe whose final instruction is to soak the beans overnight). Most problems with written instructions are likely to come from not understanding them or not reading them at all. Unless you are there to see that they are read, you will not know whether people have read and understood them.

In some cases it is best to give instructions both orally and in writing. Then one method reinforces the other. People receive the impact of the oral directive and have the written instructions for confirmation and reference.

The second step in giving instructions is to *establish a climate of acceptance.* This may be something as simple as making sure that people are not preoccupied with something else and are ready to listen. This is the point at which you explain the why of the task (if people don't know) and what's in it for them, to involve their interest and if possible, secure their commitment. Quiet surroundings free of distractions help to establish a climate of acceptance. But your surroundings and conditions will probably be less than ideal—the typical fragmentary 48-second time-pressured conversation—so you have to make the most of it.

Among the different types of people who work for you there will be those who are cooperative and enthusiastic, with whom you have a relationship of trust and goodwill. They will always be receptive and accepting. There will be other people who just plod along doing whatever they are told to do—no less, no more. You must be sure that you have their full attention and that everything is included in the instructions, because that is exactly what they will do—just enough to get by.

There will be a third type, the hostile workers, the ones who do not trust you and whom you do not trust. There are always a few of these, and they are looking for ways to beat the system, to do as little as possible, to challenge you, to show you up if they can. If you make a mistake in your instructions to them, they will follow that mistake to the letter and take delight in the trouble it makes for you. An incident at a riverboat restaurant in St. Louis illustrates the point. The manager, appalled at the total disorder of the dishroom, told the two dishwashers, "Get this place cleaned up *now*! I'll be back in 30 minutes to check it out!" When he came back 30 minutes later the room was totally clean, not a dish in sight—cleaned out. The dishwashers had simply pushed everything into the Mississippi River.

With this type of person, spell everything out—why they are given the task, exactly what they must do, and how, and why, and what results you will hold them responsible for. If it is something important, put it in writing. You cannot expect a spirit of acceptance from these people; you must force acceptance of the instructions to whatever degree you can, using your powers of enforcement as necessary.

The third step is to *deliver the instructions.* Your manner of delivery is critical. Gestures, inflection, tone of voice, facial expressions, all the nonverbal ways of communicating come into play here, as well as what you say. Give your instructions calmly and confidently. The air of confidence is critical to giving the order. You can appear confident even when you are not, by acting calm, competent, and collected, speaking lower and slower than you normally do, and talking without hesitation or groping for words. Your image as a leader is involved here, and this is one of the things that make people listen and take your directions seriously.

Where you stand or sit in relation to people you are directing can sometimes have an effect on the communication. Research has established that there are unexpressed zones of comfortable communication between people (**communication

zones). Two to three feet is **personal space**—don't come any closer unless I invite you. Four to seven feet is **social distance**—it's okay to give me instructions from this distance. Seven to twenty-five feet is **public distance,** and that's too far from me— I am not a public meeting you are addressing. These are American zones. People from some other cultures, such as Latin Americans, have much smaller zones, and you can have communication problems when one of these people tries to get close enough to speak comfortably and the other person keeps moving away to maintain personal space.

There are several ways of issuing instructions. You can *request* people to do things. This is an easy method to use, and it works well with most people—cooperative types, plodders, long-time employees, older people, and sensitive individuals.

You can *suggest* actions to certain kinds of people when you want something done and there is no set way you want it done. This is a subtle and more gentle form of direction that you cannot use with everybody because you are leaving up to the worker not only how something is done but whether it is done. It is a method to use with smart, ambitious, experienced people; they will jump on your suggestion and run with it because they want to please or impress you. It is not a good technique to use with inexperienced people or with plodders or those who are hostile.

> You can *command.* Do it now!— No alternative, no choices! Few people like to be commanded. But there are emergencies, when immediate action is needed, when a direct command is the only way to go. If the dishmachine has broken down, if you have no cups for your restaurant, if you have no sheets to put on the beds in your motel, you have no choice but to issue a command: "Get them now!" But for general use, commands cause resentment; people just don't like to be ordered around.
>
> Sometimes when you get tired you begin giving orders in this way. It is not a good practice. Not only do people dislike it, they get used to hearing you talk that way, and then when you really need to issue a command, it doesn't have the old impact.

The fourth step in giving instructions is to *verify that the instructions have been understood.* There are various ways of doing this. You can watch for spontaneous signs: the look of comprehension in the eyes, nodding of the head, a verbal okay. This means that the person thinks that he or she understands or at least wants you to think so. On the other hand, a glazed look in the eyes or a lost expression on the face can tell you that you have not gotten through.

If you ask people whether they understand, they are likely to say yes whether or not they do understand. A better way to check understanding is to ask whether they have any questions. The trouble with this is that people don't like to admit that they do not understand, especially in group situations. Sometimes they do not even understand enough to formulate a question that makes sense. They must feel at ease with you before they can handle asking you questions. Sometimes if you ask them, "Can I clarify anything for you?" they will admit there is something they have not understood.

One way to test understanding is to ask people to repeat your instructions back to you. Some people are insulted or embarrassed by this. Sometimes you can take the edge off this impact by presenting the repeating as a way of checking up on yourself: "Have I told you everything necessary?" People who know they have trouble getting things straight generally do not mind repeating things back to you. It is a technique best used selectively according to the person you are dealing with. The best proof of understanding is seeing people carry out your orders correctly. But it is risky to wait and see, and it is a bit late in the game for corrections.

The fifth and final step—*following up*—deals with just this problem. You should not consider that you have carried out your direction-giving responsibilities fully until you find out how your instructions are being carried out. Observe your people at work. Measure results where they can be measured. Give assistance and further direction where they are needed. And check back on your own performance: Did your instructions do the job? Can you do even better the next time you give directions to these unique and diverse people who carry out the work of your department?

To summarize, the steps for giving instructions are:

1. Plan what it is you are going to say (the who, what, how, when, where, and why of the task), whom you will say it to, when you will give the instruction, where you will give it, and how (orally or in writing, or both, perhaps with additional materials such as diagrams, recipes, or a manual of procedures).
2. Establish a climate of acceptance.
3. Deliver the instructions.
4. Verify that the instructions have been understood.
5. Follow up.

Check Your Knowledge

1. When directing people at work, what leads to effective management?
2. Explain the importance of sending clear messages.
3. Describe the three essential steps of getting your messages across to the people you are directing.
4. What is the importance of making a positive impact?

Business Writing

As a supervisor you are involved in all types of writing: job descriptions, policies and procedures, memos to employees and managers, performance appraisals, disciplinary action notices. It is crucial for you to be able to express yourself effectively in these different types of written documents as well as write in a clear, organized manner. Let's first take a look at some common problems, or pitfalls, in business writing.

- ⌘ Too long, too wordy
- ⌘ Too vague
- ⌘ Too much jargon, too many hard-to-understand words
- ⌘ Poorly organized
- ⌘ Purpose not clear
- ⌘ Sloppy, misspelled words; incorrect grammar and punctuation

❧ Too negative

❧ Indirect, beats around the bush

You have surely read letters, memos, and policies with some, or even most, of these problems.

Following are 10 tips for better business writing:

1. Pay attention to who the reader will be and write from his or her perspective.

2. Organize your thoughts so that your writing is then better organized and better able to communicate.

3. Use simple words to communicate your message. Stay away from jargon, slang, and big words, as they only clutter up your message and the reader may not understand them.

4. Get to the point quickly. Use only as many words as you need to get your point across. Trim all unnecessary words. Be specific about what you want to communicate. Avoid vague terms and expressions such as *somewhat, sort of, rather.*

5. Be positive and upbeat. Even when you have to give bad news, provide some good news.

6. Write as though you were talking. Be natural.

7. Write clearly. Proofread your writing for clarity.

8. Show how the reader will benefit from reading your written communication.

9. Keep the document as short as possible.

10. Always check your document for correct grammar, spelling, punctuation, and neatness.

Meetings

Mention the word *meeting* to a group of supervisors, and you might hear a few groans and comments such as "What a waste of time!" Meetings appear to have a bad reputation. Surveys help tell us why. Surveys show that meetings often have problems such as people getting off the subject, no goals or agenda is set, they last too long, people are not well prepared, and important issues are not resolved. Some things you can do to make meetings effective are as follows.

1. Be prepared for all meetings. If you are calling the meeting, plan out exactly what you want to accomplish, and formalize your list of topics to be covered in an **agenda,** a written statement of topics to be discussed.

2. Start on time, and first review the agenda.

3. Summarize at appropriate points and move on.

4. When the conversation goes off in a different direction, bring it back to the matter at hand.

5. Make sure that meeting minutes are kept and followed up.

6. Have some rules of order so that everyone has a fair chance of speaking.

7. Handle differences of opinions with respect.

When run well, meetings really can accomplish a lot, without too many groans!

Check Your Knowledge

1. List the steps for giving instructions.

2. Why is business writing important?

3. List five tips for better business writing.

∾ key points

1. Communication is the "process of creating a meaning between two or more people"[5]

2. Supervisors are involved in interpersonal communication, organizational communication, small-group communication, and sometimes mass communication.

3. Figure 4.1 shows the six elements of a successful communication.

4. Communication is important because supervisors spend most of their time communicating, as when directing people at work, giving instructions, training, interviewing, hiring, firing, and so on.

5. Figure 4.2 describes many of the obstacles to communication.

6. The following can be done to remove many obstacles to good communication: build a climate of trust and respect; send your messages clearly; use language the receiver can understand; don't assume anything; take into account the receiver's ability to receive; send your message at the best time; send your message to the right person; choose the best means of sending your message; check for understanding; listen; be objective; avoid slang and disrespectful terms; and don't communicate when you are upset.

7. Listening is the second half of the communication process—the most neglected half and sometimes the most important.

8. Bad listening practices include going off on tangents, reacting emotionally, and cutting off the flow of the message.

9. Five principles of good listening include giving the other person your undivided attention, hearing the person out, looking for the real message, keeping your emotions out of it, and maintaining your role.

10. To direct work effectively, a supervisor must send clear messages, get people to accept the messages, and make a positive impact.

[5]Tubbs Moss, *Human Communications.*

11. The steps in giving instruction include planning, establishing a climate of acceptance, delivering the instructions, verifying that the instructions have been understood, and following up.

12. Tips for effective business writing include paying attention to your reader, organizing your writing, using simple words, getting to the point quickly, being upbeat, writing as though you were talking, writing clearly, showing how the reader will benefit from reading your communication, keeping it short, and checking your document for grammar, spelling, punctuation, and neatness.

13. For meetings to work for everyone, you need to be prepared, have an agenda, follow the agenda, and respect differences of opinion.

~ key terms

active listening
agenda
body language
communications
communication zones
directing
interpersonal communication
interviewing
listening
mass communication

nonverbal communication
open communication
organizational communication
personal space
public distance
small-group communication
social distance
symbols
two-way communication

~ review questions

Answer each question in complete sentences. Read each question carefully and make sure that you answer all parts of the question. Organize your answer using more than one paragraph when appropriate.

1. Define *communication* and the five types of communication discussed in this chapter.

2. List five obstacles to communication and how to overcome each.

3. Describe briefly the five principles of active listening.

4. You need to give new instructions to the late-shift supervisor about how to close the operation for the night. Describe how you might do so.

5. Discuss briefly three problems you have seen in business writing and how you would overcome them.

6. What can be done to prevent lengthy meetings that don't accomplish anything?

❧ activities and applications

1. Discussion Questions

- Explain why two people describing the same object or the same situation may give different accounts of it. How does this interfere with communication?
- Comment on the statement, "When emotions are involved, the emotions become the message." Do you agree? Give examples to back up your answer. How does emotion block communication on the job?
- Give several examples of words that may mean different things to different people, such as *fun, soon, a little,* or *pretty.* Pick two or three words and ask several people to describe what each means to them. Compare the meanings and discuss how the differences could complicate communication.
- The supervisor is responsible not only for giving an instruction but for making sure that it is received and carried out, yet it is the worker who controls the reception. How can a supervisor deal with this problem?
- Do you know people who are really good listeners? What do they do that makes them good listeners? Do you think a first-line supervisor would be able to become an active listener? What is the best way to do this?

2. Group Activity: Communication Methods

Complete a chart listing the advantages and disadvantages of face-to-face communication, telephone communication, memos, meetings, and electronic mail. Compare your chart with those prepared by other groups.

3. Memo Critique

Critique the memo in Figure 4.5 using the criteria in the text. What could you do to make this memo more effective?

4. Are You Listening?

With the students working in pairs, one student draws two or three shapes (such as squares, rectangles, or triangles) on a blank piece of paper. The other student should not see it. Next, the first student describes what he or she drew to the second student, who tries to draw the same picture on a blank sheet of paper. The second student is not allowed to ask questions or say anything. Once completed, reverse roles. What did you learn?

5. Case Study: Meeting

Once a month, Sue, a district manager for a foodservice contract company, holds a meeting at a single location that is accessible to all the foodservice directors at her six hospital accounts. The meeting is supposed to start at 2:00 P.M. but Sue waits until the last manager arrives at 2:25.

The meeting starts as Sue thanks everyone for coming and asks how everyone is doing. Three managers start in at the same time with problems they want Sue's advice on, until one manages to outshout the others and gets Sue's attention. He complains about problems using the new computers in his hospitals. Once he's done, each manager takes a turn asking questions about concerns in his or her own

MEMO

TO: Sue

FROM: Pete

DATE:

I can't stop wondering why we always have problems when you are not at work. Today, while you were off, I had a visit from the local health department. They came to do an inspection because of a complaint from a customer about one of YOUR cafeteria employees not wearing a hairnet which is against the rules and regs! During this inspection, the inspector found several of your employees (I forget who) without hairnets and also found someone with their bare hands in the tuna fish salad! Then, he found a reach-in refrig. with pies in it not working. When I looked at the daily temperature log for the refrigs, I found that no one had filled it in for a while. If someone had done so, we might have fixed the refrig. in time. Please speak to your employees about these problems.

FIGURE 4.5 Sample memo.

operation. Their questions are all directed to Sue. By the time Sue has given each question her attention, it is almost 3:30. Since the meetings are only supposed to go until 4:00, Sue tries to share her news with everyone in 30 minutes.

After the meeting is over, Sue realizes that she forgot to mention something very important. She becomes angry with herself because she once again ran out of time and didn't write an agenda. The managers grumble and groan about wasted time as they run to their cars to return to their accounts.

QUESTIONS

1. What went well with this meeting?
2. What went poorly?
3. How could Sue make her management meetings more productive?
4. What could the managers do to make the meetings more productive?
5. Did Sue really not have enough time to write an agenda, or did she not make it a priority?

6. Case Study: The Refugee Cleaning Crew

Brian supervises the night cleaning crew at an airport catering facility. The company has always had a terrible time getting help because of its distance from the city, the working hours, and lack of public transportation. Recently, the head of recruiting persuaded Brian to take on six refugees from a country in Southeast Asia as part of a deal with a sponsoring church group that has arranged to transport a busload of people to employers in the airport area. The refugees do not speak a word of English. Brian will have to train them in their jobs. This includes cleaning techniques and routines; using and caring for equipment and utensils; using and storing cleaning compounds, sanitizers, and pesticides; and maintaining standards of cleanliness. He must also teach them the company rules that they must observe. Someone from the church will teach Brian any 10 words of the refugees' language and provide a pamphlet explaining cultural differences that might cause problems (for example, the refugees read and write from right to left).

QUESTIONS

1. What 10 words do you think would be most useful for Brian to learn?
2. What kinds of symbols should he use?
3. Besides the language barrier, what other obstacles to communication may there be?
4. What can he do to create a receptive attitude on their part?
5. Should he try to train all of them as a group, or one at a time? Why?
6. How will he be able to tell whether they are really receiving his messages as he intends them?
7. How can he communicate encouragement and approval?
8. How can he make sure that they will not get the different chemicals confused and that they will dilute them in the right proportions?
9. As a result of learning to communicate with them successfully, what will he learn that he can apply to training his other workers?

chapter 5

Creating a Positive Work Climate

Susan just started working a month ago at the front desk of an airport hotel. So far she is not very happy with the job. To begin with, she has trouble finding a parking spot every afternoon when she comes to work, although she was promised there were plenty. When she reports to work, she is lucky if she can find her boss, who is often away from the work area, to question him about her training program, which is going very slowly. Most of her peers manage to say hello, but that is usually all. She wonders if anyone would notice if she just took off out the front door and did not come back.

Randy, a cook in a downtown restaurant, loves where he works. Although his pay and benefits are good, there are many other reasons why he loves his job. He feels like part of a quality team at work, management always keeps him informed of what's going on, hourly employees frequently get promoted when there are open positions, the kitchen is comfortable to work in and he has just the equipment he needs, everyone is on a first-name basis, he gets bonuses based on the number of guests served, and the restaurant owners give him time off to go to college and pay his tuition.

Employees today want to be treated first as individuals and as employees second. They want a lot more out of work than just a paycheck. They want, for example, respect, trust, rewards, and interesting work.

In the first section of this chapter we discuss employee expectations and needs. The concept of motivation is then discussed, followed by a section on how to build a positive work climate. This chapter will help you to:

- ∾ Explain common employee expectations of their supervisors.
- ∾ Define the term *motivation* and explain the supervisor's responsibility to motivate his or her employees.
- ∾ Discuss the essential points of current theories and practices for motivating employees on the job.
- ∾ Explain the challenge of applying common motivational theories in the hospitality work environment.
- ∾ Identify nine ways to build a positive work climate by focusing on employees as individuals.
- ∾ Describe two ways a supervisor can build a positive work climate by focussing on him or herself.

Employee Expectations and Needs

When you become a supervisor, you will have certain expectations of your employees. You will expect them to do the work they have been hired to do—to produce the products and services to the quality standards set by the enterprise that is paying you both. You may wonder whether their performance will meet your expectations, and you may have some plans for improving productivity.

But you may not realize that what these people expect from *you* and how *you* meet *their* expectations may have as much to do with their performance as your expectations of them. If you handle their expectations well, if they recognize your authority willingly, you will have a positive relationship going for you, one on which you can build a successful operation. Let us look at some categories of things workers typically expect and need from the boss.

Your Experience and Technical Skills

Your people expect you to be qualified to supervise. First, they want you to have worked in the area in which you are supervising: a hotel, a hospital kitchen, a restaurant, whatever it is. Coming into a restaurant from a hospital kitchen may discount your experience and you will have to prove yourself. Coming into a big hotel from a job in a budget motel, you may also have to prove yourself. Your workers want to feel that you understand the operation well and appreciate the work they are doing. They want to feel that they and their jobs are in good hands—that you are truly capable of directing their work.

In some circumstances, being a college graduate will make you distrusted. Your workers may assume that you think you know it all and they are afraid you will look down on them. They may think that *they* know it all and that you have not paid your dues by coming up the hard way. In other places, if you are not a college graduate and other supervisors have college degrees—in a hospital setting, perhaps—you will have to work harder to establish yourself with your workers. If they are satisfied with what you have done on other jobs and how you are doing on this one, they will each decide at some point, okay, you are qualified to supervise here. But it may take time and tact and determination on your part.

Second, they want you to be not only experienced but technically competent. Every employee who works for you expects you to be able to do his or her particular job. They may not expect you to have their own proficiency or skill, but you must be able to do that job. This can become a sort of game. They will question you, they will check you, they will make you prove you know what you are doing—"Why doesn't the bread rise?" "Why doesn't the sauce thicken?"—and there will be instances when they will have sabotaged that recipe just to see if you know what is wrong. They may unplug the slicer and tell you it is broken, and you will start checking the machine and the fuses before you catch on. You are going to have to prove your right to supervise.

The Way You Behave as a Boss

Nearly everyone wants a boss who will take stands and make decisions, who will stay in charge no matter how difficult the situation is, who is out there handling whatever emergency comes up. Hardly anyone respects a boss who evades issues and responsibilities, shifts blame, hides behind the mistakes of others, or avoids making decisions that will be unpopular even though they are necessary.

Many people expect authority and direction from the boss. These people want you to tell them what to do; they do not know how to handle too much independence. Some of them will want you to supervise every single thing they do—"Is that okay?" "Is this the way you want it?" Others just want you to define the job, tell them what you want done, and let them go at it—"Hey, get off my back and leave me alone." Sometimes you will have a worker who is totally opposed to authority, who will reject everything you say simply because you are the boss; this one will give you a hard time. When you get to know each person's special needs and expectations, you can adjust your style of directing them accordingly—your style, but not what you require of them. You must do what is correct, not what pleases them.

Your people expect you to act like a boss toward them, not like one of the gang. They want you to be friendly, but they expect you to maintain an objective, work-oriented relationship with each person. They do not want you to be everyone's pal, and they do not like you to have special friends among the workers.

If you do socialize off the job with some of the people you supervise, you are running certain risks. Can you go out and party with them, form close friendships, and then come back and supervise them on the job without playing favorites or making other workers jealous? Maybe you can. But can your worker friends handle this closeness, this double relationship? Will they think they are special and that they can get away with things? These are friendships to approach with caution or to avoid altogether.

Your people expect you to treat them fairly and equally, without favoritism. The fairness that people expect is fairness as they see it, not necessarily as you see it. There may be someone on your staff that you don't like, and it is going to be difficult, if not impossible, for you to treat this person without bias. There may be someone else who you like a lot. And there is going to be a world of difference in the way you instruct, discipline, and deal with these two people. Is it fair in the minds of your employees? They may think that you are playing favorites or are really putting somebody down. You must always think of how these things look to the other workers, how it will affect their acceptance of you. Sometimes they may be right and you are not aware of it.

Fairness includes honesty with your workers and with the company. Your people expect you to evaluate their work honestly, to follow company rules, to put in your time, to fulfill your promises, and to carry out your threats. One of the worst mistakes you can make is to promise something you cannot deliver, whether it is a threat or a reward. People will not respect the authority of a boss who does this. If you do not come through for your workers, they will not come through for you.

Communication between Boss and Workers

Your workers expect several things from you in the way of communication. First, *they expect information.* They expect you to define their jobs and to give them directions in a way they can comprehend. Probably 90 percent of the people who work for you want to do a good job, but it is up to you to make it clear to them what the job is and how it should be done. It often takes a little extra time to make sure that each worker has grasped the full meaning of what you have said. But if you expect them to do a good job, they expect you to take the time necessary to tell them clearly exactly what a good job is.

Telling them what to do and how to do it should include the necessary skills training. In the foodservice industry it is typical to skip this training or to ask another worker to train the new person while the two of them are on the job. It is not uncommon to hire people to bus tables, put them to work without training, yell at them for doing everything wrong, and then fire them for breaking so many dishes. Unless they leave first. They may leave first because they expected to be told the right way to bus tables, and they were not told. Lack of clear direction is a major reason for the high rate of employee turnover in this industry. The boss does not meet the worker's expectations.

The second type of communication that people want from the boss is *feedback on their performance.* The most important thing a worker wants to know is, "How am I doing? Am I getting along all right?" Yet this expectation, this need, is usually met

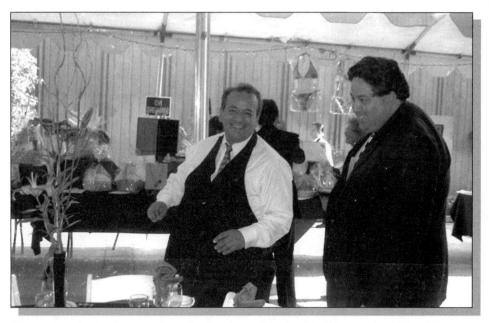

Clear communication between supervisors and associates is critical in a creative and positive work climate.

only when the worker is *not* doing all right. We tear into them when they are doing things wrong, but we seldom take the time to tell them when they are doing a good job. A few seconds to fill that basic human need for approval can make a world of difference in your workers' attitude toward you, and the work they do for you.

A third form of communication that employees expect from you is to have you *listen* when they tell you something. They can give you useful information about their jobs and your customers, and they can often make very valuable suggestions if you will take the time to listen—really listen—to what they have to say. But they do expect you to take that time and to take them seriously, because they are offering you something of their own.

Two cardinal rules on suggestions from employees are:

1. Never steal one of their suggestions and use it as your own.
2. If you cannot use a suggestion, explain why you can't, and express your appreciation.

If you violate either of these rules, suddenly your people will stop telling you anything. They are not even going to respond when you ask for their input. You have closed the door they expected to be open, and they are not going to open it again.

Unwritten Rules and Customs

In most enterprises certain work customs become established over the years, and employees expect a new supervisor to observe them. They are not written down anywhere, they have just grown up, and they are treasured by workers as inviolable rights, never to be tampered with, especially by newcomers. In many kitchens, for example, a new worker is always given the grungy jobs, such as vegetable prep or cleaning shrimp. In a hotel, a new night cleaner will have to clean the lobby and the public rest rooms. If the boss brings in somebody new and he or she isn't started off with the grungy jobs, that's just not right. If a new waiter is brought in and given the best station in the dining room—the one with the best tips or the one closest to the kitchen—there's going to be a mutiny; that's just not done.

People will lay claim to the same chair day after day to eat their lunch, they will park their cars in the same place, and if you disrupt one of these things established by usage and custom, they will take it as a personal affront. You are expected to observe the established customs, and if you want to make changes, you will be wise to approach them cautiously and introduce them gradually.

Another type of rule or custom, sometimes written down but more often unwritten, is the content of a job as seen by the person performing it. When people begin a new job, they quickly settle in their own minds what constitutes a day's work in that job and the obligations and expectations that go with it. If you as a supervisor go beyond your workers' expectations, if you ask them to do something extra or out of the ordinary, you have violated their concept of what they were hired to do and they feel you are imposing on them, taking advantage. They will resent you, and they will resent the whole idea.

Suppose that you are a dishwasher and you finish early, and the boss is so pleased that she asks you to clean the walk-in. The next day you finish early again and the boss says, "This is terrific, today we are going to clean the garbage cans." "Hey, no," you say, "I was hired to wash dishes, not to clean walk-ins and garbage cans." And you are about ready to tell her off but you think better of it; you need the job. On the third day you have only 30 people for lunch instead of your usual 300, but how long does it take you to finish the dishes? All afternoon and 30 minutes of overtime at least.

In sum, people expect the boss to observe what workers believe their jobs to be, whether they have been defined on paper by management or defined only in the workers' own minds. Rightly or wrongly, they resent being given more to do than they were hired to do, and they may refuse to do the extra work, or won't do it well, or will take overtime to do it.

One way to avoid this kind of resistance is to make clear when you hire people that you may ask them to vary their duties now and then when the work is slow or you are shorthanded or there is an emergency. An all-purpose phrase included in each job description—"other duties as assigned"—will establish the principle. However, as a new supervisor you need to be aware of the way people perceive what you ask them to do. In our example, the worker who finishes early is rewarded with two unpleasant jobs totally unrelated to running the dishmachine. There is no immediate and urgent need and no warning that the worker might be expected to fill idle time with other tasks. We will have more to say about defining job content in later chapters. A clear understanding is essential to a successful relationship between worker and boss.

Person-to-Person Relationships

Today's workers expect to be treated as human beings rather than as part of the machinery of production. They want the boss to know who they are and what they do on the job and how well they are doing it. They want to be treated as individuals, and they want to feel comfortable talking to the boss, whether it is about problems on the job or about hunting or fishing and the weather and the new baby at home. They want the boss's acceptance and approval, including tolerance for an occasional mistake or a bad day. They want recognition for a job well done. Whether they are aware of it or not, they want a sense of belonging on the job.

To your people you personify the company. They don't know the owners, the stockholders, the general manager, and the top brass. To most hourly workers, you are the company—you are it. If they have an easy relationship with you, they will feel good about the company. If they feel good about the company, they can develop that sense of belonging there. And if they feel that they belong there, they are likely to stay.

Successful supervisors develop a sensitivity to each person, to the person's individual needs and desires and fears and anxieties as well as talent and skills. They handle each person as much as possible in the way that best fills the worker's personal needs. If you can establish good relationships on this one-to-one level with all your workers, you can build the positive kind of work climate that is necessary for success.

Check Your Knowledge

1. Name expectations that employees often have of their supervisors.
2. Why is communication between boss and workers important?

Motivation

The term **motivation** refers to what makes people tick: the needs and desires and fears and aspirations within people that make them behave as they do. Motivation is the energizer that makes people take action; it is the *why* of human behavior. In the workplace, motivation goes hand in hand with productivity. Highly motivated people usually work hard and do superior work. Poorly motivated people do what is necessary to get by without any hassles from the boss, even though they may be capable of doing more and better work. Unmotivated people usually do marginal or substandard work and often take up a good deal of the boss's time. Sometimes, people are motivated by resentment and anger to make trouble for the supervisor, to beat the system, or to gain power for themselves. Such motivations are at cross-purposes with the goals of the operation and have a negative effect on productivity.

Motivation, as we have noted many times, is a major concern of the supervisor. Supervisory success is measured by the performance of the department as a whole, which is made up of the performance of individuals. Each person's performance can raise or lower overall productivity and supervisory success. The big question is how to motivate poor performers to realize their potential and raise their productivity, and how to keep good performers from going stale in their jobs or leaving for a better opportunity.

Actually, you cannot motivate people to do good work. Motivation comes from within. The one thing you as a supervisor can do is to turn it on, to activate people's own motivations. To do this you must get to know your people and find out what

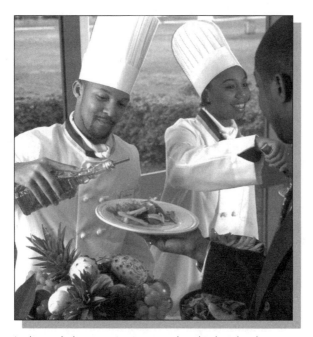

In the workplace, motivation goes hand in hand with
productivity. (Courtesy of Sodexho)

they respond to. It may be the work itself. It may be the way you supervise. It may
be the work environment. It may be their individual goals: money, recognition,
achievement, or whatever.

How do you find out what will turn people on? It isn't easy. There are many theories and few answers. What motivates one person may turn someone else off completely. Everybody is different. People do the same things for different reasons and
different things for the same reasons. People's needs and desires and behaviors
change from day to day and sometimes from minute to minute. You can never know
directly why they behave as they do, and they may not know why either, or would
not tell you if they could.

In sum, motivation is a complicated business, and motivating people to do their
jobs well has no one simple answer. It takes something of an experimental approach; you try to find out what each person responds to, and if one thing doesn't
work, maybe the next thing will.

But it need not be just a trial-and-error process. You can get quite a bit of insight into human behavior from people who have spent their lives studying the subject, and you will find much in their theories that will help you to figure out how to
motivate individual workers to do their best for you.

But the one thing that you can seldom do is to develop a set of rules applying
this or that theory to a certain person or particular situation on the job. For this reason we give you the various theories first. Then we spend the balance of the chapter investigating ways of motivating people by using your broadened understanding

of human nature along with a mixture of theory, sensitivity, and ingenuity.

Theories of Motivation

Whether they realize it or not, everyone has a theory of how to get people to perform on the job. Several of them are familiar to you, although you may not think of them as theories.

Motivation through Fear

One of the oldest ways of motivating people to perform on the job is to use fear as the trigger for getting action. This method makes systematic use of coercion, threats, and punishment: "If you don't do your job and do it right, you won't get your raise." "I'll put you back on the night shift." "I'll fire you."

This approach to motivation is sometimes referred to as a "kick in the pants." It is still used surprisingly often, with little success. Yet people who use it believe that it is the only way to get results. They are typically autocratic, high-control, authoritarian bosses with Theory X beliefs about people, and they think other theories of motivation are baloney, that you must be tough with people.

Motivation through fear seldom works for long. People who work in order to avoid punishment usually produce mediocre results at best, and fear may actually reduce the ability to perform. At the same time it arouses hostility, resentment, and the desire to get even. Absenteeism, tardiness, poor performance, and high turnover are typical under this type of supervision.

Fear will sometimes motivate people who have always been treated this way, and it can function as a last resort when all other methods have failed. But it will work only if the supervisor is perceived as being powerful enough to carry out the punishment. If the boss continually threatens punishment and never punishes, the threats have no power to motivate. In fact, not even fear works in this situation.

No one recommends motivation through fear except the people who practice it. On average, workers in the United States simply will not put up with that kind of boss unless they are desperate for a job.

Carrot-and-Stick Method

A second philosophy of motivation is to combine fear with incentive reward for good performance, punishment for bad. You may recognize this as carrot-and-stick motivation: the carrot dangled in front as a promised reward, the stick hitting the

The primary motivation to doing a job well must come from within an employee, but outside incentives can help. Toward that end, managers should find out what their employees want and design work environments that complement those desires. To determine what hotel employees want out of their job, 278 employees of 12 hotels in the United States and Canada were asked to rank the importance of good wages, tactful discipline, job security, interesting work, a feeling of being "in on things," sympathetic help with personal problems, opportunities for advancement and development, good working conditions, personal loyalty to employees, and appreciation for work accomplishments. Overall, the employees said that what they want most are good wages, job security, and opportunities for advancement and development. Responses differed somewhat depending on the age of employees and the area in which they work.

Source: Tony Simon and Cathy Enz, "Motivating hotel employees," *Cornell Hotel and Restaurant Administration Quarterly,* Vol. 36, pp. 20–27, February 1995.

worker from behind as goad and punishment. It is another high-control method, one that requires constant application. Once the reward is achieved or the punishment administered, it no longer motivates performance, and another reward must be devised or punishment threatened or applied.

In effect, the boss is pushing and pulling workers through their jobs; they themselves feel no motivation to perform well. At the same time, workers come to feel that they have a continuing right to the rewards (such as higher wages, fringe benefits), and these get built into the system without further motivating effect. Meanwhile the punishments and threats of punishment breed resentment and resistance.

Economic Man (Person) Theory

A third motivation theory maintains that money is the only thing that people work for. This classical view of job motivation was known as the **economic man (person) theory**.[1] Frederick Taylor was perhaps its most influential advocate. Taylor developed his scientific management theories on the cornerstone of incentive pay based on amount of work done. He firmly believed that he was offering workers what they wanted most, and that the way to motivate workers to increase their productivity was to relate wages directly to the amount of work produced. What he did not know was that the workers in his plant were far more strongly motivated by their loyalty to one another. In fact, for three years they united to block every effort he made to increase output despite the extra wages that they could have earned.

There is no doubt that money has always been and still is one of the most important reasons that people work. For some people it may be the most important reason. That paycheck feeds and clothes and houses them; it can give them security, status, a feeling of personal worth. For people who have been at the poverty level, it can be the difference between being hungry and being well fed or between welfare and self-support with self-respect. For teenagers it can mean the difference between owning a car and being without transportation. For most people on their first job, whether it is an hourly job or an entry-level management job, money is the primary motivator.

But the amount of money in the paycheck does not guarantee performance on the job. The paycheck buys people's time and enough effort to get by, but it does not buy quality, quantity, and commitment to doing one's work well. If people work for money, does it follow that they will work better for more—the more the pay, the better the performance? There are certainly instances in which it works: the expectation of wage increases, bonuses, tips, and rewards is likely to have this outcome. But money does not motivate performance once it is paid; the incentive comes from the *expectation* of more to come.

Furthermore, people do not work for money alone. A number of research studies have shown that, for most people, money as a motivator on the job has less importance than achievement, recognition, responsibility, and interesting work. In sum, money is only one of the resources you have for motivating people, and it does not necessarily have a direct relationship to productivity.

---

[1] A pre–women's movement phrase that included the few women who were then part of the workforce. Purists intent on degendering the language call this the **economic person theory.** You should learn to recognize it by both names. While we respect the view that language should mirror the equality of the sexes, we prefer in this instance to support historical usage.

Human Relations Theory

After the Hawthorne experiments (Chapter 1) uncovered the human factors affecting productivity, the **social man (person)** succeeded the economic man (person) in motivation theory. The human relations enthusiasts pushed their convictions that if people are treated as people, they will be more productive on the job. Make people feel secure, they said, treat them as individuals, make them feel they belong and have worth, develop person-to-person relationships with each one, let them participate in plans and decisions that affect them, and they will respond by giving their best to the organization.

Putting this theory to work brought about higher wages, better working conditions, pension plans, paid vacations, insurance plans, and other fringe benefits, making workers happier but not necessarily more productive. The question remained: What motivates people to work?

Maslow's Hierarchy of Needs

An influential answer to this question was the motivation theory of psychologist Abraham Maslow. Human beings, he pointed out, are *wanting animals,* and they behave in ways that will satisfy their needs and wants. Their needs and desires are inexhaustible; as soon as one need is satisfied, another appears to take its place. Maslow proposed a hierarchy of universal human needs representing the order in which these needs become motivators of human behavior. This **hierarchy of needs** is represented by the pyramid in Figure 5.1.

At the bottom of the pyramid are people's most basic needs—the *physiological needs* related to *survival,* such as food and water. When these needs are not being

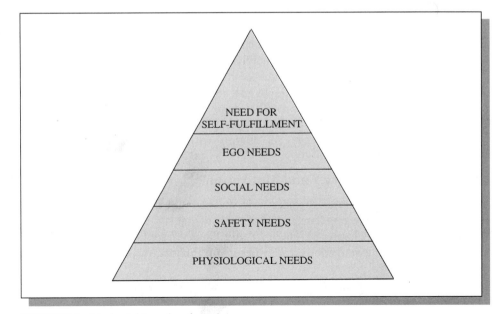

FIGURE 5.1　Maslow's hierarchy of needs.

met, every effort is directed toward meeting them. People who are truly hungry cannot think of anything but food.

But when survival needs are being met, they no longer motivate behavior, and the next level of needs comes into play. These relate to *safety;* they include protection, security, stability, structure, order, and freedom from fear, anxiety, and chaos.

As these needs in turn are more or less satisfied, *social needs* become the predominant motivators. These include the need to be with others, to belong, to have friends, to love, and be loved.

Above these three groups of needs (sometimes called *primary needs*) is a higher level of needs centered on *esteem.* These are sometimes referred to as *ego needs.* One of them is the desire for *self-esteem* or *self-respect* and for the strength, achievement, mastery, competence, confidence, independence, and freedom that provide such self-esteem. Another is the desire for the *esteem of others:* for status, fame and glory, dominance, recognition, attention, importance, dignity, appreciation. The need for esteem gives rise in some people to the need for power as a way of commanding the esteem of others. Satisfaction of the need for self-esteem leads to feelings of self-confidence, strength, and worth. When these needs go unsatisfied, they produce feelings of inferiority, weakness, and helplessness.

At the top of the hierarchy is the need for *self-fulfillment,* or what Maslow called **self-actualization.** This includes the need to be doing what one is best fitted for, the desire to fulfill one's own potential.

One or another of all these personal needs or various combinations of needs is what motivates people to do what they do. If a lower need goes unsatisfied, people will spend all their time and energy trying to fill it, and they will not experience the next level of needs until the lower needs are met. When a need is satisfied it is no longer a motivator, and the next level of needs becomes the predominant motivation.[2]

Thus motivation is an unending cycle of need and satisfaction, need and satisfaction. You have a need, you look for a solution, you take action to satisfy the need, and another need appears, because human beings are wanting animals whose needs and desires are never completely satisfied. This continuing cycle explains why workers' needs evolve and change as their own situation changes.

Maslow's theory of motivation does not give you a tool you can use directly; you cannot sit down and analyze each person's needs and then know how to motivate that person. What it *can* do is to make you aware of how people differ in their needs and why they respond to certain things and not to others. It can help you understand why some of your workers behave as they do on the job.

Theory Y and Motivation

Maslow's theories were the springboard for McGregor's Theory X and Theory Y, two opposing views of the way that supervisors and managers look at their workers (Chapter 2). Theory X and Theory Y applied Maslow's theories directly to the problem of motivating workers on the job. McGregor made two particularly significant

---

[2]Maslow's hierarchy of needs is set forth in Chapter 4 of his *Motivation and Personality,* 2nd ed. New York: Harper & Row, 1970.

contributions with Theory Y. One was to revise the typical view of the way that people look at work: It is "as natural as play or rest" when it is satisfying a need. This is a flat reversal of the Theory X view of the worker, and it suggests a clear reason why people work willingly.

McGregor's second contribution to motivational theory was the idea that people's needs, especially their ego and self-actualization needs, can be made to operate on the job in harmony with the needs and goals of the organization. If, for example, people are given assignments in which they see the opportunity for achievement, for responsibility, for growth, for self-fulfillment, they will become committed to carrying them out. They will be self-directed and self-controlled, and external controls and the threat of punishment will be unnecessary. In other words, if you can give people work that will fill some basic need, their own motivation will take care of its performance. People will work harder and longer and better for the company if they are satisfying their own needs in the process.

Herzberg's Motivation-Hygiene Theory

The work of another psychologist, Frederick Herzberg, explained why human relations methods failed to motivate performance and identified factors that truly motivate (see Table 5.1). Herzberg found that factors associated with the job environment (compensation, supervision, working conditions, company policy, and so on) create dissatisfaction and unhappiness on the job when they are inadequate; they become **dissatisfiers.**

But removing the causes of dissatisfaction (the human relations approach) does not create satisfaction, and it therefore does not motivate performance. Herzberg called these environmental factors **hygiene factors.** They are also commonly called **maintenance factors.** For example, if you think you are underpaid, if you don't get along with your boss, if the kitchen isn't air-conditioned—these things can reduce motivation and cause absenteeism, poor work, and less of it. They are related to motivation only in the sense that they reduce it. Such factors must be maintained at satisfying levels to avoid negative motivation. But air-conditioning the kitchen or raising wages will not make the cooks work harder once the novelty wears off.

In contrast, a second group of factors provides both motivation and job satisfaction. These, Herzberg found, consist of opportunities in the job itself for achievement

TABLE 5.1   ∽   Herzberg's Motivation-Hygiene Theory

Motivators	Hygiene (Maintenance) Factors
Recognition	Compensation
Responsibility	Supervision
Achievement	Working conditions
Advancement	Company policy
Work itself	

and growth—such factors as recognition, responsibility, achievement, advancement, the work itself. He called these factors **motivators.** If you give a cook who loves to invent new dishes a chance to develop a special menu item, you will see a motivator at work.

The answer to motivating employees, then, lies in the job itself. If it can be enriched to provide opportunity for achievement and growth, it will not only motivate the worker to perform well but will also tap unused potential and use personnel more effectively.[3] We look at job enrichment in more detail later in the chapter.

Behavior Modification

Behavior modification, a newer method for improving performance, simply bypasses inner motivation and deals instead with behavior change. It takes off from the behaviorist's theory that *all behavior is a function of its consequences;* people behave as they do because of positive or negative consequences to them. If the consequences are positive, they will tend to repeat the behavior; if they are negative, they will tend not to.

If you want to improve performance, then, you will give **positive reinforcement** (attention, praise) whenever people do things right. You look actively for such behavior, and when you catch people doing something right, you praise them for it.

If you were going to carry out the theory literally, you would provide some form of negative consequence for undesired behavior, but in practice negative consequences (blaming, punishment) tend to have side effects such as hostility and aggressive behavior. However, you cannot ignore the undesired behavior. You can deal with it positively without threatening the person by suggesting the correct behavior in coaching fashion. "Let me show you how."[4] But the really important side of behavior modification is positive reinforcement. It reverses the usual story of nothing but negative feedback ("The boss never notices me except when I do something wrong"), and it satisfies the need for attention with the kind of attention that builds self-worth.

The use of behavior modification has burgeoned in recent years, and it can sometimes be very effective. There have been instances where positive reinforcement has not only corrected undesired behavior but has actually increased productivity. Whatever its theoretical base, positive reinforcement can be another resource for you to try out with your people.

Check Your Knowledge

1. Explain what is meant by *person-to-person relationships.*
2. Define *motivation.*
3. Briefly discuss the motivation theories.
4. Define *behavior modification* and *positive reinforcement.*

---

[3]Herzberg's theories and their application are detailed in Frederick Herzberg, *The Managerial Choice: To Be Efficient and to Be Human,* 2nd (rev.) ed. Salt Lake City, UT: Olympus, 1982. See especially Chapter 2.

[4]Another positive approach to undesired behavior—positive discipline—is discussed in Chapter 10.

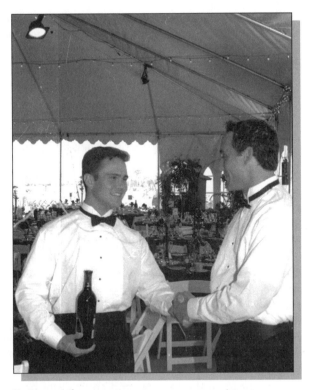

Positive reinforcements can encourage associates to improve their performance.

Applying Theory to Reality: Limiting Factors

Now, what can you do with all this theory? There is a great deal in it that you can put to work if you can adapt it to your particular situation and to your individual workers. There are also circumstances that limit how far you can go. One limiting factor that immediately comes to mind is the *nature of many jobs* in the hospitality industry. They are dull, unchallenging, repetitive, and boring. On the surface at least there does not seem to be much you can do to motivate the potwasher, the security guard, the cleanup crew, the makers of the beds, and the changers of the light bulbs to keep them working up to standard and to keep them from leaving for another job.

Even among the less routine jobs there is little you can change to make the work itself more interesting and challenging. The great majority of jobs are made up of things that must be done in the same way day after day. At the same time, many jobs depend to some extent on factors beyond your control: What people do each day and how much they do varies according to customer demand. Unless your workers happen to find this interesting and challenging (and some people do), it is difficult to structure such jobs to motivate people. But the situation is not hopeless. Later in the chapter we will see what creative management can do for even the dullest jobs.

A second limiting factor is *company policy, administration, and management philosophy.* Everything you do must be in harmony with company goals (customer-oriented and cost-effective) and must meet company rules and regulations. Furthermore, you do not control wage rates, fringe benefits, promotion policies, controls, and other companywide systems and practices. If jobs are totally standardized by scientific management methods, you cannot tamper with job content and method at all unless you go through proper channels and procedures established by the company.

The style of management characteristic of the organization will greatly influence what you can and cannot do. If the philosophy if management is authoritarian and high-control, you will have a hard time practicing another approach. In particular, your relationship with your own boss and your boss's management style will influence the nature and scope of what you can do to motivate your people.

A third factor, closely related to the second, is the *extent of your responsibility, authority, and resources.* You cannot exceed the limits of your own job. You may be limited in your authority to spend money, to make changes in job duties, and so on. Remember, too, that your boss is responsible and accountable for your results, and this goes all the way up the chain of command. If you are going to innovate extensively, you will need the blessing of your superiors. But maybe you can get it!

Another limiting factor is the *kinds of people who work for you.* If they are only working there *until,* the job does not really motivate them; they are just putting in time. They do not put forth their energy and enthusiasm because work is not the central interest in their lives. They have something going on outside—family, studies—that takes care of most of their personal needs and interests, and they don't want to work any harder than they have to.

The large numbers of workers who are dependent personalities often pose a motivation problem—they want you to tell them what to do at every turn, until they sometimes seem like millstones around your neck. How do you shake them loose and put them on their own?

The *constant pressures* of the typical day in the life of the hospitality manager tend to fix attention on the immediate problems and the work itself. It is all too easy to become work-oriented rather than people-oriented, especially if you have been an hourly worker and are more at home managing work than managing people. This is a limitation that managers can deliberately strive to overcome once they see how motivating people can help to accomplish the work better.

Another limitation is *time.* You probably think your day is already too full, and it may well be. It takes time to get to know your people. It takes time to figure out ways of changing things that will make people more motivated. It takes a lot of time to get changes through channels if that is necessary. It takes time to get people used to changes in their jobs, and it usually takes time before you begin to see results. But the effective manager will make the time and will gain time in the end by making more effective use of people.

There are limitations in the theories themselves when it comes to applying them. The primary one is that there is no law of motivation or set of laws that you can apply as you can apply scientific or mathematical formulas. This, of course, is true of everything having to do with human beings. Everyone is different, and their needs and desires and behavior respond in a kaleidoscope of change triggered by anything and everything—other people, the environment, the task, their memories, their expectations, *your* expectations, and what they ate for breakfast.

The theories themselves change. New experiments shed new light. The enthusiasms of the past give way to the fads of the future.

Who has the answers? What works? *You* have to translate the findings of others in terms of your individual workers and the jobs you supervise. These are judgments you make; there are no sure-fire answers. But there is plenty of guidance along the way.

Check Your Knowledge

1. List factors that may limit your use of motivational techniques.

Building a Positive Work Climate

A positive work climate is one in which employees can and will work productively, in which they can do their best work and achieve their highest potential in their jobs. Meeting employee expectations and needs is one way to create a positive work climate. Before we take a look at others, let's discuss a similar concept: morale.

Morale is a group spirit with respect to getting the job done. It can run the gamut from enthusiasm, confidence, cheerfulness, and dedication to discouragement, pessimism, indifference, and gloom. It is made up of individual attitudes

High morale helps keep employee turnover low. (Courtesy of Sodexho)

toward the work that pass quickly from one person to another until you have a group mood that everyone shares. It may change from moment to moment. You see it when it is very high and you notice it when it is very low; and if it is average, nobody says anything about it.

When people are unhappy in their jobs, they just plain don't feel good at work. They feel exhausted, they get sick easily and miss a lot of days, and eventually, they give up because the job is not worth the stress and unhappiness. In an industry where many people are working "until" and do not have a sense of belonging, these kinds of feelings and behavior are contagious and morale becomes a big problem. Absenteeism, low-quality work, and high employee turnover multiply production problems and cost money. It probably costs at least $1000 every time you have to replace a busperson.

High morale has just the opposite effects and is the best thing that can happen in an enterprise. Napoleon claimed that 75 percent of his success on the battlefield was due to the high morale of his troops.

To build a positive work climate, you need to focus on these three areas: the individual, the job, and the supervisor. Table 5.2 lists 40 ways to build a positive work climate. Let's look at some of the most important ways that you can make work enjoyable.

Focus: The Individual

The starting point is your individual workers—one by one. The idea that everybody works for some one thing, like money, is no longer credible. Everybody is glad to have the paycheck, but whether they are willing to work hard for that money or for something else or for anything at all is what you want to determine. Because everybody is different, you are going to need an individual strategy of motivation for each person—not a formal program, just a special way of dealing with each one that brings out their best efforts and offers them the greatest personal satisfaction.

Getting to Know Your People

Getting to know your people takes an indirect approach. People are not going to open up to the boss if you sit down with them at the coffee break and ask them questions about what they want from their jobs. They will tell you what they think you want to hear, and they will probably feel uncomfortable about being quizzed. You may have hired them for one reason, but they probably come to work for altogether different reasons, which they may think is none of your business. They have taken the job as a vehicle for getting where or what they want, but that is a hidden agenda. For some people it is money, for some it is pride, for some it is status, for some it is something to do *until*. If you can find out what kind of satisfactions they are looking for, it will help you to motivate them.

You can learn about them best by observing them. How do they go about their work? How do they react to you, to other workers, to customers? What questions do they ask, or do they ask any? How do they move—quickly, slowly, freely, stiffly? How

TABLE 5.2   ∾   **Forty Ways to Build a Positive Work Climate**

1. Write an effective vision statement.
2. Develop guiding principles.
3. Institutionalize your vision and guiding principles.
4. Give a friendly greeting to your employees each day and get to know them.
5. Actively listen to your employees.
6. Give a hand to your employees when appropriate.
7. Do not hover over your employees.
8. Treat employees fairly and consistently.
9. Never discuss an employee's performance with another employee.
10. Keep your employees informed.
11. Involve your employees.
12. When feasible, offer employee counseling and wellness programs.
13. Use up-to-date and accurate job descriptions.
14. Orient new employees.
15. Train employees to do their jobs well.
16. Coach your employees.
17. Formally evaluate employee performance at least once yearly.
18. Set corrective action guidelines and communicate them to employees.
19. Handle counterproductive behaviors using a two-step process.
20. Prevent counterproductive behaviors.
21. Reward your employees.
22. Follow employee reward guidelines.
23. Pay for performance.
24. Institute a profit-sharing or other gain-sharing program for employees.
25. Help employees see the end result of their work.
26. Let your employees make as many of their own decisions as possible.
27. Cross-train employees and rotate their positions.
28. Give employees special assignments.
29. Have a career ladder and promote from within.
30. Offer employees opportunities for personal and professional development.
31. Be honest.
32. Be able to perform the jobs you supervise.
33. Manage your time.
34. Be visible.
35. Be a good role model.
36. Establish competitive and equitable pay rates.
37. Offer a competitive benefit package suited to your employees.
38. Provide a reasonable work schedule.
39. Provide a pleasant, safe, and clean work environment.
40. Have fun while you work.

Source: Adapted from Karen Eich Drummond, *Retaining Your Foodservice Employees.* New York: Wiley, 1992.

do they look as they speak or listen? Notice their gestures and facial expressions. What makes them light up? What makes them clam up? Pay special attention to what they tell you about themselves in casual conversation. This may be an entirely new approach for you, but people-watching is really quite interesting, and you can quickly become good at spotting clues.

Clues to what? Needs and desires, discontents and aspirations. Frustrations, drive, and achievement. Ability and performance, too, and whether performance is up to par for that job and whether this person has abilities the job does not call on. But primarily needs, desires, and responses, because these are the motivators you want to channel into high performance that will satisfy both you and them.

Observing your people has a purely practical purpose. You are not going to try to psychoanalyze them, probe for hidden motives, delve into what really makes them tick. You can't. That takes years of training you don't have, and a great deal of time you don't have either. Furthermore, you shouldn't. If you are wrong in your amateur analysis, your employees will consider you unjust, and if you are right, they will feel vulnerable—you know them too well. Either way it is going to interfere with motivation rather than improve it.

Your approach, in contrast, should be practical, pragmatic, and experimental; you could even call it superficial. You observe your people and get ideas of what you might do to motivate this or that person to perform better for you as well as get more personal satisfaction from the work. You try out an idea, and if this person does not respond, you try something else. What they respond to is what is important and what you have to work with. The personal whys—the inner needs—are simply clues that you sometimes use to reach the what-to-do.

> The issue of how to motivate employees is frequently discussed by hotel owners, operators, and managers, but it is important to realize that people cannot motivate other people but can only create the environment that motivates people to do something in particular. So motivation involves setting up psychological factors that influence reactions or even attitudes. However, before setting up these factors, it is necessary to examine how employees are recruited, selected, employed, oriented, directed, and supervised. The key to motivating people lies in the direction and supervision afforded by management.
>
> *Source:* Howard Feiertag, "Environment: the foundation of motivation," *Hotel & Motel Management*, Vol. 214, p. 48, December 31, 1999.

Dealing with Security Needs

It is relatively easy to spot people with high security needs. They look and act anxious, uncertain, and tentative. They may be among those who ask you how to do everything, or they may be too scared even to ask. Fear and anxiety are demotivators; they reduce motivation. When security needs are not satisfied, people cannot function well at all; in fact, these people are among those who leave during the first few days on the job.

Here is where Maslow's theories come in handy. If you see that someone has a need for security and you can help that person satisfy that need, you ease that person along to a higher motivational level. To satisfy these needs, you do all the things that we have been recommending in earlier chapters. You tell them what to do and how to do it; you tell them exactly what you expect. You train them. All these things provide a reassuring structure to the work that protects them from the uncertainties of working. It reduces their mistakes and builds their motivation and confidence.

You let them know where they stand at all times. You support them with coaching and feedback and encouragement. You give them positive reinforcement for things they do right, and you retrain them to help them correct their mistakes. You do not solve their problems, you do not cuddle and coddle, you help *them* to do their jobs *themselves*.

You keep on making positive comments about their work even when they are fully trained and you are satisfied with their performance. It is natural for a supervisor to stop paying attention to a worker once things are going well, but even a short absence of approving comments can trigger doubt and uncertainty again in workers who are insecure. Recognition, even if it is only a big smile and a passing "Hey, keep up the good work!" is an affirmation that life on the job is, after all, not uncertain and threatening. Above all, you must avoid any use of fear as a motivator. This is the last thing that these people need.

Evaluate their work frequently, and give praise for things done right, especially for improvement of any sort. Use improvement to build confidence: Accentuate the achievement and the potential—"See how far you have come; see where you *can* go from here." Show them that you expect them to do well. Your confidence will give them confidence. And if you can build confidence, you may eventually activate self-motivation and aspiration. Satisfaction of primary needs allows these higher-level needs to emerge.

Dealing with Social Needs

Everybody has social needs (Maslow again). You may not think of work as being a place to satisfy them, but it often is. For many people a job fills the need to be with others, the need to be accepted, the need to belong. These are powerful needs. Often they will fall into Herzberg's category of hygiene factors: They cause dissatisfaction when they are unsatisfied, but they do not motivate when satisfied. But for some people they can be motivators, too.

For example, consider the homemaker who gets a job because she wants to talk to people who are more than three feet tall. If you hire her as a cashier or a switchboard operator, she probably won't be very good at it because this is not what she came to work for. But if you make her a desk clerk or a waitress or a sales rep where she can talk to people all day long, she could easily become a higher achiever.

Whether or not social needs can be turned into motivators, it is useful when people find such needs being satisfied on the job, both in terms of their individual development and in terms of the general work climate. People whose social needs are unmet may just not work very well, or they may even provoke trouble and conflict.

What can you do to help meet people's social needs? There are two specific needs you can work on, and it takes hardly any of your time. One is the *need for acceptance*. We have talked about this before: You build a person-to-person relationship and you treat each person as a unique individual who has dignity and worth. You respect their idiosyncracies (unless they interfere with the work): you speak softly to Peter because that is what Peter responds to. You scream and yell at Paul because that is your unique way of relating to Paul and you both know it, and Paul will think he doesn't matter to you anymore if you treat him any other way.

You deal with each person differently, but you treat each according to the same standards, whether she is good-looking or plain, whether his mother is on welfare or owns the biggest bank in town. Each one is a person who has value, has worth, and you treat them all that way.

You also make it clear that you value each person's work and that it is important to the organization no matter how menial it is. The well-made bed, the properly washed salad greens, the sparkling-clean rest room all please customers; the crooked bedspread, the gritty salad, the empty tissue holder send customers away. This attention to detail can be as important to the success of the hotel or restaurant as the expertise of the sommelier or the masterpieces of the chef. You can make people feel that they are an essential part of the entire organization, that you need them, that they belong there. A sense of belonging may be your most powerful ally in the long run—and it helps the long run to happen.

This *need to belong* is the other social need that you can do a lot to satisfy. Things you should be doing anyway help to satisfy this need, such as making people feel comfortable in their jobs by training them, coaching them, telling them where they stand, evaluating their work frequently. Open communications also encourage belonging; people feel free to come to you with suggestions or problems. Keeping people informed about changes that affect them is a way of including them in what is going on—and if you leave anybody out you reduce that person to a nobody. You can also include people in discussions about the work, inviting their ideas, feelings, and reactions. If you can build a spirit of teamwork, that, too, will foster a sense of belonging.

One's peer group also nurtures belonging. You need to be aware of social relationships among your workers and to realize that these relationships are just as important as their relationship with you, and sometimes more so. Often, peer pressure is more influential than the boss is.

You need to have the group on your side—if it ever comes to taking sides—and that is best done through good relationships with each person. These people work under you and they look at you as their boss. They expect you to be friendly and to sit down with them if they invite you, but they do not expect you to be one of the gang. In fact, your uninvited presence for more than a moment or two may act as a constraint to their socializing.

Groups and group socialization are a normal part of the job scene. Often, groups break into cliques, with different interests and sometimes rivalries. You should not try to prevent the formation of groups and cliques. But if competition between cliques begins to disrupt the work, you will have to intervene. You cannot let employee competition interfere with the work climate.

Rewarding Your Employees

Incentive pay, bonuses, and various kinds of nonmonetary rewards can be very effective motivators if they activate people's needs and desires or are related to their reason for working. One of the problems, of course, is that what motivates one person leaves another indifferent, yet to treat people fairly you have to have rewards of equal value for equal performance.

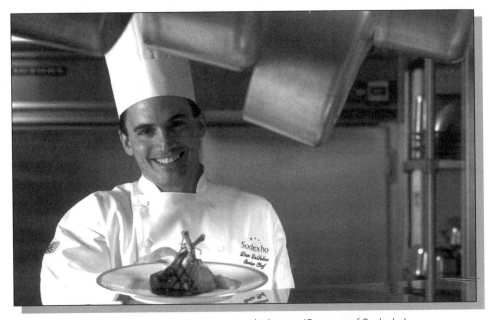

Rewarding associates contributes to a positive work climate. (Courtesy of Sodexho)

These methods of triggering motivation begin with the carrot principle of dangling a reward for good performance. When people need or want the reward, they will work hard in expectation of getting it. If they do not want the carrot, it has no effect.

Once the reward is achieved, the cycle must start again: The desire must be activated by the *expectation of reward,* as Herzberg points out. No expectation, no achievement, and performance slumps back to a nonreward level unless people begin to derive satisfaction from the achievement itself. However, there is no doubt that rewards are useful motivators. In many jobs the boring repetition of meaningless tasks precludes a sense of achievement that is fulfilling, and rewards may be the only resource you have for motivating.

The entire system of rewards, both monetary and otherwise, must be worked out with care, not only for getting the maximum motivation but also for fairness in the eyes of the employees. The performance required to achieve the reward must be spelled out carefully, and the goal must be within reach of everyone. People must know ahead of time what the rewards are and must perceive them as fair or they will cause more dissatisfaction than motivation.

How do you make rewards into effective motivators if people's needs and desires are so different? Somebody with eight children to feed might work very hard for a money reward or the chance to work more overtime. Another person might outdo himself for an extra day of paid vacation. Still another would do almost anything for a reserved space in the parking lot right near the door with her name on it in great-big letters. Such rewards might be suitable prizes in an employee contest, with the winner being allowed to choose from among them.

You might get people involved by letting them suggest rewards (keeping the final decision to yourself). Any involvement increases the likelihood of sparking real motivation. Actually, any reward can be more than a carrot. It can be a recognition of achievement, of value, of worth to the company. It can build pride; it can generate self-esteem. It can also be a goal. Once employees earn a reward, if it gives them satisfaction, they will probably go for it again. Then you have activated motivation from within, with commitment to a person's own goal. And that, in miniature, is what successful on-the-job motivation is all about—fulfilling individual goals and company goals in the same process.

Following are some additional guidelines to keep in mind when rewarding employees:

- ❧ Always give recognition in a positive and sincere manner.

- ❧ When having a contest, don't pit employees against each other in order to win only one or several prizes. When only a few people can win, most employees don't even try and are disheartened, instead of being motivated, when the winners are announced. When running a contest, make it possible for all employees to win, and have the employee compete with himself to try to beat his own goals rather than competing with a peer.

- ❧ Don't just recognize your superb performers. About 10 percent of your employees are top-notch employees who you pray never leave. If you recognize only these performers, you will frustrate the majority of your employees, who are satisfactory performers but are the backbone of your operation. In addition to the heroes, champion the average employees who come to work on time, follow rules, work safely, and so on.

- ❧ Determine which employees will be recognized using objective criteria. In this manner, managers are less likely to make their decisions based on favoritism, seniority, or pity.

- ❧ Recognize employees in a timely fashion. Don't make your recognition program so complicated and unwieldy that it takes too long to recognize your employees and hand out any awards or prizes.

- ❧ From time to time, recognize employees when they least expect it, and be somewhat unpredictable about it. For example, tell someone to take the rest of the day off.

- ❧ Rewards should be tied to true accomplishments, not to superficial or momentary gains.

- ❧ Rewards should be of appropriate value; don't forget that small rewards can be just as impressive as large ones.

- ❧ Rewards should be something desired by your employees. Ask your employees what types of rewards they prefer.[5]

---

[5]Karen Eich Drummond, *Retaining Your Foodservice Employees.* New York: Wiley, 1992. Reprinted with permission of the publisher.

Developing Your Employees

Another way of maintaining a positive work climate is to help your people to become better at their jobs and to develop their potential. This may be one of the most critical things you do. A large percentage of the people in foodservice and hospitality enterprises are underemployed, and as managers we really do not utilize the skills and abilities of the people who work for us as fully as we could. Your goal should be to make all your people as competent as you can, because it makes your job easier, it makes you look better to your superiors, and it is good for your people.

You can develop your beginning workers through training, feedback, encouragement, and support, as well as by providing the right equipment and generally facilitating their work. By the way you deal with them, you can also give them a feeling of importance to the operation, a sense of their own worth, and a feeling of achievement and growth. Concrete recognition of improvement, whether it is an award, a reward, or merely a word of praise, can add to the pride of achievement.

If you have people with high potential, you should do all these things and more. You should try to develop their skills, utilize any talents you see, challenge them by asking for their input on the work, give them responsibilities, and open doors to advancement to the extent that you can. One thing is certain: If you have trained someone to take your place, it will be a lot easier for your company to promote you. But if none of your subordinates can fill your job, the company is less likely to move you up because they need you where you are.

Developing your people also helps morale. It gives people that sense of moving forward that keeps them from going stale, marking time, moving on a treadmill. It is also important to your acceptance as a leader to have people feel that you are helping them to help themselves.

You develop your employees by involving them. Employees who are asked to influence what happens at work tend to develop a sense of ownership; this feeling of ownership breeds commitment. Employees can become effectively involved in many managerial activities, such as evaluating work methods, identifying problems, proposing suggestions, and deciding on a course of action. Your employees can tell you better than anyone else how their own jobs should be done.

For instance, McGuffey's Restaurants, a dinner-house chain based in North Carolina, asks for employee input on ways to improve service and also asks employees to elect representatives to an associate board at which employees concerns will be addressed. In some cases, when you involve your employees, you are actually empowering them. Empowering your employees means giving them additional responsibility and authority to do their jobs. Instead of employees feeling responsible for merely doing what they are told, they are given greater control over decisions about work. For example, in some restaurants, servers are empowered, or given the authority, to resolve customer complaints without management intervention. A server may decide, in response to a customer complaint, not to charge the customer for a menu item that was not satisfactory.

At McGuffey's Restaurants, the company gives employees their own business cards, which they can use to invite potential customers in for free food or beverages. The company even lets employees run the restaurants two days a year, during which they can change the menu and make other changes.

↝ profile

MANUEL LORENZO

Manuel Lorenzo is a supervisor for Sodexho Education Services at Alliant International University (AIU) and arrives to begin his shift at AIU at 9:00 A.M. Manuel's first duty is to check the catering board, where he will find a list of scheduled catering events for the day. Manuel then plans the food preparations and starts gathering the necessary equipment.

He then meets with Rick Nargi, the general manager of foodservices at AIU, to coordinate the next 48 hours. This is the time that any problems or concerns can be addressed. At 11:00 A.M., Manuel walks around to make sure that the cafeteria is ready to serve lunch. Manuel supervises the lunch operation until it ends at 1:30. After lunch, Manuel continues working on catering functions and makes sure that everything flows smoothly and is ready for dinner.

Before Manuel leaves for the day, he must check to see that all catering vehicles are tanked and running properly. Then the storerooms must be cleaned and orga-

Following are some guidelines for **empowering** your employees:

↝ Give your employees your trust and respect, two essential ingredients for empowerment of employees.
↝ Determine exactly what you want employees to be empowered to do.
↝ Train your employees in those new areas. Be clear as to what you want them to do.
↝ Create an environment in which exceptions to rules, particularly when they involve customer satisfaction, are permissible.
↝ Allow employees to make mistakes without being criticized or punished. Instead, view these times as opportunities to educate your employees.
↝ Reward empowered employees who take risks, make good decisions, and take ownership.

Finally, you should also continue to develop yourself. Chances are that you won't have much time for reading and studying, but you should keep pace with what is going on in other parts of your company and in the industry as a whole—read trade publications and attend trade association meetings. You can also watch yourself as you practice your profession, evaluating your own progress and learning from your mistakes. Make a habit of thinking back on the decisions you have made. What would have happened if you had done something differently? Can you do it better next time?

nized. Rick will also have a list of projects for Manuel to complete. These tasks usually consist of maintaining sanitation standards. Last, Manuel checks staffing levels for the rest of the week and deals with basic human resource functions.

Manuel sees time management as one of the major challenges of his career. Events are constantly pending, and he has only a very limited amount of time to plan, organize, and carry out those functions. Manuel contends that the only way to be successful in this respect is to be highly organized. Also, Manuel says that success requires one to be a "people person." This skill helps him deal with employees effectively and helps him understand the people he serves, so that he can serve them better.

Keeping the customer satisfied is another challenge for Manuel. University food-service operations have the unique and difficult task of keeping long-term boarding residents happy with food quality. Manuel solves this problem by serving a wide variety of entrées, yet maintaining consistency with daily staples.

Each catering event is different because of the variety in food served. With each new function, Manuel learns something new about food and/or culture. Manuel admits that this is one of the most interesting, exciting, and rewarding aspects of his job.

Focus: The Job

Providing an Attractive Job Environment

The worker's job environment includes not only the physical environment and working conditions but the other workers, the hours, rate of pay, benefits, and company policies and administration. You may recognize these as *hygiene* or *maintenance factors*.

As Herzberg pointed out, such job factors do not motivate. But any of them can cause dissatisfaction and demotivation, which can interfere with productivity and increase turnover. So it behooves the supervisor to remove as many dissatisfiers as possible. To the extent that you have control, you can provide good physical working conditions: satisfactory equipment in good working order; adequate heating, cooling, and lighting; comfortable employee lounges; plenty of parking; and so on. You can see that working hours and schedules meet workers' needs as closely as possible. If you have anything to say about it, you can see that wages and benefits are as good as those of your competitors or better, so that your people will not be lured away by a better deal than you can give.

There is not much that you can do about company policy and administration if it is rigid and high-control, except to work within its limits, stick up for your people, and do things your own way within your sphere of authority. We will assume that the management philosophy is not based on fear and punishment or you would not be there yourself.

Providing a Safe and Secure Work Environment

Safety hazards in hospitality operations range from knives put in a kitchen sink full of water to hazardous chemicals housekeepers use to clean hotel rooms. Cuts, falls, fires, and electric shock are all examples of accidents that can and do happen. They occur because employees are fooling around, rushing, being careless, working under the influence, not paying attention, or overdoing it. Accidents sometimes also occur because employees are ignorant or just feel that accidents are inevitable, so they don't bother trying to prevent them. There is much a supervisor can do to provide a safe and secure workplace. This topic is covered in detail in Chapter 14.

Putting the Right Person in the Right Job

If you get to know your workers, you are in a good position to figure out what jobs are right for what people. People with high security needs may do very well in routine jobs: Once they have mastered the routine they will have the satisfaction and security of doing it well. Putting them in a server's job would be a disaster. Putting people-oriented workers in routine behind-the-scenes jobs might be a disaster, too.

Many cooks enjoy preparing good things for people to eat. Even when they must follow other people's standardized recipes, there is the satisfaction of being able to tell exactly when a steak is medium rare, of making a perfect omelet, of arranging a beautiful buffet platter. Bartenders often enjoy putting on a show of their pouring prowess. These people are in the right jobs.

Pride in one's work can be a powerful motivator. Some people get a great sense of achievement from tearing into a room left in chaos by guests and putting it in order again, leaving it clean and inviting for the next guest. They, too, are in the right jobs. The professional dishwasher we have mentioned several times obviously took great pride in his work and wore his occupation as a badge of honor. He belonged in his job, and it belonged to him, and in a curious way it probably satisfied all levels of needs for him.

Another instance of finding the right job for the right person involved a supervisor in her 60s who lived in a one-room flat and had no family and no life outside her job. Yet on the job she seemed to make nothing but trouble. She couldn't manage her people, and she was always meddling in other people's work and generally disrupting things. Finally, her manager put her in charge of the laundry, where she had the entire responsibility but no one to supervise. Now she had something she was good at, something that was important and appreciated, and she belonged there. She became a whirlwind of efficiency, even reducing costs substantially.

Making the Job Interesting and Challenging

People do their best work when something about the work involves their interest and stimulates their desire to do it well. People who like what they are doing work hard at it of their own accord. People who don't like their jobs drag their heels, watch the clock, do as little as they can get by with, and are called lazy by the boss.

Different things about the work turn different people on. Some are stimulated by working with customers: They get a kick out of making them welcome, serving

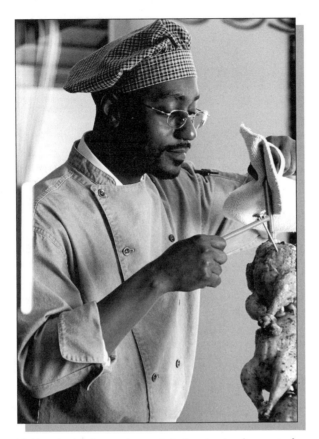

Making the job interesting and challenging is a key part of
a supervisor's job. (Courtesy of Sodexho)

them well, pleasing them, amusing them, turning an irate customer into a fan by
helping to solve a problem. Some people are miserable dealing with customers and
enjoy a nice routine job with no people hassles where they can put their accuracy
and skill to work straightening out messy records and putting things in order. Some
people like jobs where there is always some new problem to solve; others hate problems and like to exercise their special skills and turn out products they are proud of.

What these people all have in common is that something about the content of
their job both stimulates and satisfies them. Stated in theoretical terms, it satisfies
their higher needs, those related to self-esteem and self-fulfillment. Specifically, people work hard at jobs that give them opportunity for achievement, for responsibility, for growth and advancement, for doing work they enjoy doing for its own sake.

There are two ideas here that you as a supervisor can use in motivating your
people. One is to put people in jobs that are right for them as just discussed. The
other is to enrich people's jobs to include more of the motivating elements. Of
course, there are limits to what you can do, but the more you can move in this direction, the more likely you are to create a positive work climate.

Workers who are bored are underemployed: The job does not make use of their talents, their education, and their abilities. They are only there *until*—until they find a more interesting and challenging job. Not only will you have to train their replacements sooner or later, but you are not making use of abilities right now that could contribute a great deal to your department and to the entire organization. Furthermore, as we said in Chapter 1, supervisors have an obligation to develop their people.

You cannot move people into better jobs unless jobs are available, but you can look for ways to enrich their present jobs by building some motivators into them. This does not mean asking them to take on additional, but similar, tasks—this is called *job loading*. **Job enrichment** means shifting the way things are done so as to provide more responsibility for one's own work and more opportunity for achievement, for recognition, for learning, for growth.

You might start by giving people more responsibility for their own work. Relax your control; stop watching every move they make. Let them try out their own methods of achieving results as long as they do not run counter to the standards and procedures that are an essential part of the job. In other words, decrease controls and increase accountability. This must all be discussed between you, and there must be a clear understanding, as in any delegation agreement.

From there you can experiment with other forms of job enrichment. You can delegate some of your own tasks. You can rearrange the work in the jobs you are enriching to add more authority and responsibility for the workers. You can give new and challenging assignments. You can assign special tasks that require imagination and develop skills.

If, for example, you find that you have creative people in routine kitchen jobs, let them try planning new plate layouts or garnishes. If someone who majored in English is working as a payroll clerk, let her try her hand at writing menu fliers or notices for the employee bulletin board or stories for the company magazine. Look for people's hidden talents and secret ambitions and use them, and keep in mind reporting them when more suitable jobs are available.

Another idea that is being tried out in a number of industries is replacing the assembly-line method of dividing the work into minute, repetitive parts by giving a worker or group of workers responsibility for an entire unit of work or complete product, including quality control. Is there a way of avoiding assembly-line sandwich-making that would give each worker or a group of workers complete responsibility for one kind of sandwich, letting them work out the most efficient method? Could you give a cleaning team responsibility for making up an entire corridor of rooms, dividing the tasks as they see fit?

There are many jobs in which the work is going to be dull no matter what you do. But even in these a shift in responsibility and point of view can work near-miracles. A concerted program of job enrichment for cleaning and janitorial services carried out at Texas Instruments is an example of what can be done with routine low-skill tasks. These services were revamped to give everyone a role in the planning and control of their work, although the work itself remained the same. Extensive training embodying Theory Y principles was given to supervisors and working foremen, while worker training included orientation in company goals and philosophy and their part in the overall operation. A team-oriented, goal-oriented, problem-solving approach encouraged worker participation in reorganizing, simplifying, and expediting the work.

Increased responsibility, participation, and pride of achievement generated high commitment as well as better ways of doing the work. In the first year's trial the cleanliness level improved from 65 percent to 85 percent, the number of people required dropped from 120 to 71, and the quarterly turnover rate dropped from 100 percent to 9.8 percent. The annual savings to the company was a six-figure total. The average educational level of these workers was fourth or fifth grade, proving that Theory Y management is applicable all up and down the scale.[6]

A major program such as this takes a long time to develop and implement and is out of the reach of the first-time supervisor working alone. But it shows what can be done when dedicated leadership and enlightened company policies activate employee motivation.

Any job enrichment effort is likely to produce a drop in productivity at first as workers get used to changes and new responsibilities. It takes a coaching approach to begin with and a lot of support from the boss. It is also essential to initiate changes slowly and to plan them with care. Too much responsibility and freedom too soon may be more than some workers can handle, either out of inexperience or because of the insecurities involved. Again, it is a situation in which your own sensitivity to your workers is a key ingredient.

Focus: The Supervisor

Ultimately, it is the supervisor who holds the keys to a positive work climate. It is not only the steps he takes, the things she does to spark motivation; it is the way that supervisors themselves approach their own tasks and responsibilities—their own performance of their own jobs. If they themselves are highly motivated and enthusiastic about their work, their people are likely to be motivated, too. If they have high expectations of themselves and their people, and if they believe in themselves and their people, the people will generally come through for them. It is motivation by contagion, by expectation, by example.

In some operations the manager conveys a sense of excitement, a feeling that *anything is possible, so let's go for it!* You find it sometimes in the individual entrepreneur or the manager of a new unit in a larger company. If the manager is up, the people are up, too, and it is an exciting place to work. It is not unusual for people who have worked for such managers to end up as entrepreneurs themselves, putting their own excitement to work in an enterprise of their own.

Tony's Restaurant in St. Louis is a case in point. Owner Vincent Bommarito's enthusiasm, high standards, and involvement with employee development and performance, coupled with an anything-is-possible approach, have spawned at least 20 restaurants owned and operated by former employees. Of course, there are the

---

[6]A detailed account of this program is given by Earl D Week, Jr., "Job enrichment 'cleans up' at Texas Instruments," in John R. Maher, ed., *New Perspectives in Job Enrichment.* New York: Van Nostrand Reinhold, 1971.

added incentives of ownership in such cases, but it really begins with the excitement and enthusiasm of the original restaurant experience.

At the opposite extreme, supervisors who are not happy in their jobs, who are not themselves motivated, will have unmotivated workers who are faithful reflections of themselves—management by example again. You cannot motivate others successfully if you are not motivated yourself. And if you are not, you need a change of attitude or a change of job.

If you give 75 percent of your effort to your job, your people will give 25 to 50 percent. If you put forth a 100 percent effort, your people will give you 110 percent. If you expect the best of people, they will give you their best. If you expect poor performance, poor performance is what you will get. If you tell people they can do a certain thing and they believe in you, they can do it and they will. If you tell them it is beyond their ability, they won't even try.

This contagious kind of motivation can run back and forth between supervisor and workers; they can motivate you if you will let them. If you have good relationships with your people, they can spark your interest with new ideas about the work. They can help you solve problems. Their enthusiasm for the work will sustain your own motivation in the face of setbacks and disappointments. When a "we" attitude prevails, it builds belonging, involvement, and commitment.

Setting a Good Example

Whether you are aware of it or not, you set an example for your workers; they are going to copy what you do. The psychologist's term for this is **role model.** If you expect the best work from your people, you've got to give your best work to your job. If you give 100 percent of your time and effort and enthusiasm, chances are that your workers will give you 110 percent. But if they see you giving about 75 percent and hear you groaning about your problems, they will give you only 25 to 50 percent of their effort. So if you want a fair day's work from your people, give a fair day's work to them: **management by example,** it is sometimes called.

Giving your best means keeping your best side out all the time. Everybody has a good side and a bad side, and most of us are vulnerable to a certain few things that can turn that bad side out and cause us to lose our cool. This is disastrous when you are a role model, particularly if you are supervising people who deal with customers. If you lose your temper with a group of workers and shout at them, they are going to carry the echo of your voice and the feelings it arouses in them right into the hotel lobby or the dining room or the hospital floor. They are going to be impatient and hostile and heedless of the customers' needs. And there goes the training you have given them in customer relations.

Your good side is as influential as your bad side. If you want your people to treat customers courteously and serve them well, treat your workers courteously and well. If bad moods are contagious, so are good moods. Enthusiasm is contagious. If you would like your workers to enjoy their work, be enthusiastic yourself. Is that a big order? Sometimes. But if you can do it, it works.

Set your sights high; expect the best of your workers. If you expect their best, they will usually give you their best if you approach the subject positively. If you show them you believe in them and have confidence in their ability to do the job, if you cheer them on, so to speak, they will attach the same value to their performance that you do. They will take pride in their work and in their own achievements. On the other hand, if you suddenly tell them to improve their work, without warning and in a critical way, implying that they are slackers and don't measure up, they are likely to resent the criticism and resist the demand.

Establishing a Climate of Honesty

A positive work climate requires a climate of honesty. We have talked about honesty as one of the things that workers expect of the boss. It means that you are honest with them when you talk to them about their performance and their potential and their achievements and mistakes. It means that you keep your promises and give credit where credit is due. It means that you do not cheat, lie, or steal from the company: you do not take food home from the kitchen or booze from the bar, you do not take money from customers in return for a better room or a better table. You are a role model and you do not do these things, not only because they are unethical, but also because you want your workers to be honest; they are going to imitate you. Management by example again.

You do not say one thing and do another. Nothing confuses a worker more than a supervisor who gives good advice but sets a bad example. You are consistent and fair. You do not manipulate; you are open and aboveboard; you can be trusted.

A climate of honesty encourages the growth of loyalty. If you are loyal to the company that employs you and are honest and fair and open with your people, they will develop loyalty to both you and the company. If you put down the company, you destroy your entire work climate because your workers will begin to believe that the company is a lousy place. If you feel like running down the company now and then, keep it to yourself. If you feel like that all the time, get out. You cannot do a good job as supervisor with those feelings bottled up inside.

∾ key points

1. Employees want their supervisor to be qualified to supervise, be experienced, take charge, treat people fairly and equally, communicate, and treat people as human beings.

2. Motivation is the "why" of human behavior.

3. There are various theories of motivation: Use fear (McGregor's Theory X); combine fear with incentives (carrot-and-stick motivation); give money [economic man (person) theory]; give them consideration [human relations or social man (person) theory, Maslow's hierarchy of needs]; satisfy employee work needs, such as a need for growth or achievement (McGregor's Theory Y); and give positive reinforcement when a worker does something right (behavior modification).

4. Factors that may limit your use of motivational techniques include the boring nature of many jobs, company management policies, the extent of your authority and resources, the employees themselves, and the constant time pressures.

5. A positive work climate is one in which employees can and will work productively.

6. Morale is a group spirit surrounding getting a job done.

7. In order to build a positive work climate, you need to focus on the individual, the job, and yourself (the supervisor) by getting to know your people, dealing with security and social needs, rewarding and developing your people, providing an attractive job environment, providing a safe and secure work environment, making the job interesting and challenging, setting a good example, and establishing a climate of honesty.

∾ key terms

behavior modification	management by example
dissatisfiers	morale
economic man (person) theory	motivation
empowering	motivators
hierarchy of needs	positive reinforcement
hygiene factors	role model
job enrichment	self-actualization
maintenance factors	social man (person) theory

∾ review questions

Answer each question in complete sentences. Read each question carefully and make sure that you answer all parts of the question. Organize your answer using more than one paragraph when appropriate.

1. Name five expectations that employees often have of their supervisor.

2. Briefly discuss five motivational theories that make the most sense to you.

3. Which motivational theorist thinks that most people will "become all they are capable of becoming"?

4. What limits the supervisor from using motivational theories to their fullest?

5. Compare the terms *positive work climate* and *morale.* In what ways are their meanings similar, and in what ways different?

6. To what do the terms *demotivator* and *dissatisfier* refer? How do demotivators and dissatisfiers affect productivity? How can the supervisor avoid them?

7. What is meant by *develop your people?*

8. Describe management by example.

9. As a supervisor, briefly describe seven things that you can do to create a positive work climate.

❦ activities and applications

1. **Discussion Questions**
   - When you go to work, what are some of your expectations and needs? What is positive about the work climate? What is negative?
   - Why can't motivation theory be reduced to a set of rules that a supervisor can apply to maintain or increase productivity?
   - What motivates you when you are working? Does your supervisor make any effort to determine what motivates your actions and use this knowledge to increase your productivity or try a new task?
   - Do you think that one motivational theory is especially better than others in motivating workers to perform well? Defend your answer.
   - Eleven factors are mentioned in this chapter to help build a positive work climate. Which three are most important to you? Can you think of any other factors? Refer to Table 5.2 for more factors.

2. **"Dear Boss" Letter**

Write a letter to a future boss about how you want to be treated. For example, you may ask to be listened to, to be thanked, to be challenged, and so on. List at least 10 things describing how you want your future boss to work with you.

3. **Group Activity: Rewards**

Working in a group, number in priority order what you think employees want from their jobs. Then number in priority order what supervisors believe that employees want from their jobs. A real survey like this was done with supervisors and employees. The top three concerns for employees, and how supervisors ranked their concerns, are listed at the end of this chapter.

Employees Want:		*Supervisors Think Employees Want:*
_____	1. Promotion and growth	_____
_____	2. Interesting work	_____
_____	3. Job security	_____
_____	4. Feeling of being in on things	_____
_____	5. Full appreciation of work done	_____
_____	6. Good wages	_____

4. **Case Study: Keeping the Kitchen Clean**

Last week the Health Department gave the kitchen of the (fictitious) Cedar Crest Hotel a 64 percent rating along with a warning to clean up or close up. A local newspaper columnist got hold of this information and made a big story out of it. Customer counts dropped immediately, hotel reservations were canceled, and the sales department lost several pending contracts for conventions. The hotel's general manager chewed out the food and beverage director, who chewed out the executive chef, who chewed out the sous chef, who chewed out everybody in the kitchen individually and collectively. Everyone was forced to work overtime to get things into shape for the Health Department's repeat inspection three days later, which gave the Cedar Crest kitchen a passing grade of 85 percent and put it on probation. The incident left everyone shaken up. Station heads and cooks who had always been fanatics on sanitation had been treated as though guilty, while a couple of careless cooks who had caused many of the problems were secretly gloating over their escape from the spotlight. Nearly everyone is still angry with Albert, the sous chef, whose responsibility it is now to maintain and improve the 85 percent rating.

1. Albert knows that he must do something to quiet the current emotional turmoil and to motivate people to practice sanitation on a daily basis. He knows that without a change in employee motivation, sanitation will soon slip back to its former levels.

2. Evaluate the following suggestions for actions. Which ones do you think Albert can turn into effective motivators? Discuss how he could implement them effectively or modify them to make them more motivating. Explain why the others would not work or would be counterproductive. Add any suggestions of your own.

3. On the basis of your evaluations, rank the suggestions in order of importance and make a plan of action for Albert. He needs all the help he can get.

SUGGESTIONS

1. Call a meeting, give a lecture on the seriousness of the situation, hand out a set of rules and penalties, and lay down the law.

2. Fire the careless cooks who are chronic offenders, as a symbol of a new regime.

3. Admit his own failure to maintain standards in the past and plead for everyone's help in making improvements.

4. Begin a formal training program on sanitation, given by an outside specialist, with films, lectures, and hands-on training.

5. Hire a sanitation specialist to inspect the kitchen several times a day. Follow up on every violation.

6. Interview people individually, coach them, and give them positive reinforcement for improvement.

7. Delegate responsibility for sanitation to the station heads.

8. Invite suggestions for solving or avoiding persistent sanitation problems.

9. Set a goal of 95 percent or better for the next Health Department inspection and promise a big party if the goal is met.

10. Explain the importance for the hotel of the kitchen's image, and point out that the loss of clientele can mean fewer jobs in the kitchen.

Answer to (Group Activity: Rewards)

Employees: 2, 5, 4
Supervisors: 6, 3, 1

chapter 6
Developing Job Expectations

Picture a scared young employee named Joe reporting to work in a big hotel kitchen on his first job. The day's work is in full swing, nobody pays any attention to him, and he has trouble even finding Chef Paul to report for duty. When he finally finds him, Joe has to follow him around to tell him he is the new cook's helper. Paul tells him to go over and help Roger.

Roger is making salads and he tells Joe to go to the cooler and get another crate of romaine. Joe doesn't know what a cooler is, or where it is, or what romaine is. He feels like heading for home. Joe doesn't know what his job is. Roger knows that Joe is supposed to be his helper, but it doesn't occur to Roger to tell Joe what that means. Even Chef Paul doesn't think to tell Joe what his duties are—he assumes that what Roger will tell him to do is all that is needed.

Many operations are as casual and disorganized as this. A supervisor can quickly go crazy trying to run such a department because things will constantly go wrong and the chief management activity will be coping with this or that crisis. Fortunately, there are ways of bringing order out of this kind of chaos by defining each job and telling people what it is and how to do it.

One of the most useful tools for sorting out this kind of confusion is a job description that incorporates performance standards. Once you start to grasp these concepts and learn how to use them, they will become some of the most useful devices in your entire supervisory repertoire.

In this chapter we explain how to develop job descriptions and performance standards and examine their use in standardizing routine jobs. It will help you to:

∾ Define *job analysis* and describe the process for creating one.

∾ Explain the importance of defining jobs clearly and telling employees the what, how, and how-wells of their jobs.

∾ Define *performance standard* and list several examples of performance standards that might be used in the hospitality industry.

∾ Write a job description using performance standards.

∾ Describe how performance standards can be used to develop a system of managing employees and their work.

∾ Explain why some performance standard systems succeed and others fail.

When we start to discuss job descriptions there are many related terms that come up, such as position, job analysis, job specification, and job evaluation. Before beginning this chapter, let's define some of these terms.

A **position** consists of duties and responsibilities performed by one employee. For example, in an operation there are four cook positions occupied by four employees, yet each of them has only one job or job classification, that of *cook*. A **job** is a group of positions with the same duties and responsibilities. It is the entirety of the work, the sum total of what a person is paid to do. Other common hospitality jobs include server, housekeeper, and front desk clerk.

Job analysis is the process that tries to present a picture of how the world of work looks for a specific job. A job analyst determines the content of a given job by breaking it down into units (work sequences) and identifying the tasks that make up each unit. For instance, for a cashier, there are a number of tasks or steps involved in ringing up sales. The primary purpose of job analysis is to form the basis of the job description.

The **job description** describes what the job is as a whole. It explains *what* the employee is supposed to do, *how* to perform job duties, and *how well* they are to be done. As such, it describes a fair day's work and sets the performance standards. The job description also explains the context of the job (or the conditions in which the work takes place), including the factors of working conditions (often hot and steamy) and the social environment (hopefully, warm and friendly).

The **job specification** spells out the qualifications that a person must have in order to get the job. Qualifications often fall into the following areas: knowledge, skills and abilities, work experience, education, and training.

Job evaluation is the process of examining the responsibilities and difficulties of each job in order to determine which jobs are worth more than others. Job evaluation is used primarily to determine which jobs should pay more than others. There are several ways to perform job evaluation.

Before discussing job descriptions, it is important first to talk about analyzing a job.

Job Analysis

Every job in the hospitality industry or in a managed services setting includes several distinct work segments or **units of work.** For example, the job of server in a restaurant includes taking orders, serving food, serving wine, and so on. Each of these is a separate unit of the work that, when combined, comprise a job. Figure 6.1 shows a typical list of units of work for a server. You will see that our list includes such units as dress and grooming, sanitation, and guest relations, which are not true work sequences but are, nevertheless, critical activities in the server's job. They require the setting of standards, training, and evaluation just as the actual work sequences do. Such units appear in other jobs as well, and the same standards will apply in each case.

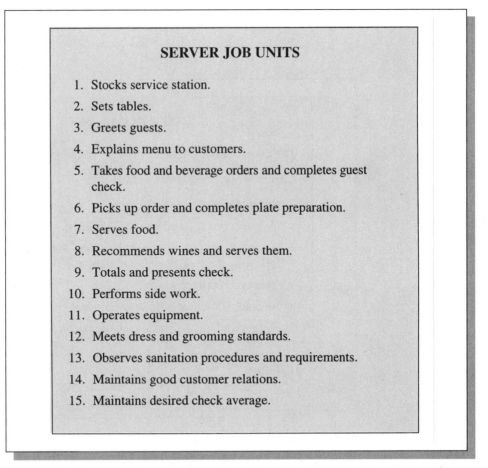

SERVER JOB UNITS

1. Stocks service station.
2. Sets tables.
3. Greets guests.
4. Explains menu to customers.
5. Takes food and beverage orders and completes guest check.
6. Picks up order and completes plate preparation.
7. Serves food.
8. Recommends wines and serves them.
9. Totals and presents check.
10. Performs side work.
11. Operates equipment.
12. Meets dress and grooming standards.
13. Observes sanitation procedures and requirements.
14. Maintains good customer relations.
15. Maintains desired check average.

FIGURE 6.1   Example of job analysis: breakdown of one job classification into units (page from a procedures manual for one operation). Unit lists will vary from one operation to another.

An important concept of job analysis is that the analysis is conducted of the job, not the person. Although job analysis data may be collected from incumbents through interviews or questionnaires, the product of the analysis is a description or specifications of the job, not a description of the person.

Source: Anonymous, "HR Guide to the Internet: Job Analysis: Overview," www.hrguide.com/data/G000.htm, 1999.

Each unit consists of a number of **tasks**—perhaps 5, 10, 20, or 100 things that the server has to do in carrying out the work of that unit. A task is an identifiable activity that constitutes a skill or activity necessary to complete a unit of the job. For example, what are the tasks performed in taking an order? Figure 6.2 lists the tasks in order of performance. You may have trouble at first deciding what is a unit and what is a task that is part of a unit. Is *explains menu* a separate unit or is it part of *takes order*? The line between unit and task is fluid at times, and you could go either way. You can even set it up both as a separate unit and as a task in another unit.

Once you have a list of tasks or procedural steps for each unit, you have the complete description for that job (Figure 6.3): the entirety of the work, the sum total of what each person in that job is paid to do, the fair day's work. Now let's see how we use units of work and tasks in writing job descriptions.

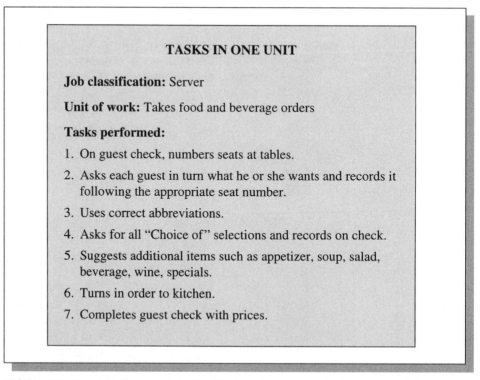

TASKS IN ONE UNIT

Job classification: Server

Unit of work: Takes food and beverage orders

Tasks performed:

1. On guest check, numbers seats at tables.

2. Asks each guest in turn what he or she wants and records it following the appropriate seat number.

3. Uses correct abbreviations.

4. Asks for all "Choice of" selections and records on check.

5. Suggests additional items such as appetizer, soup, salad, beverage, wine, specials.

6. Turns in order to kitchen.

7. Completes guest check with prices.

FIGURE 6.2   Example of task analysis: these tasks make up one unit of the server job (page from a procedures manual).

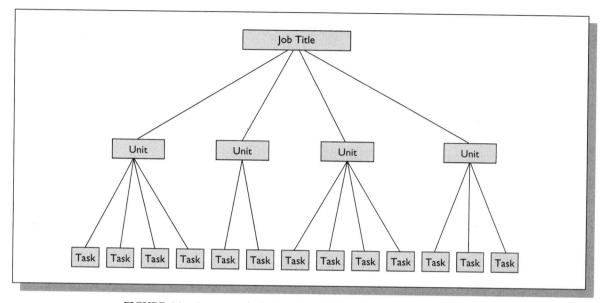

FIGURE 6.3 Anatomy of job classification. This diagram represents the content of an entire job. Numbers of units and tasks vary with the job and often from one enterprise to another. The sum of all the parts represents the total work requirements of that job.

Job Description

There are five major reasons for low productivity and high turnover among people working at routine hospitality jobs:

1. Workers don't know what they are supposed to be doing.
2. They don't know how to do what they are supposed to be doing.
3. They don't know how well they are doing what they are supposed to be doing.
4. The supervisor has not given them any direction, help, or support.
5. The workers have a poor relationship with the supervisor, largely for the first four reasons.

You could certainly lump all these reasons together as communications failures. However, far more than communication is involved. It is likely that the supervisor has never really defined the whats, how-tos, and how-wells of the jobs. (It is likely that no one has defined the supervisor's job in these terms either.) There are probably all sorts of gray areas in the supervisor's mind about who does what and how. Who, for instance, is supposed to clean the bar floor and dispose of the empty bottles: the bartender or the cleanup staff? Who is supposed to replace burned-out lights in hotel rooms and report television sets that don't work? In a hospital, who is supposed to serve the food to the patients, and who is supposed to pick up all the dirty trays from the rooms? How much work can one waiter or cleaning person or cook's helper be expected to do in one shift? In fact, what is a "fair day's work" for any job? What's more, how many people are doing a fair day's work right now? Enter the job description with performance standards. Let's start with a discussion of performance standards.

Performance Standards

Performance standards form the heart of the job description and they describe the whats, how-tos, and how-wells of a job. Each performance standard states three things about each unit of the job:

1. What the employee is to do
2. How it is to be done
3. To what extent it is to be done (how much, how well, how soon)

Traditionally, job descriptions have simply listed the duties and responsibilities (what the employee is to do) for each job. Although this approach is better than no approach, a job description using performance standards is much more useful, as will be discussed soon.

Here is an example of a performance standard for one unit of the waiter or waitress job at a certain restaurant: "The server will take food and beverage orders for up to five tables with 100 percent accuracy, using standard house procedures." Figure 6.4 breaks this standard down for you to give you the structure of a performance standard. The "what" of the standard is the work unit. The tasks become the "hows" that make up the standard procedure. When you add a performance goal for each unit, you set a performance standard: how much, how many, how good, how fast, how soon, how accurate—whatever it is that is important for establishing how well that unit of work should be done in your operation.

Supporting materials explaining or illustrating the specifics of the how (in this case, "standard house procedures") are necessary to complete each performance standard. They explain the action to be taken in order to reach the goal or standard.

Other Parts of the Job Description

Figure 6.5 is a sample job description for a server. Although there is no standard format for a job description, it usually includes the following:

Ken Blanchard, the renowned management author, gives a great example of Jim, whose work performance is only "so-so" but who is the star of the Wednesday night bowling league. The story goes . . . imagine that you are Jim as he is about to bowl . . . and a curtain comes down so that he can't see where to bowl the ball. Sounds familiar—there are numerous associates who are not clear as to what they are aiming at—in other words, they have no clear goals. So Jim knocks down six skittles, but he doesn't know that because no one tells him—also sounds familiar—well, thousands of associates carry on working without any feedback on how well they did. Suppose that a supervisor stood there and said "Jim, you missed four skittles"—we would know how Jim would feel. But guess how many times this actually happens to associates. Wouldn't it be better to have no certain and clear goals—to knock down all 10 skittles—but have immediate feedback and encouragement?

Source: From an address to the National Restaurant Association by Ken Blanchard, May 14, 2001.

ANATOMY OF A PERFORMANCE STANDARD

Job classification: Server (waiter/waitress)

Unit of work: Takes food and beverage orders.

Performance standard:

The server will take food and beverage orders for up to five tables with 100 percent accuracy using standard house procedures.

Breakdown:

The server will:

What:	*take food and beverage orders*
How:	*using standard house procedures*
To what standard:	*for up to five tables with 100 percent accuracy*

FIGURE 6.4 Anatomy of a performance standard.

- **Job title,** such as cook or server
- Job summary; a brief one- or two-sentence statement of the major or overall duty and purpose of the job
- Units of work, preferably in the format of performance standards
- **Job setting,** including physical conditions, physical demands, and work hazards
- Social environment: information on the extent of interpersonal interaction required to perform the job

Some operators also put qualifications, such as education and experience, into the job description. Although qualifications are technically included in the job specification, many operators put them in the job description for convenience. The job-setting section describes the conditions under which the job is to be done. This should include physical conditions, such as the temperature, humidity, noise, and ventilation in a kitchen (be honest—they are usually disagreeable). Physical demands, such as frequent heavy lifting and work hazards, such as hot surfaces and slippery floors, also need to be noted. Job setting also includes the personal contacts required by the job—in other words, who the employee interacts with.

In addition to the job title, you may want to include some or all of the following descriptive information at the beginning of the job description: the department name, grade level, location of the job, whether the job is exempt or nonexempt, work hours, and reporting relationship. When discussing the reporting relationship, include the title of the person supervising this employee (and when applicable, who this employee supervises).

JOB DESCRIPTION

JOB IDENTIFICATION

JOB TITLE <u>Server</u>

DEPARTMENT <u>Dining Room</u> REPORTS TO <u>Dining Room Manager</u>

HOURS <u>10:30 AM – 2:30 PM, 2:30 – 6:30 PM, 4:30 – 10:30 PM</u>

EXEMPT OR NONEXEMPT <u>NONEXEMPT</u>

GRADE <u>6</u>

JOB SUMMARY

Serve guests in a courteous, helpful, and prompt manner.

PERFORMANCE STANDARDS

1. Stocks the service station for one serving area for one meal completely and correctly, as specified on the Service Station Procedures Sheet, in 10 minutes or less.

2. Sets or resets a table properly, as shown on the Table Setting Layout Sheet, in not more than 3 minutes.

3. Greets guests cordially within 5 minutes after they are seated and takes their order if time permits; if too busy, informs them that he or she will be back as soon as possible.

4. Explains menu to customers: (a) accurately describes the day's specials (as posted); (b) if asked, accurately describes the quality or cut, portion size, and preparation method of each menu entrée and specifies items accompanying it; (c) if asked, accurately specifies allowable substitutions for items on a complete meal menu; (d) if asked, accurately describes ingredients and taste of any menu item.

5. Takes food, wine, and beverage orders accurately for a table of up to six guests; accurately and legibly completes guest check as specified on the Guest Check Procedures Sheet; prices and totals check with 100 percent accuracy.

6. Picks up order and completes plate preparation correctly as specified on the Plate Preparation Sheet.

7. Serves a complete meal to all persons at each table in an assigned station in not more than 1 hour per table using the tray service method correctly as specified in the Tray Service Sheet.

FIGURE 6.5 Sample job description.

8. If asked, recommends wines appropriate to menu items selected, according to the What Wine Goes with What Food Sheet; opens and serves wines correctly as shown on the Wine Service Sheet.

9. Totals and presents check and carries out payment procedures with 100 percent accuracy, as specified on the Check Payment Procedures Sheet.

10. Performs side work correctly as assigned, according to the Side Work Procedures Sheet and to the level required on the Sanitation Checklist.

11. Operates all preparation and service equipment in the assigned area correctly according to the operations manuals and the safety regulations prescribed on the Operational Procedures Sheet.

12. Meets at all times all the uniform, appearance, and grooming standards specified in the Appearance and Grooming Checklist.

13. Observes at all times the sanitation procedures specified for serving personnel in the Sanitation Manual; maintains work area to score 90 percent or higher on the Sanitation Checklist.

14. Maintains good customer relations at all times according to the Customer Relations Checklist; maintains a customer complaint ratio of less than 1 per 200 customers served.

15. Maintains a check average of not less than $5.00 per person at lunch and $11.00 per person at dinner.

JOB SETTING

CONTACTS   Guests, dining room personnel, cooking staff.

WORKING CONDITIONS   Works in temperature controlled dining room and service area which become congested at busy times.

PHYSICAL DEMANDS   Standing and walking most of the time, frequent lifting of heavy trays.

WORK HAZARDS   Hot surfaces, steam, wet floors, heavy lifting, sharp knives

Approval Signature _____

Approval Signature _____

Date _____

FIGURE 6.5   *(Continued)*

Always keep in mind that a job description should not refer to the person doing the job, since the job description refers to a job, not to the people doing the job. As the employee's supervisor, you need to approve and sign the job description for each of the job classifications under your control. Depending on your operation, your job descriptions may also have to be approved and signed by a representative from the human resources department and/or your superior.

Luckily, there are now sources of generic job descriptions available to hospitality supervisors. The National Restaurant Association has available a publication titled *Model Position Descriptions,* which contains 117 job descriptions for both lodging and restaurant occupations. The National Skills Standards Board *(www.nssb.org)* has available sample job descriptions and additional information on a number of foodservice and lodging jobs as well.

Uses of the Job Description

Job descriptions are used often in recruiting, evaluating applicants, and training. They are also useful in assigning work, evaluating performance, and deciding on disciplinary action. In the next section we discuss the uses and benefits of performance standards in more detail.

Check Your Knowledge

1. Define the following terms:
    a. Position
    b. Job analysis
    c. Job description
    d. Job specification
    e. Job evaluation
2. What is meant by *performance standards?*

What a Good Performance Standard System Can Do

If you develop a full set of performance standards for each job classification that you supervise, you have the basis for a management system for your people and the work they do. You can use them to describe the jobs, to define the day's work for each job, to train workers to meet standards, to evaluate workers' performance, and to give them feedback on how they are doing. You can use performance standards as a basis for rewarding achievement and selecting people for promotion. You can use them as diagnostic tools to pinpoint ineffective performance and as a basis for corrective action. You can also use them in disciplining workers as a means of demonstrating incompetence. They provide the framework for a complete system of people management. This system operates successfully in many areas of supervisory responsibility.

Performance standards answer the question: How will the employee and the performance manager know when the employee is meeting or exceeding expectations for his or her position?

Source: Guide to Performance Management: Standard of Performance, Human Resources, University of California, San Diego, 2000.

On the Job

Intelligent and consistent use of a performance standard system reduces or eliminates those five major reasons cited earlier for low productivity and high turnover. Employees are told clearly what to do. They are taught how to do it. They know how well they are doing because there is an objective standard of measurement. The supervisor helps and supports them with additional training or coaching when standards are not being met. All this makes for much better relationships between workers and supervisor.

Performance standards improve individual performance. When people are not given explicit instructions but are left to work out their own ways of getting their work done, they usually choose the easiest methods they can find. If this meets your standards, well and good, but often it does not. People also begin to find certain parts of their job more to their liking than other parts and will slack off on the parts they like least. The procedures and standards put all these things into the right perspective.

Once workers know what to do and how to do it, they can concentrate on improving their skills. Improved skills and knowledge, coupled with goals to be met, encourage people to work more independently. If a reward system is related to achievement—as it should be—people will respond with better and better work. Better and better work means better productivity, better customer service, more sales, and higher profits. Who could complain about that?

Performance standards help ensure quality and consistency. (Courtesy of Sodexho)

∾ profile

TANIA GONZALES

Courtesy of Tania Gonzales

Every time I think about the word *supervision*, the two other words that come into my mind are *super* and *vision*. According to the *New Scribner Bantam English Dictionary*, the word *super* means "excellent; over and beyond; exceeding; greater than other of its kind; superior to." The word *vision* means "act or faculty of seeing; that which is seen; perception of mental images." The word *supervision* is a composition of these two words. To me the word signifies the ability to oversee one's surroundings with great attention to detail. For a more technical definition the dictionary describes it as, "to direct, oversee; superintendent." With this said, the characteristics that a supervisor should possess are many: Only a couple will be looked at from a housekeeping perspective.

The first quality that a housekeeping supervisor should have is the ability to pay attention to detail. Attention to details begins when the rooms are distributed to the housekeepers at the beginning of their shift. The correct number of rooms needs to be given to each housekeeper. If one gets more than the other, you (as a supervisor) will have to explain why one associate gets less than the other. Also, the rooms that need to be placed on maintenance need to be reviewed carefully. The supervisor

Morale benefits greatly. People feel secure when they know what to do and how to do it, and when their work is judged on the basis of job content and job performance. If they have participated in developing the objectives, they have a sense of pride and a commitment to seeing that the objectives work. Participation also contributes to their sense of belonging and their loyalty to the company.

A performance standard system can reduce conflict and misunderstanding. Everybody knows who is responsible for what. They know what parts of the job are most important. They know the level of performance the boss expects in each job. This reduces the likelihood that one person is doing less than another who is being paid the same wage—often a cause for discontent and conflict.

Well-defined standards can eliminate problems caused by the overlapping of functions or duties. Sometimes in a restaurant, for example, the functions of busing and serving overlap. Who resets the tables after customers leave? Both the busperson and the server may try to do it and run into each other, or each of them may think it is the other's job and it does not get done, and the table is out of service while people are waiting to be seated. At the front desk of the hotel, who will do the report for the housekeeper, the night auditor, or the early morning desk clerk, and will there be two reports or none? In the hospital, who picks up all the dirty trays, the kitchen personnel or the aides on the floor, or do they sit in the patients' rooms all day? All these gaps and overlaps will be eliminated in a perform-needs to be aware of those guests who are occupying the room that needs to be fixed and make arrangements with the front desk to accommodate the guests. These are only a couple of examples of what a housekeeping supervisor needs to pay attention to.

The ability to work well with other associates is an important aspect of being a supervisor. A supervisor needs great people skills. To be able to delegate, he or she needs to get along with every member in his or her department. If there is a personality barrier between a supervisor and an employee, the job performance of the department will suffer. Either the job will not get done, or a bad job will be done. An example of this is when a front desk associate places an order for a rollaway with the supervisor, the supervisor goes to the houseman, and they have an issue. The houseman ignores the supervisor and the rollaway never gets delivered. The supervisor needs to implement some type of corrective action so that this does not occur again, but more important than the corrective action is the ability to get along well with that person.

One last thing that a supervisor should be able to do is to correct and recognize employees in the housekeeping department. Correcting an employee is not the most exciting thing to do, but a corrective action needs to be taken so that whatever occurred does not happen again. On the other hand, rewarding an employee is rewarding to the supervisor. This is when a supervisor feels good about the job that he or she has done because the employees have done a good job.

ance standard system because the responsibility for performing the tasks will be spelled out.

In Recruiting and Hiring

The typical job description spells out in general terms the content of the job, the duties, and perhaps the kind of experience or skill desired. Performance standards, on the other hand, clearly define the jobs and the duties, the methods of performing the duties, and the competencies required. This will help you as a supervisor to find the right people and to explain the jobs to prospective employees. It will also help in planning and forecasting personnel needs, because you will know exactly what you can expect from each trained employee. If you are looking for experienced people, performance standards are helpful for testing skills.

> Five years of experience listed on somebody's application may have been five years of doing third-rate work and forming bad habits rather than developing good skills.

When you select a new employee, you have a ready-made definition of the day's work for the job. You and your new worker can start off on the right foot with a clear understanding of what is to be done in return for the paycheck. It is a results-oriented approach to defining the job.

We discuss recruiting and selection more fully in Chapter 7.

In Training

A complete set of performance standards gives you the blueprint for a training program. Each standard sets the competency goals for on-the-job performance toward which the training is guided. The training that forms the heart of a successful performance standard system begins with a written procedure. Developing a training program is discussed at length in Chapter 8.

In Evaluating Performance

A complete performance standard system should include periodic evaluations of each worker's performance, with feedback to the workers on how they are doing. Realistic and well-developed standards of performance form a solid basis for objective evaluation. After evaluation, the supervisor is responsible for helping those who are working below standard to improve their performance.

An evaluation system based on performance standards can pinpoint specific deficiencies needing corrective training. It is a positive approach; the focus is on the work, not the person; it does not put the person down. The problem is addressed and corrected, and everyone benefits. A performance standard evaluation system can also help you to identify superior workers by the way they meet or exceed the standards set. Such people merit your attention as candidates for development and promotion. Evaluation is discussed at length in Chapter 9.

In Your Job and Your Career

A performance standard system will simplify your job as supervisor. Once it is in place and running, you will spend less of your time supervising because your people will be working more independently and things will run more smoothly of their own accord. You will have fewer misunderstandings, fewer mistakes in orders, fewer broken dishes, and fewer irate customers. You will have more time to spend in planning, training, thinking, observing, and improving product and method instead of managing on a crash-and-crisis basis.

After experiencing the standard-setting process, you will have a much better conceptual grasp of your own department, your own area of command, and everything that goes on there. You will be able to coordinate better the various aspects of the work you are responsible for, be able to see how things can better be organized, and be able to run a tight ship. It will be a growth experience for you, and it will make you a better manager. The experience will stand you in good stead as you pursue your career, and so will the improved results in your department.

Check Your Knowledge

1. What can a good performance standard system do?
2. The performance standard system operates successfully in many areas of supervisory responsibilities. What are these areas?

Setting Up a Performance Standard System

Developing a complete performance standard system is not something you can do overnight. There are a number of steps to the process, and there are certain essentials for success that must be included in the planning and operation.

Three essentials for successful operation must be built into the system from the beginning. The first is *worker participation*. The people who are currently working in a given job category should work with you as you analyze that job, set the standards for performance, develop the standard procedures, and determine a fair day's work. One worker's input is very important to you. Often, they know the job better than you do, particularly the procedural steps involved.

The give and take of discussion will often produce better results than one person working alone. In many cases your workers will set higher standards of performance than they would have accepted if you alone had set them. In the end, there must be mutual agreement between supervisor and workers on the procedures and the standards and the fair day's work, although the supervisor always has the final say.

Helping to hammer out the *whats, hows,* and *how-wells* will inevitably commit workers to the goals. They will work much harder for something they have helped to develop than for something handed down by the boss. The experience will make them feel recognized, needed, and important, as well as helping to build that sense of belonging that is so necessary to morale.

The second essential for a successful system is *active supervisory leadership and assistance throughout.* As supervisor, you will make the final decisions on the work units to be included and their relative importance. You will determine how much leeway to give your people in working out the procedures and standards of performance. As leader, you will be in charge at all times. But you will all work together as much as possible in identifying the units, specifying the methods and procedures, and setting the performance standards. Under your leadership, performance standards will represent a joint acceptance of the work to be done and responsibility for achieving it.

In training and on the job, the supervisor's leadership continues. Now your role is the supportive one of facilitating the learning of skills, giving feedback, and providing additional training as necessary. Frequent evaluations, whether formal appraisals or a "Hey, you're doing fine," must be an integral part of the system. If the supervisor neglects this aspect of the system, the entire system will soon deteriorate.

The third essential is a *built-in reward system* of some sort, with the rewards linked to how well each worker meets the performance standards. People who do not want to work hard must understand that the better shifts, the promotions, and the other rewards will go to those whose work meets or exceeds the standards set. In some instances you may not have a great deal of leeway in handing out rewards, but you can always give the extra word of praise or written note of thanks for a job well done. Often, this means as much as a material reward. People feel that you are recognizing them as individuals and are appreciating their contributions.

For some people in some jobs, the sense of achievement measured against a defined standard of excellence is a reward in itself, as long as it is recognized *and not taken for granted.* This probably does not operate so effectively in dull and repetitive jobs such as washing dishes and vacuuming carpets. But in such jobs as desk clerk or server, dealing with customers offers many challenges, and the worker can take pride in improving skills and handling difficult situations well. There is nothing in this system that limits excellence to the standards set, and workers should be encouraged to excel.

There is a definite order of steps to be taken in developing a performance standard system. Figure 6.6 is a flowchart depicting the entire process. The next several pages will follow in detail each progression on the chart. As you read, you will find it helpful to refer back to the flowchart to see the relationship of each step to the whole process.

Defining the Purpose

The first step is to define the purpose for which the standards are to be used. Our purpose here is to develop a system for one job classification that can be used to define a day's work, set standards, develop training plans, and evaluate on-the-job performance. A performance standard is to be developed for each unit of the work.

Analyzing the Job

Once you have defined your purpose, your next step is to analyze the job and break it down into units. First, your employees can help to identify all the different work units they perform. When your list of units is complete, you and your crew should list in order of performance all the tasks or steps to be taken in completing that unit of work.

Once you have agreed on a list of tasks or procedural steps for each unit, you have the data for the first two parts of each performance standard that you are going to write. The unit is the *what* of the objective. The tasks become the *hows* that make up the standard procedures. When you add a standard for each unit, you have a complete performance standard.

The supervisor and the people working at the job should set the standards of performance together, as already discussed. Although the supervisor has the final say in the matter, it is critical to have the workers' input on the standard and their agreement that it is fair. If they don't think that it is fair, they will stop cooperating and your entire system will fail. They will let you succeed only to the degree that they want you to succeed.

Sometimes it is appropriate to define three **levels of performance:** an optimistic level, a realistic level, and a minimum level. An **optimistic level** is your secret dream of how a fantastic crew would do the work. A **realistic level** is your estimate of what constitutes a competent job and the way that good steady workers are doing it now. A **minimum level** is rock bottom—if people did any less, you would fire them.

It is best to write your performance standards for a realistic level. A minimum level simply sets the standard at what a worker can get away with—and some of them will. This level is appropriate only for trainees or new employees during their first days on the job.

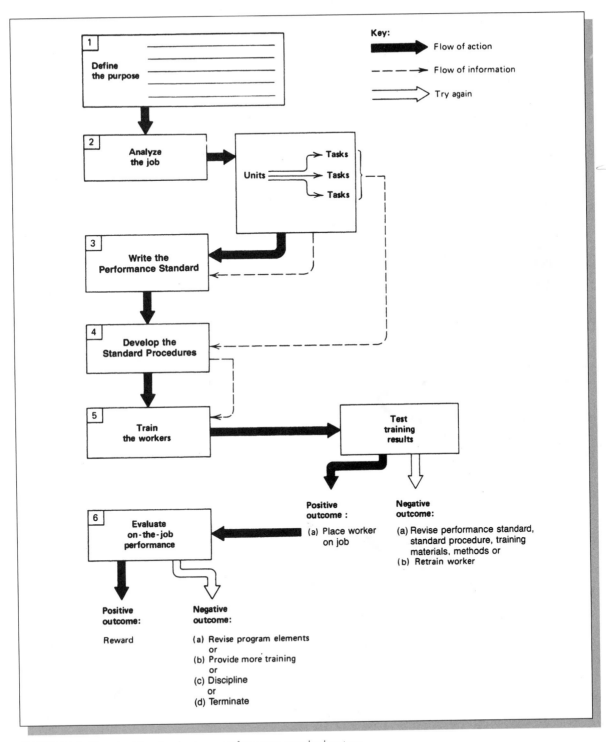

FIGURE 6.6 Flowchart for developing a performance standard system.

An optimistic level is appropriate for the high achiever who is not challenged by a goal that is too easy. Achievement on this high level must be rewarded if you want that kind of effort to continue.

When you have determined all the elements of each performance standard in a given job—the *what,* the *how,* and the actual standard itself for each unit—you should rate each unit in terms of the importance that you, as a supervisor, attach to it in on-the-job performance, as is done in Figure 6.7 for the job of server. This value scale should be made very clear to your servers and should carry considerable weight in a formal evaluation and in any reward system you set up. You may want to ask your servers for their ideas about relative importance, but the final decisions are your responsibility alone. You are the one with the management point of view and the company goals in mind. It will help your people if you explain clearly just why you rate the units as you do. In Figure 6.7, their relative importance is shown by assigning a point value to each unit. The rewards go to those people with the highest total points on their evaluation score.

SERVER UNIT RATINGS	
1. Stocks service station.	4 points
2. Sets tables.	4
3. Greets guests.	8
4. Explains menu to customers.	8
5. Takes food and beverage orders and completes guest check.	8
6. Picks up order and completes plate preparation.	4
7. Serves food.	6
8. Recommends wines and serves them.	8
9. Totals and presents check.	8
10. Performs side work.	4
11. Operates equipment.	4
12. Meets dress and grooming standards.	8
13. Observes sanitation procedures and requirements.	8
14. Maintains good customer relations.	10
15. Maintains desired check average.	8
	100

FIGURE 6.7 Server unit ratings. Point values represent the importance of good performance in each unit of work (page from a procedures manual).

Writing the Performance Standards

Now we are ready for step 3 on the flowchart (Figure 6.6), writing the performance standards for each unit of the job. First, let us review the essential features of a performance standard. It is a concise statement made up of three elements that together describe the way a unit of work is to be carried out in a given operation:

1. What is to be done?
2. How is it to be done?
3. To what extent (quality, quantity, accuracy, speed) is it to be done?

You can use the form in Figure 6.8 and simply fill in the blanks as we go. Let us take the first unit on the server list (Figure 6.1) and go through the process step by step. The first unit is *stocks service station*. You make this abbreviated description more precise by limiting the scope of the work sequence: "The server will stock the service station for one serving area for one meal. . . ." Notice two things here:

1. You must use an action verb: the server will *do* something, will perform—not "be able to" or "know how to" or "understand," but actually *do* something. (The other phrases are used in objectives written for training purposes. Here we are writing objectives for day-in, day-out, on-the-job performance.) Use Table 6.1 for help choosing a verb.
2. You limit the action as clearly and precisely as possible—which service station, what for. Limiting the action in this way makes it easier to measure performance.

Writing performance standards is crucial to setting up a performance standard system. (Courtesy of Sodexho)

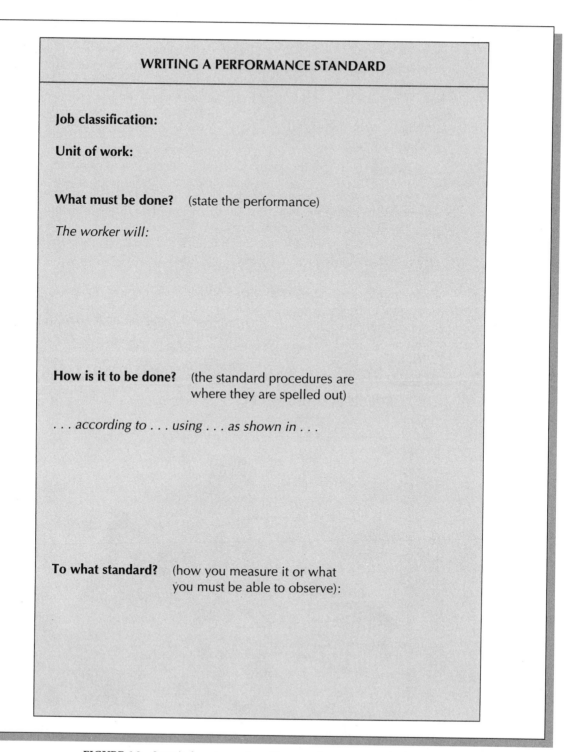

FIGURE 6.8 Sample form to use in writing a performance standard.

TABLE 6.1 ∾ Active Verbs for Performance Standards

Knowledge

Cite	Label
Define	List
Describe	Name
Discuss	Point out
Explain	Recite
Give example	State
Identify	Tell in one's own words

Skills

Application/analytical skills	Practice
Analyze	Prepare
Apply	Proceed
Assess	Produce
Calculate	Repeat
Compute	Try
Determine	*Attitude*
Distinguish	Accept
Evaluate	Acknowledge
Modify	Agree to
Operate	Assist
Organize	Be aware
Prepare	Be interested
Show	Be willing
Solve	Behave according to
Use	Communicate
Perceptual skills	Cooperate
Detect	Exemplify
Feel	Exhibit
Recognize	Notice
See	Participate willingly
Smell	Respond to
Taste	Service
Manual skills	Show awareness
Assemble	Show concern
Conduct	Show interest
Demonstate	Support
Make	Tolerate
Operate under supervision	Use resources to

Source: Karen Eich Drummond, *Developing and Conducting Training for Foodservice Employees,* Section VIII, 1992. Reprinted courtesy of the American Dietetic Association.

Next you define the *how:* "... as described in the Service Station Procedures Sheet ..." or "... following standard house procedures...." The standard simply states how or where this information is spelled out.

Finally, you state the standard of performance: "... completely and correctly in 10 minutes or less...." That is, everything must be put in its assigned place within 10 minutes and nothing must be missing.

Now you can put together the whole performance standard: "The server will stock the service station for one serving area for one meal as described in the Service Station Procedures Sheet. The server will stock the station completely and correctly in 10 minutes or less."

Actually, you do not even need to make sentences. A completed form such as the one in Figure 6.8 will tell the whole story.

Here are the requirements for the finished product: a good, useful, workable performance standard.

1. *The statement must be specific, clear, complete, and accurate.* It must tell the worker exactly what you want. Instructions cannot be vague so that it is not misinterpreted or misread. If it is not specific, clear, complete, and accurate, it can be more confusing than anything else.

2. *The standard of performance must be measurable or observable.* "Good" and "well" are not measurable or observable; they are subjective judgments. "Correct" and "accurate" are measurable *if there is something to measure by*—a set of instructions, a diagram, mathematical accuracy. The waiter delivers the order correctly if he serves the customer what the customer ordered. The bartender measures accurately if she pours 10 two-ounce martinis and 20 ounces are gone from the gin bottle. There are ways to measure these performances. There *must* be a measurable or observable way for the supervisor to tell whether a person is meeting the performance standard.

3. *The standard must be attainable.* It must be within the physical and mental capabilities of the workers and the conditions of the job. For example, servers cannot take orders at a specified speed because they have no control over the time it takes customers to make up their minds. Sometimes a standard is set too high the first time around. If nobody can meet it, expectations are unrealistic and you should reexamine the objective.

4. *The standard must conform to company policies, company goals, and applicable legal and moral constraints.* It must not require or imply any action that is legally or morally wrong (such as selling liquor to minors or misrepresenting ingredients or portion sizes).

5. *Certain kinds of standards must have a time limit set for achievement.* This applies to training objectives and performance improvement objectives, to be discussed shortly.

Figure 6.5 includes a set of performance standards for the job of server in a specific restaurant, developed for the units of work identified in Figure 6.1.

Performance standards are a specialized and demanding form of communication, and writing them may be the most difficult part of developing a performance standard system. But it is precisely this process that requires you to make things clear in your own mind. If you have problems with writing performance standards, don't worry—even experts do. But try it anyway. If it forces you to figure out just what you as a supervisor expect of your workers, you will have learned a tremendous lesson.

Check Your Knowledge

1. Name the three essentials to setting up a successful performance standard system.

2. What is meant by *optimistic level, realistic level,* and *minimum level?*

Developing Standard Procedures

The fourth step on the flowchart (Figure 6.6) is to develop standard procedures. Standard procedures complete each package and in many ways are the heart of the matter. The procedures state what a person must do to achieve the results—they give the instructions for the action. They tell the worker exactly how things are supposed to be done in your establishment. Spelling out, step by step, each task of each unit in a given job develops them. There may be many tasks involved—5, 10, 20, 100—whatever is necessary to describe precisely how to carry out that unit of the job. Turn back to Figure 6.2 to refresh your memory.

The standard procedures have two functions. The first is to standardize the procedures you want your people to follow; the second is to provide a basis for training. You can use various means of presenting the how-to materials that make up each standard procedure: individual procedure sheets, pages in a procedural manual, diagrams, filmstrips, videotapes, slides, and photographs. It depends on what will be easiest to understand and what will best meet the requirements of the individual standard. For stocking the service station you might use a list of items and quantities along with a diagram showing how they are placed. For opening a wine bottle you might have a videotape or a series of slides or pictures showing each step. For dress and grooming you would have a list of rules (Figure 6.9). The important thing is to have them in some form of accessible record so that they can be referred to in cases of doubt or disagreement and so that the trainers can train workers correctly. Show-and-tell is not enough in a performance standard system.

Two areas of caution: Don't get carried away with unnecessary detail (you don't need to specify that the menu must be presented right side up), and don't make rigid rules when there is a choice of how things can be done (there are many acceptable ways to greet a customer). You do not want your people to feel that they have tied themselves into a straitjacket in helping you to develop these procedure sheets. In fact, this entire process should free them to work more creatively. You simply specify what must be done in a certain way and include everything that is likely to be done wrong when there are no established procedures. The rest should be left up to the person on the job as long as the work is done and the standards are met.

> Assessments used in making performance standards must be useful and reliable. Even though there is some subjectivity, the results should be fairly uniform and reproducible when done by different team members or on different shifts.
>
> *Source:* William T. Doggette, "New OSHA ergonomics standard emphasizes importance of training," *Management Side of Engineering,* January 2001, p. 18 (Cahners Business Information: Plant Engineering, 2001).

> ### APPEARANCE AND GROOMING CHECKLIST
>
> *Immaculate cleanliness is required.*
> 1. Clean body: take a daily shower or bath, and use deodorant.
> 2. Clean teeth and breath: brush your teeth often, use mouthwash after meals if brushing is impossible.
> 3. Clean hair: shampoo at least once a week.
> 4. Clean hands and nails at all times: wash frequently.
> 5. Clean clothing, hose, and underwear daily.
> 6. Clean shoes: polish well, in good repair.
>
> *Grooming must be neat and in good taste.*
> 7. Hair neatly styled.
> 8. Nails clean, clipped short, no polish.
> 9. Minimal makeup.
> 10. No strong scents from perfume, cologne, after-shave, soap, or hair spray.
> 11. No jewelry except wedding ring and/or service award pins.
>
> *Uniforms will be issued by hotel. You must care for them.*
> 12. Clean, wrinkle free, in good repair at start of shift.
> 13. Hose required.
> 14. Closed-toe shoes, low heels.
>
> *Health and Posture*
> 15. Report any sickness, cuts, burns, boils, and abrasions to your supervisor immediately.
> 16. Stand straight, walk tall, and look confident!

FIGURE 6.9 Standard procedures for the unit on appearance and grooming: 16 tasks must be completed to meet the objective (page from a procedures manual).

Training Workers to Meet the Performance Standards

Training is the fifth step in developing a performance standard system (see Figure 6.6). A training program should have its own **training objective** for each standard. Each training objective will have a time limit added within which the worker must reach a required performance standard. For example: "After 1 hour of training and practice, the trainee will be able to stock the service station for one serving area for one meal completely and correctly in 15 minutes or less following standard house procedures." You will notice that the performance time limit is changed from the previous example because this is a training goal and not an on-the-job goal. In training, the procedures form the basis of the training plans and the training itself. We talk about this in Chapter 8.

At the end of the training period, the results of the training will be tested. In a new performance standard program this is a test of both the worker and the various elements of the program. If the results are positive, you can put the worker right into the job (or that part of the job for which training is complete). If the results are negative, you have to consider where the problem lies. Is it the worker? The standard? The procedures? The training itself? Something calls for corrective action.

Evaluating On-the-Job Performance

The final step in developing a performance standard system (see Figure 6.6) is to evaluate worker performance on the job using the performance standards that apply to that job. This first evaluation is a test of both the workers and the system so far. If a worker meets all the standards, the outcome is positive and a reward is in order. A positive outcome is also an indication that your standards and procedures are suitable and workable.

If a worker rates below standard in one or more areas, you again have to diagnose the trouble. Is the standard too high? Are the procedures confusing, misleading, or impossible to carry out? Or is it the worker? If it is the worker, what corrective training does he or she need? If the worker is far below standard in everything, is there hope for improvement, or should the worker be terminated?

Implementing a Performance Standard System

Once you have fine-tuned your system, you have a permanent set of instruments for describing jobs, defining a fair day's work for each job, training workers to your standards, evaluating performance, and rewarding achievement. How well can you expect it to work?

How to Make a Performance Standard System Pay Off

The first key to making your system work is the *workers' cooperation* in the developmental stage and their agreement to the standards of performance. If they have participated fully in developing them, they will participate fully in carrying them out. If, on the other hand, the development sessions were full of wrangling, bargaining, and manipulation, and in the end you more or less forced your people to agree to your decisions, they will find ways to sabotage the system. They will also be resentful and uncooperative if they are required to put in time and work in addition to their regular duties and hours without extra compensation or reward.

The second key to success is to *put the system to work slowly* over a period of time, one job at a time. It cannot be done in a day or a week or a month. A performance standard system is a total management system, and it takes a great deal of time to develop it and put it in place. It takes a long time to develop good standards, to standardize the procedures, to translate the standards and procedures into training programs, and to train your people to meet the performance standards. It takes total commitment to the system, and if you do not have that commitment it will never work for you.

The third key to success is *an award or incentive system*. This is something you work out alone, since you are the only one who knows what you have to offer. It

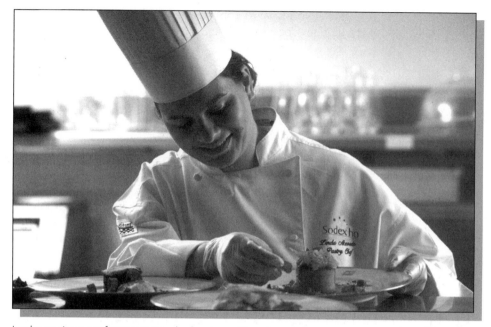

Implementing a performance standard system will work as well as everyone wants it to. (Courtesy of Sodexho)

could be money: a bonus, a prize, a pay raise, a promotion. But it does not have to be money; it could be a better shift, an extra day off, a better serving area, a bottle of champagne, or a certificate of merit displayed for all to see. Whatever it is, it is important that all your people understand what the rewards are for and how they are allotted, that they feel the system is fair, and that you practice it consistently.

The fourth key to success is to *recognize your workers' potential* and use it as fully as you can within the limits of your authority. Performance standards tend to uncover talent that has been hidden under day-after-day drudgery. Numerous surveys have shown that many people in the hospitality industry are truly underemployed. If they are encouraged to become more productive, to take more responsibility, to learn new skills, you will get a higher return. Human assets are the most underutilized assets in the hospitality industry today. A performance standard system gives you new ways to capitalize on them. Better products, better service, more customers—who knows how far you can go?

The fifth key to continued success is to *review your system periodically*, evaluating and updating and modifying if your ways of doing things have changed. For example, you may have changed your menu or your wine list. Have you also changed the list of what wine goes with what food? You may have put in some new pieces of equipment. Have you adapted your procedures to include training the workers to use them properly?

If you do not keep your materials up-to-date, if you begin to let them slide, you may begin to let other things slide, too—the training, the evaluations, the reward system. It will run by itself for a time, but not indefinitely. It works best when everyone is actively involved in maintaining it.

How a Performance Standard System Can Fail

Performance standards do not work everywhere. Good, clear, accurate, understandable standards are often hard to write unless you or one of your workers is good at putting words together. (This may be one of those hidden talents that the process uncovers.) *If the standards are not clearly stated and clearly communicated to everyone, they can cause confusion instead of getting rid of it.* The objectives are communications tools, and if they do not communicate well—if the people do not understand them—the program will never get off the ground.

The supervisor can cause the system to fail in several ways. The worst thing that you can do is to change standards without telling your people. You just do not change the rules of the game while you are playing it, especially without telling anyone. You can make changes—often you have to—but you have to keep your people informed, especially when such critical matters as evaluations and rewards are at stake.

Another way in which the supervisor can bring about the failure of the system is to neglect its various follow-up elements. It is especially important to help your people attain and maintain the performance standards you and they have set—to correct underperformance through additional instruction and training, and to do this in a positive, supportive way rather than criticizing or scolding. You must help, and you must maintain a helping attitude.

If you neglect the follow-up elements—if you do not help underperformers, if you fail to carry out a consistent reward system, if you do not recognize superior achievement and creativity, if you do not analyze individual failures and learn from them—all these things can make a system die of neglect. *Similarly, it will die if your people find no challenge or reward in the system—if the goals are too low to stimulate effort, if the supervisor is hovering around all the time "evaluating," or if for some reason the system has not succeeded in putting people on their own.*

What it often comes down to is that if the supervisor believes in the system and wants to make it work, it will, bringing all its benefits with it. If the supervisor is halfhearted, you will have a half-baked system that will fail of its own deadweight.

Sometimes a supervisor can become so preoccupied with maintaining the system that the system will take over and become a straightjacket that prevents healthy change in response to new ideas and changing circumstances. This happens at times in large organizations where the deadweight of routine and paperwork stifles vitality and creativity. It can also happen with a rigid, high-control supervisor whose management style leans heavily on enforcing rules and regulations. A performance standard system should not lock people in; it should change and improve in response to changes in the work and the needs of the workers.

Sometimes the system is administered in a negative way: "You didn't meet your objectives." "You won't get a raise." "You're gonna be fired if you don't meet these standards." People can experience it as a whip or a club rather than as a challenge, and that is the end of its usefulness. This is not the fault of the system, however, but of the way in which it is administered. Truly, the supervisor is the key to success.

Check Your Knowledge

1. Explain the two functions of standard procedures.
2. What are the keys to making a performance system work?

Some Alternatives

One obvious drawback of a performance standard system is the time and effort necessary for developing it. Most first-line supervisors would have trouble finding the time, and in fact they might not have the authority to develop such a system on their own initiative. It is more suited to the job of manager of a large unit or an individual restaurant. Sometimes it is made part of a companywide system in which individual supervisors are directed to develop such a system for their own units within a prescribed framework and with company training.

Another way of developing a company is to hire an outside expert to do the job analysis and write the objectives. However, a homegrown system developed by a supervisor together with the workers who actually carry out the duties and tasks is more likely to succeed than is a system grafted onto an operation from outside. A system developed by outsiders is not likely to provide the same motivation to make it succeed. It is better to have imperfectly phrased objectives embodying the spirit of the homegrown product than technically correct standards imposed from the outside that no one has any interest in meeting.

Many large companies approach the problems of defining jobs and standardizing procedures without using performance standards. Job analysis and procedures manuals are used widely and successfully, especially in organizing, recruiting, and training. They avoid the time and effort of developing a performance standard system. But they also lose its advantages. They go halfway, without taking the final step of developing performance standards. Without the goals and standards this approach does not have the challenge or the controls of a performance standard system. It does not tie together all aspects of managing people—daily performance, selection, training, evaluation, recognition, and rewards—as a proper system does. It does not ensure that workers will be told what to do and how to do it and to what standard. It does not go far enough.

As a supervisor, you can derive great benefit from understanding and applying these concepts even if you never have the chance or the desire to develop a written system. You can use the *what, how-to,* and *how-well* principles to analyze and organize your jobs, train your workers, and let them know how they are doing. You can formulate clearly in your own mind what you want them to do, how you want them to do it, and what standard of performance you expect without formalizing anything in writing. Then, if you can communicate it all to your people and establish it as a way of life on the job and a system of management for yourself, you have the best part of a formal written system. But it may take just as much thought and effort and just as long a time.

∾ key points

1. Every job in the hospitality industry includes several distinct work segments or units of work. Each unit of work is made up of a number of tasks.
2. Job descriptions often include job title, job summary, units of work (preferably in the format of performance standards), job setting, and the social environment.

3. Performance standards form the heart of the job description and describe the whats, how-tos, and how-wells of a job.

4. If you develop a full set of performance standards for each job that you supervise, you have the basis for a management system for your people and the work they do. You can use them in recruiting, training, and evaluation. You can use them with employees to reduce conflict and misunderstanding. Everyone knows who is responsible for what.

5. Three essentials to setting up a successful performance standard system are worker participation, active supervisory leadership and assistance throughout, and a built-in reward system.

6. Figure 6.6 depicts how to develop a performance standard system: define the purpose, analyze the job, write the performance standard, train the workers, and evaluate on-the-job performance.

7. Figure 6.8 shows a sample form to be used when writing performance standards.

8. Performance standards must be specific, clear, complete, accurate, measurable or observable, attainable, and in conformance with company policies and legal and moral constraints.

9. The first key to making your system work is the workers' cooperation and agreement in the developmental stage. The second key to success is to put the system to work slowly over a period of time, one job at a time. Other keys to success include having an award or incentive system, recognizing your workers' potential, and reviewing the system periodically.

10. A performance standard system can fail if the standards are not clearly stated and communicated to everyone, if the supervisor does not follow up properly, if the supervisor does not provide enough challenge or reward, or if the system is administered in a confining or negative manner.

❧ key terms

job	tasks prescribed as a unit of work
job analysis	levels of performance: optimistic level, realistic level, minimum level
job description	performance standards
job evaluation	position
job setting	tasks
job specification	training objective
job title	units of work

❧ review questions

Answer each question in complete sentences. Read each question carefully and make sure that you answer all parts of the question. Organize your answer using more than one paragraph when appropriate.

1. How is a job different from a position?
2. How is a job description different from a job specification?
3. How is a job evaluation different from job analysis?
4. List four possible units of work for a baker.
5. Describe common parts of a job description.
6. What is a job description used for?
7. Briefly describe how you would set up a performance standard system in a restaurant or hotel. How would you implement it? What would you do to make sure that it was successful?
8. Think of a unit of work performed by a hospitality worker, such as taking reservations or setting up a salad bar, and write a possible performance standard for that unit. Did your performance standard meet the five standards mentioned in the book?

❧ activities and applications

1. Discussion Questions

- Describe the goals of a performance standard system as you see them. How must the performance standards be used to attain these goals?
- What elements of scientific management are contained in a performance standard system? Of human relations theory? Of participative management? Explain each answer.
- What managerial style would go best with a performance standard system? Why do you think so?
- In your opinion, what are the chief values in using a performance standard system? What are the chief drawbacks? Do you think it is worthwhile or even possible to develop such a system in an industry with such high turnover?

2. Group Activity: Critique of Job Descriptions

Using a variety of job descriptions from student workplaces, or other hospitality operations, critique them using this chapter as a guide. What works well with each job description? What could be improved, and how would you improve it? In your personal experience, do hospitality operations really rely upon job descriptions to recruit, hire, train, and evaluate?

3. Writing Performance Standards

The following standards represent first attempts by a housekeeping supervisor to write some of the standards for the job of room cleaner in a motel. They are for on-the-job performance. You are to evaluate them according to the criteria listed here and correct any that do not meet the criteria. Then discuss each one as it was and as you have rewritten it. (This is not intended to be a complete list for the job.)

DRAFTS OF STANDARDS

1. Before starting work, the cleaner will load the cleaning cart correctly according to the Cleaning Cart Diagram and Supply Sheet.
2. The cleaner will make all beds using the procedures shown on the Bedmaking Procedures Sheet.
3. The cleaner will scrub the tub, shower, basin, floor, and toilet according to the Bathroom Cleaning Procedures Sheet, using the cleaning supplies and utensils specified on that sheet. The result must score 90 percent or higher on the Cleanliness Checklist for each room cleaned.
4. The cleaner will vacuum carpeting according to the instructions on the Vacuum Cleaning Procedures Sheet.
5. The cleaner will operate all cleaning equipment correctly and safely.
6. The cleaner must be able to clean 15 rooms per day in an average time of 25 minutes per room.

CRITERIA FOR EVALUATION

- Specific, clear, and complete: states what, how, and how well
- Measurable or observable standard of performance
- Attainable, possible
- Correct verb type for on-the-job performance

4. Case Study

Labor turnover for the past 12 months at Maria's restaurant was 220 percent. For every person who came to work at the restaurant, two others left. Maria had no idea of the exact cost of this turnover, but she knew that some things had to change. The manager she had hired, Joe, had excellent references, but he had not worked out as she had hoped. Many of the older employees complained that Joe showed favoritism in scheduling, giving the better-tipping shifts to people he liked most. Saturday night was an absolute disaster—the restaurant was full, with a wait list; food was slow in coming out of the kitchen; and the service seemed to be disorganized. Servers seemed to be wandering about the restaurant without any direction or station being allocated to them.

New staff was expected to learn what to do from existing servers and busers. It seemed as if no one had really determined what needed to be done, when it needed doing, and who should do it. The resulting chaos meant that guests were constantly complaining, and guest counts were down over the same period last year.

Maria has asked you, as a consultant, to make specific recommendations advising her what needs to be done to make the restaurant successful.

QUESTION

1. What are your top 10 recommendations?

chapter 7

Recruiting and Selecting Applicants

overview

~ You've run an ad in the Sunday paper for a weekend housekeeper, but the only person to put in an application is a high school student looking for her first job. So you interview her, and you look at the housekeeper's work schedule and realize that if you don't hire her today, you'll have to spend the weekend doing housekeeper duties yourself. So you hire her, and the next day, when she starts, you ask an experienced (but not very friendly) housekeeper to get the new hire started. By next Saturday, she has quit, so you put another ad in the Sunday paper and you think, "There's got to be a better way."

How do you find the people you need? How can you choose people who will stay beyond the first week, do a good job, and be worth the money you pay them? Does it always have to be the way it is today?

No, it doesn't. There is no foolproof system: Human beings are unpredictable and so is the day-to-day situation in the typical hospitality operation. But the knowledge and experience of people who have faced and studied these problems can be helpful to you, even though you must adapt it to your own situation.

In this chapter we examine the processes and problems of recruiting and selecting hourly employees for hospitality operations. It will help you to:

- ∞ Describe the typical characteristics of entry-level jobs in the hospitality industry.
- ∞ Identify common sources of workers for the hospitality industry.
- ∞ Define a job's qualifications.
- ∞ List factors that affect forecasts of personal needs.
- ∞ List and briefly describe U.S. laws related to equal employment opportunities and fair employment practices.
- ∞ Identify and avoid discriminatory language and practices in recruiting, interviewing, and selecting.
- ∞ Describe the most used methods of recruiting and evaluate their usefulness.
- ∞ Discuss and evaluate the standard tools and practices for screening people and selecting the best person for the job.

The Labor Market

The term **labor market** refers to (1) the supply of workers looking for jobs as well as (2) the jobs available in a given area. When you need people to fill certain jobs, you are looking for people with certain characteristics—knowledge, abilities, skills, personal qualities—and you have a certain price you are willing or able to pay for the work you expect them to do. The people who are in the market for a job are looking for jobs with certain characteristics—work they are qualified to do or are able to learn, a place they can get to easily, certain days and hours off, a pleasant work environment, people they are comfortable working with and for, and a certain rate of pay (usually, the most they can get). The trick is to get a good match between people and jobs.

When jobs are plentiful and few people are unemployed, employers have a harder time finding the people they want, and workers are more particular about the jobs they will accept. When many people are looking for jobs and jobs are scarce, employers have a better choice and workers will settle for less. The number of employers looking for the same kinds of people also affects the labor market. You are always in competition with other hospitality operations like your own, as well as retail stores, which also offer many part-time entry-level jobs.

The Industry of Choice study, released by the Foodservice Research Forum of the National Restaurant Association's Educational Foundation, predicts that by 2005, 1.3 million new foodservice jobs will be created. If you also take into account people who will retire and will need to be replaced, the total job openings between 1996 and 2005 will be almost 4 million! The study suggests that there will be enough people to fill these vacancies if you take into account factors such as the increasing number of women and immigrants entering the workforce. However, both food-service and lodging jobs will continue to have stiff competition from retail and health care, industries that have typically drawn workers from the same pool. Both foodservice and lodging will have to continue improving its image to potential workers and offering competitive wages, benefits, and incentives.

Jobs to Be Filled

Many of the jobs in food and lodging operations demand hard physical labor. In kitchens, dining rooms, cafeterias, bars, and storerooms and in bell service, house-keeping, laundry, maintenance, engineering, and security, people are on their feet all day and much of the work is physically exhausting. About the only people who sit down are telephone operators, typists, cashiers, reservationists, and many clerical workers. Kitchens are hot and filled with safety hazards. At busy times pressure is intense and tension is high. Many jobs are uninteresting and monotonous—eight hours of pushing a vacuum cleaner, running an elevator, polishing silver, washing vegetables, spreading mayonnaise on bread.

In most of these jobs the pay is low, usually minimum wage, and there is little hope of promotion. It is not surprising that the duller and more demanding a job is, the harder it is to fill it with a good worker and the more often you have to fill it. The main thing that is attractive about such jobs is that they are available and you are willing to take people with no experience and no skills.

For certain jobs you must look for specific skills and abilities. Front desk clerks, servers, and bartenders must have several kinds of skills: verbal and manual skills and skill in dealing with customers. Cooks must have technical skills, varying in complexity with the station and the menu. All these jobs require people who can function well under pressure. The rate of pay goes up for skilled workers, except for waiters and waitresses, who are usually paid minimum wage or less and make most of their money in tips.

Days and Hours of Work

In the foodservice industry, people needs have a pattern of daily peaks and valleys, with the peaks forming around mealtimes and the valleys falling between. This makes for some difficulty in offering the regular eight-hour day that many people are looking for. You also have some very early hours if you serve breakfast, evening hours if you serve dinner, and late-night hours if you operate a bar or feature entertainment or serve an after-theater clientele. This irregular kind of need encourages split shifts, part-time jobs, and unusual hours, which can work both for you and against you in finding workers. Sometimes you cannot guarantee a certain number of hours of work per week: Workers are put on a call-in schedule and must simply take their chances of getting as many hours as they want. But if they cannot count on you, you may not be able to count on them.

You also have varying needs according to days of the week. These form a fairly predictable pattern, predictable enough for you to plan your hiring and scheduling. In restaurants, staff needs are light during the week and heavy on weekends, which closes your doors to people looking for a Monday-to-Friday week. In hotels the pattern is the reverse, heavy during the week and light on weekends. Restaurant employees typically work when other people are playing—evenings, weekends, and holidays—which complicates finding people to fill your jobs. Restaurants may also have urgent temporary needs for parties and promotions and emergencies when regular employees are out sick or leave without warning. This requires a banquet waiter call-in system or overtime for regular employees.

In some facets of the foodservice industry, the timing of people needs is regular and predictable. In hospitals and nursing homes the population is generally steady seven days a week, and the only variation in need comes with the daily peaks and valleys of mealtimes. Schools have steady Monday–Friday patterns with short days built around lunch, and they follow the school calendar, closing down for vacations, when they lose many people. Business and industry feeding follows the workweek of the business or plant.

In hotels the pattern of need is likely to be irregular but fairly predictable. Reservations are typically made ahead except in the restaurants, and need is generally geared to coming events in the community or in the hotel itself, or to predictable vacation and travel trends. Often, a hotel will require large numbers of temporary workers for single events such as conventions and conferences. Temporary extra help is often supplemented by having regulars work overtime. Where needs vary widely and frequently, supervisors can spend a great deal of time on staffing and scheduling alone.

The types of jobs, unusual working hours and days, minimum wages, and the up-and-down character of the need for workers limits the appeal of hotel and foodservice jobs to people who can fit this pattern or can slip in and out of it easily. Accordingly, it attracts people who are looking for short-term jobs, or part-time work, or jobs requiring no skills or no previous experience. Some people deliberately seek the unusual hours to fit their own personal schedule: people going to school, moonlighters, parents who must have a spouse at home to take care of the kids. Many people are looking for temporary work and have no interest in long-term employment or a career in the industry. "I am only working here until I can find a *real* job" is a common attitude.

Sources of Workers

The source of workers continues to change as the composition of the U.S. labor forces changes. The majority of new workers entering the workforce are women, minorities, and immigrants. Why is this? It is due to the combination of a shrinking, older, white U.S. population; a younger, growing minority population; recent easing of immigration restrictions; and increasing numbers of women entering or returning to work. These groups and others are discussed in this section.

If the job you need to fill is anything above the lowest level in terms of pay, interesting work, and decent hours, *the first place to look for someone to fill it is inside your own operation*. Upgrading someone whose attitudes and performance you already know is far less risky than hiring someone new and will probably assure you of a good, loyal worker. You will spend less time in training, and the adjustment will be smoother all around.

Consider also how people would feel if you brought someone in from outside to fill a job or a shift they would like to have. It is important for morale to give your workers first chance, even when you might find it easier to fill the vacant job from outside than to fill the job your current employee will vacate. It is part of being a good leader to consider your own people first and to move them along and develop their capabilities for better jobs.

In the labor market at large, a major source of workers for foodservice and lodging jobs consists of *people looking for their first job*. Of these, most are teenagers. The percentage of teenagers in the total population is not as large as it used to be. This valuable source of labor has shrunk while our need for workers has grown. Overall, the hospitality industry employs many younger workers.

As an industry, we are always looking for people, and we are among the few employers who will hire people without experience. Usually, first-timers want the jobs for the money, the experience of working, and the advantage it gives them in getting their next job. A few, but not many, apply because they think the work will be interesting. Often, they choose a particular place because a friend is working there or because it is close to home. Many are looking for part-time work because they are students. Many are working *until*—until school starts or until they get enough money to buy a car.

Another group of potential hospitality employees is *women* who want to go to work to supplement the family income or simply to get out of the house. In addition to money, women are looking for acceptance in a different role; the woman wants to be a person in her own right and not just somebody's wife or mother. She may be very happy with part-time work, three or four hours spanning the lunch period while the kids are at school, or an evening shift when her husband can take care of the children.

First-time job hunters apply for lodging and foodservice jobs because the jobs are available. (Courtesy of Sodexho)

Another group of part-time workers is interested in evening work: the *moonlighters*, people looking for a second job. This is not ideal for either you or them, since they may be tired from working their first job. However, students and homemakers also carry a double load, so perhaps moonlighting is no more difficult.

Another source of workers is the *unemployed*. If they have worked in an operation like yours, they may have skills and experience useful to you. If they were in another line of work, you may be competing with unemployment compensation, which is often more than the wages you pay. Workers from the automobile industry, for example, may have been making $25 an hour, and although their unemployment compensation is not as high as that, it is still above hospitality wages. If compensation runs out and they go to work in a hotel or restaurant, workers from higher-paying industries rarely find satisfaction in their jobs. They are likely to see both the pay and the work as a step down from the jobs they lost. They are truly *until*-type employees.

Unfortunately, the unemployed often include disproportionate numbers of young African-Americans and Hispanics. Members of both groups frequently see hospitality jobs as menial labor with little status, pay, or opportunity for advancement. They often think of foodservice jobs, in particular, as just flipping hamburgers for minimum wage. To get more blacks and Hispanics into hospitality jobs, it will be necessary to meet their needs of having a respectable job with satisfactory compensation and opportunities for advancement.

Some people seek work in hotels or restaurants just to get away from what they have been doing. Sometimes, recent college graduates find that they are not happy with the jobs they have taken or the field they prepared for, and they just want to get out. Sometimes these people just want a breather, some time to think things over and make new plans. Sometimes they are thinking of switching to the hotel or restaurant field and want to experience it from the inside before they make up their minds. A number of people today are interested in learning professional cooking because the pay at the top is high and a certain glamor goes with it.

Still another group of workers is made up of *aliens or immigrants from other countries.* Wages here are higher than they were at home, and many aliens are willing to take almost any kind of job. Aliens are not permitted to work while they are in the United States unless they come under a special category in the Federal Immigration and Nationality Act. Aliens may be permitted to work in certain jobs where there are not enough qualified U.S. citizens to do the work.

Due to a lack of employees for the U.S. hospitality industry, some companies are seeking J1 visas to allow workers from foreign countries to come to the United States for periods of 6 to 18 months. Other visas (such as an H1) may be obtainable for specialized or managerial positions. Local immigration offices can provide up-to-date information or visit the U.S. Department of Justice Web site.

An examination of the 1998 filings of 11 U.S. hotel chains with the Equal Employment Opportunity Commission shows that nearly half of the managers are women. A sample of over 470 hotels found that the split between male and female managers was 54 percent to 46 percent. However, just over 15 percent of the general managers were women, and most of the women were clustered in just a few management positions. Women were also underrepresented on hotels' executive committees. Still, the overall picture is one of progress.

Source: Robert H. Woods and Douglas Viehlan, "Women in hotel management," *Cornell Hotel and Restaurant Administration Quarterly,* Vol. 41, No. 5, pp. 51–54, October 2000.

The leading challenge in the food industry is finding people to work the hourly jobs. The food and beverage director Alex Fewell also encountered this problem in Myrtle Beach Manor. Myrtle Beach is a tourist area and during the tourist season people leave to find better-paying jobs. Alex still needed workers, so he decided to work with Horry County Department of Disabilities and Special Needs to hire people to fill the empty slots. He now oversees five disabled people who wash dishes six hours a day five days a week. "The work that the five of them do could probably be done by one full-time person, but they are all good workers. They like to work and they're proud of themselves." When there was a state inspection "The inspector said he had never seen such a clean sink." Fewell said that the most amazing part is that the state charges only $50 a day for the entire crew versus $5.50 per hour plus benefits. As Gerry Fernandez, president of Multicultural Foodservice & Hospitality Alliance, put it: "The social benefits are immeasurable in hiring the disabled. After working with someone who's disabled, employees are a lot less shy about interacting and being courteous to people—including customers—who look different."

Source: Kathy Blake, Print Media Subtitle, *Weekly Newspaper of the Food Service Industry,* Vol. 2, No. 8, p. 22, September 1999.

Hiring *retired people* is becoming more commonplace, although the number of retired people who do return to work is still quite small. The over-65 group is growing and will increase to 20 percent of the population in 2030 from 12 percent in 1987. Retirees often want to work to fill some empty time or perhaps to supplement their income. Although some of our jobs may not be suitable because of physical demands and odd hours, this is not a labor source you should dismiss routinely. Not only is it against the law to discriminate based on age, but also, older workers often have stability and an inner motivation that younger people have not yet developed. One national fast-food chain has made a special effort to develop jobs and hours that fit the availability and skills and talents of the retired. They have found this group to be an excellent source of employees; they are dependable, work-oriented people who are happy to have the jobs. In general, retirees have proven to be loyal, willing, and service-oriented workers. They come to work on time, have much prior work experience on which to draw, and do their jobs well. Unfortunately, senior citizens have an unfavorable opinion of foodservice jobs and are skeptical about their chances in this area.[1] This is due partly to myths concerning older employees' problems with productivity, absenteeism, flexibility, and higher health insurance costs—which are just that, myths.

Then there are the *disabled.* A disabled person is someone who has a physical, mental, or developmental impairment that significantly limits one or more of life's major activities. For example, a disabled person may have a visual or hearing impairment or may be mentally retarded. Although you may spend more time training disabled employees, they tend to be loyal, enthusiastic, hardworking, and dependable. There are disabled employees doing many different hospitality jobs. For instance, a cashier or payroll clerk can work from a wheelchair, a hearing-impaired person can do some food preparation tasks, or a mentally retarded person may be able to wash dishes and pots. It is illegal not to hire a disabled worker unless the disability would interfere with the person's ability to perform the work.

As supervisor, you need to be aware of the fact that your employees may be reluctant to work with a disabled person. This is usually due to a fear of the unknown; most of your employees probably don't know what it is like to interact and work with someone who is disabled. It is your job to build a supportive environment in which the disabled employee, and your other employees, will work well together. Discussing with your employees ahead of time what the new employee will be doing and what to expect can do this. Encourage your employees to talk honestly about how

[1]"Study: Seniors lukewarm about jobs in hospitality," *Nations Restaurant News,* Vol. 34, No. 22, p 4, May 29, 2000.

they feel and about their concerns. Be positive about the place of disabled people in the workplace and what they can accomplish.

Often, we set up qualifications for jobs we want to fill that are totally unrealistic (and quite possibly illegal), and if we get what we say we are looking for we will have overqualified and unhappy people. We do not need high school graduates to make beds, bus tables, cook hamburgers, wash vegetables, push vacuum cleaners, or wash pots or floors.

Setting such requirements, in fact, can be interpreted as discriminatory. For some jobs, people do not even need to be able to read and write. All they need is the ability to perform the required tasks. The human requirements we set up for a job must be based on the requirements of the work.

Check Your Knowledge

1. To what does *labor market* refer?
2. Compare and contrast the need for staff in a restaurant and in a hotel.

Characteristics of Your Labor Area

You will find it helpful to know something about the labor market in your own area: such things as prevailing wages for various kinds of jobs, unemployment rates for various types of workers, the makeup of the labor force, and the kinds of enterprises that are competing with you for workers, both in and out of your own industry. You should know something of the **demographics** of your area: ethnic groups, income levels, education levels, and where in your area different groups live. Where do low-income workers, young marrieds, immigrants, and the employable retired typically live?

There are other useful things to know about your community. Where are the high schools and colleges that can provide you with student workers? What agencies will work with you to find suitable disabled workers? What are the transportation patterns in your area? Are there buses from where your potential workers live that run at hours to fit your needs? Can workers drive from their homes in a reasonable length of time? Operations such as airports or in-plant cafeterias in outlying areas often find transportation the greatest single problem in finding employees.

In a large organization your human resource or personnel department may have such information. In fact, your human resource or personnel office may take care of much of the routine of recruiting. But the more you participate and the better you know the labor resources of the area, the more likely you are to know how to attract and hold the kind of people you want.

Determining Labor Needs

If you are a busy supervisor and you see a heading like this, your first reaction may be to laugh. What the heck, you need people all the time. You've got no time to make out lists, you need whoever walks in the door, and you are just afraid nobody will walk in. But what if you could turn things around and avoid panic and crisis by hiring workers who are right for the job and will not walk off and leave you in the lurch? And do you realize the hidden costs when you hire unqualified people or people who are wrong for the jobs you ask them to do?

Hiring such workers is worse than useless. Either you will keep those workers and suffer their shortcomings, or you will have to fire them and start all over—and perhaps make the same mistakes. If you train those workers and the ones you replace them with, your training costs will skyrocket and the work will suffer until you get them trained. If you do not train them, they will not do their jobs right and they will waste things and break things and turn out inferior products and give inferior service.

If they are unhappy or incompetent, they will be absent a lot and late a lot, and their morale will be poor and so will everyone else's. They will not get the work done on time, and you will have to pay overtime. They will give poor service and drive customers away, and your sales will dwindle. When you finally do fire them, your unemployment compensation costs will go up and you will have to hire people to take their places: and the next people you hire may be even worse. It is a very, very costly way to choose people, and in time it could cost you your reputation as a good employer, your job, or your business. There are better ways to go about hiring people based on the thinking and experience of experts, and the place to start is to figure out exactly what to look for.

Defining Job Qualifications

To define a job's qualifications, you need to list the knowledge, skills and abilities, work experience, and education and training required. This is known as a **job specification.** Figure 7.1 shows a sample job specification.

Knowledge consists of the information needed to perform job duties. For example, a cook must know that one cup holds eight ounces, and other measurements, just as the dietary manager in a hospital kitchen must know which foods are not allowed on modified diets. You can use verbs such as *knows, defines, lists,* or *explains* to begin a knowledge statement.

Skills and abilities refer to competence in performing a task or behaving in a certain manner. Must a person be able to lift 100-pound bags and boxes? Add and subtract and multiply? Convert recipes? Mix *x* number of drinks per hour? Cook eggs to order at a certain rate? Have a responsive, outgoing approach to people? Be as specific as possible.

Performance standards, if you have them, will tell you the specific skills you are looking for. You must decide whether to buy these skills or do your own skills training. If you plan to train, you need to define the qualities that will make people train-

---

IHOP in south Florida had been having a hard time trying to retain workers with in-depth knowledge of each position. So it was decided that a training and rewards program would help to increase worker determination and performance. In this program hourly employees receive raises for every level of testing they pass. Once they pass the test for the third and final level, their health insurance premium is on FMS. FMS therefore took the program further by increasing the level of training and standards for job performance. Although it is true that paying full cost for health insurance is an extra expense, the company is actually saving money because it costs around $2000 to hire a new cook and $1000 for a server. The company realizes that the real reward is earning better-trained employees for a longer amount of time.

Source: Dina Berta, Print Media Subtitle, *Weekly Newspaper of the Food Service Industry,* Vol. 35, No. 4, p. 14, January 22, 2001.

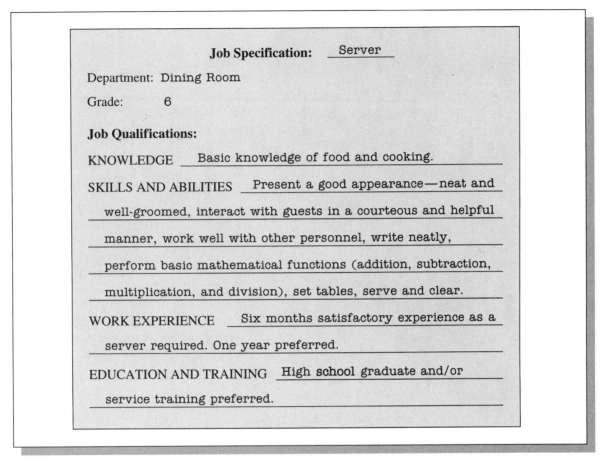

Job Specification: __Server__

Department: Dining Room

Grade: 6

Job Qualifications:

KNOWLEDGE __Basic knowledge of food and cooking.__

SKILLS AND ABILITIES __Present a good appearance—neat and__ __well-groomed, interact with guests in a courteous and helpful__ __manner, work well with other personnel, write neatly,__ __perform basic mathematical functions (addition, subtraction,__ __multiplication, and division), set tables, serve and clear.__

WORK EXPERIENCE __Six months satisfactory experience as a__ __server required. One year preferred.__

EDUCATION AND TRAINING __High school graduate and/or__ __service training preferred.__

FIGURE 7.1 Job specification.

able for a given job. A bartender, for example, needs manual dexterity. Desk clerks and serving personnel need verbal skills.

The qualifications that you list in your job specification must not discriminate in any way on the basis of race, national origin, gender, age, marital or family status, religion, or disability. Stuttering, for example, would interfere with taking telephone reservations, but not with busing tables. On the other hand, a person with only one arm could not bus tables but could take phone reservations. The place to begin in avoiding discrimination is with your job specifications. It is important that you phrase them in concrete terms of what each job requires and that you think in these terms as well.

Forecasting Personnel Needs

Anticipating your needs for workers will give you time to look for the right people. If you need extra people for holiday and vacation periods, hire them ahead of time or your competitors will beat you to the best people. Records of past sales or occupancy

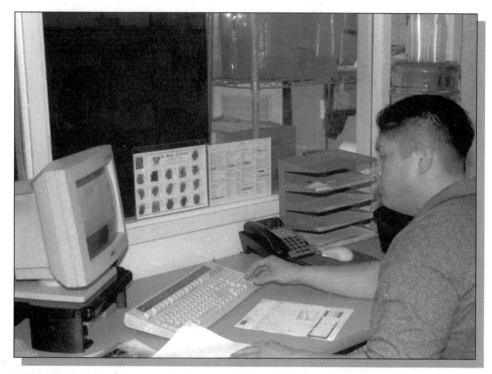

Scheduling is an important task which when well done helps ensure a smooth-running operation.

or special events may indicate trends in people needs. Look ahead to changes in your business: Is your employer planning to expand? And how will it affect your department's need for people?

Scheduling is a key factor. Your work schedules form a day-to-day forecast of the people you need at each hour of the day. Plan them in advance. Make sure that your workers are aware of any changes you make, and make sure that they tell you well in advance of any changes that they have in mind.

"Motivation makes a difference" and is the secret to maintaining good workers, according to Van Slyke, former senior manager in the human-capital advisor services–consulting area in New York City. Employees need an environment that motivates them and offers benefits. Let employees know that you value their opinion. If at all possible, allow schedules to be flexible. This gives employees a feeling of control and the comfort of knowing that if something comes up, they will not be criticized. Today, more people are demanding that their personal lives be taken as seriously as their work lives. People want to be taken seriously; they are concerned about pursuing their own personal goals. Your employees need to feel respected by you.[2]

As an employer it is important that you try to meet the needs of both your employees and the company. Examine your scheduling as a whole. First, does it provide efficiently for your needs? Second, are there ways of organizing the shifts that would

[2]Phillip Perry, "A carrot a day," *Restaurants USA*, January–February 2001.

be more attractive to the type of person you would like to hire? Do you ask people to work short shifts at unattractive hours, such as early in the morning or late at night? A country club advertised a split shift of 11 to 3 and 5 to 11 three days a week—is that likely to appeal to anyone? That's a 10-hour day with hardly enough time between shifts to go home, yet it is not a full 40-hour week.

Consider revamping your schedules with people needs and desires in mind. Look at your hours from their point of view. How far do they have to travel? How much useful personal time does your schedule leave them? How much money do they make for the time involved in working for you, including travel times? Ask your present workers how they feel about their days and hours, and try to devise schedules that will not only fill your needs but will be attractive to new people as well. Your people will appreciate it if you give them a chance to move to a shift they like better before you hire someone new to fill a vacancy. Often, before making decisions it is important to implement new plans or policies with the staff. Include staff in decision-making process and find out how they feel on certain policies; you may be surprised at what they have to say.

Another key factor in forecasting personnel needs is *downtime,* the length of time that a position is vacant until a new employee who can fully perform the job fills it. Let's consider how long downtime might normally be: An employee resigns and gives you only two days' notice. It's not unusual, particularly if you don't make a point of requiring proper notice and withhold something of value to the employee, such as accrued vacation time, if proper notice is not given. Once the employee resigns, depending on your employer's procedures, you may have to fill out an **employment requisition form** (Figure 7.2). A requisition is something like a purchase order that must be signed by the appropriate person before you can begin the recruiting process.

Let's say that this takes one week. If you want to advertise the job, you will probably have to wait another week before the ad appears and you get responses. Now you can probably plan on from one to two weeks to screen applicants, interview and test applicants, check references, and make a final selection. Often, the person you hire must give his or her current employer two weeks' notice, so you wait a little more.

Now if you believe in magic, when the new employee shows up for the first day of work, you will think your problems are over and put the new employee right to work. Wrong! Now it will take at least one week, probably more, before your new employee gets up to speed in the new position. It has now been about six to seven weeks since your employee resigned. One way to help reduce downtime is to forecast your personnel needs periodically. Figure 7.3 shows a form that can be used every two months to help determine when to hire new employees so that downtime is minimized.

Training versus Buying Skills

In determining your personnel needs, you must decide whether to buy skills or to train new people yourself. Most managers will tell you they simply don't have time to train people—they are too busy with the work itself. They look for people who

---

Employment Requisition

Department: _____

Position: _____

Reason for vacancy: _____ Incumbent leaving the company

Name: _____

Separation Date: _____

_____ New Position

Is position budgeted? _____ Yes _____ No

Is position temporary _____ or permanent _____?

Is position full-time _____ or part-time _____?

Hours of position/days off: _____

When needed? _____

Job qualifications: _____

_____

_____

_____

_____

_____

Approvals Department Head _____

General Manager _____

Director, Human Resources _____

FIGURE 7.2 Employment requisition.

have experience in the jobs they are hiring for, even when they have to pay a higher wage.

There is no security in hiring experience, however. You may pay more to break someone of five years of forming bad habits than it would cost you to train an inexperienced person from scratch. For exactly this reason, a number of corporations hire

PERSONNEL FORECAST

Department: _____ Date: _____

Positions	Number Full Staff	Staff on Hand	Current Openings	Anticipated Openings	Total to Be Hired	Time Required to Recruit and Train

FIGURE 7.3 Personnel forecast form.

only people with no experience for certain jobs. If you do hire experience, it is important to verify it by checking references and to evaluate it by testing performance.

Training takes the time of both trainer and trainee, and that is expensive. But putting people in jobs without enough training is likely to be more costly in the end. The worker does not perform well and is not happy, the customer suffers and is not happy, and you will suffer too and you will not be happy. You really don't have time *not* to train people. There is more on this subject in Chapter 8.

Check Your Knowledge

1. Discuss why it is important to know the characteristics of your labor needs.
2. Explain what is known as *job qualification.*

Legal Aspects of Recruiting and Selection

Equal Employment Opportunity Laws

Equal employment opportunity is a concept which means that people should be treated equally in all employment matters. Table 7.1 lists important federal laws commonly referred to as **equal employment opportunity** (EEO) **laws.** In general, EEO laws make it unlawful for you to discriminate against applicants or employees with respect to recruiting, hiring, firing, promotions, compensation, or other employment-related activities, on the basis of race, color, religion, gender, nationality, age, or disability. Discrimination can be thought of as making employment decisions based on factors that have nothing to do with a person's ability to do the job.

The starting point for EEO laws was probably passage of the **Equal Pay Act of 1963.** This law requires equal pay and benefits for men and women working in jobs requiring substantially equal skills, effort, and responsibilities under similar working conditions.

Congress passed the **Civil Rights Act of 1964, Title VII** (amended in 1991), to bring about equality in employment decisions. The act makes it unlawful for you to discriminate against applicants or employees with respect to recruiting, hiring, firing, promotions, or other employment-related activities, on the basis of race, color, religion, gender, or national origin. Other employment-related activities include, but are not limited to, wages, overtime pay, job assignments, training opportunities, leaves of absence, and retirement plans.

Title VII does not require you to hire, promote, or retain employees who are not qualified. The law does provide for you to hire a person of a particular gender if it is based on what is called a *bona fide occupational qualification* (BFOQ). For instance, it is permissible to hire a man to clean lounges and rest rooms reserved for men.

The **Equal Employment Opportunity Commission** (EEOC) was created by the Civil Rights Act of 1964, and it is responsible for enforcing the employment-related provisions of the Civil Rights Act of 1964 as well as other EEO laws. Employees with the EEOC, which also develops and issues guidelines to enforce EEO laws, can file complaints of discrimination.

Age discrimination was addressed in the **Age Discrimination in Employment Act of 1967** (ADEA), amended in 1978 and 1986, which makes it unlawful for you to discriminate in compensation, terms, or conditions of employment because of a person's age. The ADEA applies to all people 40 years of age and older. This act also bans forced retirement.

The **Pregnancy Discrimination Act of 1978** makes it unlawful for you to discriminate against a woman on the basis of pregnancy, childbirth, or related medical conditions. You cannot refuse to hire (or promote) a woman just because she is

TABLE 7.1 ∾ **Equal Employment Opportunity Laws**

Federal Laws	Type of Employment Discrimination Prohibited	Employers Covered
Equal Pay Act of 1963	Gender differences in pay, benefits, and pension for substantially equal work	Almost all companies, private and government
Title VII, 1964 Civil Rights Act (amended in 1991)	Discrimination in all human resource activities based on race, color, gender, religion, or national origin; established Equal Employment Opportunity Commission to administer the law	Companies with 15 or more employees
Age Discrimination in Employment Act of 1967 (amended in 1986)	Age discrimination against those 40 years of age or older	Companies with 20 or more employees
Pregnancy Discrimination Act of 1978	Prohibits discrimination in hiring, promoting, or terminating because of pregnancy; pregnancy to be treated as medical disability	Same as Title VII
Immigration Reform and Control Act (1986 and 1990)	Prohibits discrimination on the basis of citizenship status and nationality	Companies with 4 or more employees
Americans with Disabilities Act (1990)	Bars discrimination of disabled persons in hiring and employment	Businesses with 15 or more employees
Family Medical Leave Act of 1993	Mandates 12 workweeks of leave for husband or wife upon birth or adoption of a child or sickness in the family	Companies with 50 or more employees
Fair Employment Practice Acts of States and Local Governments	Bar discrimination; varies	Varies

pregnant. According to this law, pregnancy is a temporary disability and women must be permitted to work as long as they are physically able to perform their jobs. Employers cannot determine the beginning and ending dates of a pregnant employee's maternity leave.

The **Immigration Reform and Control Act** (IRCA; 1986 and 1990) was prompted by the problems associated with the increasing numbers of immigrants living in the United States. This act makes it illegal for you to discriminate in recruiting, hiring, or terminating based on a person's national origin or citizenship status. In these kinds of cases, fines can be charged and judges can order employers to provide back pay, pay court charges, and reinstate an employee. Although Title VII of the Civil Rights Act of 1964 has long prohibited this type of discrimination, IRCA covers employers with four or more employees, and Title VII covers employers with 15 or more employees.

The only people you can discriminate against are those you are not legally allowed to hire (or continue to employ): illegal aliens. IRCA imposes penalties for hiring unauthorized aliens. To help ensure that you don't hire an illegal alien, IRCA requires employers to verify that the people they hire are eligible to work in the United States. This is done by completing an I-9 Employment Eligibility Verification form within three days after hire. Using this form, the employer may ask for certain documents that establish the person's identity (such as a driver's license) and employment eligibility (such as a U.S. birth certificate or valid Immigration and Naturalization Services' Employment Authorization Card). To be fair and nondiscriminatory, you cannot request certain work status documentation from some applicants but not others.

The **Americans with Disabilities Act** (ADA) makes it unlawful to discriminate in employment matters against the estimated 43 million Americans who have a disability. Under the ADA, a person has a disability if he or she has a physical or mental impairment that substantially limits one or more major life activities, such as hearing, seeing, speaking, or walking. It also covers recovering alcohol and drug abusers (as long as they are in a supervised treatment program) and people infected with the HIV virus.

It is unlawful to ask an applicant whether he or she is disabled or about the disability itself. You can ask an applicant questions about his or her ability to perform job-related functions as long as the questions are not phrased in terms of a disability. You can also ask the applicant to describe or demonstrate how (with or without reasonable accommodation) he or she will perform job duties. The ADA does not interfere with your right to hire the best-qualified applicant, and a disabled applicant must satisfy your job requirements and be able to perform essential job functions (with or without reasonable accommodation).

Reasonable accommodation refers to any change or adjustment to a job or the work environment that will enable someone with a disability to perform essential job functions. For example, a worktable may be lowered to enable someone to work while seated, a work schedule may be modified, or a job may be restructured. Employers are not required to lower quality or quantity standards to provide an accommodation, nor are they required to make an accommodation if it would impose an *undue hardship* on the operation of the business. Undue hardship is defined as an "action requiring significant difficulty or expense" and is determined on a case-by-case basis.

In addition to the federal EEO laws, state and local governments have fair employment practice acts (FEPs) that often include further conditions. For example, some states forbid employment discrimination on the basis of marital status. It is important to learn about EEO laws because you need to be able to select applicants in a fair and nondiscriminatory manner.

The **Family and Medical Leave Act of 1993** allows employees to take an unpaid leave of absence from work for up to 12 weeks per year for any of the following reasons.

1. Birth or adoption of a child
2. Serious health condition of a child

3. Serious health condition of a spouse or parent

4. Employee's own serious health condition

When the employee returns from leave, he or she is entitled to his or her former position or an equivalent position. To be eligible for a leave of absence, the employee must have worked for the employer for at least 12 months. If it was provided before the leave was taken, the employer is obligated to maintain group health insurance during the leave.

EEO Laws and the Hiring Process

Table 7.2 lists recommended ways to ask questions of job applicants, whether on job applications or during interviews, to avoid charges of discrimination. The kinds of questions that are not allowed relate to race, gender, age (except to make sure that the applicant's age meets labor laws), family and marital status, religion, national origin, appearance, and disabilities unrelated to the job.

Job requirements or qualifications, such as those regarding education and work experience, must be relevant to the job, nondiscriminatory, and predictive of future job performance. Although requiring a high school diploma for an entry-level food-service job, such as server, seems to be acceptable, there are certainly many servers who do their jobs well without the diploma. The requirement of a high school diploma when it is not related to successful performance of the job can be viewed as discriminatory because it tends to screen out minority applicants.

Any type of preemployment test must be valid, reliable, and relevant to the job. To be valid, tests must be related to successful performance on the job. To be reliable, tests must yield consistent results. Tests should be given to all applicants, with a single standard for rating scores, and must be given under the same conditions. Even when a test is given to all concerned, it may be considered discriminatory if the test eliminates members of protected groups (the groups protected or covered by EEO laws) more frequently than members of nonprotected groups.

To avoid charges of discrimination, be sure that you can answer "yes" to the following five questions when evaluating and selecting job applicants:

1. Are the qualifications based on the actual duties and needs of the job, not on personal preferences or a wish list?

2. Will the information requested from the applicant help me to judge his or her ability to do the job?

3. Will each part of the selection process, including job descriptions, applications, advertising, and interviews, prevent screening out those groups covered by EEO laws?

4. Can I judge an applicant's ability to do the job successfully without regard to how he or she is different from me in terms of age, gender, race, color, nationality, religion, or disability?

5. Is the selection process the same for all applicants?

TABLE 7.2 ∾ **Equal Employment Opportunity: Appropriate and Inappropriate Questions Sometimes Used in Hiring a New Employee**

Subject	Inappropriate Questions (May Not Ask or Require)	Appropriate Questions (May Ask or Require)
Gender or marital status	Gender (on application form) Mr., Miss, Mrs., Ms.? Information about spouse (name, employment, etc.) Married, divorced, single, separated? Number and ages of children Pregnancy, actual or intended Maiden name, former name	In checking your work record, do we need another name for identification?
Race	Race? Color of skin, eyes, hair, etc. Request for photograph	(A photograph may be required after hiring for identification)
National origin	Questions about place of birth, ancestry, mother tongue, national origin of parents or spouse What is your native language? How did you learn to speak Spanish (or other language) fluently?	If job-related, what foreign languages do you speak fluently?
Citizenship, immigration status	Of what country are you a citizen? Are you a native-born U.S. citizen? Questions about naturalization of applicant, spouse, or parents	Are you a U.S. citizen? If hired, can you show proof that you are eligible to work in the United States?
Religion	Religious affiliation or preference Religious holidays observed Membership in religious clubs	Can you observe regularly the required days and hours of work?
Age	How old are you? Date of birth	Are you 18 or older? (to comply with labor laws) Are you 21 or older? (for positions serving alcohol)
Disability	Do you have any disabilities? Have you ever been treated for (certain) diseases? Are you healthy?	
Questions that may discriminate against minorities because of economic status, etc.	Have you ever been arrested?	Have you ever been convicted of a crime? If yes, give details. (If crime is job-related, as embezzlement is to handling money, you may refuse to hire.)

TABLE 7.2 ～ **Equal Employment Opportunity: Appropriate and Inappropriate Questions Sometimes Used in Hiring a New Employee (Cont'd)**

Subject	Inappropriate Questions (May Not Ask or Require)	Appropriate Questions (May Ask or Require)
	List all clubs, societies, and lodges to which you belong.	List membership in professional organizations relevant to job performance.
	Do you own a car? (Unless required to do the job)	Do you have a reliable means of getting to work?
	Type of military discharge	Military service: dates, branch of service, education, and experience (if job-related).
	Questions regarding credit ratings, financial status, wage garnishment, home ownership	
Assumptions related to gender, age, race, disability, etc.	Work is too heavy for women or handicapped	Can you do the job?
	Stereotypes: buspersons should be men, room cleaners and typists should be women, bartenders should be under 40, etc.	

Check Your Knowledge

1. Define *equal employment opportunity*.
2. List four important federal laws commonly referred to as equal employment opportunity laws.
3. What is the function of equal employment opportunity laws?

Negligent Hiring

Could your employer be sued if a guest was injured by a hostile employee who had a violent background that would have been uncovered if a reference check had been done? Yes, your employer could be sued for **negligent hiring.** In the past 10 years, lawsuits for negligent hiring have been on the rise. If a violent or hostile employee injures a guest or employee, the injured party may sue the employer and will probably win if he or she can prove that the employer did not take reasonable and appropriate precautions to avoid hiring or retaining the employee.

As a supervisor, you have the responsibility of taking reasonable and appropriate safeguards when hiring employees to make sure that they are not the type to harm guests or other workers. Such safeguards include conducting a reasonable investigation into an applicant's background and, especially, inquiring further about suspicious factors such as short residency periods or gaps in employment. You also have a re-

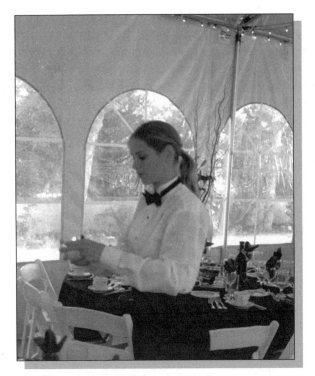

Recruiting excellent candidates is requisite to ensuring
excellent morale and guest satisfaction.

sponsibility to counsel or discipline your employees when they become abusive, violent, or show any other deviant behavior. Follow up on complaints your employees and customers may make about another employee's negative behaviors. Use your employer's policies to dismiss dangerous or unfit employees after appropriate warnings.

Recruiting

Now that you understand the EEO laws and have defined the jobs to be filled, you are ready to look for applicants. How do you reach people who are likely to be interested in food and lodging jobs?

General Recruiting Principles

Recruiting—looking actively for people to fill jobs—is a form of marketing. You are in the labor market to sell jobs to people who might want them. Because your need is constant and urgent, because you have many competitors, and because many of your jobs are not the most exciting ways of making a living, you really need to work at making your recruiting effective.

The first word to keep in mind is *appropriate*. You must put out your message in appropriate places and angle it toward people you would like to hire. Use techniques appropriate to your image and to the kinds of people you want to attract. A "Help Wanted" sign in a dirty and flyspecked window is going to reach only people who pass by and attract only people who reflect that image themselves—if it attracts anyone at all. "Now Hiring" hanging in a clean window is only one step up.

Take a look at some of the classified ads found in Figure 7.4. Which one might you respond to? Can you decipher what all the abbreviations mean? Which advertisement tells you the most about the restaurant and the nature of the jobs available? If you project an image of being a desirable employer through your advertisements, you are probably going to attract desirable applicants.

Your message must be appropriate: Tell them what they want to know. They want to know (1) what the job is, (2) where you are, (3) what the hours are, (4) what qualifications are needed, and (5) how to apply. "Bartender Wanted" and a phone number is not going to pull them in until after they have tried everyone else. They are also interested in (6) attractive features of the job, such as good wages and benefits.

It is also essential to use channels of communication appropriate to the people you want to reach, the same channels that they are using to look for jobs. You must get the message to the areas where they live and use media of communication they see and hear.

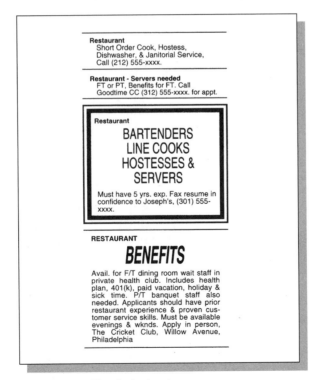

FIGURE 7.4 Classified advertisements.

∾ profile

PATRICK ACCORD

*Courtesy of
Patrick Accord*

Regardless of industry, supervision is a key constant: *key* because the quality of supervision affects the bottom line as well as most of the operations required to reach that point; *constant* because you can be assured that there will always be someone looking over your shoulder. Regardless of industry, there are certain qualities and characteristics that define a good supervisor. My personal experience, based on work as a kitchen/chef supervisor, coupled with other experiences as an employee under supervision, has taught me that certain traits common to the most effective supervisors cross industry boundaries.

While supervising a kitchen, I learned quickly that personal communication is one of the main ingredients needed by an effective supervisor. Actually, I think I learned this while working under supervisors who weren't able to communicate effectively. There is nothing more disheartening for an employee than when he or she is blamed for something that was altered or lost in the channels of communication. To minimize the chance that information is lost in the chain of command, shorten the chain. The most effective supervisors and managers that I've witnessed are the ones who are in the field with employees, talking with them and keeping lines of communication intact. There is no need to ask cook 1 what cook 2 has been doing when you can just ask cook 1 himself.

The second word to keep in mind is *competitive.* You are competing with every other hotel and foodservice operation in your area for the same types of people. For unskilled labor you may also be competing with other types of operations as well: retail stores, light industry, and so on. You must sell your jobs and your company at least as well as your competitors sell theirs, if not better.

The third word to remember is *constant.* It is a good practice to be on the lookout for potential employees all the time, even when you have no vacancies. Even the best and luckiest of employers in your field will probably replace at least six out of every 10 employees in a year's time, and many operations run far higher than that. Keep a file of the records of promising people who apply each time you fill a job, and look through them the next time you need to hire.

You will also have drop-in applicants from time to time. Pay attention to them; they have taken the initiative to seek you out. Have them fill out an application even though you are not hiring at the moment, and add it to your files. Give them a tentative date to call back, and be cordial. They should leave with a feeling of wanting to work for you; remember that you are marketing yourself as a good employer, and you may need them tomorrow.

The final words of wisdom are: *use a multiple approach.* Do not depend on a single resource or channel; try a variety of methods to attract people. There are many chan-

Through hard work and communication, a supervisor can then begin to foster a team atmosphere. A supervisor shapes a group's atmosphere or company culture through his work ethic, attitude, and set regulations. The supervisor must set the standard for hard work, do it in an affable manner, and set rules for the benefit of the entire unit. These rules might include a certain dress code or even a dress-down day. Functioning as a group in the workplace, so that the work can be accomplished efficiently, is the key to profitability.

Hopefully, a supervisor who begins to foster a good atmosphere will be able to retain employees. Quality in almost any industry is synonymous with consistency. Two out of the four employees left during my first week of supervising the kitchen. Even though they had served notice and we started training in preparation, their loss set our consistency off for almost a month. Customers were complaining that their favorite recipes over the last several years tasted different and they weren't going to give us another chance. I stress the importance of consistency in everything that a supervisor does.

Obviously, good supervision is multidimensional and much more involved than the limited discussion above indicates. But I believe that the basic tenant of open lines of communication leads to good relationships, a good working environment, and retention of employees. Quality is consistency, and as we keep employee turnover at a minimum and build a valued and trusted staff, our jobs as supervisors become that much easier and more profitable.

nels: schools and colleges giving hotel and foodservice and bartending courses, well-chosen word-of-mouth channels such as current employees, notices on the right bulletin boards (the student union, the school financial aid office, even the Laundromat if you are after a part-time homemaker), newspaper and radio ads, trade unions, employment agencies, community organizations, summer job fairs, and organizations working to place certain groups of people such as refugees or minorities or disabled persons. You can also go out into the field and recruit workers directly wherever they are.

Let us look at some of these resources and channels in more detail.

Internal Recruiting

Internal recruiting is the process of letting your own employees know about job openings so that they may apply for them. Often, the most successful placements occur through people who already work for you. Internal recruiting often results in **promoting from within,** a practice in which current employees are given preference for promotions over outside applicants with similar backgrounds. Promoting from within has several advantages: It rewards employees for doing a good job, it motivates employees and gives them something to work toward, and it maintains consistency within the enterprise.

Now how can you be sure of letting all employees know about open positions? Using a practice called **job posting,** a representative (usually from the human resources or personnel department) posts lists of open positions (Figure 7.5) in specific locations where employees are most likely to see them. Usually, employees are given a certain period of time, such as five days, in which to apply before applicants from the outside will be evaluated. In most cases, employees must meet certain conditions before responding to a job posting. For instance, the employee may be required to have a satisfactory rating on his or her last evaluation and have been in his

---

JOB POSTING

Date: Friday, June 3, 2002

Department: Kitchen

Job Title: Cook

Grade: 8

Hours: 9:00 AM – 5:00 PM

Job Qualifications:

KNOWLEDGE   Cooking terminology and ingredients

SKILLS AND ABILITIES   Measure, use a knife, identify and use various pieces of small and large kitchen equipment, read and follow recipes, do basic math (addition, subtraction, multiplication and division), use any cooking method, determine degree of doneness in cooked foods, use portion control tools, garnish, work well with others.

WORK EXPERIENCE   One year of satisfactory experience as a cook required. Two to three years cooking experience preparing a variety of menu items preferred.

EDUCATION AND TRAINING   Culinary training preferred.

FIGURE 7.5   Job posting. (Adapted from Karen Eich Drummond, *Staffing your Foodservice Operation.* New York: Van Nostrand Reinhold, 1991.

or her current position for at least six months. These conditions prevent employees from jumping around too often to different jobs, a practice that benefits neither you nor your employee.

When you can't find a current employee to fill an open position, your employees may refer their friends and acquaintances to you. Some employers give a cash or merchandise reward to employees who bring in somebody who works for at least a certain time, such as 90 days. Many employers trying to draw in new employees have used these types of programs, called **employee referral programs,** very successfully. Employees who refer applicants are usually asked to fill out a referral form or card that may be handed in with the applicant's application form.

The idea behind this type of program is that if your present employees are good workers and are happy working for you, they are not likely to bring in someone who won't suit you or who won't fit into the work group. Bringing a total stranger into a group of workers can be very disruptive. Sometimes employees bring in relatives. Among employers there are two schools of thought about this: Some say that it is an absolute disaster, whereas others find that it works out well. It probably depends on the particular set of relatives. If a family fights all the time, you do not want them working for you. Some people point out that if one family member leaves or is terminated, the other will probably quit too, and then you will have two jobs to fill. You have a similar problem when there is a death in the family; you will be short both employees.

Other internal recruiting methods include speaking with applicants who walk in, call in, or write in. These applicants should be asked to fill out an application form and should be interviewed when possible.

External Recruiting

The remaining recruiting methods are all considered **external recruiting,** that is, seeking applicants from outside the operation. An advantage of bringing in outsiders is that they tend to bring in new ideas and a fresh perspective.

Check Your Knowledge

1. What is *negligent hiring?* As a supervisor, what responsibilities should you have to take into consideration?
2. Discuss briefly the principles for recruiting.
3. What are *internal recruiting* and *external recruiting?*

Advertising

The classified ad section of the Sunday paper is probably the most common meeting place for job seekers and employers. It is also the best source for reaching large numbers of applicants, although it does not necessarily bring in the best candidates. Probably 90 percent of employers looking for non-college-educated employees advertise in newspapers, which makes it a competitive job market as well as a popular one for job seekers. You can run an ad at a better rate for seven days or for three days than for one, but Sunday is your best day.

There are two types of ads: classified and display. Because they take up less space, classified ads are less costly than display ads. However, display ads using the company's logo attract more attention and set your ad apart from others (Figure 7.6). Regardless of the type of ad, be sure to include information on (1) what the job is, (2) where you are, (3) what the hours are, (4) what qualifications are needed, and (5) how to apply. Regarding how to apply, there are two types of ads: *open,* which

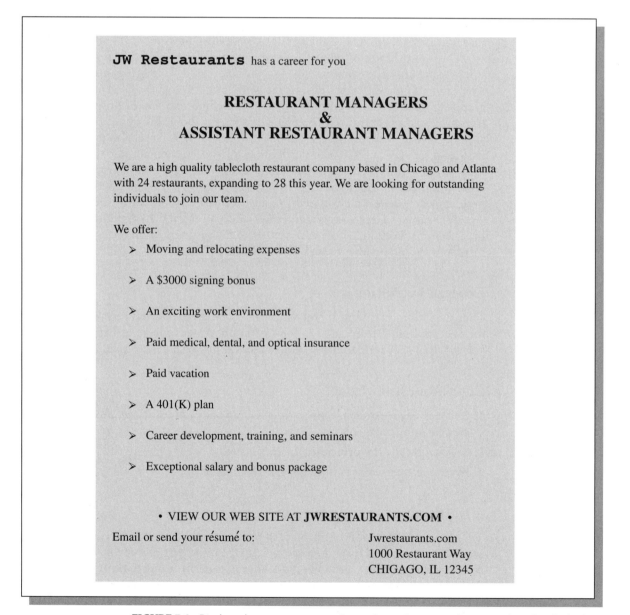

FIGURE 7.6 Display ads attract more attention and can give more information than classified ads.

give your company name and address, and *blind,* which do not reveal company identity, but instead, give a box number for responses. Blind ads pull in fewer responses than open ads because readers don't know who the company is (it could even be their current employer). The open ad brings in larger numbers of applicants, or it can screen applicants by listing job requirements in detail.

Another way to screen is to include a specific instruction such as "Call Joe 9–11 A.M." The people who call Joe at 2 P.M. obviously do not follow written instructions, so if the job requires following written instructions, you can eliminate these callers then and there (unless nobody calls between 9 and 11 and you are in a panic). Your company name and address will screen out people who do not want to work there for whatever reason.

> Heyman says that the boutique hotel experiences relatively light employee turnover, which points out an advantage of such properties in tight labor markets. "The exclusive nature of the hotel and its restaurant actually creates a tightknit family that works here," she says. "That really helps us find and keep our employees."
>
> *Source:* Ron Ruggless, Print Media Subtitle, *Weekly Newspaper of the Food Service Industry,* Vol. 34, No. 14, pp. 61–66, April 3, 2000.

When you are writing job advertisements, avoid discriminatory terms such as *busboy* or *hostess.* These terms indicate that the applicants should be male in the case of the busboy, or female in the case of the hostess. This is discriminatory, and therefore illegal, but you see it frequently in the newspapers. Also, avoid references to age, such as "young" or "recent high school graduate."

The number of applicants an ad pulls will vary greatly with the state of the economy. In good times even an enticing ad may pull fewer responses than you would like. But when unemployment is high, even your most careful attempts to screen will not keep the numbers down. People who need that job are going to apply for it no matter what your ad says. You may have 250 applicants for one pot washing job.

If you are going to advertise in the paper, it is well worth studying the ad pages to see what your competition is doing. Read all the ads with the mind-set of a job seeker, and then write one that will top them all. Display ads such as those in Figure 7.6 attract attention and project a good image. Many ads mention incentives such as benefits, equal opportunity, job training, career growth, and other attractions. Usually, such ads are for large numbers of jobs (hotel openings, new units of chains, and so on) or for skilled labor or management jobs. If you are only looking for one potwasher, you may not want to go all out in your ad, but if you want a competitive potwasher, run a good-looking, competitive ad.

Some companies advertise all the time. There are two types: the third-rate place whose third-rate ad isn't pulling anyone in ("Needed: intelligent, well-groomed person for nightclub work; call Pete") and the large corporation that runs a two-line ad to keep its name in the job seeker's consciousness ("TGI Friday's, have a nice day!" or "Plaza of the Americas Hotel is the finest").

In addition to advertising in the major area paper, consider running ads in special places where your potential workers will see them. Many cities have special area newspaper and shopping guides. Place your ads in those areas where your target workers live—people within commuting distance who may be candidates for your types of jobs. For instance, if Hispanics represent a potential group of employees, run ads in Spanish-language newspapers. Other special places are the school and college newspapers in your area.

In addition to newspaper advertising, some employers use radio and television. These media can reach many more people and do so, of course, at a much higher price. The higher price is due in part to the cost of using an advertising agency to develop the ad for you. Radio and television can be used very effectively to reach certain groups, such as teenagers.

A low-cost place to advertise is right in your operation. You can use any of the following to bring in applicants: placemats, indoor or outdoor signs (only if done professionally), receipts, or table tents, to name just a few. The mini–application form shown in Figure 7.7 is easy for customers to fill out and hand in. Finally, you can advertise open jobs by posting notices in supermarkets, libraries, churches, synagogues, community centers, and health clubs.

Employment Agencies

Employment agencies are a resource you should look into under certain circumstances. We will look at three common types of agencies: private, temporary, and government. **Private employment agencies** normally charge a fee, which is not collected until they successfully place an applicant with you. In most cases, if this person does not work out during a certain period of time, the agency must find a suitable applicant or return the fee. The fee is often 10 percent of the employee's first-year salary. These types of agencies most often handle management or high-skills jobs and should be used only if they specialize in your field.

Temporary agencies have recently grown in size and importance, and now a small number specialize in filling positions, including entry-level positions, for hotels, restaurants, and caterers. Temporary agencies charge by the hour for personnel who work anywhere from one day to as long as needed. Using temporary employ-

FIGURE 7.7 Mini–application form.

ees is advantageous during peak business periods or other times when emergency fill-in personnel are needed. However, you can't expect a temporary employee to walk into your operation and go straight to work. You must be willing and able to spend time and money to orient and train these employees.

Another source of employees, at no cost, is the U.S. Employment Service, a federal and state system of employment offices called **Job Service Centers.** Your local Job Service Center will screen and provide applicants for entry-level jobs. The centers have lots of unemployed people on their books who are looking for jobs; it is a question of whether they are well enough staffed to be able to sift through the people and send you suitable applicants who will not waste your time.

Direct Recruiting

Direct recruiting, going where the job seekers are, is practiced primarily by large organizations seeking management talent or top-level culinary skills. Such organizations send recruiters to colleges that teach hospitality management or culinary skills to interview interested candidates. There are also certain situations in which direct recruiting is appropriate for entry-level and semiskilled personnel. For example, when a hotel or restaurant closes, you might arrange to interview its employees. A large layoff at a local factory might be another such situation. It may also be worthwhile to interview foodservice students in secondary or vocational schools.

Some large cities hold job fairs in early summer to help high school students find summer work. This would be an appropriate place for direct recruiting. Summer employees, if they like the way they are treated, can also become part-time or occasional employees during the school year that follows.

One of the advantages of direct recruiting is that you may get better employees than you would by waiting for them to drop around or to answer your ad in the Sunday paper. Another advantage is the image-building possibilities of direct recruiting. You are not only hiring for the present; you are creating a good image of your company as a place of future employment.

Additional External Recruiting Sources

Organizations that are involved with minorities, women, disabled workers, immigrants, or other special groups will usually be very cooperative and eager to place their candidates. Examples of such organizations include the National Association for the Advancement of Colored People, the National Organization of Women, and the American Association for Retired Persons. However, they may not be familiar with the demands of your jobs, and it is absolutely necessary that you be very clear and open and honest about what each job entails. Here again your detailed job descriptions and performance standards are available. In addition, community organizations such as church groups, Girl Scouts, and Boy Scouts can be sources of employees.

It is a good idea to tell people with whom you do business when you are trying to fill a job. Many of the salespersons you deal with, for example, have wide contacts in the field, and they have good reason to help you out if you are a customer.

Sometimes friends and acquaintances in other fields know of someone who needs a job. Ministers, priests, and rabbis whose parishioners have confided their financial problems can be sources of good people. Sometimes parents are looking for jobs for their children. Through individual contacts you often reach people who are not yet actively looking for jobs but intend to start soon.

Many people say that one person's telling another that yours is a good place to work is the best advertising there is and that it will provide you with a steady stream of applicants. Whether the stream of applicants appears or not, there is no guarantee that it will send you the people you want. You are more likely to get the type of people you are looking for through a systematic marketing plan to reach your target groups. But one thing is true: If yours is a good place to work, you will not need as many applicants because they will stay with you longer.

Evaluating Your Recruiting

To determine which sources give you the best workers, you need to evaluate the results over a period of time. What is your successful rate of hire from each source? What is the cost, not only the cash paid out for ads but the hire ratio to numbers interviewed from each source? Interviewing is time consuming, and if interviewing people from a certain source is just an exercise in frustration, that is not a good source.

What is the tenure of people from each source: How long on average have they stayed? How many have stayed more than 30 days or three months? How good is their performance? If you find that you are getting poor workers from a particular source, you should drop that source. If you are getting good people from a certain source, stick with it.

You should also evaluate your own recruiting efforts. Are you staying competitive? Do you explain the job clearly and completely and honestly, or do you oversell the job? Do you project a good image for your enterprise, or do you oversell the company? If you oversell, your mistakes will come back to haunt you.

Selecting the Right Person

Let us suppose that you now have a number of applicants for a job you want to fill. Ten applicants for one job is considered by experts to be a good ratio, but in good times, when jobs are plentiful, you probably will not come close to that. In bad times, when jobs are scarce, you may get 200 people who want desperately to clean your floors. Up to a point, the more you have to choose from, the better your chances are of finding someone who is right for the job. But even if you have only one applicant, you should go through the entire selection procedure. It may save you from a terrible mistake.

Assuming that you have already established job specifications and have done some preliminary screening through your ads or on the phone, the selection procedure from here on has five elements:

1. The application form
2. The interview and evaluation
3. Testing
4. The reference check
5. Making the choice

Application Form

An application form is a fact-finding sheet for each applicant. It is a standard form (Figure 7.8) that asks relevant and job-related questions such as name, address, and phone number, type of job wanted, work history, education, references, and how the applicant heard about the job. The kinds of questions that are not allowed relate to race, gender, age, family and marital status, religion, national origin, and disabilities unrelated to the job (refer to Table 7.2). You should instruct applicants to complete everything, especially the work history, including places and dates of employment and names of supervisors.

Before you interview an applicant, you should familiarize yourself with the material on the application and jot down questions. What about gaps in employment? Unanswered questions? The way applicants fill out applications can also be very revealing. Do they follow instructions? Can they read and write? Do they understand the questions? Are they neat or messy? Is their handwriting legible? Did they complete everything? Such things may relate to the job requirements.

Interview

The first essential for a good interview is a quiet place free of distractions and interruptions, and the first task is to put the candidate at ease. You can tell how they feel by looking for nonverbal clues: a worried look on the face, tensed posture. If you can make them feel comfortable and nonthreatened, they are more likely to open up and be themselves, and this is what you are after. Listen attentively; this calls for your best listening skills. And remember that you want to impress them favorably on behalf of your hotel, restaurant, club, or hospital. A careless mistake in the beginning can ruin the entire interview.

With lower-level jobs it is best to follow a preplanned pattern for the interview, so that you cover the same territory with every applicant. You can start off with general information about the job and the company. The interview involves a two-way exchange of information: you want to know about the applicant, and the applicant wants to know about the job. Some employers use a highly structured type of interview known as a **patterned interview,** in which the interviewer asks each applicant a predetermined list of questions. There may also be additional questions on the interviewer's form that are not asked of the applicant but are provided to help the interviewer interpret the applicant's responses. The training required for a patterned interview is minimal compared to other methods, and the standardized questions help to avoid possible charges of discrimination.

You are after two kinds of information about the applicant: hard data on skills and experience, and personal qualities important to the job. As you go over the

APPLICATION FOR EMPLOYMENT
PLEASE PRINT ALL INFORMATION

Date

| Month | Day | Year |

Equal Opportunity Employer

The Company will not discriminate against an applicant or employee because of race, sex, age, religious creed, political affiliation, national origin, sexual preference, disability, or any veteran status.

| Last Name | First | Middle Initial | Social Security Number |

| Present Address (Street & Number) | City | State | Zip Code | Home Phone Number ( ) |

| Address where you may be contacted if different from present address | Alternate Phone Number ( ) |

Are you 16 years of age or older?   ☐ YES ☐ NO

U.S. Citizen or Resident Alien?   ☐ YES ☐ NO

If no, indicate type of Visa

JOB INTEREST

| Position you are applying for: | Type of position you eventually desire: |

Available for:
☐ Full-Time   ☐ Day Shift   ☐ Weekends
☐ Part-Time   ☐ Evening Shift ☐ Other _____
☐ Per Diem   ☐ Night Shift

When would you be available to begin work?

Have you previously been employed by us?   ☐ Yes ☐ No   If yes, when

Previous Position(s)

Have you previously submitted an application to us?   ☐ Yes ☐ No   If yes, when

How were you referred to the Company?   ☐ Employment Agency   ☐ Your Own Initiative
☐ Advertisement - Publication _____   ☐ Employee Referral - Name _____

EDUCATION

School	Name and Address	Circle Highest Year Completed	Type of Degree	Major Subject
High School Last Attended		1 2 3 4		
College, University, or Technical School		1 2 3 4		
College, University, or Technical School		1 2 3 4		
Other (Specify)				

FIGURE 7.8 Application for employment.

PREVIOUS EMPLOYMENT — BEGIN WITH PRESENT OR MOST RECENT POSITION

1. Employer

Employed _____ to _____

Address (include Street, City, and Zip Code)

May we contact?   ☐ Yes   ☐ No

Telephone Number   (   )

Starting Position

Salary

Last Position

Salary

Name and Title of Last Supervisor

Telephone Number   (   )

Brief description of duties:

Reason for Leaving:

Disadvantages of Last Position:

2. Employer

Employed _____ to _____

Address (include Street, City, and Zip Code)

May we contact?   ☐ Yes   ☐ No

Telephone Number   (   )

Starting Position

Salary

Last Position

Salary

Name and Title of Last Supervisor

Telephone Number   (   )

Brief description of duties:

Reason for Leaving:

Disadvantages of Last Position:

3. Employer

Employed _____ to _____

Address (include Street, City, and Zip Code)

May we contact?   ☐ Yes   ☐ No

Telephone Number   (   )

Starting Position

Salary

Last Position

Salary

Name and Title of Last Supervisor

Telephone Number   (   )

Brief description of duties:

Reason for Leaving:

Disadvantages of Last Position:

FIGURE 7.8   *(Continued)*

IF MORE THAN THREE PREVIOUS EMPLOYERS, PLEASE LIST OTHERS HERE

Employment Dates		Company and Address	Position or Type of Work	Salary or Wage	Reason for Leaving
From	To				

Please indicate if you were employed under a different name than the one shown on the first page of this application in any of your previous positions.

Employer	Name Used

U.S. MILITARY RECORD (If related to the job you are applying for)

Branch of Service _____

Active Duty _____ From _____ To _____

Nature of Duties _____

CONVICTIONS/COURT RECORD

Have you been convicted of a crime within the last 7 years?

_____ Yes   _____ No   The existence of a record of convictions for criminal offenses is not considered an automatic bar to employment.

Date of Conviction _____   Describe circumstances: _____

ACKNOWLEDGMENT

I understand that this employment application and any other Company documents are not contracts of employment and that any individual who is hired may voluntarily leave employment upon proper notice and may be terminated by the Company at any time and for any reason. I understand that no employee of the Company has the authority to make any agreement to the contrary and I acknowledge that any oral or written statements to the contrary are hereby expressly disavowed and should not be relied upon by any prospective employee.

I hereby grant permission for the authorities of the Company, or its agents, to investigate my references, and I release the Company and all previous employers, educational institutions, persons, and law enforcement agencies from any and all liability resulting from such an investigation. Upon my termination, I authorize the release of information in connection with my employment.

I certify that the statements made on this application are true and correct, and thereby grant the Company permission to verify the information contained herein.

I understand that giving false information or the failure to give complete information requested herein shall constitute grounds, among others, for rejection of my application or my dismissal in the event of my employment by the Company.

DATE:_____   SIGNATURE OF APPLICANT: _____

FIGURE 7.8   *(Continued)*

application in the interview, fill in all details that the applicant left unanswered and ask questions about gaps of 30 days or more on the employment record. Often, people will not list jobs on which they had problems. If they have something to hide, they will hide it, and these are exactly the things you need to find out. Don't hesitate to probe if you are not satisfied with either the applicant or his or her answers to your questions. Take care to avoid questions that could be considered discriminatory.

As to personal qualities, you may never really know what they are like until you put them to work. If you can get them talking, you can judge such traits as verbal skills or ease with people. But you will not be able to tell anything about motivation, temperament, absenteeism, honesty, reliability, and all the other things you are looking for.

Getting people to talk may be agonizing the first time you interview. The best method is to avoid questions that have yes or no answers. Ask: "What did you do at . . . ?" "What did you like best about . . . ?" "Tell me why. . . ." One owner always asked server applicants what the funniest thing was that ever happened to them on the job. He would not hire people who said that nothing funny had ever happened to them because he believed that they could not deal with people effectively if they couldn't see the funny side of things. You should talk only about 20 percent of the time, with the candidate filling in the remaining 80 percent.

Make notes. You can do this during the interview if it does not inhibit the applicant; otherwise, do it immediately after, lest you forget. Avoid writing down subjective opinions or impressions; instead, write down specific job-related facts and direct observations. Be objective, factual, and clear.

Evaluate the applicant immediately on your list of specifications for the job, using a rating system that is meaningful to you, such as a point system or a descriptive

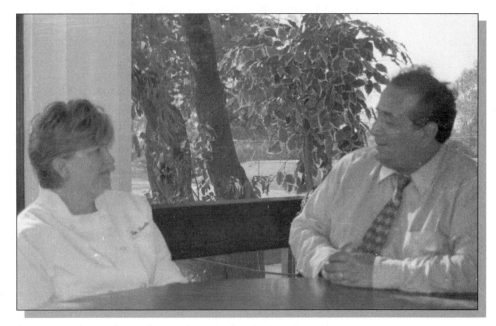

Getting people to talk may be agonizing the first time you interview.

ranking: (1) exceptional, hire immediately; (2) well qualified; (3) qualified with reservations; (4) not qualified. Some large companies have evaluation forms or systems they may require you to use. Look at the applicant from the perspective of what they can do and what they will do. **Can-do factors** include the applicant's job knowledge, past experience, and education—in other words, whether the applicant can perform the job. **Will-do factors** examine an applicant's willingness, desire, and attitude toward performing the job. You want the person who you hire to be both technically capable to do the job (or be trainable) and willing to do the job. Without one or the other, you are creating a problem situation and possibly a problem employee.

Evaluation is a subjective business; it is based primarily on feelings and emotions. People turn you off or they turn you on; you like them or you don't; and you will make your decision to hire or not to hire primarily on this interview, whether your judgment is valid or not. Studies have shown that there is very little correlation between interview evaluation and success on the job. They also show that interviewers make up their minds in the first 4 minutes.

Yet you would not dare skip the interview. So how can you get the most value out of it? If you are aware of what is going on in your head and in the other person's behavior, it will help you to evaluate applicants more objectively.

One thing that is happening is that applicants are giving you the answers they think you want to hear and projecting the image they think you are looking for, and they may not be like that at all in real life. Yet often they let their guard down when the interview is just about over and reveal their true selves in the last few minutes. If you are aware of this, perhaps you can exchange the first 4 minutes with the last few in making your evaluations.

It is very easy, in that first 4 minutes, to be influenced by one or two characteristics and extend them into an overall impression of a person. This is known as the **halo effect** or **overgeneralization.** You may be so impressed with someone who is articulate and well-dressed that you jump to the conclusion that this applicant will make a great bartender. The first day on the job, this impressive person has drunk half a bottle of bourbon two hours into the shift.

A negative impression may be just as misleading. One restaurant manager interviewed a man for a dishwasher job and was so shaken by what he perceived as a wild look in the man's eyes that he was literally afraid to have the man in the place at all. So in the usual panic and crisis, he hired a young kid. He told a friend in the business about the wild-looking man, and the friend said, "You have just turned down the only absolutely professional dishwasher in this entire city." So after the young kid quit two days later, the manager got in touch with the wild-looking man, who accepted the position, stayed 15 years, never was absent, never was late, never broke anything, kept the dishroom spotless, polished the dishmachine every day, and retired on a company pension.

Another form of overgeneralization is to assume that all applicants from a certain school or all people your pot-washer knows personally and says are okay are going to be good workers. This is not necessarily so; it is a generalization about personality rather than knowledge or skill.

Another thing that happens easily is to let *expectations* blind you to reality. If someone has sent you an applicant with a glowing recommendation, you will tend to see that applicant in those terms, whether or not they are accurate.

Still another thing that is easy to do is to see some facet of yourself in someone else and to assume that this person is exactly like you. You discover that this person grew up in your old neighborhood, went to the same school that you did, had some of the same teachers, and knows people you know. A spark is kindled and you think, "Hallelujah, this person has got to be great!" This reaction is known as **projection**—you project your own qualities onto that person. Furthermore, you are so excited about finding someone exactly like you (you think) that you may even forget what that has to do with the job for which you are interviewing this person.

What it all comes down to is that in interviewing and evaluating, you need to stick closely to the personal qualities needed *on the job* and to be on guard against your subjective reactions and judgments. Do not make snap judgments and do not set standards that are higher than necessary. A security guard or busperson does not need to be enthusiastic, articulate, or well educated, so don't be turned off by a quiet school dropout who can't put six words together to make a sentence.

When it comes to telling applicants about a job, you should be open and honest and completely frank. If they will have to work Sundays and holidays, tell them so. One supervisor told an applicant she would work a five-day week. The applicant assumed that it was Monday through Friday, and that was fine. But when she reported for work and they told her it was Wednesday through Sunday, she quit then and there. She felt that the supervisor had cheated, and from that point on the trust was gone.

Be frank about days and hours and overtime and pay and tips and uniforms and meals and all the rest, so the new employee will start the job with no unpleasant surprises. You might call this **truth in hiring.** Sure, you want to sell your jobs, but overselling will catch up with you.

Explain your pay scale and your promotion policy: "This is what you start at, this is what you can make with overtime, this is what you can realistically expect in tips, this is what you will take home, this is as high as you can go in this job, these are the jobs you can eventually work up to, these are your chances of that happening." Give them a chance to ask questions, and then end the interview. Tell them when you will make your decision and ask them to call you the day after that if they have not heard from you. Altogether it should take you 20 to 30 minutes to interview an applicant for an entry-level job and up to 60 minutes for a supervisory position. Tips for interviewing are summarized in Table 7.3.

Testing

Some companies use tests as an additional method of evaluating applicants. Sometimes tests are given before the interview to screen out candidates. Sometimes they are given after interviews to the small group of candidates still in the running, to add objective data to subjective evaluations. Various kinds of tests are used:

∾ Skills tests measure specific skills.
∾ Aptitude tests are intended to measure ability to learn a particular job or skill. Manual dexterity tests are a form of aptitude test and measure manipulative ability.

TABLE 7.3 ❧ **Tips for Interviewing**

1. Be nonjudgmental during the entire interview process. Do not jump to conclusions. A poor interviewer reaches a decision in the first 5 minutes.
2. Recognize your personal biases and try not to let them influence you. Be objective. Do not look for clones of yourself. Do not let an applicant's age, gender, attractiveness, or verbal fluency influence your opinions.
3. Spend most of your time listening attentively. Allow the candidate to do at least 70 to 80 percent of the talking. Listen to each answer before deciding on the next question. Do not interrupt.
4. Make notes so that vital information is not forgotten.
5. Repeat or paraphrase the applicant's statements to make sure that you understand the applicant and perhaps get more information, or you may repeat the last few words the applicant just said with a questioning inflection. Also, summarize the applicant's statements periodically to clarify points and to bring information together. A summary statement may begin with, "Let's state the major points up to now. . . ." In this manner, the applicant can confirm or clarify what has been discussed.
6. Another technique to get a quiet applicant to talk and show interest is to ask open-ended questions (questions without a yes or no answer) and use pauses. Pauses allow the applicant to sense that more information is desired and hopefully, the interviewee will feel compelled to fill the silence.
7. Use body language to show interest and elicit information. Use direct eye contact, nod, smile, and lean forward slightly.
8. Do not be bashful about probing for more information when it is needed.
9. Instead of asking about an applicant's "weaknesses," refer to areas of improvement.
10. Paint a realistic picture of the job. Be honest.
11. Always be sincere, respectful, courteous, friendly, and treat all applicants in the same way.
12. Allow the applicant to ask questions of you.

❧ Psychological tests are designed to measure personality traits; large companies often use them in hiring management personnel.

❧ Medical examinations measure physical fitness.

Except for medical examinations and skills tests, most hospitality enterprises do not use tests for nonmanagement jobs. There are several reasons for this. One is the time it takes to give tests and score them. Another is that many of the tests available have little relevance to the requirements of nonmanagement jobs. A third is that many tests, having been constructed for populations of a certain background and education, discriminate against applicants who do not have that background and education. It is illegal to use such tests either in hiring or in promotion.

To be usable, a test must be valid, reliable, and relevant to the job. To be valid, it must actually measure what it is designed to measure. To be reliable, it must be consistent in its measurement, that is, give the same result each time a given person takes it. To be relevant, it must relate to the specific job for which it is given. The user of any test must determine that it meets these criteria and must use it properly as its publisher designed it to be used. All in all, the complications of testing, the risks of discrimination, and the possibilities for error at the hands of an untrained user make most tests more trouble than they are worth.

Skills tests and specific aptitude tests such as manual dexterity tests are the exceptions. Your best bet, and the one most closely geared to your job needs, is a set of skills tests derived from your performance standards. They must be adapted somewhat since the applicant will not know all the ins and outs of your special house procedures, but this can be done. It will give you an objective measure of an applicant's ability to perform on the job and an indication of how much additional training is needed.

Psychological tests are available that test for honesty and even broader qualities such as integrity. These tests are based on the assumption that honest and dishonest people have different values and see the world differently. Some employers use honesty tests in the hopes of providing a secure workplace for their employees.

Using honesty tests properly requires some work. First, some states and localities do not allow such testing, so check the regulations. Next, you need to examine independent reviews and validity tests (provided that the instrument actually tests what it is supposed to test) of the instrument you want to use. Even if you find a good instrument and they are legal in your location, don't forget that testing also requires money and time and that the results are not a substitute for any of the other selection steps you take, such as interviewing or making reference checks.

A medical examination can be required only after a job offer has been made to the applicant. When a job offer is made prior to the medical exam, it is considered a conditional job offer because if the applicant does not pass the medical exam, the job offer is normally revoked.

The **Employee Polygraph Protection Act of 1988** prohibits the use of lie detectors in the screening of job applicants. Although lie detectors have been used in the past in some states, they are now illegal to use in the employment process.

Check Your Knowledge

1. What are the elements that the selection process includes?
2. Give a tip that is useful when interviewing.
3. What does the Employee Polygraph Protection Act of 1988 prohibit?

Reference Check

You have now narrowed your choice to two or three people. The reference check is the final step before hiring. It is a way to weed out applicants who have falsified or stretched their credentials or who in other jobs have been unsatisfactory. Reference information can be thought of in two ways: substance and style. *Substance* concerns the factual information given to you by the applicant. *Style* concerns how the person did in previous jobs, how he or she got along with others, how well he or she worked under pressure.

First, verify the substance issues, such as dates of employment, job title, salary, and so on. You may wonder why applicants would falsify information on an application, but they do. One applicant writes that he graduated from a culinary school that he only attended briefly, another says that she was the front desk manager when in reality she filled in twice for the regular manager. If your job requires a particular educational degree or certification, ask applicants to supply a copy of the appropriate document. Otherwise, get the applicant's written permission to obtain a transcript.

Once you have confirmed that the person is who they say they are on paper, you can start checking previous work references. Often, former employers will only reveal neutral information such as job title, dates of employment, and salary, because of fear of being charged with libel, slander, or defamation of character by the former employee. Although there is nothing wrong with providing objective documented information, such as an attendance problem, past employers are often reluctant to discuss this sort of concern or even answer the one question you really need an answer to: "Would you rehire?" To reduce any possible liability, you should ask applicants to sign a release on the application form (Figure 7.8) that gives you permission to contact references and holds all references blameless for anything they say.

Because it is fast, checking references by phone is very common. Be sure to document your calls on a form such as the one shown in Figure 7.9. Ask to speak to the employee's former supervisor. Always identify yourself and your company, and explain that you are doing a reference check. Start by asking for neutral information such as salary and job title and work your way up to more telling information.

Despite the importance of checking references, few people in the hospitality industry bother with a reference check. It may be habit or tradition, or it may be fear and desperation: fear of finding out there is a reason not to hire and desperation to fill the job. It may just be too time consuming or you may think that your gut feeling or intuition says it all. But it is really a serious mistake to neglect the reference check and thus run the risk of hiring a problem worker.

Making the Choice

Choosing a new employee is your decision and your responsibility. Making the choice may mean choosing between two or three possibilities or looking further for the right person for the job. When making the hiring choice, avoid making any of these common mistakes:

1. Don't jump to hire someone who went to school with you, came from the same town, or simply reminds you of yourself. Also try not to fall prey to the halo effect. Look at the big picture!

2. Many problems in hiring come about when you hire too quickly. Use the time involved in the selection process to go through each step thoughtfully. Aim to hire the best candidate, not simply the first reasonably qualified applicant who comes forth.

3. Don't rush to hire the applicant who interviewed the best. Although the interview process can certainly tell you a lot about an applicant, the applicant with the best interviewing skills (which can be learned and practiced by anyone) is not necessarily the best person for the job. Also keep in mind that during an interview, some applicants will use their charismatic personalities and ability to ten you what you want to hear to get top consideration for the job in question.

Applicant Name _____

Position Applied for _____

Name of Company, Location, and Phone Number _____

_____

Name/Title of Person Supplying Reference _____

_____

1. What are the dates of employment when he/she was employed
by you? _____

2. What was his/her title when he/she started working for you, and
when he/she left the company? _____

_____

3. What was the starting and ending salary? _____

_____

4. What were his/her primary job duties and responsibilities?

_____

_____

_____

5. How much supervision did he/she receive? _____

_____

6. How were his/her attendance and lateness records? _____

_____

7. What was this person's reason for leaving? _____

_____

8. Did he/she do a satisfactory job? _____

_____

9. In what areas were job skills excellent? In what areas were
job skills weak? _____

_____

10. Did this individual get along well with others? _____

_____

11. Would you rehire this individual? Why or why not? _____

_____

_____   _____
           Date   Name

FIGURE 7.9 Sample telephone reference check form. (From Karen Eich Drummond, *Staffing Your Foodservice Operation.* New York: Wiley, 1991. Reprinted with permission of the publisher.)

4. Don't hire someone just because your "gut feeling," or intuition, says that this applicant is the best. Intuition is fine to use, but always combine it with the other tools of the trade, such as reference checking and testing.

5. Don't hire someone just because they come highly recommended. Perhaps an applicant comes highly recommended as a breakfast cook, but you are looking for an experienced pizza maker. It's fine to listen to a recommendation for an applicant, but as usual, that's only part of the story.

Every time you hire someone, even when you feel confident about your choice, there is the chance that you have made a mistake. You will not know this, however, until your new people have been with you awhile and you can see how they do the work, whether they follow instructions and learn your ways easily and willingly, how they relate to the customers and the other workers, whether they come in on time, and all the other things that make good workers. To give yourself the chance to make this evaluation, it is wise to set a probationary period, making it clear that employment is not permanent until the end of the period.

If you see that some of your new people are not going to work out, let them go and start over. Do not let them continue beyond the end of the probation period. It is hard to face the hiring process all over again, but it is better than struggling with an incompetent employee. It may be as hard to fire as it is to hire, but that's another story.

Making the Offer

Offers for all jobs should be made in writing. The offer letter typically is sent, or given, to the new hire after an offer has been made and accepted over the phone. When you are making an offer, be sure to include all the conditions that were discussed with the applicant. The following points should appear in the offer letter, as appropriate:

- Department
- Position title
- Supervisor
- Location
- Rate of pay
- Schedule of shift, days off
- When jobs start, where to report, whom to report to
- Clothing and equipment needed

- Meal arrangements
- Parking
- Arrangements for orientation/training
- Brief description of benefits
- Probationary period
- Appointment time or whom to call for an appointment concerning filling out additional personnel forms (such as the I-9 form)

❧ key points

1. *Labor market* refers to the supply of workers looking for jobs and the jobs available in a given area.

2. Many hospitality jobs require hard physical labor, and the pay is often low. The days and hours of work vary, but many employees work part-time hours, including weekends and evenings.

3. Most new workers entering the labor force are women, minorities, and immigrants.

4. Possible sources of workers include those already working in your operation, people looking for their first job, women, immigrants, retired people, moonlighters, the unemployed, the disabled, and people who just want to get away from what they have been doing.

5. You will find it helpful to know something about the labor market in your own area, such things as prevailing wages for various jobs, unemployment rates for various types of workers, demographics, and the kinds of companies you are competing with for workers.

6. To determine labor needs, you must define the qualifications for each job in a document called a job specification. Job qualifications include knowledge, skills and abilities, work experience, and education and training.

7. When forecasting personnel needs, look at your schedules and consider the amount of time it takes to replace an employee and get the new employee trained. Anticipate openings using a personnel forecast form, shown in Figure 7.3.

8. Table 7.1 lists important federal laws commonly referred to as equal employment opportunity (EEO) laws. In general, EEO laws make it unlawful for you to discriminate against applicants or employees with respect to recruiting, hiring, firing, promotions, compensation, or other employment-related activities, on the basis of race, color, religion, gender, nationality, age, or disability.

9. Table 7.2 states recommended ways to ask questions of job applicants to avoid charges of discrimination.

10. Recruiting should be appropriate, competitive, constant, and use a multifaceted approach.

11. Recruiting is either internal or external. Examples include employee referral programs, direct recruiting, advertising, employment agencies, community organizations, personal contacts, and word of mouth.

12. The selection process includes the application form, the interview and evaluation, testing, the reference check, and making the choice.

13. Tips for interviewing are given in Table 7.3.

14. To be usable, a test must be valid, reliable, and relevant to the job.

15. Checking references by phone using a form such as that shown in Figure 7.9 is common.

∾ key terms

Age Discrimination in Employment Act of 1967
Americans with Disabilities Act
can-do factors
Civil Rights Act of 1964, Title VII

demographics
direct recruiting
Employee Polygraph Protection Act of 1988
employee referral programs

employment requisition form
equal employment opportunity
Equal Employment Opportunity
   Commission
Equal employment opportunity
   laws
Equal Pay Act of 1963
external recruiting
Family and Medical Leave Act of 1993
halo effect (overgeneralization)
Immigration Reform and Control Act
internal recruiting
job posting
Job Service Centers

job specification
labor market
negligent hiring
patterned interview
Pregnancy Discrimination Act of 1978
private employment agencies
projection
promoting from within
reasonable accommodation
recruiting
scheduling
temporary agencies
truth in hiring
will-do factors

❧ review questions

Answer each question in complete sentences. Read each question carefully and make sure that you answer all parts of the question. Organize your answer using more than one paragraph when appropriate.

1. Describe the labor market in the area in which you live. What jobs are available? Are there many jobs advertised in the classified section of the newspapers? Is it hard to get a job because of a large number of applicants?

2. Describe five sources of potential employees.

3. List the job qualifications detailed in a job specification.

4. What is an EEO law? List four EEO laws (including the Civil Rights Act of 1964) and describe the type of discrimination that each one forbids.

5. Which of the following questions are okay to ask applicants?

   • Do you own a car?

   • Do you own a home?

   • In this job, you will be lifting boxes up to 50 pounds. Can you lift 50 pounds?

   • Are you healthy?

   • Can you supply a photograph?

   • If you came from Greece, are you a Greek citizen?

   • Are you married?

   • What professional organizations do you belong to?

   • What ages are your children?

   • What clubs do you belong to?

   • Are you 40-something?

- Do you have any disabilities?
- Are you able to perform the job I have just described?
- Do you have any outside activities that would keep you from observing the required days and hours of work?

6. What is negligent hiring? How can you avoid it?
7. Describe two methods of internal recruiting and three methods of external recruiting.
8. Discuss three methods you might use to evaluate your recruiting efforts.
9. How would you review a group of five applications for a cook's position?
10. List seven do's and seven don'ts for interviewing.
11. Why is checking references so important? Why is it so difficult to check references?

∾ activities and applications

1. **Discussion Questions**
   - What recruiting methods would be most appropriate to the situation in your area?
   - Which is better in your opinion: to hire experienced workers or to train people? Defend your opinion. Are there other alternatives?
   - How can you guard against your own subjectivity in an interview?
   - How could performance standards be used in recruiting and selection?
   - Do you think you have ever been discriminated against while trying to get a job? If so, describe.
   - Describe various experiences you have had when taking a job interview. Which interviewers struck you as being good? What did poor interviewers do or forget to do?

2. **Role-Play: Interviewing**

Using the job description for a server that was presented in Chapter 6, work in groups of four to develop a series of interview questions for a part-time server position (Thursday through Saturday evenings) in an Italian restaurant serving pizza, pasta, and other Italian meals. When completed, have two students role-play an interview, with the two extra students acting as observers. When the first role-play is done, the observers will act as interviewer and interviewee. The role of the observers is to look for questions that are illegal and also to judge the ability of the interviewer to do a good job.

3. **Group Activity: Job Specifications**

Working in groups of four, each group decides on a job classification, such as cook or housekeeper, for which they will write a job specification. Use the format in Figure 7.1.

4. **Case Study: The One That Got Away**

Dennis is dining room manager in the coffee shop of a large hotel. He is about to interview Donna, a drop-in applicant who is filling out an application form. A natural waitress type, smiling, good voice, well-groomed. He'd like to hire her to replace Rosa—these married women with kids don't show up half the time.

Dennis is on duty as host for the lunch-serving period. He is seating a party of customers when Donna brings him her application. "Enjoy your lunch!" he says to the customers as he hands them the menus. Then he hurries over to ask Eleanor, a waitress who sometimes acts as hostess, to sub for him for a few minutes, and seats Donna at a table near the entrance. He can keep an eye on things while he interviews her.

He glances at the application. A year as waitress at Alfred's Restaurant—good! A high school graduate taking a couple of courses at the community college—good! The application is filled out neatly and carefully—good! He looks up to compliment her but sees Eleanor waving at him.

"Excuse me, I'll be right back," he says to Donna. He deals quickly with a customer who wants to get a recipe.

Donna is fiddling with a spoon and looks up soberly when he comes back. "I'm sorry," he says. "Now, where were we? Oh yes, I was going to tell you—" Another waitress presents herself at the table. "Listen, Dennis," she says, "tell Eleanor to get off my back. I'm not taking orders from her, she's not my boss." "Look, Dolores, I'll talk to you in a minute. The customer at Table 9 is signaling you. Go tend to her."

Donna has a fixed smile on her face. "I really think you'd like it here," says Dennis, "there's never a dull moment. Now tell me about your job at Alfred's." After getting a chance to discuss Donna's work experience, he sees that Eleanor is gesturing that he is wanted on the phone, so he excuses himself. "Yes, of course, I'll take care of it," he says to his boss, and rushes back to Donna, who is sitting with hands folded, looking straight ahead. "Now tell me about yourself."

"Well . . . what would you like to know?" She smiles politely.

"Are you married?" Dennis asks abruptly.

"Yes." Not so good.

"Any kids?"

"A baby boy." Worse! She looks at him levelly and says, "My mother takes care of him."

"Would you—oh damn!" Eleanor is gesturing madly and a customer looking like very bad news is heading his way. He rises hastily.

Donna rises, too. "I have to go," she says.

"I'll call you," Dennis says over his shoulder before facing a furious man with a long string of complaints.

The day goes on like this, one thing after another. The next morning he thinks about Donna again. Never mind about the baby: He decides to hire her on a probationary basis. When he finally finds time to call her, she tells him she has taken a job at the hotel across the street.

QUESTIONS

1. Dennis has made a number of mistakes in this interview. Identify as many as you can and discuss their adverse effects.

2. What did he find out about Donna during the interview?

3. What did he tell her about the job? What did she learn about the job in other ways?
4. On what basis did Dennis decide to hire her? Is it a good basis for making a hiring decision?
5. Do you think Donna would have decided to work for Dennis if he had gone about the interview differently?

Employee Training and Development

overview

~ An agitated coffee shop manager was overheard shrieking into the telephone: "But Shirley, you can't leave me like this . . . but Shirley, I've got a new server coming in tomorrow morning . . . but Shirley, you've got to come in tomorrow morning at six and train her for me . . . *but Shirleeee* . . . !"

Chances are good that Shirley did not come in at 6 A.M.—she has left for good. Chances are even better that if Shirley did come in, she would give her replacement a sketchy run-through of the job little better than a magic apron, plus a full-scale account of the difficulties of working with Ms. Manager. Yet this method of training is not at all uncommon in the hospitality industry.

We give many excuses for not training: We don't have the time, we don't have the money, people don't stay long enough to make training worthwhile, they don't pay attention to what you tell them anyway, they'll pick it up on the job, and so on. There is an edge of truth to all of this, but the edge distorts the truth as a whole. When you look at the whole picture, you find that the money saved by not training is likely to be spent on the problems that lack of training causes. And those problems involve more than money; they involve customer satisfaction and the well-being of the enterprise.

In this chapter we explore the subject of training in detail and offer a system for developing a training program tailored to a particular enterprise. It will help you to:

∾ Discuss the importance of training in the hospitality industry.

∾ Cite both the benefits of training and the problems encountered providing it.

∾ Outline factors that help employees learn.

∾ Explain steps for developing a job training program.

∾ List the major steps in job instruction training and describe how to apply them.

∾ List the six skills necessary for effective classroom training.

∾ Identify when retraining is needed and how to retrain.

∾ Explain the importance of orientation and enumerate the kinds of information that should be covered.

∾ Identify the essential elements in a successful training program and the major steps in developing such a program.

Importance of Training

In a hospitality setting, **training** simply means teaching people how to do their jobs. You may instruct and guide a trainee toward learning knowledge (such as certain facts and procedures), skills necessary to do the job to the standard required (such as loading the dishmachine), or attitudes (such as a customer-oriented attitude). Three kinds of training are needed in food and lodging operations:

1. **Job instruction** is just that, instruction in what to do and how to do it in every detail of a given job in a given enterprise. It begins on the first day and may be spread in small doses over several days, depending on how much needs to be taught and the complexity of the job.

2. **Retraining** applies to current employees. It is necessary when workers are not measuring up to standards, when a new method or menu or piece of equipment is introduced, or when a worker asks for it. It takes place whenever it is needed.

3. **Orientation** is the initial introduction to the job and the company. It sets the tone of what it is like to work for the company and explains the facility and the

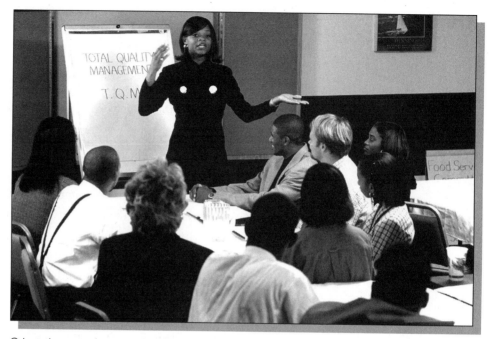

Orientation acquaints new associates with the organization and with its policies and procedures relating to the job. (Courtesy of Sodexho)

nitty-gritty of days and hours and rules and policies. It takes place at the beginning of the first day at work.

Need for Training

In our industry as a whole, we do very little of all three kinds of training. There is always that time pressure and that desperate need for someone to do the work right now, so we put untrained people to work and we hassle along with semicompetent or incompetent workers. Yet somehow we expect—or hope—that they will know how to do the work or can pick it up on the job, because we are not quite sure ourselves exactly what we want them to do.

As an industry, we are spoiled by our history in this respect. Our early inns and taverns were family affairs. The innkeeper was the host, the wife did the cooking, and the family did the chores with perhaps a servant or two, and there was no need for special training because the work was just extended housekeeping. In the nineteenth century, as hotels and restaurants and taverns followed the railroads across the country, we had floods of immigrants from Europe who had grown up as servants or had served long apprenticeships in hotel or restaurant kitchens. In the 1920s new immigration laws dried up this source of trained labor, but during the Depression we had willing workers from other industries who worked hard at learning their jobs because they needed them to survive.

It was during World War II with its shortage of workers that our labor problems really began and our need for training became acute. The capable people who were not off fighting the war worked in well-paying jobs in war plants, while hotels and restaurants had to get along with untrained, unskilled workers who couldn't find any other work but left as soon as they found jobs they liked better.

We have been struggling with such problems ever since. We are nearly always short-handed; we don't take time to train; we need a warm body on the job and that is what we hire and put to work. How do people manage people if they do not train them? We have mentioned the magic apron training method—if you put them to work, they can learn the job. Anyone can make a bed. Anyone can carry bags and turn on the lights and the television set. Anyone can take orders and serve food. Anyone can push a vacuum cleaner, wash dishes, and bus tables. That is the prevalent wishful thinking.

Many employers assume that experience in a previous job takes the place of training—a busboy is a busboy; a salad person can make any salad. They depend on these people to know how to do the job to their standard and according to their methods.

The coffee shop manager who tried to persuade Shirley to come in at 6:00 A.M. and train her replacement was practicing another common method of training—having the person who is leaving a job train the person who will take it over. This method is known as *trailing* if the new worker follows the old one around. Another method is to have a **big sister** or **big brother** or **buddy system;** an old hand shows a new worker the ropes, often in addition to working his or her own job.

None of these training methods provides any control over work methods, procedures, products, services, attitudes toward the customers, and performance standards. You do not control the quality of the training, and you do not control the results.

You may serve a 1-ounce martini on Thursday and a 3-ounce martini on Friday because your two bartenders got their experience at different bars. The blankets may pull out at the foot of the beds because no one showed the new housekeeper how much to tuck in. The cups may be stacked three deep in the dishmachine because no one trained the new dishwasher—anyone can run a dishmachine. The draft beer gets a funny taste because they did not have draft beer where the new bartender worked before and no one has told him how to take care of the lines. The fat in the fryer takes on a nauseating smell, but the new fry cook does not know it should be changed or filtered because on his last job someone else took care of that. (In fact, he was not even a fry cook, but you didn't check his references.)

Food costs may be high because kitchen personnel have not been trained in waste and portion control. Breakage may be high because servers, bartenders, bus personnel, and dishwashers have not been trained in how to handle glassware and dishes. Equipment breaks down frequently because no one has been trained in how to use it. Health department ratings are likely to be low because sanitation always suffers when training is poor, and pretty soon the local television station may send around an investigative reporting crew to expose your shortcomings to the entire community.

When good training is lacking, there is likely to be an atmosphere of tension and crisis and conflict all the time because nobody is quite sure how the various jobs are supposed to be done and who has responsibility for what. Such operations are nearly always shorthanded because someone did not show up and somebody else just quit, and people are playing catch-up all the time instead of being on top of their work. Service suffers. Customers complain or they just do not come back, and managers begin to spend money on extra advertising that they could have spent on training and avoided all these problems. Yes it is true that "proper food safety training and more sophisticated equipment are more costly. But in the long run customers gain

∾ profile

MAIRA SOMMERHAUZER HORTA

*Courtesy of
Maira Horta*

Throughout my experience in the hospitality industry, I have always played on what I call my *Brazilian jeitinho*, which embraces some qualities I have gained from growing up in Brazil. *Jeitinho* is the Brazilian optimistic attitude of being especially creative in a variety of ways suitable to work out certain situations, such as making extra efforts to satisfy guests and employees when resolving certain issues. Indeed, most things can be accomplished somehow, in order to please guests and employees, as long as you keep your goals in mind.

First of all, let me tell you a little about myself. Upon my graduation from high school in 1993, I promised myself I would continue my education. In fact, I decided to study hospitality management at Alliant International University in San Diego, California, because AIU has a great hospitality management program, and San Diego is a beautiful city, with a high volume of tourism. Shortly after I moved to San Diego and started going to school, I wanted to experience the hospitality industry. I started at the front desk of a major hotel and I did not see working my way through college as a hardship, but rather as an opportunity, requiring that I manage my time and priorities and exert every effort to be productive. Although I started at a front desk position, my curiosity and initiative took me all over many departments of the hotel industry, such as reservations, sales and marketing, and the food and beverage division.

Moreover, my greatest accomplishment was to supervise one of the food and beverage departments of another major hotel in San Diego. My new target customers were East Coast companies that sent groups of employees to our hotel in San Diego, mostly for work and conferences. We provided these preferred guests with a friendly, welcoming "happy hour," featuring a complimentary buffet and a full bar,

confidence in restaurants that are well run."[1] The benefits of training indeed outweigh the cost in the long run.

A small mistake or oversight made by a poorly trained employee can have enormous impact. This lesson was brought home a few years ago when a night clerk whose training was obviously incomplete turned off a fire alarm "because it was bothering me" and several people died in the fire.

Benefits of Training

Perhaps you are already beginning to think that what is needed is some sort of system like performance standards that would define the last detail of every job so that each person could be trained to do the job correctly. You are absolutely right. Each

---

[1]Pamela Parseghian, "For raw recruits, training is the best defense against food poisoning," *Nation's Restaurant News*, Vol. 34, No. 33, August 14, 2000.

from Monday through Friday. We usually had baseball, basketball, or football games playing on a big-screen TV during happy hour, what made an even more relaxed and fun atmosphere in which to "hang out." I found it very much fun to develop a relationship with some of these guests, especially because they always came back to our hotel. Some of them stayed for weeks, sometimes months; and some of them came back for a week every month of the year. I believe that most of these guests always came back because they got to meet a lot of people in our happy hour, and they felt very comfortable.

Next, as a supervisor, I found it effective to have a vision, or to set goals you want to accomplish during a given period of time. Then, communicate these goals to the team. Goals should be achievable given sufficient effort, and it must be possible to tell when they have been achieved. Recognizing and prizing employees who are accomplishing goals and devoting themselves to their work is crucial for employee motivation and satisfaction, leading to a higher quality of work.

Furthermore, I found it wonderful to build strong relationships with employees; you can understand them, and get sincere feedback from them on many aspects of work; and they can understand you, including what you expect from them. Supervisors make a great impact on an employee's performance; it is important to be aware of this fact. Whenever you have to correct a certain behavior or employee attitude, always mention the good things about that employee, building his or her self-esteem before criticizing the person's work.

In conclusion, I believe that effective supervising is, essentially, using common sense when making decisions in every situation. Also treating people fairly and with respect; recognizing and prizing their good work; and knowing how to criticize someone's conduct, if needed, without hurting their feelings, is very important. Finally, supervisors should listen to employees and guests and have a good sense of humor and a little *jeitinho* to please guests and employees while complying with the set goals for the company.

new person would learn the same information and procedures as everyone else. Everybody would learn the same ways of doing things. Job content, information, methods, and procedures would be standardized, and performance goals would be the same for everyone. The new employee would end up producing the same product or service to the same standards as everyone else doing that job.

Suppose that you had such a system in place and used it to train your people. *How would it help you on the job?*

❧ *It would give you more time to manage.* You would not have to spend so much time looking over people's shoulders, checking up, filling in, putting out fires, and improving solutions to unexpected problems.

❧ *You would have less absenteeism and less turnover,* because your people would know what to do and how to do it, they would feel comfortable in their jobs, and you would spend less of your time finding and breaking in new people.

∾ *It would reduce tensions between you and your people.* You would not be correcting them constantly, and you would have more reason to praise them, which would improve morale. It would also reduce tension between you and your boss. When your people are performing smoothly, the boss is not on your back. You worry less, sleep better, and work with less tension.

It is no surprise that we all struggle to tap effectively into the youth workforce of tomorrow, but truly understanding the Generation Y mentality will better position your organization to train and retain front-line employees. To some extent, those of us at Hard Rock Café have tried to cater to this common-sense principle. Realizing this, Hard Rock Café has taken a very proactive approach to aligning training with the way that people learn today. This is not to stereotype an entire generation, but the young adults that make up this rebellious generation require information to be presented to them in the same method in which they are accustomed to receiving it. Fortunately, the strong Hard Rock culture allows and supports the type of training systems they desire. The Hard Rock approach is to: think visually, provide immediacy, emphasize fun, and leverage benefits.

Source: Jim Knight, "Generation Y: how to train it and retain it," *Restaurant Hospitality,* Vol. 84, No. 5, May 2000.

∾ *It would be much easier to maintain consistency of product and service.* When you have set standards and have taught your people how to meet these standards, the products and the service are standard, too. Customers can depend on the same comfort, the same service, the same excellence of food, the same pleasant experience they had the last time.

∾ *You would have lower costs*—less breakage, less waste, fewer accidents, less spoilage, better cost control. New workers would be productive sooner. You might be able to get the work done with fewer people because everyone would work more efficiently.

∾ *Trained personnel would give you happier customers and more of them.* The way that employees treat customers is the single most important factor in repeat business. One worker untrained in customer relations can make several guests per day swear that they will never set foot in your place again.

∾ *Training your workers can help your own career.* Your performance depends on their performance. And if you have not trained anyone in your job, you may never be promoted because you will always be needed where you are.

Good training will benefit your workers, too. Here are some things that it can do for them:

∾ *It can eliminate the five reasons why people do poor work:* not knowing what to do, or how to do it, or how well they are doing; not getting any help from the supervisor; not getting along with the supervisor at all. Good training can get them through those first painful days and make them comfortable sooner.

∾ *Trained employees do not always have to be asking how to do things.* They have confidence; they can say to themselves, "Hey, I know my job; I can do my job." This gives them satisfaction, security, and a sense of belonging, and it can earn praise from the boss.

∾ *Training can reduce employee tension.* The boss is not on their backs all the time with constant negative evaluations, and they are not worried about how they are doing.

∾ *Training can boost employee morale and job satisfaction.* When employees know exactly what the boss expects from them, they tend to be more satisfied and relaxed with their jobs. Wouldn't you be?

∾ *It can also reduce accidents and injuries.* If you have been trained how to lift heavy luggage or cases of food, you are not going to hurt your back. If you have been trained how to handle a hot stockpot, you are not going to scald yourself.

∞ *Training can give people a chance to advance.* The initial training, even at the lowest levels, can reveal capabilities and open doors to further training, promotion, and better pay.

Good training will benefit the entire enterprise. Training that reduces tensions, turnover, and costs and improves product, service, and customer count is certainly going to improve the company image and the bottom line. Many corporations recognize this and have developed systematic training programs.

However, not everyone in the industry sees training as an investment that pays its way. Many managers of small operations consider training an exercise in futility because, they say, it takes more time than it is worth, because people do not stay, because people are not interested in being trained, because it does not work, because it should not be necessary. The myth persists that people in entry-level service jobs should be able to do these jobs without training. When times are bad, with lack of volume and low customer counts, training is the first thing that a manager gives up, as though it were a frill.

It is hard to convince these people that training is worth the investment. It is difficult to measure and prove the difference that training makes because there are always many variables in every situation. Perhaps the best way to be convinced that training pays off is to compare individual operations where the training is good with those that do little or no training. The differences will be obvious in atmosphere, in smoothness of operation, in customer enjoyment, and in profit.

Among larger establishments, there are some that have gained a reputation for their training, that train people so well they are hired away by other firms. It is a nice reputation to have—a nice image for bringing in customers as well as attracting good workers. How do you measure an image? Usually, you do not have to.

On the downside there have been instances where cutting down on training to cut expenses has proved to be false economy and has resulted in deterioration of service, decline in customer count, and eventually the demise of the enterprise.

Think back to the theory that ROI means *return on individuals.* Training is an investment in people. In an industry whose every product and service depends almost entirely on individual people at work—people who deal directly with customers—investing in training those people is a major key to ROI of any sort.

Check Your Knowledge

1. What is *training?*
2. List the three kinds of training needed in hospitality operations.
3. What are the benefits of training your new personnel? Briefly explain each benefit.

Problems in Training

Managers who do not train their people are not all stubborn fools or cynics; the problems are real. Perhaps the biggest problem is *urgent need;* you need this person so badly right now that you don't have time to train, you can't get along without this pair of hands. You put the person right into the job and correct mistakes as they happen and keep your fingers crossed.

A second critical problem is *training time:* your time and the worker's time. While you are training, neither of you is doing anything else, and you do not have that kind of time. Your time and the worker's cost the company *money.* A training program requires an immediate outlay of money, time, and effort for results that are down the road. This is especially a problem for the small operation with cash-flow problems and a day-to-day existence. Training is an investment in the future they cannot afford; their problems are here today.

A fourth problem is *turnover*—people leave just as you get them trained, and you have spent all that time and money and effort for nothing. Training may reduce turnover, but it does not eliminate it, given the easy-come, easy-go workers in the hospitality industry.

The *short-term worker* is a training problem in many ways. People who do not expect to stay long on a job are not highly motivated. They are not interested in the job and they are not interested in getting ahead; they just want the paycheck at the end of the week. They do not like training programs. They do not like to read training materials. They do not get anything out of lectures. Most of them have poor listening, reading, and studying skills. They do poorly with the general, the abstract, and the complex. They are impatient; they are looking for a *now* skill—something they can do this afternoon.

The *diversity of workers* can be a training problem. Some are pursuing college degrees; others are poorly educated. Many have never had a job before; others have been in the industry for years. (Some of these are floaters who move from one operation to another; they like to work openings, stay about a month, and move on.) Some are know-it-alls; others are timid and dependent. Some are bright; others are below average in intelligence and aptitudes. Some do not speak English. Overall, they are not a promising classroom crowd. How can you train such different people for the same jobs and expect the same performance standards?

We also have problems with the *kinds of jobs* we train for. One type is the dull, routine job that takes no high degree of intelligence or skill: vacuuming carpets, mopping floors, prepping vegetables, and running a dishmachine. The problem here is the very simplicity of these jobs: We tend to overlook the training. Yet these jobs are very important to the operation, and it is essential that they be done correctly.

Most housekeeping jobs, for example, involve sanitation. Yet because sanitation can be technical and at times boring, and much of it is not visible to the untrained eye, it is easy to skip over it lightly. Techniques may not be properly taught or their importance emphasized—the sanitizer in the bucket of water, the indicator on the temperature gauge in the right place, the dishmachine loaded so that the spray reaches every dish and utensil.

Also overlooked are techniques of doing routine tasks quickly, efficiently, and safely. The optimum stroke of the vacuum cleaner, the order of tasks in cleaning a room, how to handle your body in making a bed or scrubbing a tub so that you don't strain your back—these little things can make a critical difference to efficiency, absenteeism, and employee well-being.

At the other extreme is the *complexity* of jobs containing up to 200 or 300 different tasks, plus the subtle skills of customer relations. Such jobs—server, bartender, and desk clerk—are so familiar to people who supervise them that they do not stop to think how much there is for a new person to learn. Training time for these multiple tasks can be a real problem. Therefore, you skimp on the training, you rush it, or you hire experienced people and skip the training. You forgo the control, the consistency of product and service, and the high-grade performance of people you have trained to your own standards.

The final typical training problem is *not knowing exactly what you want your people to do and how*. If you do not know this, how can you train them?

What you need is a system of training that defines what your people are to do and how, trains everyone to the same standards, adapts to individual needs and skills, and lends itself to one-on-one training. We talked in Chapter 6 about using performance standards in such a system, and we are going to discuss in detail how to develop a training program for this kind of system. Although not many people are going to take the trouble to develop a full-blown system, you can still see how its principles and techniques apply in training, and you can go as far as you find practical in applying them.

Before we look at the three different types of training, let us first consider who will do the training and how employees learn best.

Who Will Do the Training

We have mentioned various ways of assigning the training responsibility: the magic apron, having an employee who is leaving train her replacement, the buddy or big brother/sister system. They do not work because such training is haphazard and incomplete, but most of all because the wrong person is doing the training.

With the magic apron, people train themselves. They are the wrong persons to do the training. They make a mistake and are yelled at, and what they train themselves to do is what will keep them from being yelled at. They will also train themselves to do things the easiest way and, in general, to do what is to their own best interest, and often, these things are opposed to the interests of the house.

Shirley is leaving or has already left. She will do only enough to placate Ms. Manager and get her paycheck. She will tell her replacement only what she knows, which may be very little, and only what she can cram into the shortest possible time, and she will not care whether the new person learns anything. She will also teach shortcuts and ways of getting away with breaking rules.

Big brother, big sister, and buddy will also teach only what they know, and only as much of that as they happen to think of, and they too will not care how well the new person understands. Unless they are paid extra for training, they may resent the assignment. They may also resent the new person as a competitor. In addition, they will hand on to the new worker all their own bad habits and all their accumulated gripes, and they will condition the trainee to their view of the job, the boss, the customers, and the pay.

The logical person to train your people is you, the supervisor. It is your responsibility, whether you delegate it or do it yourself. Training is one of those obligations to your people that goes with your job—giving them the tools and knowledge to do theirs. However, you have a thousand other responsibilities and your day is interrupted every 20 to 48 seconds.

If you can possibly make the time, you owe it to yourself to do the training. It is the beginning of leadership. A good teacher forms a lasting impression in the learner's mind, a special regard that will color the relationship from that point on. It gives you a chance to get to know your new people, to establish that one-to-one relationship necessary to being an effective leader.

On the other hand, you may have someone on your staff with the right potential who might be able to train new people even better than you can, considering all the demands on your time and attention. If you have established a good training program, you can delegate the training to someone like this.

Such people must be trained. They must know how to do everything they have to teach. They must learn the skills needed to train others: how to treat people as individuals, how to put themselves in the learner's place, how to gear the lesson to the learner, how to increase motivation, how to lead—all the good things you have been learning yourself.

It is essential for these people to receive appropriate compensation: extra pay for extra work, a promotion, whatever fits the situation. They must also want to do the training. You remain responsible for the training, and if it is not done well, it will come back to haunt you.

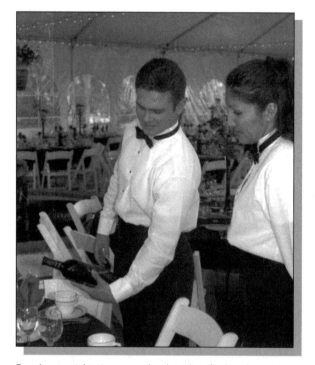

Good potential trainers need to be identified and receive additional compensation for training.

By the way you train, you are teaching more than rules, procedures, skills, and job standards. You are teaching basic attitudes toward work, personal standards of performance, the importance of the person, getting along with other people (both customers and colleagues), your own work values, and many subtle but lasting lessons in human relations and values. People on their first jobs are particularly susceptible to this type of learning. Their first job will probably affect their attitude toward work performance, work relationships, and work values for the rest of their lives. It is important to be aware of this. You do not have to save their souls, but you do owe it to them to set high standards and a good example and to teach a work ethic of being on time, meeting standards, and giving their best efforts to the job. You owe it to yourself, too, and to the organization.

"Generation-Xers do not respond to the more traditional authoritarian educational methods." One of the biggest pitfalls of trainers is that they feel they are all-knowing. When training Gen-X workers it is important that your focus is trying to understand them, not change them. People are doing well at their primary jobs so they simply don't have a need to "wait on tables for additional income." Kids are not working as much either because their parents are doing well; extra money is not a necessity. Therefore, restaurant staffs will not stand for an "authoritative trainer on their management team." Gen-X staff will respect authority that will respect them. Always explain to employees what you are doing. Today's youth will not follow blindly; they were raised to be self-sufficient. When training members of the Gen-X culture, keep in mind the following guidelines: (1) Explain yourself and your qualifications; (2) state your purpose with clarity; (3) be self-deprecating; (4) get them involved; (5) make them laugh.

Source: James Dunne, "Training Gen-Xers takes understanding and fairness, not traditional iron fist," *Nation's Restaurant News,* Vol. 34, No. 49, December 4, 2000.

How Employees Learn Best

Training is a form of communication, and as in all communication, the sender (trainer) controls only the first half of the interaction. The second half, the receiving of the message—the learning—depends on the trainee. **Learning** is the acquisition of knowledge, skills, or attitudes. How do adults learn best? Many of the following tips for helping employees learn are derived from a field of study called **adult learning theory.**[2]

1. *Employees learn best when they are actively involved in the learning process.* When employees participate in their own training, they retain more of the concepts being taught. To get employees involved, you need to choose appropriate **teaching methods.** Teaching methods are the ways we convey information to learners. You are no doubt familiar with the lecture method because it has dominated U.S. education for many years. Using the lecture method, content is delivered primarily in a one-way fashion from a trainer to the participants. Little or no interaction occurs between the trainer and the participants. Although the lecture method may be an efficient method to get across needed information to employees, it is most inefficient at getting employees to use the information. Table 8.1 lists teaching methods that more actively involve employees.

2. *Employees also learn best when the training is relevant and practical.* Adult learners are picky about what they will spend their

[2]Adapted from "Inservice training: how do employees learn best?" *Hospital Food & Nutrition Focus,* Vol. 6, No. 4, pp. 1–4, © 1989, Aspen Publishers, Inc. Reprinted with permission.

TABLE 8.1   ∾   **Teaching Methods to Promote Employee Involvement in Training**

Discussion	Simulation
Demonstration	Dramatization
Practice/skill rehearsal	Instructional games
Case study	Brainstorming
Guest speaker	Field trip
Role-play	

time learning. They often pursue learning experiences in order to cope with life-changing events such as a job change. Learning must be especially pertinent and rewarding for them.

3. Besides being relevant, *training material needs to be well organized and presented in small, easy-to-grasp chunks.* Adults need to be able to learn new skills at a speed that permits mastery. Unlike children, adults come to the classroom with prior experience, so they need to integrate new ideas with what they already know. Using visual aids, such as posters, during training helps to focus employees' attention, reinforce main ideas, save time, and increase understanding and retention.

4. *The optimal learning environment for employees is an informal, quiet, comfortable setting.* The effort you put into selecting and maintaining an appropriate environment for training shows your employees how important you think the training is. You give a message that training isn't that important when employees are stuffed into your office, made to stand in a noisy part of the kitchen, or when you allow yourself to be interrupted by phone calls. Employees like to feel special, so find a private room, and consider having beverages, and perhaps some food, available.

5. In addition to training in an appropriate setting, *employees learn best with a good trainer.* Table 8.2 lists characteristics of successful trainers, some of which we have already discussed. As you go through the table, you will see that the characteristics listed also apply to successful supervisors. A good supervisor is usually a good trainer.

6. Toward the end of training, employees are generally evaluated on how well they are doing. *Employees learn best when they receive feedback on their performance and when they are rewarded* (perhaps with a certificate or pin) for doing well.

Check Your Knowledge

1. What are some of problems you may come across when you do not train your employees?

2. Who will train your employees?

3. When do employees learn best?

TABLE 8.2   ∾   **Characteristics of a Successful Trainer**

1. Is knowledgeable
2. Displays enthusiasm
3. Has a sense of humor
4. Communicates clearly, concisely, and in a straightforward manner
5. Is sincere, caring, respecting, and responsive toward employees
6. Encourages employee performance
7. Is patient
8. Sets an appropriate role model
9. Is organized
10. Maintains control and eye contact with employees
11. Listens well
12. Is friendly and outgoing
13. Keeps calm
14. Tries to involve all employees
15. Positively reinforces employees

Source: Adapted from "Inservice training: how do employees learn best?" *Hospital Food & Nutrition Focus,* Vol. 6, No. 4, p. 4, © 1989, Aspen Publishers, Inc.

Developing a Job-Training Program

A good job-training program should be organized as a series of written **training plans,** each representing a learnable, teachable segment of the job. Once you have prepared such plans, you can use them for every new person you hire for the job: They are all ready to go. You can use as much or as little of each plan as you need, depending on what the new employee already knows.

Performance standards provide a ready-made structure for a training program for a given job: Each unit of the job with its performance standards provides the framework for one training plan. In this section we describe how to develop a training program using performance standards. Although you may not complete the system in every detail, you can apply the principles and content to any training program.

Establishing Plan Content

Even if you do not have performance standards, you still have to go through pretty much the same procedures to develop a good training program. You must analyze the job as a whole, identifying all the units that make up that job classification and then the tasks that make up each unit. Then you must decide how you want each unit and task done and to what standard. You then develop a procedure manual or some other way of showing how the tasks are to be carried out. These steps are described in detail in Chapter 6. When you have done all this, you are ready to prepare training plans, one plan for each unit of the job.

Figure 8.1 traces the progress of one training plan from its beginning to its implementation on the job. Let us follow it through, using an example from the bartender's job. The job of bartender contains a dozen or so units, such as setting up the bar, mixing and serving drinks, recording drink sales, operating the cash register, and so on. You will write a training plan for each unit. Your first training plan will be for *setting up the bar.*

1. Write your performance standard: "The bartender will set up the bar correctly according to standard house procedures in half an hour or less."

2. Write a **training objective** derived from your performance standard: "After 3 hours of instruction and practice, the trainee will be able to set up the bar correctly according to standard house procedures in 45 minutes." This training objective expresses what you expect the person to do after training, the training goal. It differs from the on-the-job performance objective in three ways:

    a. A time limit is set for the training.
    b. The verb expresses trainee achievement rather than on-the-job performance.
    c. The performance standard is lower for this learning level (45 minutes) than for the day-in, day-out performance level.

3. Incorporate your standard procedures that you may already have developed. If not, here is what you do. You list all the tasks of the unit in the order in which they are performed, and you spell out each task in the form of a procedures sheet or visual presentation stating or showing exactly how you want that task carried

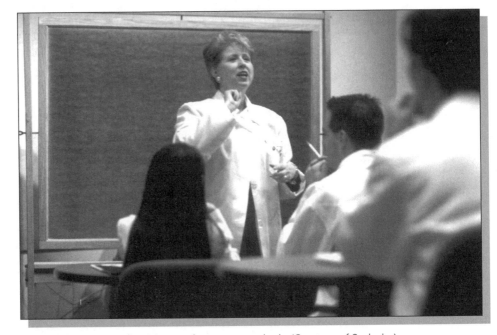

Training objectives are based on performance standards. (Courtesy of Sodexho)

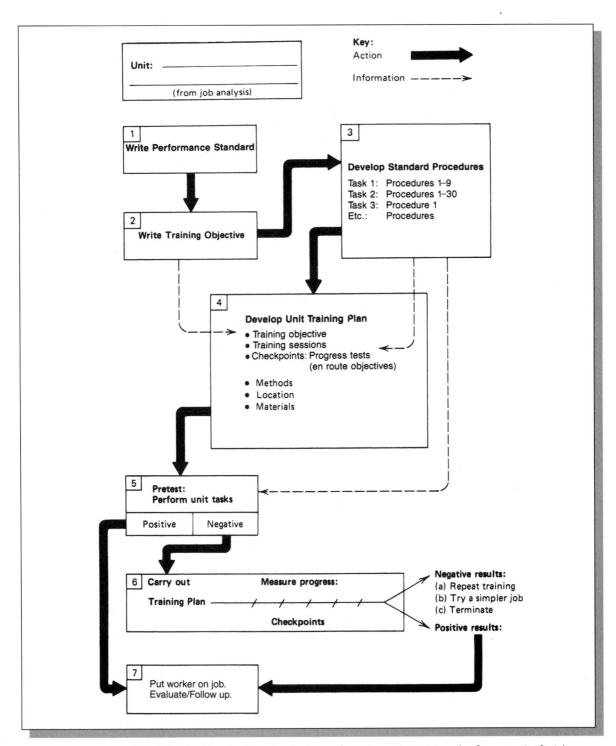

FIGURE 8.1 Flowchart for developing and carrying out a training plan for one unit of a job.

out in your operation. Figure 8.2 is a procedures sheet for the first task of setting up the bar. Figure 8.3 goes with it to illustrate some of the procedures. All the procedural materials taken together define the content of the instruction for the unit, and they become both guides and standards for the training. You are now ready to plan the training itself.

Developing a Unit Training Plan

A training plan (Figure 8.1, step 4) sets forth not only what you will train someone to do, but how, and when, and where, what supplies and materials you need, and how much training you will do at one time. Figure 8.4 is an example of a training plan for the first unit of the bartender job. Let us go through that plan item by item.

Notice first that the training objective is stated, so that you can keep the goal in mind and shape the training to reach it. The unit is taught in several *training sessions*. The primary reason for this is to avoid giving the trainee too much to learn at once. Another reason is to avoid tying up the person doing the training for too long a time. In this particular case it is also to avoid tying up the bar itself.

The tasks are taught in the order in which they are performed on the job. (Some tasks do not have an order; in Dress and Grooming, for example, all "tasks" are carried on simultaneously.) One training session may include several tasks, some taking as little as 5 or 10 minutes. Length of time for each session will vary according to the trainee's previous experience. An experienced bartender, for example, will learn your par-stock-empty-bottle-requisition routine far more quickly than someone who has never tended bar before. (Most operations look for experienced bartenders because training from scratch takes too long, but even an experienced bartender must be trained in *your* bar and *your* procedures.)

The training plan should provide *checkpoints* along the way, as shown in step 6 of Figure 8.1. These allow you to measure a worker's progress toward achieving the objective. They may follow groups of tasks within the unit of work, or they may follow the whole unit with a series of less demanding performance standards (a more lenient time limit, a greater margin for error). You can write special intermediate objectives for the checkpoints or set several successive levels of performance for the entire unit of work.

The *method of training* must include two elements: (1) showing and telling the trainee what to do and how to do it, and (2) having the trainee actually do it and do it right. These elements are combined in a widely used formula known as *job instruction training*, which we examine in detail shortly. There are various ways to show and tell: demonstration, movies, videotapes, CD/ROMs.

The closer the training method and setup are to the on-the-job situation, the better the training. You can teach table setting by actually setting up tables for service, teach bed making while you are actually making a room ready for the next guest. But there are many things you cannot teach while doing them on the job. In such cases you simulate on-the-job conditions as closely as you can: You use the real equipment and real supplies and you set up the equipment and the task as realistically as possible.

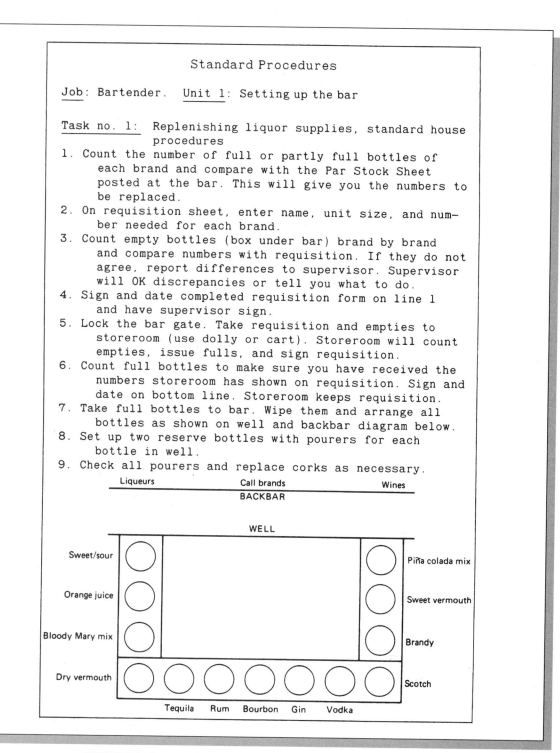

Standard Procedures

Job: Bartender. Unit 1: Setting up the bar

Task no. 1: Replenishing liquor supplies, standard house
            procedures

1. Count the number of full or partly full bottles of
   each brand and compare with the Par Stock Sheet
   posted at the bar. This will give you the numbers to
   be replaced.
2. On requisition sheet, enter name, unit size, and number needed for each brand.
3. Count empty bottles (box under bar) brand by brand
   and compare numbers with requisition. If they do not
   agree, report differences to supervisor. Supervisor
   will OK discrepancies or tell you what to do.
4. Sign and date completed requisition form on line 1
   and have supervisor sign.
5. Lock the bar gate. Take requisition and empties to
   storeroom (use dolly or cart). Storeroom will count
   empties, issue fulls, and sign requisition.
6. Count full bottles to make sure you have received the
   numbers storeroom has shown on requisition. Sign and
   date on bottom line. Storeroom keeps requisition.
7. Take full bottles to bar. Wipe them and arrange all
   bottles as shown on well and backbar diagram below.
8. Set up two reserve bottles with pourers for each
   bottle in well.
9. Check all pourers and replace corks as necessary.

Liqueurs   Call brands   Wines
                  BACKBAR

                  WELL

Sweet/sour   Piña colada mix

Orange juice   Sweet vermouth

Bloody Mary mix   Brandy

Dry vermouth   Scotch

        Tequila Rum Bourbon Gin Vodka

FIGURE 8.2 Portion of a procedure for setting up the bar: procedures for one task (page from a procedures manual for the job of bartender).

REQUISITION

DEPT _Bar_   DATE _June 12_

Item (Brand)	Unit	Quantity Requested	Quantity Issued	Unit Cost	Total Cost
J & B	L	2			
Chivas	L	1			
Jim Bean	L	1			
C. C.	L	1			
Beefeater	L	2			
Smirnoff	L	3			
Teq - Cuervo	L	2			
Bacardi	L	2			
Brandy - C.B.	L	1			
Amaretto	750	1			
Baileys IC.		1			
Cr. Cacao-W		1			
Burgundy - Gal	1.75	1			
Chablis - Alm	1.75	4			
Cinzano dry	750	1			
Mary mix	case	1			

REQUISITIONED BY _Mike Smith_   DATE   6/12

SUPERVISOR   DATE

ISSUED BY   DATE

RECEIVED BY   DATE

FIGURE 8.3 Example of a requisition filled out by a bartender (part of a procedures manual for the job of bartender).

```
                           TRAINING PLAN

Job classification:  Bartender

Unit 1:  Setting up the bar

Learning objective: After 3 hours of instruction and
practice, trainee will be able to set up the
bar correctly according to standard house procedures in
45 minutes.

Training sessions:   1. Replenish liquor (Task 1, training
                        time 30 minutes)
                     2. Replenish other supplies (Tasks
                        2-6, training time 30 minutes)
                     3. Set up draft beer, check soda
                        system (Tasks 7-8, training
                        time 20 minutes)
                     4. Prepare garnishes (Tasks 9-13,
                        training time 30 minutes)
                     5. Set up register (Tasks 14-15,
                        training time 20 minutes)
                     6. Set up ice bins, glasses, sinks,
                        mixing equipment, bar top,
                        coffee (Tasks 16-21, training
                        time 25 minutes)

Method:  Demonstrate and do (JIT), one on one. Video-
         tape on beer setup.

Location:  Bar, 1 hour before opening (bar must be as
           left after closing)

Materials:  Liquor and all other    Cocktail napkins
              supplies as of         Ice
              closing                Bar knife and cutting
            Liquor empties from        board
              previous day           Bar spoon, jiggers
            Par Stock Sheet          Mixing glasses
            Requisition forms        Guest checks
            Well and backbar         Credit card slips
              diagram                Cash register
            Pourers, replacement     Opening bank
              collars                Dolly or cart
            Ashtrays                 Coffee machine and
            Matches                    coffee
            Picks                    Procedure sheets, Tasks
            Snacks                     1-21

Checkpoints:  After each task
```

FIGURE 8.4   Training plan for one unit (page from a training manual).

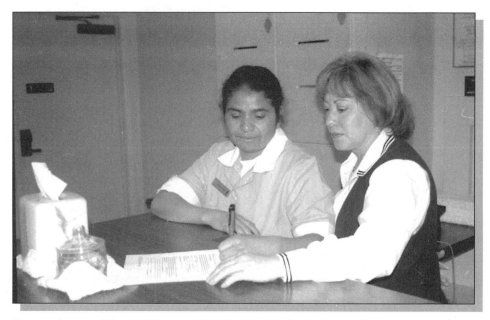

Training plans need checkpoints to measure the trainees' progress.

One-on-one training generally works best. In a classroom, a person does not learn as well. Everybody absorbs the material at different rates or has different problems with it. The slow learners are lost and the fast learners are bored. The classroom also causes anxiety and inhibits everyone except the know-it-all.

However, group presentations have certain advantages. They are useful for giving general information and background that may be overlooked by the individual trainer. Because group presentations can be more closely controlled, it is a good way to convey company policy so that it is always stated accurately and everyone gets the same message. Groups are also used for material presented in movies and videos.

A number of chains use audiovisual presentations such as videotapes or slide-tapes that are developed at headquarters and are sent out for use by individual stores or several stores in an area. Training in customer relations, for example, can be given in this fashion. It is effective and ensures not only a consistent message but also consistent training quality.

The *location* of the training should be a quiet place free of interruptions. Ideally, training is done in the actual job setting during off hours. Some corporations have special training facilities completely equipped to simulate the actual job environment.

Your *training materials* should include the same equipment and supplies that will be used on the job, and they should all be on hand and ready before the training starts. You must prepare your entire session in advance if training is to be effective.

Developing a written training plan helps you to think out all the aspects of the training and to orient everything to the new employee and the details of the job. Each completed plan gives you a checklist for readiness and a blueprint for action.

Like many good things prepared for a well-run operation, training plans take a long time to develop, and the manager or supervisor will have to do one plan at a time one piece at a time, probably over a long period. It may be helpful to schedule development along the lines of an improvement objective (Chapter 6), setting overall goals and interim goals. Then each completed piece of the plan will provide a feeling of achievement and the momentum to continue. Of course, if you already have job analyses, performance objectives, and procedures manuals, your work is half done at the outset.

Moving from Plan to Action

Now you are ready to train the worker. But before you train new employees you must find out how much training they really need. If they have knowledge and skills from previous experience, it wastes both their time and yours to teach them things they already know. For this reason the training of people who have some experience begins with a **pretest** (Figure 8.1, step 5): You have them actually do the unit of work. If the unit consists of operating the dishmachine, you have them operate the dishmachine; if it is serving wine, you have them serve wine; if it is setting up the bar, you have them set up the bar.

You observe the new worker's performance and confine your training to what the person does not know, what does not measure up to your standard, what varies from your special ways of doing things, and what the person must unlearn in the way of habits and procedures from other jobs. Experienced workers should end up meeting the same standards as people whom you train from scratch.

Not all units and tasks are suitable for pretesting. Some are too complex, and some are different every day. In this case you can ask experienced new workers to describe how they would carry out the tasks in question and then adjust the training accordingly.

Now suppose that you are training Gloria and David, who have never had a job before. You carry out your first unit training plan (Figure 8.4), teaching each of them every task in the unit's action plan. You test them at every checkpoint to make sure that they are following you and are putting it all together and meeting your time requirements. Finally, when you have taught all the tasks in the unit, you evaluate Gloria and David by having them perform the entire unit in sequence.

Does Gloria meet the performance standard of your learning objective? If so, you move on to the second unit of the job and the second objective. Suppose that David fails to meet the standard for the first unit. You retrain him in those procedures that he is not doing correctly. If he did not meet the time requirement, you have him practice some more.

If he just can't get it all together, you might try him on the second unit anyway. If he can't do that either, he may not be able to handle the job, and you may have to place him in a less demanding job. It is also possible that your training was at fault, and you have to take a hard look at that. If you do not have a simpler job, or if he cannot team that simpler job either, you may have to let him go. The training has not been wasted if it has identified an untrainable employee in time to save your paying unemployment compensation. (It sure was frustrating, though!) Don't frustrate yourself with someone who cannot or will not learn.

Ideally, you will put a new employee on the job (Figure 8.1, step 7) after training for all units of the job has been completed. But you may need Gloria and David so badly that you will have them work a unit of the job as soon as they have been trained for that unit. In complex jobs it may even be easier for them to work certain units of the job for awhile before going on to learn the entire job.

Once the formal training process is completed, there is still one very important step: evaluation. Making an evaluation is the crucial process of determining whether training objectives were met. It can occur both during and after training. **Formative evaluation** uses observation, interviews, and surveys to monitor training while it is going on. **Summative evaluation** measures the results of the training after the program is completed, looking at it in five ways.

1. *Reaction:* Did the employees like the training?
2. *Knowledge:* Did the employees learn the information taught?
3. *Behavior:* Are the employees using the new skills or behavior on the job?
4. *Attitudes:* Do the employees demonstrate any new attitudes?
5. *Productivity:* Did the training increase productivity, and was it cost-effective?

Various techniques can be used to answer these questions. Participants can report on what they liked and did not like about the training by filling out evaluation forms. Tests are frequently given at the end of training sessions to determine whether the employees know the information and/or skills covered. For instance, a dishwasher may be asked the correct temperature for the final rinse and then asked to demonstrate how to pick up dishes without contaminating them. Results can also be measured through observation of employee behavior and monitoring of critical indicators such as the number of guest complaints, level of repeat business, and so on. After collecting information from various sources, the person doing the evaluation needs to compare the results to the learning objectives to determine whether the training indeed succeeded in bringing about the desired changes.

Job Instruction Training

Successful training observes the flow of the learning process. During World War II, when war plants had to train millions of workers quickly, a training method was developed that took maximum advantage of the learning flow. It was so successful that it has been used in various forms ever since in all kinds of training programs in all types of industries. This is **job instruction training** (JIT), sometimes also called on-the-job training.

The Ritz-Carlton Hotel is one of the leading hotels in the travel market. One of the main reasons behind the Ritz's success is the fact that the company puts a lot of time, money, and effort into customer service training. Every one of its 16,000 employees must undergo customer service training. Even before a new person is hired, behavior traits are explored to see if the person's personality is compatible with that of the company and its expectations. The entire training system is a combination of two elements: customer service philosophy and technical skills. After workers are taught a task, they are reviewed, and ultimately, their trainer certifies them. Each employee is also taught resolution techniques and is given the power to resolve customer challenges. This helps to create loyalty with customers. The focus is on hospitality. They adapt to the local citizens and their way of hospitality. At Ritz they realize that it is important to please workers as well as customers. If workers are not satisfied, the needs of the customers will not be met. They believe that "a better human being will be a better professional."

Source: Scott Hays, "Exceptional customer service takes the 'Ritz' touch," *Workforce,* Vol. 78, No. 1, January, 1999.

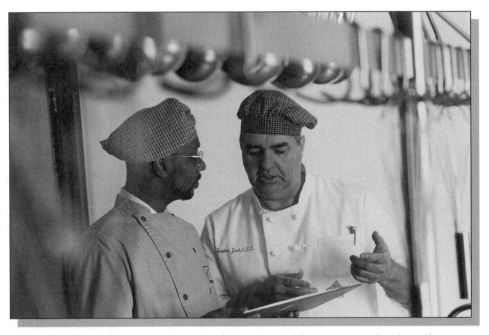

Job instruction training prepares the worker for training and demonstrating what the worker is to do (show and tell). (Courtesy of Sodexho)

The method consists of four steps:

1. Prepare the worker for training.
2. Demonstrate what the worker is to do (show and tell).
3. Have the worker do the task, as shown, repeating until the performance is satisfactory.
4. Follow through: Put the worker on the job, checking and correcting as needed.

These four steps are applied to one task at a time. Figure 8.5 shows the steps and the relationship to learning flow.

Step 1, preparing the worker (call him Bob), consists of several things you do to let him know what is coming, make him feel at ease, and motivate him to learn. One thing is telling Bob where his job fits into the overall operation and why it is important to the operation. Another is giving Bob a reason to learn ("It will benefit you." "It will help you to do your job." "You will be rewarded in such and such a way.") A third is telling him what to expect in the training and expressing confidence that he can do the job.

Step 2, demonstrating the task, is show-and-tell: "This is what I want you to do and this is how I want you to do it." You explain what you are doing and how you are doing it and why you are doing it the way you are. You use simple language and stress the key points. You tell Bob exactly what he needs to know but no more (unless he asks). If you tell him too much, you will confuse him. You do not go into the theory

FIGURE 8.5 Learning flow in job instruction training.

of the dishmachine: the temperature it has to reach, the bacteria that have to be killed, and why bacteria are such an issue. You tell him, "The dish must get very hot. The needle must be at this number." The core of the action stands out clearly—no theory, all application. You take care to demonstrate well, because what you do is going to set the standard of performance, along with teaching the how-to. You cannot give a second-class demonstration and expect the worker to do a first-class job.

Step 3, having Bob do the task as you showed him, is really the heart of the training. The first time is a tryout. If he can do it correctly right off, he is stimulated. If he cannot, you correct the errors and omissions in a positive way and have him do it again, showing him again if necessary. As he does it, have him tell you the key points and why they are done the way they are; this will reinforce the learning. Have him do the task several times, correcting himself if he can, telling you why he made the correction, letting him experience the stimulation of his increasing understanding. Encourage his questions, taking them seriously no matter how simpleminded they sound to you. Praise him for his progress and encourage him when he falters or fails. Have him repeat the task until you are satisfied that he can do it exactly as you did, to the standard you have set for him. Let him see your satisfaction and approval.

Step 4, following through, means putting Bob on his own in the actual job. You do this not for individual tasks but for units or groups of units or when the worker has learned the entire job. You stay in the background and watch him at work. You touch base frequently, correct his performance as necessary, and let him know how he is doing. Now, briefly, you are a partner in his success. You praise and reward as promised. When he continues to do things just the way you have trained him to do, you can leave him on his own.

Classroom Training

The classroom is an appropriate place to communicate information to groups of employees and may be used at times for job instruction or retraining. For example, you want your servers to start using suggestive selling techniques. You may get them together to explain what suggestive selling is and what it is not, and to describe some suggestive selling techniques. You may then use videotapes showing how these techniques are used. Up to this point, you have used the classroom to educate your staff about suggestive selling, but your staff is not actually trained to run out and sell suggestively to the guests. That can now be done on the job with the help of managers and supervisors.

Teaching in a classroom requires certain skills. We will discuss six different areas of classroom skills.[3]

1. When teaching a group, *be aware of and use appropriate body language and speech.* Show that you are comfortable with the group through natural, positive body language, including good posture and keeping your hands away from your face. Make good eye contact with everyone in your group. Pay close attention to the pace, volume, and tone of your voice. The pace should be neither too fast, nor too slow; you should speak at the appropriate volume for everyone to hear you. Vary the tone of your voice to avoid sounding boring. Avoid speech habits such as "um" or "you know." Smile and nod to employees frequently to show positive reinforcement.

2. *The way you talk to employees greatly influences how receptive they are to your leadership,* so do the following: Convey respect and appreciation by making statements such as "Thanks for taking the time from your busy jobs to be here today." Share what you have in common with employees, such as certain knowledge, skills, and frustrations. Use informal, familiar language and phrase your directives gently, as in "Let's start today's class by doing an exercise." Encourage employee comments, both positive and negative, and give your employees lots of praise and support. When employees bring up different points of view, make a positive statement about this, such as "It's always interesting to hear several points of view." Finally, correct in a calm, positive, and friendly manner.

3. *Handle problem behaviors in an effective manner.* For example, when an employee disagrees, complains, or argues, do not take it personally and do not let it ruffle your feathers. Say, "You've got a good point," even if you disagree with the employee, or ask the employee to discuss the matter with you after class. Make sure that you use a warm but businesslike tone of voice. In this type of situation, you may also want to use some humor, as long as you are not being sarcastic or patronizing to the

[3]The following six paragraphs are adapted from Karen Eich Drummond, "Developing and Conducting Training for Foodservice Employees" (audiocassette), 1992. Courtesy of the American Dietetic Association.

❧ corporate profile

ARBY'S

Arby's is one of today's leading fast-food chains. The Raffel Brothers opened it in 1964 as the only Arby's. Today, the company has expanded and there are more than 3000 restaurants worldwide.

Arby's has been in a constant struggle for corporate improvement, which is not uncommon in the fast-food industry. There is no doubt that in the hospitality industry, maintaining good employees is an ongoing battle. In an effort to build employee loyalty, a series of multilingual training tapes were produced.

These training tapes are available in five languages: Spanish, Chinese, French, Vietnamese, and Russian. Each tape contains common courtesies and greetings that can help managers to communicate with workers from all types of backgrounds. All of the tapes also include key words for managers, such as "Please clean this area," "Do you need a break?" and "Thank you." The tapes have English translations and subtitles so that employees can learn the English language.

employee. When an employee seems to be monopolizing the class, summarize what he or she has said and move on to the next topic. Another technique to use is to ask other employees to participate. When employees are having private conversations during class, try making eye contact, moving closer, and asking one of them a question. These techniques are often helpful in ending these distracting conversations.

4. *Avoid time-wasters.* Always start on time and stay on track. Classes sometimes get off track; when this happens, it is important to redirect the group back to your outline. Another time-waster is passing out handouts during class. This can easily be avoided by passing out handouts either as employees come in or leave.

5. *Facilitate employee participation and discussions* by doing the following: Ask questions that are neither too easy nor too hard for the employees to answer. Express appreciation to participants who ask questions or make comments, especially for those that are interesting or insightful. Make a comment, such as "Thank you for bringing that to my attention." Never criticize anyone for contributing. Paraphrase what someone has said so that the employee knows that he or she has been understood and the other employees get a short summary. Bring into the discussion employees who are not participating. Energize a discussion by being funny or asking the group for more participation. Ask employees to clarify their comments when you or the employees are not sure of their meaning. Summarize the major points or different viewpoints being discussed.

6. Use visual aids to avoid referring constantly to notes. There are certain rules for using visual aids effectively. First, do not block the visual aid and do not put your back to employees when using the visual aid. Next, talk to the employees, not the visual. Do not read your visual; paraphrase what it says. After you have explained a visual's message, remove it from view. When using an overhead projector, turn the

The multicultural training tapes were put together in an effort to build employee loyalty by treating workers of varying ethnicities as team members. The tapes give job instructions in native languages, with English translations following. In today's labor force, 30 percent of workers speak languages other than English at home. Lynne Weisenfels is the director of training and development for the Atlanta-based roast-beef-sandwich chain. She explains: "Every indication is that diversity in our industry will increase as the white workforce drops in numbers, and if we are going to be the industry of choice, we'd better have a way of communicating with this huge multicultural workforce."

The key to success in the future is through caring. Workers want to know that they have an employer who cares for them personally. When a worker knows that their employer is acting in the best interest of their welfare, they are more willing to be loyal. Not many restaurant chains offer training tapes in a variety of languages. It is important to demonstrate right from the start that your workers are valued and that you want them to succeed.

Source: "Arby's deploys five multilingual training tapes to build loyalty," *Nation's Restaurant News*, Vol. 34, No. 21, May 22, 2000; also at www.arbys.com/arb01.html.

lamp off when not in use, use a pen to direct attention to one part of the transparency, and place a sheet of paper on the transparency to show information a little at a time. When using a flipchart, face the audience and turn pages with the hand nearest the flipchart. Flip to a blank page when not in use.

Check Your Knowledge

1. Why is evaluating important?
2. Briefly explain the four steps of job instruction training.

Retraining

Training people for jobs does not always take care of their training needs. Further training is necessary in several instances.

One such situation arises when changes are made that affect the job. You might make some changes in the menu. You might put in a different type of cash register. Your boss might decide to use paper and plastic on the hospital trays instead of china and glasses. Your food and beverage director might decide to install an automatic dispensing system for all the bars.

When such changes affect the work of your people, it is your responsibility to tell them about the changes and see that they are trained to deal with them. If the changes are large, you might develop new performance standards, procedural sheets, and training plans and run your people through additional training sessions. If the changes are small, such as a new kind of coffeemaker or a new linen supplier with different routines and delivery times, they still affect people's work, but in the usual daily rush it is easy to overlook letting people know or to assume they will find out and know what to do. Even posting a notice or a set of instructions is not enough; a person-to-person message is in order, with show-and-tell as called for.

It is as important to keep your people's knowledge and skills up-to-date as it is to train them right in the first place. They cannot do the job well if the job has changed, and it makes them feel bad to know that no one has thought to tell them of the change and show them what to do.

A second kind of training need arises when an employee's performance drops below par, when he or she is simply not meeting minimal performance standards. It may be caused by various things—difficulties involving the job itself or other people, personal problems outside the job, or simply job burnout—disenchantment with doing the same old thing day after day and lack of motivation to do it well any more.

Suppose that Sally's performance as a cocktail waitress has deteriorated noticeably in the last few weeks and there have been customer complaints of poor service, ill temper, and rudeness. The old-style manager, of course, would be on Sally's back yelling at her and ordering her to shape up, but threats and coercion are not going to do the trick. Nor will it help to ignore the problem. A person whose previous work has been up to standard is usually well aware of what is happening. If you tolerate Sally's poor performance, it will reduce her respect for you, for the job, and for herself.

This situation calls for a positive one-on-one approach, generally referred to as **coaching.** Coaching is a two-part process involving observation of employee performance and conversation focusing on job performance between the manager and the employee. It is discussed in detail in Chapter 9.

A few other situations also call for retraining. For example, you may notice that a worker has never really mastered a particular technique (such as cleaning in the corners of rooms) *or has gone back to an old bad habit* (such as picking up clean glasses with the fingers inside the rims). In such cases, you simply retrain the person in the techniques involved.

In other instances, people themselves may ask for further training. If you have good relationships with your people, they will feel free to do this, and of course, you should comply. It is testimony to your good leadership that they feel free to ask and that they want to improve their performance.

Orientation

Orientation is the prejob phase of training. It introduces each new employee to the job and workplace as soon as he or she reports for work. It is not uncommon in the hospitality industry for people to be put to work without any orientation at all: "Here is your workstation; do what Virginia tells you." You don't even know what door to come in and out of and where the rest rooms are, and on payday everyone else gets paid and you don't, and you wonder if you have been fired and didn't even know it.

The primary purpose of orientation is to tell new staff members (1) what they want to know, and (2) what the company wants them to know. As with any training, it takes time—the new person's time and the supervisor's time—anywhere from 30 minutes to most of the day.

Nevertheless, it is worth the time needed to do it and to do it well. It can reduce employee anxiety and confusion, ease the adjustment, and tip the balance between leaving and staying during the first critical days. In addition, it provides an excellent opportunity to create positive employee attitudes toward the company and the job.

Therefore, you have two goals for an orientation:

1. Communicating information: getting the messages through
2. Creating a positive response to company and job

Let us look at the second one first because it makes the first one easier and because it is more likely to be overlooked.

Creating a Positive Response

If you do not have an orientation for each new employee, somebody else will—your other workers. Their orientation will be quite different from yours, and it may have a negative impact. They want to give a new person the inside story, the lowdown, and it will include everybody's pet gripes and negative feelings about the company and warnings to watch out for this and that, and your new worker will begin to have

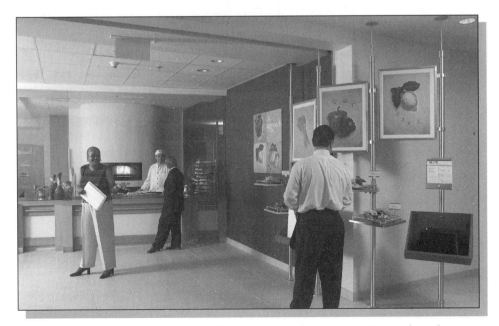

Orientation seeks to give important job information and creates a positive image about the company and job. (Courtesy of Sodexho)

an uneasy feeling that this is not such a good place to work. People are always more ready to believe their co-workers, their peer group, than their boss, so it is important for you to make your impact first. Then, in the days that follow, you must live up to what you have told them in your orientation or their co-workers may undermine the impression you have made.

You want to create an image of the company as a good place to work. You also want to foster certain feelings in your new people: that they are needed and wanted, that they and their jobs are important to the company. You want to create the beginnings of a sense of belonging, of fitting in. You want to reduce their anxieties and promote a feeling of confidence and security about the company and the job and their ability to do it. This is the beginning of establishing that positive work environment discussed in Chapter 5.

You do all this not only through what you say but how you say it and even more through your own attitude. You speak as one human being to another; you do not talk down from a power position. You avoid Theory X assumptions; you assume that each is a person worthy of your concern and attention who can and will work well for you. You do not lay down the law; you inform. You treat orientation as a way of filling *their* need to know rather than *your* need to have them follow the rules (although it is that, too). You accentuate the positive.

If you can make a favorable impact, reduce anxieties, and create positive attitudes and feelings, new employees will probably stay through the critical first seven days. It will be much easier for you to train them, and they will become productive much more quickly.

Communicating the Necessary Information

Employees want to know about their pay rate, overtime, days and hours of work, where the rest rooms are, where to park, where to go in and out, where the phone is and whether they can make or receive calls, where their workstation is, to whom they report, break times, meals, and whether their brother can come to the Christmas party. The company wants them to know all this plus all the rules and regulations they must follow; company policy on holidays, sick days, benefits, and so on; uniform and grooming codes; how to use the time clock; emergency procedures; key control; withholding of taxes; and other boring and bewildering things. They must also fill out the necessary forms and get their name tags, and they should have a tour of the facility and be introduced to the people they will work with.

It is a lot to give all at once. It is best to give it one-on-one rather than waiting until you have several new people and giving a group lecture. A lecture is too formal, and waiting several days may be too late.

You can have it all printed in a booklet, commonly called an **employee handbook**. But you cannot hand people a book of rules and expect them to read and absorb it. It will really turn them off if you ask them first thing to read a little booklet about things they cannot do. *Tell them.* Give them the booklet to take home.

An orientation checklist, shown in Figure 8.6, is an excellent tool for telling your employees what they need to know. It lists sample topics covered during an orientation program, such as how to request a day off. These topics are grouped into

INTRODUCTION TO THE COMPANY

_____   Welcome.

_____   Describe company briefly, including history, operation (type of menu, service, hours of operation, etc.) and goals (be sure to mention the importance of quality service).

_____   Show how company is structured or organized.

POLICIES AND PROCEDURES

_____   Explain dress code and who furnishes uniforms.

_____   Describe where to park.

_____   How to sign in and out and when.

_____   Assign locker and explain its use.

_____   Review amount of sick time, holiday time, personal time, and vacation time as applicable.

_____   Review benefits.

_____   Explain how to call in if unable to come to work.

_____   Explain procedure to request time off.

_____   Review salary and when and where to pick up check, as well as who can pick up the employee's paycheck. If applicable, explain policy on overtime and reporting of tips.

_____   Discuss rules on personal telephone use.

_____   Explain smoking policy.

_____   Explain meal policy, including when and where food can be eaten.

_____   Review disciplinary guidelines.

_____   Explain guest relations policy.

_____   Review teamwork policy.

_____   Explain property removal policy.

_____   Explain responsible service of alcohol, if applicable.

_____   Explain Equal Employment Opportunity policy.

_____   Discuss promotional and transfer opportunities.

_____   Explain professional conduct policy.

_____   Explain guidelines for safe food handling, safety in the kitchen, and what to do in case of a fire.

_____   Explain notice requirement if leaving your job.

THE NEW JOB

_____   Review job description and standards of performance.

_____   Review daily work schedule including break times.

_____   Review hours of work and days off. Show where schedule is posted.

_____   Explain how and when employee will be evaluated.

_____   Explain probationary period.

_____   Explain training program, including its length.

_____   Describe growth opportunities.

_____   Give tour of operation and introduce to other managers and co-workers.

FIGURE 8.6   Sample orientation checklist.

three categories: "Introduction to the Company," "Policies and Procedures," and "The New Job." One benefit of using such a checklist is that it ensures consistency among managers and supervisors who are conducting orientation and makes it unlikely that any topic will be forgotten.

Similarly, you cannot expect new employees to soak up everything you say. As you are aware, communication is a two-way process, and you can send message after message but you cannot control the receiving end. They will listen selectively, picking out what interests them. Try to give each item an importance *for them*. (For example: "You can get any entrée under $5 free." "The employee parking lot is the only place that isn't crowded." "The cook will poison your lunch if you come in through the kitchen.") Give reasons. ("The money withheld goes to the government.") Phrase things positively. ("You may smoke on breaks in the employee lounge" rather than "Smoking is forbidden on the job.")

Watch your workers carefully to make sure that you are understood, and repeat as necessary. Encourage questions. ("Can I clarify anything?") Be sure you cover everything (use a checklist). Even so, you will need to repeat some things during the next few days.

Taking the trouble to start new employees off on the right foot will make things easier as you begin their training for the job. They will feel more positive, less anxious, and more receptive to the training to come.

Overcoming Obstacles to Learning

When you think of the many barriers to communication that we discovered in Chapter 4, it should not be surprising that training should have its share of obstacles. Some of them are learning problems, and some have to do with teaching, the trainer, or the training program. (You can see the two halves of the communication process again: sending and receiving the message.)

One problem for the learner may be fear. Some people are afraid of training, especially if they did not finish school and never really learned how to learn. This kind of anxiety clouds the mind and makes learning difficult. Some people have fear as their basic motivation. Contrary to prevalent belief in this industry, fear is usually a barrier to learning, not a motivator. It interferes with concentration and inhibits performance. People who are afraid of the boss or the instructor will not ask questions. They will say that they understand when they do not.

You can reduce fear and anxiety with a positive approach. Begin by putting the new employee at ease, conveying your confidence that he or she can learn the job without any trouble. Everyone will learn faster and better if you can reduce their anxieties and increase their confidence. Work with the trainee informally, as one human being to another, and try to establish a relationship of trust. Praise progress and achievement.

Some people have little natural motivation to learn, such as ambition, need for money, desire to excel, desire to please, and self-satisfaction. If they don't see anything in the training for them, they will learn slowly, they will not get things straight, and they will forget quickly.

There are several ways of increasing motivation.

1. *Emphasize whatever is of value to the learner:* how it will help in the job, increase tips, or make things easier. As you teach each procedure, point out why you do it as you do, why it is important, and how it will help.

2. *Make the program form a series of small successes for the learner.* Each success increases confidence and stimulates the desire for more success.

3. *Perhaps the most important motivator is to build in incentives and rewards for achievement as successive steps are mastered.* These can range from praise, a progress chart, and public recognition (a different-colored apron, an achievement pin) to a bonus for completing the training.

Some people are not as bright as others. They may have trouble with the pace and level of the instruction: too fast, too much at once, too abstract, too many big words. They may be capable of learning if the teaching is adjusted to their learning ability. *One-to-one instruction, patience,* and *sensitivity* are the keys here. Often, things learned slowly are better retained.

Some people are lazy and indifferent. And if they are lazy about learning the job, they will probably be lazy about doing it. Others will resist training because they think they know it all. They expect to be bored and they pay little attention to the instruction. These are potential problem types and they will be either a challenge or a real headache.

Sometimes we do not deal with people as they are. We assume that they know something they do not know, or we assume that they don't know something they do know. Either way, we lose their attention and their desire or ability to learn what we want them to learn. To overcome this obstacle, we need to *approach training from the learner's point of view.* Instead of teaching tasks, teach people. Put yourself in their place, find out what they know, teach what they do not know, and interest them in learning it.

Keep it simple, concrete, practical, and real. Use words they can understand: familiar words, key words they can hang an idea on. Involve all their senses: seeing, hearing, feeling, experiencing. It is said that people remember 10 percent of what they read, 20 percent of what they hear, 30 percent of what they see, 50 percent of what they hear and see, and they remember more of what they do than what they are told. Teach by show, tell, and do—hands-on.

Sometimes the training program is the problem. If it is abstract, academic, impersonal, or unrealistic, it will not get across. If you have not carefully defined what you want the trainee to learn and you have no way of measuring when learning has taken place, the trainee may never learn the job well. If the training sessions are poorly organized, or if the training materials are inadequate or inappropriate, or if the setting is wrong (noisy, subject to constant interruptions, lacking in equipment or other on-the-job realism), the sessions will be ineffective. If the program does not provide incentives to succeed, the program itself will not succeed.

Sometimes the instructor causes the learning problems. Trainers need to know the job well enough to teach it. They need to be good communicators, able to use words other people will understand, sensitive enough to see when they are not getting through. They need to be able to look at the task from the learner's point of view, a very difficult thing when you know it so well that it is second nature to you. They need patience. They need leadership qualities: If people do not respond to the trainer as a leader, they do not learn willingly from that person.

Above all, trainers must not have a negative attitude toward those they are training. Never look down on either the person or the job, and take care to avoid Theory X assumptions (people are lazy, dislike work, must be coerced, controlled, and threatened). Assume the best of everyone.

When a mistake is made, correct the action rather than the person, and correct by helping, not by criticizing. A useful technique is to compliment before correcting. Say, for example, "You are holding the bottle exactly right and you have poured exactly the right amount of wine. What you need to do to avoid spilling is to raise the mouth and turn the bottle slightly before you draw it away from the glass" (instead of "Look what you did, you dribbled wine all over the table; don't *do* that, I *told* you to raise the mouth!"). Emphasize what is right, not what is wrong.

Be patient. Hang onto your temper. Praise progress and achievement. Think success. Cheer your people on as they learn their jobs, and stick with them until they have reached your goals.

❧ key points

1. Training means teaching people how to do their jobs. You may instruct and guide a trainee toward learning knowledge, skills, or attitudes.

2. Three kinds of training are needed in hospitality operations: job instruction, retraining, and orientation.

3. Training has the following benefits: more time to manage, less absenteeism and less turnover, less tension, higher consistency of product and service, lower costs, happier customers and more of them, and enhancement of your career. By making sure that your employees know what to do, tension is reduced, morale and job satisfaction are boosted, the number of accidents and injuries are reduced, and your workers have a better chance of advancing.

4. The problems involved in training are real: urgent need for trained workers, lack of time, lack of money, short-term workers, diversity of workers, kinds of jobs and skills, complexity of some jobs, and not knowing exactly what you want your people to do and how.

5. The logical person to train your people is you, the supervisor. It is your responsibility, whether you delegate it or do it yourself. Training is one of those obligations to your people that goes with your job—giving them the tools and knowledge to do theirs.

6. Employees learn best when they are actively involved in the learning process, when the training is relevant and practical, when the training materials are or-

ganized and presented in small chunks, when the setting is informal and quiet, when the trainer is good, and when employees receive feedback on their performance and reward for achievement.

7. Figure 8.1 portrays the steps involved in developing and carrying out a training plan.

8. Once the formal training process is completed, there is still one very important step: evaluation. Formative evaluation uses observation, interviews, and surveys to monitor training while it is going on. Summative evaluation measures the results of the training after the program is completed, looking at it in five ways: reaction, knowledge, behavior, attitudes, and productivity.

9. The procedure for job instruction training is illustrated in Figure 8.5.

10. Classroom training may be used at times for job instruction or retraining. Teaching in a classroom requires certain skills: Be aware of and use appropriate body language and speech, convey respect and appreciation, use informal and familiar language, correct in a positive and friendly manner, handle problem behaviors effectively, avoid time-wasters, facilitate employee participation and discussions, and use visual aids properly.

11. Retraining is needed when changes are made that affect the job, when an employee's performance drops below par, or when a worker simply has never really mastered a particular technique.

12. Orientation is the prejob phase of training that introduces each new employee to the job and workplace. Your goals for orientation are to communicate necessary information, such as where to park and when to pick up a paycheck, and also to create a positive response to the company and job.

13. Some keys to training include the following: Use a positive approach to reduce fear and anxiety, look at ways to increase employee motivation, such as building in incentives and rewards as steps are mastered; adjust the teaching to the employee's learning ability; don't assume anything; approach training from the learner's point of view; keep it simple and practical; and make sure that the trainer is doing a good job.

❧ key terms

adult learning theory
big sister/big brother or buddy
    system
coaching
employee handbook
formative evaluation
job instruction
job instruction training
learning

orientation
pretest
retraining
summative evaluation
teaching methods
training
training objective
training plan

❧ review questions

Answer each question in complete sentences. Read each question carefully and make sure that you answer all parts of the question. Organize your answer using more than one paragraph when appropriate.

1. Define the three kinds of training needed in hospitality operations.
2. State why supervisors find it hard to train and the benefits that training can bring.
3. Why is the supervisor the logical person to do training?
4. How do employees learn best?
5. Discuss the steps involved in developing and implementing a training plan.
6. Give an example of formative and summative evaluation.
7. If you had to teach an employee how to clean a hotel room, how could you use job instruction training to do so?
8. List 10 tips for training in a classroom (group) situation.
9. When is retraining necessary?
10. Why is orientation important? What happens during orientation?
11. Discuss briefly six keys to successful training.

❧ activities and applications

1. **Discussion Questions**
   - In your opinion, what is the most serious consequence of not training? What is the most persuasive reason for not training? How can you weigh one against the other?
   - Why can't people simply be trained by working alongside another employee until they learn the job? In what kinds of jobs would this work best? In what situations would it be impossible or undesirable?
   - Have you ever started a new job and received little or no orientation? Describe what kinds of orientation programs you've received from past or present employers. What were some of their good features? Was orientation helpful?
   - A server for a well-known Italian restaurant chain has finished her training. As the supervisor, how might you evaluate her training?

2. **Brainstorming: My Favorite Teacher**

As a class, brainstorm the personal qualities and characteristics of teachers you've had in the past who you thought were excellent at teaching. How does your list compare to the list in Table 8.2?

3. Group Activity: Cost/Benefit Analysis

Cost/benefit analysis is a way to evaluate training by comparing its costs to its benefits to see which are greater. In groups of four students, make a list of possible costs (such as the trainer's and trainees' salaries) involved in training kitchen staff about preventing accidents. Next, make a list of the possible benefits to be derived from this training. Which costs and benefits did you list that can be quantified into dollars and cents? Under what circumstances might an accident-prevention program have more benefits than costs?

4. Group Activity: Develop a Training Plan

The general manager at Nighty-Night Hotels suspects a problem with sexual harassment among some staff members. He needs a training plan to educate staff on this topic. Form groups of four and discuss how you would go about using Figure 8.1 (steps 1 through 4) to develop such a training plan.

5. Case Study: A Quick-Fix Training Program

Tom is assistant manager of a restaurant having about 40 people on the payroll. He reports to Alex, the manager. Tom has full charge of the restaurant on the 7-to-3 shift, figures the weekly payroll, takes care of all the ordering and receiving, and carries out special assignments for Alex. He couldn't be any busier. Then this morning Alex handed him the biggest headache yet.

"Tom," said Alex, "things are going downhill here and we've got to do something. Sales are off, profits are down, our employee turnover is high and getting higher, and customer complaints are going up. They complain about the food, the service, the drinks, the prices, everything. I really don't think any of our people are doing the best they could, and maybe some more training would help. Look into it for me, would you, and see if you can figure out how you and I between us can find time to train our people to do a better job? I want to start tomorrow—I've got two new waiters and a grill cook coming in at 10:00 A.M." And he handed Tom a copy of a book called *Supervision in the Hospitality Industry* and told him to read Chapter 8.

QUESTIONS

1. What can Tom come up with between now and tomorrow morning? Is Alex expecting the impossible of Tom?
2. What kind of training can he provide for the three new people starting to work at 10:00 A.M.? What might he do that he was not doing before?
3. What should Tom and Alex consider in deciding which category of current employees should be trained first?
4. How can Alex and Tom sell the entire process to current employees and get their cooperation?
5. How can either Alex or Tom find time to carry out the training, and when should it be carried out in relation to employee time?
6. Should Tom recommend bringing in outside help? Why or why not?
7. How can the two of them determine what training is needed?
8. How long do you think it will be before they can expect perceptible results?
9. What kind of long-range, permanent training plans and policies should Tom recommend?

Evaluating Performance

Among the five reasons why people do poor work or leave their jobs entirely is that they don't know how well they are doing. This chapter is about finding out how well they are doing and telling them about it.

Good supervisors are out among their people every day, observing, coaching, evaluating: "Hey, that's a great job!" "Here, let me show you how to do that." "Look, there's a quicker way." Informal evaluation or coaching is an everyday part of their involvement with their people. It goes with getting the work done, achieving the results they are responsible for. They may not think of it as evaluation, but they are on the lookout all the time to see if people are doing what they are supposed to do in the way they are supposed to do it. And if they have good human relations skills, they let their people know in a positive, upbeat fashion.

Unfortunately, the hospitality industry also has its share of supervisors who are not long on human relations skills. They may be out there every day, too, watching, checking up, looking for mistakes, and getting after people when they are doing something wrong. They take a totally negative approach, and their people receive continuous negative evaluations or none at all. If they are doing all right, the boss sees no need to comment. However, the absence of negatives does not add up to a positive. This makes people uneasy.

We need a systematic approach to evaluation that will let people know how well they are doing and help them to improve. We cannot get along without the day-by-day approach, but we need to stop and assess performance over a period of time. This provides a chance to recognize achievement, point out paths to improvement, and formalize it all for the record.

This chapter deals with day-to-day coaching and periodic performance evaluations and how they can contribute to increased production, employee satisfaction, and supervisory success. It will help you to:

∾ Describe the concept of coaching, and outline the guidelines of effective coaching.

∾ Explain the complementary relationship between ongoing day-by-day evaluation and periodic performance reviews.

∾ Enumerate the purposes and benefits of performance reviews.

∾ Outline the steps of the performance review process.

∾ Explain common hurdles to evaluating employee performance fairly and objectively.

∾ Describe how to handle an appraisal interview, and list mistakes that commonly occur during appraisal interviews.

∾ Explain how follow-up can extend the benefits of performance review.

Success in foodservice and lodging operations depends on the individual performance of many people. We have said this often. To get the results you are responsible for, all your workers must be performing up to standard—to the standard you have set and trained them for. Are they? That is what evaluation is all about. First, we look at coaching, then performance evaluation.

> No hotel can have excellent operations without excellent employees, and that requires excellent human resources practices. In today's competitive environment, high-performing organizations have learned how to deploy human resources practices to enhance competitive advantage. The five categories of the best practices are:
>
> 1. Leader development
> 2. Training and knowledge building
> 3. Employee empowerment
> 4. Employee recognition
> 5. Cost management
>
> *Source:* Cathy A. Enz and Judy A. Siguaw, "Best practices in human resources," *Cornell Hotel and Restaurant Administration Quarterly.* Vol. 41, No. 1, pp. 48–61, February 2000.

Coaching

Coaching is a two-part process involving observation of employee performance and conversation focusing on job performance between the manager and the employee. Coaching can take place informally at the employee's workstation or formally by having coaching sessions in an office. It is different from **counseling,** a process used to help employees who are performing poorly because of personal problems such as substance abuse.

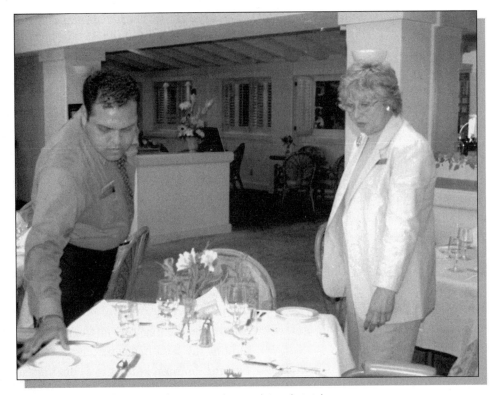

The first step in coaching is to observe employees doing their jobs.

The overall purpose of coaching is to evaluate work performance and then to encourage optimum work performance either by reinforcing good performance or confronting and redirecting poor performance. Coaching therefore provides your employees with regular feedback and support about their job performance and helps you to understand exactly what your employees need to know. It also prevents small problems from turning into big ones that may require much more attention later.

If coaching employees is so beneficial, why do supervisors often avoid it? Possible reasons are:

∾ Lack of time (In most cases, coaching requires only a few minutes.)

∾ Fear of confronting an employee with a concern about his or her performance (A mistake—the problem not faced may only get worse, not better.)

∾ Assuming that the employee already knows that he or she is doing a good job, so why bother saying anything? (Your employee would love to hear it anyway.)

∾ Little experience coaching (You can start practicing now.)

∾ Assuming that the employee will ask questions when appropriate and does not need feedback (Many employees are too proud or shy to ask questions.)

The first step in coaching is to observe employees doing their jobs. Be sure you are completely familiar with pertinent performance standards and job duties. If an employee is doing the job well, do not hesitate to say so. Everyone likes to be told that they are doing a good job, so praise employees as often as you can. Work on catching your employees doing things right, and then use these steps.

1. Describe the specific action you are praising.
2. Explain the results or effects of the actions.
3. State your appreciation.

In some cases you may want to write a letter of thanks and make sure that a copy goes into the employee's personnel file. You could instead use a standard form, which is quicker to complete.

When observing employees, sometimes you'll see what appears to be a problem with performance. If Ted left a pallet of canned goods outside the storeroom, ask him: "Is there a reason why these canned goods aren't put away yet?" If Sally isn't using the new procedure for cleaning flatware, ask her, "Are you aware of the new procedure for washing flatware?" before you assume that she is trying to get away with something. It could be that Ted stopped putting the canned goods away when a delivery of milk (which has to be put in the refrigerator immediately) came in, or perhaps Sally was on vacation when the cleaning procedure was changed. Consider the following questions *before* correcting an employee.

∾ Does the employee know what is supposed to be done, and why?
∾ Are there any reasons for poor performance that the employee can't control, such as inadequate equipment?
∾ How serious are the consequences of this problem?
∾ Has the employee been spoken to about this concern before?

By asking questions before you point a finger at someone, you help maintain the self-respect of the employee. After asking questions, if it is obvious to you that a correction is needed, be careful not to correct one employee in front of another. No one likes being corrected in front of his or her peers. Arrange to talk privately with the employee to define the performance problem, agree on why it is happening, make your standards clear, and work with the employee to set goals for improvement.

Let's say that Kim's performance as a cocktail waitress has deteriorated noticeably in the last few weeks and there have been customer complaints of poor service, ill temper, and rudeness. If you tolerate her poor performance, it will reduce her respect for you, for the job, and for herself. So you arrange to talk to her privately and try to get her to do most of the talking. You get Kim to tell you what is wrong and let her know how you perceive the problem as well. The goal is to resolve the problem, and you encourage her to make her own suggestions for doing this. This leads to her commitment to improve. You make sure that she understands the performance you expect, and you get her to set her own improvement goals: measurable performance goals such as a specific reduction in customer complaints within a certain period of time.

If the problem is related to the job, you do what you can to solve it. For instance, one fast-food employee's poor performance turned out to be caused by a large puddle of water in which she had to stand while working. The supervisor had the plumbing fixed and that solved the performance problem. Kim's problem may have an equally simple solution.

If the problem involves other people on the job, the solution may be more complex, but you do everything you can to resolve it. In the meantime you have a management obligation to help Kim meet performance standards.

If the problem is personal, it may help Kim to talk about it, but you cannot solve it for her. You can only listen in order to help her overcome its interfering with her work.

If the problem is burnout, you may be able to motivate her with some change of duties and responsibilities that would add variety and interest to her job. In any case, she will probably respond to your supportive approach, and when she has set her own goals, she will feel a commitment to achieving them.

When goals have been set that you both agree to, establish checkpoints at which you meet to discuss progress (get Kim to set the times—perhaps once a week or every two weeks). You express your confidence in her ability to meet her goals, make it clear that you are available when needed, and put her on her own.

During the improvement period, you observe discreetly from the sidelines, but you do not intervene. Kim is in charge of her own improvement; you are simply staying available. You compliment her when you see her handle a difficult customer; you give her all the positive feedback you can; you keep her aware of your support.

You wait for the checkpoints to discuss the negatives, and you let Kim bring them up. You use the checkpoints as informal problem-solving sessions in which you again encourage Kim to do most of the talking and generate most of the ideas.

To summarize, make sure that a counseling session includes the following:

1. Speak in private with the employee. Be relaxed and friendly.
2. Express in a calm manner your concern about the specific aspect of job performance you feel needs to be improved. Describe the concern in behavioral terms and explain the effect it has. Do so in a positive manner.
3. Ask the employee for his or her thoughts and opinions, including possible solutions. Discuss together these solutions and agree mutually on a course of action and a time frame.
4. Ask the employee to restate what has been agreed upon to check on understanding. State your confidence in the employee's ability to turn the situation around.

At a later time, you should follow up and make sure that the performance concern has been addressed. Table 9.1 lists general coaching guidelines.

In many operations, you will be asked to document (meaning you will need to write on paper) coaching sessions. Some supervisors document coaching sessions in a supervisor's logbook, which is much like a diary of day-to-day events in the operation. Depending on the policy, coaching sessions may be recorded on forms intended for that purpose. Any documentation of coaching sessions should include the date and place of the coaching and a summary of the coaching session. Although you may feel this is time-consuming, documentation is essential if you ever need to terminate an employee or simply to do yearly performance evaluations, the next topic.

TABLE 9.1   ᴄᴏ   General Coaching Guidelines

1. Be specific about the employee's job performance.
2. Focus on the employee's behavior, not the employee. Always maintain the self-respect of the employee. To reduce employee defensiveness, use "I" statements rather than "you" statements.
3. Reinforce or confront job performance issues as soon as possible after observation. However, if you are at all angry or upset, do not confront the employee until you have cooled down.
4. Praise in public, correct in private. We are all very sensitive about being told in front of our peers that we are doing something wrong. Unless the error could have serious consequences, wait until you can at least take the employee aside long enough to discuss it.
5. Explain the impact of the employee's job performance on the work group and the entire operation.
6. Be a coach, not a drill sergeant.
7. Allow some time each day to walk around and coach employees.
8. Document coaching sessions.

Check Your Knowledge

1. What is *coaching?* What is the overall purpose of coaching?

Essentials of Performance Evaluation

In management terms, the phrase **performance evaluation** refers to a periodic review and assessment of each employee's performance during a given period: three months, six months, a year, or a certain number of hours worked. The assessment is recorded, usually on a company rating form, and is then discussed with the employee in an interview that answers the perennial question, "How am I doing?" and explores the possibilities for improvement.

Other terms used for this process are **performance appraisal** and **performance review.** We will use these terms to distinguish the system of periodic evaluation from the informal performance evaluation that is a daily part of the supervisor's job.

Performance reviews are not always used for hourly workers in the hospitality industry. This is partly because supervisors are so busy, partly because so many workers do not stay long enough to be evaluated, and partly because so many operations are under the immediate direction of the owner. But the practice is increasing, especially in chain operations. It is part of their general thrust toward maintaining consistency of product and service, improving quality and productivity, and developing the human resources of the organization.

A performance review does not substitute in any way for the informal evaluations you make in checking on work in progress. Where things happen so fast, where so many people are involved and so much is at stake in customer satisfaction, you cannot just train your people, turn them loose, and evaluate their performance six months later. You must be on the scene every day to see how they are doing, who is not doing well, and how you can help those who are not measuring up. This is an informal blend of evaluation and on-the-job coaching and support to maintain or improve performance right now and to let people know when they are doing a good job. Performance reviews every six months or so cannot substitute for it. Feedback must be immediate to be effective.

In fact, if you had to choose between periodic reviews and daily evaluations, the daily evaluations would win hands down. But it isn't a choice; one complements the other.

Purpose and Benefits

If you are evaluating people every day, why do you need a performance review? There are several good reasons or purposes.

1. *In your day-to-day evaluations you tend to concentrate on the people who need to improve,* the people you have trouble with, the squeaky wheels who drive you crazy. You may also watch the outstanding performers, because they make you look good and because you are interested in keeping them happy and in developing them. But you seldom pay attention to the middle-of-the-road people. They come in every day, they are never late, they do their work, they don't cause any problems, but they never get any recognition because they do not stand out in any way. Yet they really are the backbone of the entire operation and they ought to be recognized. Everybody who is performing satisfactorily should be recognized. In a performance review you evaluate everybody, so you will notice these people and give them the recognition they deserve.

2. *Looking back over a period of time gives you a different perspective.* You can see how people have improved. You will also look at how they do the entire job and not just the parts they do poorly or very well. You evaluate their total performance.

3. *A performance review is for the record.* It is made in writing, and other people—the personnel department, your own supervisor, someone in another department looking for a person to fill another job—may use it. It may be used as data in a disciplinary action or in defending a discrimination case. It may be and should be used as a basis for recognition and reward.

4. A performance review requires you to get together with each worker to discuss the results. *It lets people know how well they are doing.* You may forget to tell them day by day, but you cannot escape it in a scheduled review. And if you know you will have to do ratings and interviews at evaluation time, you may pay more attention to people's performances day by day.

The evaluation of employee performance is intended to be a continuous communication between employees and supervisors and to have several purposes, including the following:

1. To evaluate each employee's effectiveness in performing assigned duties and responsibilities

2. To identify factors that can improve job performance

3. To clarify performance standards as they relate to the current job description

4. To assist employees in developing additional knowledge, skills, and abilities for job advancement

5. To recognize exceptional performance

6. To document shortcomings or substandard performance

7. To determine retention of an employee at the end of the probationary period

8. To identify training and development needs

Source: Human Resources, Southwest Missouri State University, Springfield, MO, December 12, 2000.

5. *A performance review not only looks backward, it looks ahead.* It is an opportunity to plan how the coming period can be used to improve performance and solve work problems. It is a chance for setting improvement goals, and if you involve the worker in the goal setting, it increases that person's commitment to improve. The improvement goals then become a subject for review at the next appraisal, giving the entire procedure meaningful continuity.

Performance reviews have many uses beyond their primary concern with evaluating and improving performance. *One is to act as the basis for an employee's salary increase.* This type of salary increase is called a **merit raise** and is based on the employee's level of performance. For example, an employee who gets an outstanding evaluation may receive a 6 percent increase, the employee who gets a satisfactory evaluation may receive a 4 percent increase, and the employee with an unsatisfactory evaluation may not receive any increase. In one survey of U.S. businesses, 75 percent of respondents reported using appraisals to determine an employee's raise.

Another use is to identify workers with potential for advancement: people you can develop to take over some of your responsibilities, people you might groom to take your place someday or recommend for a better-paying job in another department. As you know, managers have an obligation to develop their people, and a performance review is one tool for identifying people capable of doing more than they are doing now.

Other managers may use your performance reviews. Since they are a matter of record, others may use them to look for people to fill vacancies in their departments.

If they are going to be used this way, it is important that you make your evaluations as accurate and objective as you can. (It is important anyway—more on this subject later.) If someone has been promoted on the basis of your inaccurate evaluation and the promotion does not work out, you may be in hot water.

Your boss, to rate your own performance as a supervisor, may use your performance reviews. If the records show that most of your workers are poor performers, this may indicate that you are not a very good supervisor.

Performance reviews can *provide feedback on your hiring and training procedures.* When workers turn out to lack skills they should have been trained in, it may indicate that your training procedures were inadequate. Workers you hired who rate poorly in every respect reflect on your hiring practices. Both indicate areas for improvement on your part. (Good selection and training programs were discussed in Chapters 7 and 8.)

Workers who rate poorly across the board are of special concern and may be candidates for termination. Performance evaluations can help to identify such workers. If they do not respond to attempts to coach and retrain, their performance evaluations may document inadequacies to support termination and help protect your employer from discrimination charges.[1]

Finally, *performance reviews may provide the occasion for supervisors to get feedback from employees about how they feel about their job, the company, and the way they are treated.* Supervisors who are skilled interviewers and have good relationships and

[1]Performance appraisals are not enough by themselves. We discuss this subject further in Chapter 10.

open communication with their people may be able to elicit this kind of response. It takes a genuine interest plus specific questions such as "How can I help you to be more effective at your job?" "Are there problems about the work that I can help you solve?" Many people will hesitate to express anything negative for fear it will influence the boss to give them a lower rating, but questions with a positive, helpful thrust can open up some problem areas.

When carried out conscientiously and when there is constant communication between reviews, performance reviews have many benefits. They help to maintain performance standards. By telling workers how they are doing, they can remove uncertainty and improve morale. By spotlighting areas for improvement, they can focus the efforts of both worker and supervisor to bring improvement about. They can increase motivation to perform well. They provide the opportunity for improving communication and relationships between supervisor and worker. They can identify workers with unused potential and workers who ought to be terminated. They can give feedback on supervisory performance and uncover problems that are getting in the way of the work.

All these things have great potential for improving productivity, the work climate, and person-to-person relations. And all this benefits the customer, the company image as an employer, and the bottom line.

Steps in the Process

A performance review is a two-part process: making the evaluation and sharing it with the worker. There should also be a preparation phase in which both supervi-

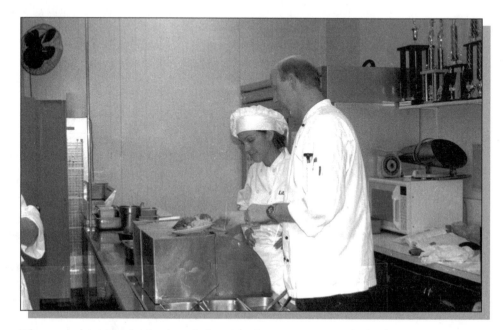

When carried out conscientiously and when there is constant communication between reviews, performance reviews have many benefits.

sors and workers become familiar with the process, and there should be follow-up to put the findings to work on the job. In all there are four steps:

1. Preparing for evaluation
2. Making the evaluation
3. Sharing it with the worker
4. Providing follow-up

Companies that use performance review systems usually give supervisors some initial training. They are told why the evaluation is important and what it will be used for: promotions, raises, further employee training, whatever objectives the company has. They are given instruction in how to use the form, how to evaluate performance fairly and objectively, and how to conduct an appraisal interview. This initiation may take the form of a briefing by the supervisor's boss, or it may be part of a companywide training program. It depends on the company.

The people being evaluated should also be prepared. They should know from the beginning that performance reviews are part of the job. Good times to mention it are in the employment interview, in orientation, and especially during training, when you can point out that they will be evaluated at review time on what they are being trained to do now. Showing people the evaluation form at this point can reinforce interest in training and spark the desire to perform well.

People must also know in advance when performance reviews will take place, and they must understand the basis for evaluation. They should be assured that they will see the completed evaluation, that they and the supervisor will discuss it together, and that they will have a chance to challenge ratings they consider unfair.

Making the Evaluation

The performance evaluation is typically formalized in an **evaluation form** that the supervisor fills out. There are probably as many different forms as there are companies that do performance reviews, but all have certain elements in common. Figures 9.1 and 9.2 are sample evaluation forms.

Performance Dimensions

An evaluation form typically lists the **performance dimensions or categories** on which each worker is to be rated. Examples include the quality and quantity of the work itself, attendance, appearance, work habits such as neatness or safety, and customer relations. The dimensions of job performance chosen for an evaluation form should be:

∾ Related to the job being evaluated
∾ Clearly defined in objective and observable terms, as in a performance standard

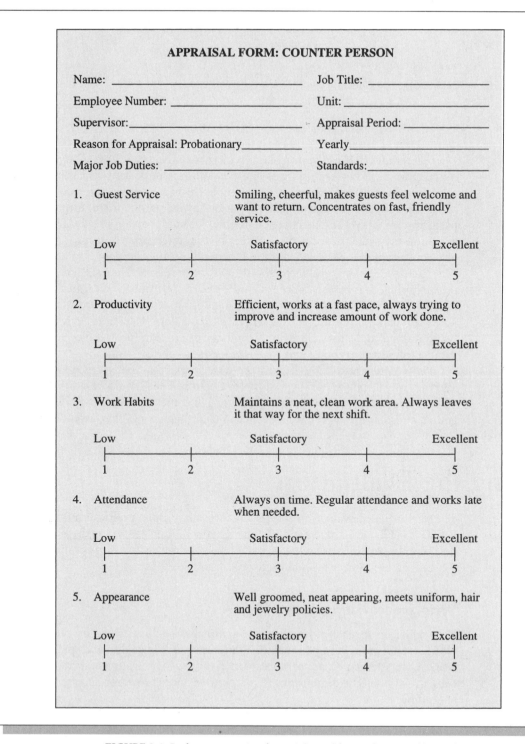

FIGURE 9-1 Performance review form. Adapted from a form used by Carl's Jr.

6. Team Oriented

Works well with others and is concerned about the entire team.

Low   Satisfactory   Excellent
├──────────┼──────────┼──────────┼──────────┤
1   2   3   4   5

7. Station Proficiency

Meets the standards of quality, proper portioning, waste control, and speed of service of each station worked.

Low   Satisfactory   Excellent
├──────────┼──────────┼──────────┼──────────┤
1   2   3   4   5

8. Safety

Works safely. Follows all safety procedures and precautions. Identifies unsafe conditions immediately.

Low   Satisfactory   Excellent
├──────────┼──────────┼──────────┼──────────┤
1   2   3   4   5

Overall Assessment: _____ Total Score: _____

_____

_____

_____

_____

Goals for Improvement for the Next Review Period. Based on the evaluation on the front of this form, develop specific improvement goals for the employee to accomplish by the next review period.

1. _____

_____

_____

2. _____

_____

_____

FIGURE 9-1 (Continued).

3. _____

_____

_____

<u>Employee's Reaction to the Performance Review.</u> Please be specific in describing your agreement or disagreement on the evaluation as well as identifying areas in need of further clarification or discussion.

_____

_____

_____

_____

_____

_____

Management Signature _____ Date _____

Employee's Signature _____ Date _____

Restaurant Manager's Signature _____ Date _____

FIGURE 9-1 (Continued).

Many evaluation forms go beyond specific performance to include such personal qualities as attitude, dependability, initiative, adaptability, loyalty, and cooperation. Such terms immediately invite personal opinion; in fact, it is hard to evaluate personal qualities in any other way. The words mean different things to different people, the qualities are not in themselves measurable, and they do not lend themselves to objective standards. Yet some of these qualities may be important in job performance. Some evaluation forms solve the problem by defining the qualities in observable, job-related terms. For instance, dependability can be defined as "comes to work on time."

Some qualities that are pleasant to have in people who work for you are not really relevant to doing a certain job. A dishmachine operator does not have to be "adaptable" to run the dishmachine. A "cooperative" bartender may cooperate with customers by serving them free drinks. "Initiative" may lead people to mix in areas

SERVER PERFORMANCE EVALUATION

Name: _____

Position: _____

Date of Hire: _____ Yearly or 60-Day Evaluation: _____

Department: _____

Please use COMMENT section whenever "Exceeds" or "Does Not Meet" is checked. POINTS: Exceeds—5, Meets—3, Does not meet—0.

Performance Standards	Exceeds	Meets	Does Not Meet
1. Stocks the service station for one serving area for one meal completely and correctly, as specified on the Service Station Procedures Sheet, in 10 minutes or less.	___ Comments:	___	___
2. Sets or resets a table properly, as shown on the Table Setting Layout Sheet, in not more than 3 minutes.	___ Comments:	___	___
3. Greets guests cordially within 5 minutes after they are seated and takes their order if time permits; if too busy, informs them that he or she will be back as soon as possible.	___ Comments:	___	___
4. Explains menu to customers: accurately describes the day's specials and, if asked, accurately answers any questions on portion size, ingredients, taste, and preparation method.	___ Comments:	___	___

Performance Standards	Exceeds	Meets	Does Not Meet
5. Takes food, wine, and beverage orders accurately and legibly for a table of up to six guests according to Guest Check Procedures; prices and totals check with 100 percent accuracy.	___ Comments:	___	___
6. Picks up order and completes plate preparation according to Plate Preparation Procedure.	___ Comments:	___	___
7. Serves a complete meal to all persons at each table in an assigned station in not more than 1 hour per table using the Tray Service Procedures.	___ Comments:	___	___
8. If asked, recommends wines appropriate to menu items selected, according to the What Wine Goes with What Food Sheet; opens and serves wines correctly as shown on the Wine Service Sheet.	___ Comments:	___	___
9. Accepts and processes payment with 100 percent accuracy as specified on the Check Payment Procedures Sheet.	___ Comments:	___	___
10. Performs side work correctly according to the Side Work Assignments Sheet and as requested.	___ Comments:	___	___
11. Operates all equipment in assigned area according to the Safety Manual.	___ Comments:	___	___

FIGURE 9-2 Performance appraisal form based on performance standards.

Performance Standards	Exceeds	Meets	Does Not Meet
12. Meets at all times the Dress Code requirements.		Comments: ___	
13. Uses at all times the sanitation procedures specified for serving personnel in the Sanitation Manual; maintains work area to score 90 percent or higher on the Sanitation Checklist.		Comments: ___	
14. Maintains a "Good" or higher rating on the Customer Relations Checklist; maintains a customer complaint ratio of less than 1 per 200 customers served.		Comments: ___	
15. Maintains a check average of not less than $7 per person at lunch and $15 per person at dinner.		Comments: ___	
16. Is absent from work less than 12 days in a year.		Comments: ___	
17. Is late to work less than 12 times in a year.		Comments: ___	
18. Can always be found in work area during work hours or supervisor knows where he or she is.		Comments: ___	
19. Attends or makes up all required meetings and training.		Comments: ___	
20. Supervisor receives positive feedback from peers with minimal complaints.		Comments: ___	

OVERALL RATING:

Outstanding Performance: 75–100 points (must meet or exceed all standards)

Good Performance: 50–74 points

Marginal Performance, Reevaluate in 60 Days: Below 50 points

EVALUATOR'S COMMENTS: _____

EMPLOYEE'S COMMENTS: Please comment freely on this evaluation.

_____
_____
_____

EMPLOYEE'S OBJECTIVES: What would you like to accomplish in the next 12 months? _____

_____
_____

EMPLOYEE'S OBJECTIVES FOR THE NEXT 12 MONTHS:

(Plan should be specific, realistic, measurable, and include target dates.)

_____
_____
_____

SIGNATURES:

_____   _____   _____
Employee   Evaluator   Reviewer

Date: _____

FIGURE 9-2 *(Continued)*.

where they have no authority or competence or to depart from standard procedures (change recipes or portion size).

Sometimes the personal qualities found on company evaluation forms are included because they are important in assessing potential for advancement. But where you are concerned only with evaluation of the performance of routine duties, it is not appropriate to include such qualities in an overall evaluation on which rewards may be based. People who polish silver or wash lettuce should not be penalized for lacking initiative. In such cases the question can be answered "NA," not applicable. Concern with promotions should not be allowed to distort an evaluation system intended primarily for other purposes.

Performance Standards

A quality evaluation form defines each performance dimension in measurable or observable terms by using performance standards (Figure 9.2). There should be standards, measurable or observable standards, wherever possible to make evaluation more objective. Unfortunately, subjective evaluations are not legally defensible if an employee for matters such as employment discrimination ever takes you to court. To be legally defensible, your evaluation of job performance should be based on measurable and objective performance standards that are communicated to employees in advance.

On the face of it, an evaluation based on performance standards may look intricate and difficult to carry out. But supervisors who have used performance standards in training and in informal day-by-day evaluations find them to be a very simple way to rate performance. Usually, they don't have to test people; they recognize performance levels from experience.

Probably not many organizations have such a system, and not all jobs lend themselves to this kind of evaluation. It is best suited to jobs where the work is repetitive and many people are doing the same job, a situation very common in hospitality operations.

Performance Ratings

Many evaluation forms use a **rating scale** ranging from outstanding to unsatisfactory performance. A common scale includes ratings of outstanding, above average, average, needs improvement, and poor. In the case of performance standards, you can simply check off that the employee either meets or does not meet the standard. In some systems, there is also a category for "exceeds standard" (Figure 9.2).

The major problem with ratings such as outstanding or excellent is figuring out what they mean in performance terms. What constitutes excellent? What is the difference between fair and poor? If there is no definition, the ratings will be entirely subjective and may vary greatly from one supervisor to another. Where raises and promotions are involved, the results are not always fair to everyone. And nothing bugs employees more than seeing an employee who puts in half the amount of work they do receive the same raise as everyone else.

Some forms take pains to describe what is excellent performance, what is average, and so on. The more precise these descriptions are, the fairer and more objective the ratings will be. In some cases, point values are assigned to each performance dimension (Figure 9.3), indicating its relative importance to the job as a whole. These point values add up to 100 percent, the total job. A different set of point values is used to weight each level of performance (3 points for superior, 2 for competent, 1 for minimum, 0 for below minimum). After evaluating each item you multiply the point value by the performance level. Then you add up the products to give you an overall performance rating. This will provide a score for each person based entirely on performance; raises can then be based on point scores. This system allows you to rate performance quality in different jobs by the same standard—a great advantage. Perhaps the most valuable feature of this rating method is that it pinpoints that part of the job the employee is not doing well and indicates how important that part is to

Performance (abbreviated here)	Point Value		Performance Level*		Overall Evaluation**
1. Stocks service station	4	×	2	=	8
2. Sets/resets a table properly	4	×	2	=	8
3. Greets guests	8	×	3	=	24
4. Explains menu	8	×	3	=	24
5. Takes orders	8	×	3	=	24
6. Picks up and completes order	4	×	2	=	8
7. Serves meal	6	×	3	=	18
8. Recommends and serves wines	8	×	1	=	8
9. Totals and presents check	8	×	3	=	24
10. Performs side work	4	×	0	=	0
11. Operates equipment	4	×	2	=	8
12. Meets dress and grooming standards	8	×	3	=	24
13. Observes sanitation procedures	8	×	2	=	16
14. Maintains good customer relations	10	×	3	=	30
15. Maintains check average	8	×	3	=	24
	100				248

*Superior	= 3	**Overall rating of 300 = outstanding: highest reward
Competent	= 2	250–300 = superior: middle reward
Minimal	= 1	200–250 = competent: minimum reward
Below minimum	= 0	100–200 = improvement needed
		100 = marginal
		below 100 = hopelessly inadequate

FIGURE 9-3 Performance dimensions rated using point values.

the whole. It gives you a focus for your discussions with the worker in the appraisal interview, and it shows clearly where improvement must take place.

The evaluation forms in Figures 9.1 and 9.2 achieve a good balance in what they ask of the supervisor. They are simple, yet they require a fair amount of thought. The required ratings provide both a means of assessing excellence for reward purposes and a way of determining where improvement is needed. Both evaluation forms feature another element often used in the overall review process—improvement objectives. Each evaluation considers how well past objectives have been met and sets new objectives for the upcoming period. This tends to emphasize the ongoing character of the performance review process rather than a report-card image.

No evaluation form solves all the problems of fairness and objectivity. Probably those that come closest are designed exclusively for hourly workers, for specific jobs, and for evaluating performance rather than promotability. Some experts suggest that a single form cannot fulfill all the different purposes for which performance reviews are used, and that questions needed for making decisions on promotion and pay be eliminated where reviews are used primarily for feedback, improvement, and problem solving.

The form you encounter as a supervisor will probably be one developed by your company. Whatever its format and its questions, its usefulness will depend on how carefully you fill it out. You can make any form into a useful instrument if you complete it thoughtfully and honestly for each person you supervise.

If your company doesn't have an evaluation system, you can develop your own forms, tailored to the jobs you supervise. If they evaluate performance rather than people and are as objective as you can make them, they will serve all the basic purposes of performance review on the supervisory level: feedback, improvement, incentive, reward, and open communication between you and your people.

Pitfalls in Rating Employee Performance

Whatever form or system you use, evaluating performance consists of putting on paper your ratings of each person's work over the period since hiring or since the last performance review. It is based on your day-to-day observations plus relevant records such as attendance records. No matter how well you think you know an employee's work, the process demands thought and reflection and a concentrated effort to be fair and objective.

There can be many pitfalls on the way to objectivity. We have noted how the *form itself* may in some cases encourage subjective judgments. Another pitfall is the *halo effect,* which you encountered in Chapter 7 in the selection interview. Something outstanding, either positive or negative, may color your judgment of the rest of a person's performance. Kevin may sell more wine than anyone else, so you may not observe that he comes in late every day. Sharon broke a whole tray of glasses her first day on the job, so you don't even notice that she has not broken anything since and that her check average has risen steadily.

Letting your feelings about a person bias your judgment is another easy mistake. If you don't like someone, you see their mistakes and forget about their achievements. If you like someone, you reverse the process.

Comparing one person with another is another trap: If John were as good as Paul . . . if he were even half as good as Paul . . . But Paul really has absolutely nothing to

ᴗ profile

DEMIAN RODILES

*Courtesy of
Demian Rodiles*

I used to work in a restaurant in Dallas, Texas. I started out there as a waiter and quickly moved my way up the ladder. I went from a waiter to a headwaiter, who was responsible for taking the money from all the staff at the end of a shift. Then I made my way into the bar and in no time at all I was the head bartender. I stayed in the bar for a while and then found that I was not doing what I really wanted to do—and that was working in the kitchen. After I worked in the kitchen and learned all the positions, management felt that I was not being used to my full potential. So they asked me if I would like to become a manager. This was great, but I guess that at the time I really did not want all that responsibility, so we came to an agreement; I became a head cook, which is something like an assistant sous chef.

While being a head cook I learned a lot about supervising, both good and bad things about supervising. As supervisor I had to choose how I acted with the other employees a little differently than when I was just a cook like them. You have to treat everyone as an equal and try not to show any favoritism. I had to respect what my su-

do with John. You have to compare John's performance with the job standards, not John with Paul.

Sometimes supervisors' feelings about the entire evaluation process will affect their ratings. They may be impatient with the time that evaluations take and the cost of taking people away from work for interviews. Even supervisors who believe in evaluation and practice it informally all the time may resent putting pencil to paper (and the interviews too) as an intrusion into their busy days. Some supervisors do not take evaluations seriously and simply go through the motions. Some are really not familiar with the details of their employees' work. Some simply hate paperwork and feel that daily informal evaluation and feedback are enough.

Some supervisors let concern about the consequences influence their ratings. They may fear losing good workers through promotions if they rate them high. They may fear worker anger and reprisals if they rate them low. They may not want to be held responsible or take the consequences of being honest, so they rate everybody average. That way they do not have to make decisions or face the anger of people they have rated negatively, and nobody is going to argue.

Procrastination is another pitfall. Some people postpone ratings until the last minute on grounds of the press of "more important" work. Then the day before evaluations are due they work overtime and rush through the evaluation forms of 45 people in 45 minutes. Obviously this is not going to be a thoughtful, objective job.

Another pitfall is the *temptation to give ratings for the effect they will have.* If you want to encourage a worker, you might give her higher ratings than her performance warrants. If you want to get rid of somebody, you might rate him low—or periors wanted and work toward achieving their goals. I do not mean that I treated anyone badly; it just meant that I had to keep a professional relationship with employees while we were at work. Since I was friends with some of the employees outside work, they knew that at work we interacted as professionals and did not let anything at work affect our relationships as friends. This sounds like it is easy to do, but there were difficult times determining where the lines were drawn. One thing I feel that gave me so much success was that I had earned respect from the kitchen staff because I had worked as one of them and performed at an equal or higher level than some of the staff. It was very noticeable how they would act when I would ask for something to be done as opposed to another supervisor, who were actually managers, but could not perform on the line and would sometimes ask for things that were unreasonable. I also began to notice that the kitchen staff would not perform to their maximum output when this particular manager was working. Or just the opposite, they would work fast and try to show him up and make him look bad in front of the wait staff. It was clear that they did not respect him and it became a problem later on down the line. It was interesting that I did not notice this until I started to look at it from a supervisor's position. So I believe that to be a good supervisor, this is a very important part of being successful. Whatever job it is you are asking your employees to do, make sure that you can do the job as well as, if not even better than, they can.

recommend him for promotion. If you want to impress your boss, you might rate everybody high to show what a good supervisor you are.

If you are a *perfectionist*, and few employees measure up to your standards, you might rate everyone poorly. Another pitfall occurs when you *rate employees on their most recent performance* because you kept insufficient documentation of their past performance. This often results in vague, general statements based only on recent observations. This can upset the employee, especially if earlier incidents of outstanding performance are forgotten.

Sooner or later, false ratings will catch up with you. Unfair or wishy-washy evaluations are likely to backfire. You are not going to make a good impression with your superiors, and you will lose the respect of your workers. Such evaluations tend to sabotage the entire evaluation system, the value of which lies in accuracy and fairness.

The defense against such pitfalls and copouts lies in the supervisor's own attitude. You can never eliminate subjectivity entirely, even by measuring everything. But you can be aware of your own blind spots and prejudices, and you can go over your ratings a second time to make sure that they represent your best efforts. You can make the effort needed to do a good job. You can also do the following:

∾ Evaluate the performance, not the employee. Be objective. Avoid subjective statements.

∾ Give specific examples of performance to back up ratings. Use your supervisor's log or other documentation to keep a continual record of past performance so that doing evaluations is easier and more accurate.

∾ Where there is substandard performance, ask "Why?" Use the rule of finger, which means looking closely at yourself before blaming the employee. Perhaps the employee was not given enough training or the appropriate tools to do the job.

∾ Think fairness and consistency when evaluating performance. Ask yourself, "If this were my review, how would I react?"

∾ Get input from others who have some working relationship with the employee. Write down some ideas to discuss with the employee on how to improve performance.

∾ If you set out to be honest and fair, you probably will be. If you keep in mind what evaluations are for and how they can help your workers and improve the work, you will tend to drop out personal feelings and ulterior motives and to see things as they are.

Employee Self-Appraisal

As part of some performance appraisal systems, some employees are asked to fill out the performance appraisal and evaluate themselves. **Employee self-appraisal** is surprisingly accurate. Many employees tend to underrate themselves, particularly the better employees, whereas less effective employees may overrate themselves. If the employee is given the chance to participate, and the manager really reads and takes the self-appraisal seriously, the employee gets the message that his or her opinion matters. This may result in less employee defensiveness and a more constructive performance appraisal interview. It may also improve motivation and job performance. Self-appraisal also helps put employees at ease because now they know what will be discussed during their appraisal. Employees may also tell you about skills they have or tasks they have accomplished that you may have forgotten. Self-appraisal is particularly justified when an employee works largely without supervision.

Check Your Knowledge

1. Why do you as a supervisor need to conduct a performance review?
2. What are the four steps in the performance review process?
3. What is the purpose of a rating scale?

The Appraisal Interview

The **appraisal interview (evaluation interview, appraisal review)** is a private face-to-face session between you and an employee. In it you tell the worker how you have evaluated his or her performance and why, and discuss how future performance can be improved. The way you do this with each person can determine the success or failure of the entire performance review.

Planning the Interview

Each interview should take place in a quiet area *free of interruption.* Schedule your interviews in advance, and allow enough time to cover the ground at a comfortable pace. A sense of rush or hurry will inhibit the person being appraised. If you encourage people to feel that this is a time with you that belongs to them alone, they are likely to be receptive and cooperative.

It is important to review your written evaluation shortly before the interview and to plan how you will communicate it to the employee for best effect. Indeed, in some companies you may give a copy of the evaluation to the employee ahead of time. Your major goal for the interview is to establish and maintain a calm and positive climate of communication and problem solving rather than a negative climate of criticism or reprimand. Although you may have negative things to report, you can address them positively as things that can be improved in the future rather than dwelling on things that were wrong in the past. If you plan carefully how you will approach each point, you can maintain your positive climate, or at the very least stay calm if you are dealing with a hostile employee.

You will remember that in communications the message gets through when the receiver wants to receive it. Successful communication is as much a matter of feeling as of logic, so if you can keep good feeling between you and the worker, you have pretty much got it made. Your own frame of mind as you approach the interview should be that any performance problems the worker has are your problems, too, and that together you can solve them.

Conducting the Interview

Usually, a bit of small talk is a good way to start off an interview—a cordial greeting by name and some informal remarks. You want to establish rapport; you want to avoid the impression of sitting in judgment, talking down, or laying down the law. You want to be person-to-person in the way you come across. You want your workers to know you are there to help them do their jobs well, not to criticize them. Criticism diminishes self-esteem, and people who have a good self-image are likely to perform better than people who don't.

Workers who are facing their first appraisal interview may be worried about it. Even though they have been told all about it before, it may seem to them like a day of judgment or like getting a school report card. *It is important to make sure that they understand the evaluation process:* the basis for evaluation, its purpose, how it will be used, and how it affects them. Stress the interview as useful feedback on performance and an opportunity for mutual problem solving. Conveying your willingness to help goes a long way toward solving problems: "How can I help you to do a good job?"

After explaining the purpose of the interview, *it is often used to ask people to rate their own performance on the categories listed on the form.* If you have established clear standards, they usually know pretty well how they measure up. Often, they are harder on themselves than you have been on them. The two of you together can then compare the two evaluations and discuss the points on which you disagree.

Stress the positive things about their work, and approach negative evaluations as opportunities to improve their skills with your support.

Encourage them to comment on your judgments. Let them disagree freely with you if they feel you are unfair. You could be wrong: You may not know the whole story or you may have made a subjective judgment that was inaccurate. Do not be afraid to change your evaluation if you discover that you were wrong.

Get them to do as much of the talking as possible. Ask questions that make them think, discuss, and explain. Encourage their questions. Take the time to let them air discontent and vent feelings. Let them tell you about problems they have and get them to suggest solutions. (The problem of the worker standing in the puddle of water mentioned in Chapter 7 surfaced in the open communication of a good appraisal interview.)

Be a good listener. Don't interrupt; hear them out. Maintain eye contact. If the people being reviewed feel that you are not seeing their side, if they begin to feel defensive, you have lost their cooperation. An evaluation that is perceived as unfair will probably turn a complacent or cooperative employee into a hostile one.

Although you encourage them to do most of the talking, you do not relinquish control of the interview. Bring the subject around to improvement goals and *work with them on seeing objectives for improvement.* Many evaluation systems make goal setting a requirement of the appraisal interview. The worker, with the supervisor's

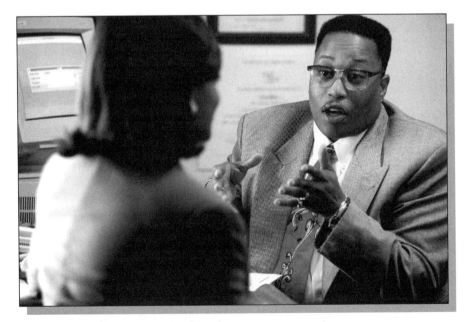

Be a good listener. Do not interrupt; hear them out.
Maintain eye contact.

help and guidance, sets goals and objectives with specific performance standards to be achieved between now and the next appraisal. These goals are recorded (as in Figure 9.1) and become an important part of the next evaluation. It is best to concentrate on two or three goals at most rather than on the whole range of possibilities. Goals should be measurable and attainable.

If you can get people to set their own improvement goals, they will usually be highly motivated to achieve them because they themselves have made the commitment. You should make it clear that you will support them with further training and coaching as needed to meet their goals.

It is a good idea to *summarize the interview* or ask the worker to summarize it and to make sure that you both have the same understanding of what the employee is to do now. Have the employee read the entire evaluation and sign it, explaining that signing it does not indicate agreement and that he or she has the right to add comments. Discuss your reward system openly and fully and explain what is or is not forthcoming for the person being interviewed. Make sure that the employee receives a copy of the completed evaluation form.

End the interview on a positive note—congratulations if they are in order, an expression of hope and support for the future if they are not. Your people should leave their interviews feeling that you care how they are doing and will support their efforts to improve, and that the future is worth working for.

Common Mistakes in Appraisal Interviews

A poorly handled appraisal interview can undermine the entire evaluation process, engender ill feeling and antagonisms, cause good people to leave, and turn competent workers into marginal performers and cynics. Interviewing is a human relations skill that requires training and practice.

If you have established good relations with your people, the appraisal review should not present any problems. It is simply another form of communication about their work—a chance to focus on their problems, reinforce acceptable behavior, and help them improve—no big deal for either of you. If you are new to supervision or if you are a hard-driving, high-control type of person, you may have difficulty at first in carrying out the human relations approach recommended for a productive appraisal review. But you will find it worth the effort. Here are some major mistakes to avoid.

If you take an *authoritarian approach* (this is what you have done well, this is how I want you to improve, this is what you will get if you do, this is what will happen if you don't), it will often antagonize employees rather than produce the improvements you want. It may work with the employee who thinks you are right or with dependent types of people who are too insecure to disagree. But people who think your evaluations are unfair in any way and do not have a chance to present their point of view may not even listen to your message, and they probably won't cooperate if the message does come through. *You* cannot improve their work; only *they* can improve their work, and few will improve for a carrot-and-stick approach unless they desperately need the carrot or truly fear the stick. They will leave, or they will remain and become hostile and discontented. Discontented people complain about you to each other, morale declines, and problems multiply. Improvement does not take place.

The *tell-and-sell approach* is a mild version of the authoritarian approach: The supervisor tells the worker the results of the evaluation and tries to persuade the employee to improve. It is a presentation based on logic alone, rather like a lecture. It seems to be a natural approach for someone who has not developed sensitivity in handling people.

The assumption is that the worker will follow the logic, see the light, and respond to persuasion with the appropriate promise to improve. No account is taken of the feelings of the people being evaluated, and the supervisor has no awareness of how the message is being read as the interview proceeds. There is also the assumption that the supervisor's evaluation is valid in every respect, so there is no need for the worker to take part in discussing it.

The result for the people being evaluated is at best like getting a report card; it is a one-sided verdict handed down from the top, and it leaves them out of the process. Usually, they sit silent and say nothing because the format does not invite them to speak. If they do challenge some part of the evaluation, the supervisor brushes aside the challenge and doubles the persuasion (being sure that there are no mistakes or perhaps being afraid to admit them). The supervisor wins the encounter but loses the worker's willingness to improve. The results are likely to be the same as in the hard-line authoritarian approach.

Certain mistakes in interviewing technique can destroy the value of the interview.

- ❧ *Criticizing and dwelling on past mistakes* usually make people feel bad and may also make them defensive, especially if they feel you are referring to them rather than to their work. Once they become defensive, communication ceases. The best way to avoid such mistakes is to talk in terms of the work, not the person, and in terms of the future rather than the past, emphasizing the help and support available for improvement.

- ❧ *Failing to listen, interrupting,* and *arguing* make the other person defensive, frustrated, and sometimes angry. Avoiding these mistakes requires you to be aware of yourself as well as of the other person and to realize continuously what you are doing and the effect it is having. It takes a conscious effort on your part to maintain a cooperative, problem-solving, worker-focused interview.

- ❧ *Losing control of the interview* is a serious mistake. There are several ways this can happen. One is to let a discussion turn into an emotional argument. This puts you on the same level as the worker: You have lost control of yourself and have abdicated your position as the boss. Another way of giving up control is to let the worker sidetrack the interview on a single issue so that you do not have time for everything you need to cover. You can recoup by suggesting a separate meeting on that issue and move on according to plan. Still another way of losing control is to allow yourself to be manipulated into reducing the standards for one person (such as overlooking poor performance because you feel sorry for someone or in exchange for some benefit to yourself). Although you may think you have bought future improvement or loyalty in this way, you have actually given away power and lost respect.

Your first appraisal interviews may not be easy. Many supervisors have trouble telling people negative things about their work in a positive, constructive way. As with so many other management skills, nobody can teach you how; it is something you just have to learn by experience, and if you are lucky you will learn it under the skillful coaching of a good supervisor. A good interview comes from preparing yourself, from practicing interviewing for other purposes (hiring, problem solving), from knowing how to listen, from knowing the worker and the job, from staying positive, and from keeping tuned in to the interviewee, whose feelings about what you are saying can make or break the interview. It is probably one of the best learning experiences you will have in your entire career in the industry.

Finding and keeping qualified employees is a major challenge. Yet most firms track traditional measures such as staff turnover and employee morale. To improve your scorecard, think about the behavior or performance you want to achieve before deciding on performance measures. Do not measure things that may be easy to count but provide meaningless information, eliminate measures that drive the wrong behavior, develop leading indicators that predict meaningful outcomes (profits, repeat business), and measure things that you can track frequently.

Source: Mark Graham Brown, "Keeping score," *Human Resources Planning*, Vol. 17, No. 11, p. 16, November 2000.

Follow-Up

The evaluation and the appraisal review have let employees know how they are doing and have pointed the way toward improved performance. If you have done the reviews well, they have fostered momentum for improvement in responsive employees. You have become aware of where people need your help and support and probably also of where your efforts will be wasted on people who will not change or are unable to meet the demands of their job. So the appraisal review has marked the end of one phase and the beginning of a new one. How do you follow up?

The first thing you do is to see that people receive the rewards they have coming to them. You must make good on rewards promised, such as raises in pay, better shifts, better stations, and so on. If there is some problem about arranging these things, devise several alternative rewards and discuss them promptly with the people concerned. Never let people think you have forgotten them.

For people you have discovered need more training, arrange to provide it for them. For people you feel will improve themselves, follow their progress discreetly without hovering or breathing down their necks. Coaching is in order here, day-to-day counseling as needed. Remember that in the appraisal review you emphasized your help and support. It doesn't take much time: just touching base frequently to let people know you will come through for them, frequent words of praise for achievement, readiness to discuss problems. Put them on their own as much as possible, but do not neglect them.

There will be some people who you are sure will make no attempt to improve, who will continue to get by with minimum performance. Reassess them in your mind: Was your appraisal fair? Did you handle the interview well? Is there some mistake that you are making in handling them? Are you hostile or merely indifferent? Are *they* able to do better, or is minimal performance really their best work? Would they do better in a different job? Is their performance so poor on key aspects of the job (customer relations, absenteeism, sanitation, quality standards) that discipline is in order? Should they be retrained? Should they be terminated (hopelessly unwilling or unable to do the job)?

If employees are complacent or indifferent, you might as well give up trying to make them improve unless you can find a way to motivate them. If employees are hostile, you should try to figure out how to turn them around or at least arrive at an armed truce so that they will do the work and get their pay without disrupting the entire department. We have more to say on motivation and discipline in later chapters.

There are two important facets of follow-up. One is actually carrying it out. If, after you have done your reviews, you let the process drop until the next appraisal date, you will let all its potential benefits slip through your fingers. The other important facet is using all you have discovered about your people and yourself to improve your working relationship with each person you supervise. It can be a constantly expanding and self-feeding process, and it will pay off in the morale of your people and in your development as a leader.

Check Your Knowledge

1. List four common mistakes in appraisal interviews.
2. List the steps to follow when conducting an interview.

Legal Aspects of Performance Evaluation

Four major equal employment opportunity laws affect the process of performance evaluation: Title VII of the Civil Rights Act of 1964, the Equal Pay Act, the Age Discrimination in Employment Act, and the Americans with Disabilities Act (Table 7.1). Knowing how to avoid violations of these laws in the evaluation process can save time and money as well as create goodwill with your employees and a positive public image. Following are ways to ensure fair and legal evaluations:

1. Evaluation of performance should be based on standards or factors obtained from a job analysis of the skills, tasks, and knowledge required to perform the job.
2. Performance standards should be observable, objective, and measurable.
3. Keep a positive rapport during your discussions with the employee. This helps tremendously to avoid complaints of being unfair and, possibly, charges of discrimination.
4. Do not enter into discussions that focus on qualities of employees based on their membership in a group protected by EEO laws. If employees refer to their membership, it is best not to respond. For example, suppose that Jack, who is 60, says: "At my age it gets harder to see the small details. I guess that explains my trouble with this." It would be appropriate for you to focus on how to ensure that Jack is able to see well enough to perform his job. It would be an error for you to make

any mention of his age, both to him or anyone else, and certainly not on the written part of his appraisal, even though he brought up the subject.[2]

5. Employee performance should be documented more frequently than once a year at appraisal time. An employee should not be surprised at performance appraisal time.

6. If an employee disagrees with his or her evaluation, he or she should be able to appeal.

ೞ key points

1. The overall purpose of coaching is to evaluate work performance and then to encourage optimum work performance by either reinforcing good performance or confronting and redirecting poor performance. Table 9.1 lists coaching guidelines.

2. Performance evaluation refers to the periodic review and assessment of each employee's performance during a given period, such as a year. This is in addition to the informal performance evaluation that is a daily part of a supervisor's job.

3. When carried out conscientiously and when there is constant communication between reviews, performance reviews have many benefits. They help to maintain performance standards. By telling workers how they are doing, they can remove uncertainty and improve morale. By spotlighting areas for improvement, they can focus the efforts of both worker and supervisor to bring about improvement. They can increase motivation to perform well and provide the opportunity for improving communication and relationships. They can identify workers with unused potential and workers who ought to be terminated. They can give feedback on supervisory performance and uncover problems that are getting in the way of the work.

4. The performance review process includes these four steps: preparing for evaluation, making the evaluation, sharing it with the worker, and providing follow-up.

5. An evaluation form typically lists the performance dimensions or categories on which each worker is to be rated. The performance dimensions should be related to the job being evaluated and defined clearly in objective and observable terms, as in a performance standard.

6. A rating scale is used for each performance dimension, such as outstanding to unsatisfactory. The more precise the descriptions for each rating, the more objective the ratings will be.

7. No evaluation form solves all the problems of fairness and objectivity. Probably those that come closest are designed exclusively for hourly workers, for specific jobs, and for evaluating performance rather than promotability.

[2]Adapted from William S. Swan, *How to Do a Superior Performance Appraisal.* New York: Wiley, 1991.

8. Some pitfalls when rating employee performance include the halo effect, letting your feelings about a person bias your judgment, comparing one person with another, letting your feelings about the evaluation process affect rating, procrastination, giving ratings for the effect they'll have, and being too lax or too much of a perfectionist.

9. Evaluate the performance, not the employee.

10. Employee self-appraisals are especially justified when an employee works largely without supervision.

11. Plan a quiet location for appraisal interviews, review your written evaluation shortly beforehand, and plan how you will communicate it to the employee for best effect.

12. When conducting the appraisal interview, start with a bit of small talk. Make sure that the employee understands the evaluation process, ask the employee to rate his or her own performance first, encourage employees to comment on your judgments, get the employee to do most of the talking. Work with them on setting improvement objectives, summarize the interview, and end on a positive note.

13. Common mistakes in appraisal interviews include taking an authoritarian or tell-and-sell approach, criticizing, dwelling on past mistakes, failing to listen, and losing control of the interview.

14. Follow-up after performance appraisals is crucial. If you let the process drop until the next appraisal date, you will let all its potential benefits slip through your fingers.

15. Equal employment opportunity laws apply to performance evaluation, so the evaluation process needs to be nondiscriminatory.

∾ key terms

appraisal interview (evaluation interview, appraisal review)

coaching

counseling

employee self-appraisal

evaluation form

merit raise

performance appraisal (performance evaluation, performance review)

performance dimensions or categories

rating scale

∾ review questions

Answer each question in complete sentences. Read each question carefully and make sure that you answer all parts of the question. Organize your answer using more than one paragraph when appropriate.

1. Compare and contrast coaching and performance evaluation. How are they different? How are they the same? What is the purpose(s) of each? What is the benefit(s) of each?

2. Briefly discuss five coaching guidelines, explaining why each is important.

3. Describe the major points in each of the four steps in a performance review: preparing for evaluation, making the evaluation, sharing it with the employee, and providing follow-up.

4. What are five pitfalls in performance evaluation, and how can you overcome each?

5. Which equal employment opportunity laws affect the process of performance evaluation?

6. What can you do to ensure legal evaluations?

∾ activities and applications

1. Discussion Questions
- What is the relationship between ongoing day-by-day evaluations and periodic performance reviews? Is either one valid without the other? Defend your answer.
- Explain the following statement: "Performance appraisals are about as beloved as IRS audits." As a supervisor, what can you do to reduce employee fear and anxiety about performance appraisals?
- Do you think periodic performance reviews are worth the time and trouble they take? Why or why not?
- What type of evaluation form do you think is most suitable for hourly employees in hospitality operations? Consider performance dimensions, performance ratings, length, and ease of completion. Explain your choice.
- In your opinion, which part of the appraisal review is most important: the written evaluation, the interview, or the follow-up? Explain.
- Explain the following statement: "A poorly handled appraisal interview can undermine the entire evaluation process." Give examples of poor handling and their effects.
- When you allow employees to do a self-appraisal, do you think they can rate their own performance accurately? What are the advantages and disadvantages of having an employee do a self-appraisal?

2. Role-Play: The Appraisal Interview
In a group of four, complete one of the performance evaluation forms in this chapter for a fictitious person. While two students role-play the supervisor and employee in an appraisal interview, the other two students can be observers. When the role-play is done, the observers can take a turn doing the appraisal interview.

3. Group Activity: Coaching
As the head housekeeper at a 100-room budget hotel, you discover that one of your employees, Luisa, is not following the new room cleaning procedure. She is continuing to do things the old way. How would you handle this situation?

4. Case Study: The First Appraisal Interview

Sandy is sitting outside her boss's office awaiting her first appraisal interview. She is nervous, but confident. She has improved tremendously since she dropped that whole tray of dinners when she first came to work three months ago. Her boss has stopped coming around and telling her not to do this and that, so she thinks that she's doing all right (although, of course, you never know). She gets along very well with the customers, and in fact, sometimes people ask to be seated at her tables. Her tips are higher than almost anyone else's, and that must mean something.

The door opens and the boss motions her to come in and sit down. "Good morning, Sally," he says. "We're a little bit rushed for time, so I'll just go through this evaluation form with you—er—Sandy. Read it over, won't you? Then we'll talk."

Sandy glances through the ratings: Average, Average, Average, Needs improvement. Well, she has to admit she still has trouble opening wine bottles and sometimes breaks the cork. Average, Average, Average.

She sighs, hands the form back to her boss, sits back in her chair, folds her hands tightly, and looks down at them.

"Well, what do you think, Sandy? Do you agree? We need to make a plan for your improvement on wine service. I know you sometimes ask Charlie to open your bottles and that's not really what good customer service is all about. Why don't you get Charlie to give you some tips on what you're doing wrong? Then maybe next time you'll get a better rating. Now, do you have any comments or questions?"

"What's average?" Sandy asks.

"Well, I guess it means no better and no worse than anyone else. Actually, it means you're doing okay, you're just not as good as people like Ruth and Charlie. But you certainly don't need to worry about losing your job or anything like that— you're all set here! Anything else?"

"Well," Sandy begins, gathering up her courage, "I thought I was really above average in customer service—people ask for me and they tip me a lot, so I must be—"

"But don't forget the time you dropped the dishes, Sandy! I do think you're doing very well indeed now, but we're talking about the whole evaluation period! Now, if you'll just sign this. . . ."

QUESTIONS

1. What do you think of the boss's ratings and his defense of them?
2. How do you think Sandy feels? Will she be motivated to improve? Is it enough to know you are not going to lose your job?
3. List the mistakes the boss makes in his interview. How could he have handled things better?
4. What do you think of the boss's improvement plan? How will Charlie feel about it?
5. If the boss's supervisor could have heard this interview, what would have been the supervisor's opinion of it? What responsibility does the boss's boss have for the way that interviews are handled? What means could be set up for evaluating supervisors on their interviews?

chapter 10

Discipline and the Marginal Employee

overview

Here are five true–false statements about the serious subject of discipline; one of them is true. Do you know which it is?

- Discipline = punishment.
- Whether or not you are plagued with discipline problems is a matter of how lucky you are in the people you supervise.
- A supervisor who is fairly relaxed about enforcing rules is likely to have fewer discipline problems than one who makes people toe the line.
- "You do that once more and you're fired!" is a good way to make a worker shape up.
- Most employees really want to obey the rules and do their jobs well.

The last one is true: Most of your employees will come to work each day, do their jobs satisfactorily, and leave without causing any problems. The first four statements are in most cases false; each is discussed in this chapter.

There is more to discipline than meets the eye. Discipline is not a black-and-white issue; there are many shades of gray. It is a fluctuating product of the continual interplay between the supervisor and the people supervised within the framework of the rules and requirements of the company and the job.

As a whole, the hospitality industry is not famous for disciplinary success. Often, discipline is administered across a crowded room at the top of the lungs, and disciplinary measures make a direct contribution to the high rate of employee turnover in the industry.

In this chapter we explore the subject of discipline from several points of view. It will help you to:

❧ Define the four essential elements of successful discipline and explain the importance of each.

❧ Compare and contrast the negative and positive approaches to discipline.

❧ State basic guidelines for administering discipline, and explain how to avoid common mistakes and pitfalls.

❧ Weigh and discuss the problems of terminating a worker who has under performed.

❧ Discuss the legal implications of termination and learn how to avoid unwarranted charges of discrimination.

❧ List guidelines for conducting a termination interview.

❧ Explain the basics of dealing with sexual harassment and substance-abuse problems.

Essentials of Discipline

If you were to walk around your work area one day and ask your employees what discipline is, it is very likely that the most frequent response would be that discipline means punishment. Does discipline really mean punishment? Let's take a closer look.

The word **discipline** has two somewhat different but related meanings. One refers to a *condition* or *state* of orderly conduct and compliance with rules, regulations, and procedures. If everyone follows the rules and procedures and the work moves along in an orderly fashion, we say that discipline is good in this department or operation. But if people are not following the rules and procedures, and maybe do not even know what the rules and procedures are, and the work is not getting done and people are fighting and the place is in chaos and nobody is listening to what the supervisor is trying to say, we say that the discipline is terrible.

The second meaning of the word *discipline* refers to *action* to ensure orderly conduct and compliance with rules and procedures. When people break rules, you discipline them; you take disciplinary action. Disciplinary action, depending on

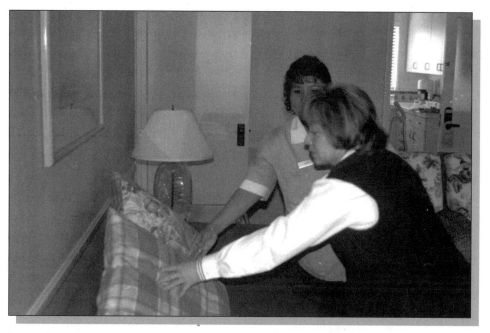

Ensure that associates know what the rules and procedures are by telling and showing them what to do.

your policy, may or may not include punishment such as a written warning or suspension. If your employees are relatively self-disciplined, it is not necessary to discipline often.

In this chapter we are concerned with both kinds of discipline. We are concerned with maintaining a condition of discipline, and we are concerned with the most effective kinds of disciplinary action to ensure compliance to rules. *Both sides of discipline are the responsibility of the supervisor, and discipline, in both senses of the word is essential to supervisory success.*

The discipline process contains three steps:

1. Establishing and communicating ground rules for performance and conduct
2. Evaluating employee performance and conduct through coaching, performance appraisals, and disciplinary investigations (Coaching and performance appraisals are discussed in Chapter 9.)
3. Reinforcing employees for appropriate performance and conduct and working with employees to improve their performance and conduct when necessary

As a supervisor, you are involved in each step of this process, as discussed throughout this chapter. Let's start by looking at the *four essentials of successful discipline:*

1. A complete set of rules that everyone knows and understands
2. A clear statement of the consequences of failing to observe the rules

3. Prompt, consistent, and impersonal action to enforce the rules

4. Appropriate recognition and reinforcement of employees' positive actions

The first essential—a complete set of rules—consists of all the policies, regulations, rules, requirements, standards, and procedures that you and your workers must observe in your job and theirs. These should include:

- Company policies, regulations, and directives that apply to your department and your people. Of particular importance to you are company policies and procedures relating to disciplinary action (Figure 10.1).

- **Work rules** relating to hours, absences, tardiness, sick days, meals, use of facilities and equipment, uniforms and grooming, conduct on the job (smoking, drinking, dealing with customers, patients, or guests).

Discipline Policy and Procedure

Policy: It is necessary to establish rules of conduct to promote efficient and congenial working conditions and employee safety. Further, it is our intention to provide equality in the administration of discipline when these rules of conduct are violated. Discipline is to be administered fairly without prejudice and only for just cause.

Procedure: In order that all disciplinary actions by supervisors are consistent, one of the following actions will be used according to the seriousness of the offense.

1. Oral warning with documentation
2. Written warning
3. Suspension
4. Termination

An employee will be subject to disciplinary action ranging from oral warning to discharge for committing or participating in any of the acts listed below. The normal level of discipline is also listed. All suspensions, terminations, or exceptions must have the approval of the Director of Human Resources.

1. False statements or misrepresentation of facts on the employment application — termination
2. Absence for one day without notifying the department manager prior to the start of the shift — written warning
3. Absence for two consecutive work days without notifying the department manager prior to the start of the shift — suspension
4. Absence for three consecutive work days without notifying the supervisor prior to the start of the shift — termination
5. Excessive absenteeism with or without medical documentation — within a calendar year —
     6 absent incidents — oral warning with documentation
     8 absent incidents — written warning
     9 absent incidents — suspension
     10 absent incidents — totaling 13 days or more — termination
6. Excessive lateness — within a calendar year —
     8 latenesses — oral warning with documentation
     12 latenesses — written warning
     16 latenesses — three-day suspension
     20 latenesses — termination

FIGURE 10.1 Discipline policy and procedure.

7. Falsification of time sheets, recording another employee's time or allowing others to do so — termination
8. Failure to record own time when required — oral warning with documentation
9. Leaving work area without permission — written warning
10. Leaving the facility without permission during normal working hours — written warning
11. Stopping work early or otherwise preparing to leave before authorized time, including meal periods — oral warning with documentation
12. Sleeping on the job — suspension
13. Failure to carry out job-related instructions by the supervisor where the failure is intentional — suspension
14. Threats or intimidation to managers, guests, or other employees — termination
15. Use of abusive language to managers, guests, or other employees — suspension
16. Stealing or destruction of company or guest's property — termination
17. Not performing up to performance standards — oral warning with documentation
18. Disorderly conduct during working time or on company property — suspension
19. Violations of sanitation and safety regulations — level 2, 3, or 4 depending on situation
20. Reporting to work unfit for duty — written warning
21. Possession or use of alcohol or nonprescribed drugs during working time or on company property — termination
22. Possession of explosives, firearms, or other weapons during working time or on company property — termination

Multiple or Cumulative Violations

1. Subsequent violations of a related nature should move to the next higher step in the discipline pattern (e.g., a related violation following a written warning will call for a 3-day suspension, etc.).
2. Violations of an unrelated nature will move to the next higher level after two disciplinary actions at the same level (e.g., after two written warnings for unrelated violations, the next unrelated violation would call for a suspension rather than another written warning).
3. Cumulative violations that occur more than 12 months before the violation in question will not be used to step up the discipline for an unrelated violation.
4. The above listed violations are the basic ones and are not intended to be all-inclusive and cover every situation that may arise.

FIGURE 10.1 *(Continued).*

∾ Legal requirements and restrictions, such as health code provisions, fire and safety regulations, liquor laws.

∾ Job requirements, performance standards, and job procedures for each job you supervise.

∾ Quality and quantity standards required (such as standardized recipes, portion sizes, drink sizes, guestroom amenities).

All this material will form a basic operations and procedures manual for your department. From it you can prepare a manual for new employees and plan their first-day orientation (Chapter 7). Then you can use it in developing your training programs (also Chapter 8), incorporating all the rules, procedures, and penalties that the workers must know, so that they start out well-informed. You can use your manual as a reference for verifying the proper ways of doing things and for settling any disputes that arise. Keep it in loose-leaf form so that you can update it easily when policies, regulations, and procedures change.

It is your responsibility to see that all your people know the rules and procedures that apply to them and to their jobs. These rules and procedures form a set of boundaries or limits for employee behavior, a framework within which they must live their occupational life. You might compare it to a box or a fence that encloses them while they are on the job (Figure 10.2). Most employees really want to do a good job, and if they know what they are supposed to do and not do, most of them will willingly stay in the box and abide by the rules. Knowing the rules and the limits makes most people more comfortable in their jobs.

The second essential is to make very clear the consequences of going beyond the limits, of not following the rules and procedures. If there are penalties for breaking the rules, people must know from the outset what the penalties are. This information should be stated in matter-of-fact terms: "This is what we expect you to do; this is what happens when you don't." *It should not take the form of warnings and threats.* There should be no hint of threat in either your words or your tone of voice.

The penalties for breaking rules are usually written into your disciplinary policy and procedures (Figure 10.1). The policy and procedures may prescribe the specific disciplinary action for each rule violation each time a given employee breaks that rule, or the penalties may be more loosely defined.

Knowing the consequences has its own security: People know where the boss stands, and they know what will happen if they go beyond the limits. Even when the penalties seem severe, and even when people do not like their supervisor personally, you often hear them say, "At least with the boss, you know where you stand."

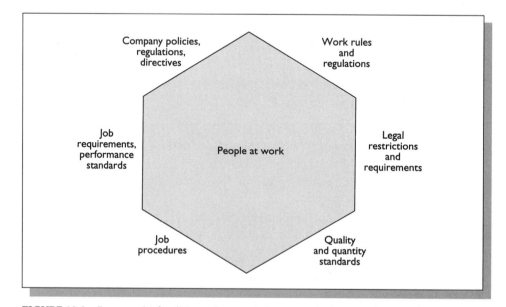

FIGURE 10.2   Framework of policies, rules, restrictions, standards, procedures, and requirements within which employees carry out their work.

The third essential is to enforce the rules promptly, consistently, and impersonally and to comply with the rules yourself. It is very common for supervisors to threaten punishment—"If you are late once more, I'm gonna fire you"—and never carry out the threat. After a while, other people see that the threat is never carried out and they begin to think, "Why should I be here on time?" And pretty soon, the supervisor has lost control and the workers are setting the rules and standards. Once you have made a threat, you have no choice but to carry it out or back down.

The principle applies not only to threats but also to rule breaking in general. If you pay no attention when people break rules, if you walk on by and do nothing, everyone will begin to break the rules and discipline will crumble. And if you break rules yourself, people will have no respect for you because you are applying a double standard. They will think, "What is good enough for you is good enough for me, too," and you will have problems with compliance. There won't be any ground rules left.

Many people suggest the hot stove as the perfect model of administering discipline[1]:

- It gives *warning*. You can feel the hot air around it.
- Its response is *immediate*. The instant you touch it, it burns your finger.
- It is *consistent*. It burns your finger every time you touch it.
- It is *impersonal*. It reacts to the touch, not the person who touches.

These are all sound guidelines to follow with any approach to discipline. You *give warning* by making sure that people know the rules and the consequences—what to do and how to do it and what happens if they don't. Your response is *immediate;* by tomorrow the mistake or transgression is past history and the worker has gotten away with something and three others have seen it happen and will try it today. You are *consistent:* You hold everybody to the same rules all the time; and you are *impersonal:* You are matter-of-fact, you don't get angry, you don't scold, you don't preach, you simply act as an adult. You deal with the specific incident, not with the person's bad attitude or thick skull. You eliminate your personal feelings about individual people: you do not prejudge someone you don't like, and you do not let favoritism creep in.

But there is more. Although impersonal, discipline ought to be carried out as part of a positive human relations approach to the people who work for you. In disciplining, you must focus on things that people do wrong, but your people can handle this negative feedback better if you use a lot of that positive reinforcement we talked about in the last chapter. Don't be like the manager who said, "Every time you do something wrong I'll be there to catch you. But when you do something right—well, that's what I pay you for."

The fourth essential is to recognize and reinforce your employee's positive actions. Discipline is not just making sure that employees follow rules, but includes recognizing those who are following rules and performing up to standards. Recognizing your employees need not be a laborious process; it can be as simple as saying, "Thanks for taking care of our guests in such a prompt and courteous manner," or filling out a positive action memo (Figure 10.3). Other ways to recognize your employees are discussed in Chapter 5.

[1]The original hot-stove model is generally attributed to Douglas McGregor of Theory X and Theory Y fame. It gave warning by being red hot.

You've Done A Great Job!

For: _____Denise Smith, Cook_____

From: _____Joe Brown, Chef_____

Date: _____8/22/92_____

Thank you for giving two of our long-term customers, Mr. and Mrs. Jones, the extra-special treatment last night. They were most unhappy about their meal until you came out of the kitchen to help them make another selection. You did a great job of reassuring them and keeping their visit enjoyable. Thanks for going the extra mile.

FIGURE 10.3   Positive action memo.

Approaches to Discipline

There are two different approaches to disciplinary action. One is the negative approach of discipline by punishment. The other is the positive approach of discipline by information and corrective training. Philosophically, they divide along Theory X and Theory Y views of people and management styles.

Negative Approach

Most people associate discipline with punishment. The theory is that if you enforce the rules by punishing people who break them, those people will learn not to break the rules and the punishment will be a warning to others that will keep them in line. It is the old theory of motivation through fear. The punishment may be anything from a public dressing-down or threat of dismissal or private reprimand to penalties tailored to fit the violation, culminating in termination.

Negative discipline has been used a great deal in the foodservice and lodging industries. It is commonly used by the rigid, high-control, autocratic, Theory X–style manager who believes that people are lazy and irresponsible and that you have to be on them all the time. Never mind the reason it happened: If they break rules, they've got to be punished; it's the only way to get it through their heads. It is also used by managers who are civilized and friendly but simply believe that punishment is the way to enforce rules.

The fear-and-punishment approach has never worked very well. Punishing one person may deter others from breaking rules, but it does not correct the behavior of the person punished. Punishment simply does not motivate employees to shape up and do their work in an orderly and obedient manner. It may motivate them to avoid the punishment a second time—"Hey, you got me once, but you will never get me again"—but from then on, they will do just enough work to get by.

Fear and punishment are in fact *demotivators*. People who are punished feel embarrassed, defensive, angry, and hostile. It often arouses a desire to get back at the boss and to get the other workers on their side. They look for ways to cause trouble for the boss without getting caught, and the boss is probably going to have to punish them again and again. Punishment almost never turns a first offender into a good worker. It is, however, likely to turn that worker into an adversary.

Managers who are rigid rule followers are usually very conscious of their right to punish and their duty to control, so they go by the book: If a rule is broken, punishment follows. Rigidity is the strongest feature of this kind of discipline: It is consistent. It does deter rule breaking, and it maintains a certain kind of controlled order.

On the other hand, punitive managers tend to have chronic discipline problems, which they are likely to blame on their "no-good workers." They do not recognize how their own shortcomings as managers and leaders have contributed to the problem: They probably haven't explained the rules, communications are poor, people don't like the constant negative feedback, don't like working for them, and so on. Some Theory X managers are really very insecure people, and their inability to control their workers' behavior makes them even more insecure. They vent their anger and frustration on their workers, reassuring themselves that the workers, not they, are to blame.

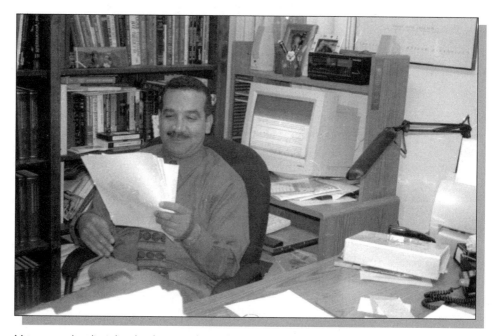

Managers who discipline by threat and punishment tend to be rigid rule followers.

In a fear-and-punishment approach to discipline there is a traditional four-stage formula for disciplinary action:

- ∾ An *oral warning*, stating the violation and warning the employee that it must not happen again
- ∾ A *written warning*, stating that the offense has been repeated and that further repetition will be punished
- ∾ *Punishment*—usually suspension without pay for a specific period, typically one to three days
- ∾ *Termination* if the employee continues to repeat the offense after returning to work

This four-stage formula is called **progressive discipline** because of the progressive severity of each stage. (The term does not in any way imply a forward-looking or humanitarian approach.) The stages are similar to those specified in most union contracts and written into most company policy manuals. The formula is not confined to hard-line Theory X managers: It is widely used with hourly employees in all types of industries.

Over all the years that negative discipline has been used, it has never been successful at turning chronic rule breakers into obedient and cooperative employees. There is nothing in it that will motivate change that will help anyone to become a better employee. It generally creates adversarial relationships and a sort of underground power struggle between worker and boss that is harmful to the work climate and the general morale. This is a power struggle that the supervisor must win if relationships with other workers are to be successful.

Positive Approach

If you stop thinking discipline = punishment and start thinking discipline = rule compliance, you can begin to see that other ways of enforcing the rules are possible. For example, what is the most frequent cause for breaking rules or going against company policies or failing to follow procedures? Up to 90 percent of the time, people do not know that they are doing something that they are not supposed to be doing. They didn't know that you must not leave the hollandaise sitting all day on the back of the range. They didn't know they shouldn't let the patient in Room 302 have the sugar packets left on other patients' trays. They didn't know that champagne had to be chilled. They didn't know that they had parked in the general manager's parking space. They didn't know that guests weren't allowed in the wine cellar and you taught them that the customer is always right.

So when rules are broken, the action you take is to inform and correct. Even though you have handed out employee manuals and have told people the rules and trained them in their jobs, there are still things they don't know, or don't understand, or don't recognize in a new situation, or forgot, or they saw somebody else doing something and thought it was all right. So the positive approach to discipline is continuous education and corrective training whenever the rules and procedures are not being observed.

The philosophy behind the corrective approach is a Theory Y view of people: By and large people are good, they will work willingly, they want to learn, they welcome responsibility, they are capable of self-direction and self-discipline. They will do their job right if you tell them what you want them to do. The approach to discipline is educative and developmental: You inform people why the rule or procedure is important and how to carry it out correctly. The goal is to turn workers into productive employees who are self-motivated to follow the rules and procedures.

This approach to discipline is really an extension of the coaching process—observation, evaluation, and continued training as needed. It approaches rule breaking as a problem to be solved, not as wrongdoing to be punished. It does not threaten people's self-respect, as punishment does; rather, it enlists their efforts in solving the problem.

There will still be some people who go on breaking rules, people who are irresponsible or lazy or hostile or who just don't care. So there must still be some last-resort disciplinary action if rule breaking persists. But persistent rule breaking doesn't happen nearly as often as it does with the punishment approach.

For chronic rule breakers, there is a three-stage formula for disciplinary action that parallels the stages of negative discipline. However, it is not punitive: Rather, it places the problem of correction squarely in the hands of the offender. The employee now has the responsibility for discipline.[2]

∽ *Stage 1: oral reminder.* In a friendly way, you point out the rule violation as you see it happen. You talk to this person—let us say that it is Jim—formally about the seriousness of the offense, the reason for the rules, and the need to obey them. You listen to what Jim has to say in explanation and express confidence that he will find a way to avoid repeating the action.

∽ *Stage 2: written reminder.* This follows further rule breaking. You discuss privately, in a very serious manner, the repeated or continual violation of the rules, and you secure Jim's agreement that he will conform in the future to company requirements. Your attitude is that of counselor rather than judge or law enforcement officer: You avoid threatening him. Following this meeting you write a memorandum summarizing the discussion and agreement, which both you and Jim sign. It is wise to have a third party present at this discussion to act as a witness if needed later. This memo goes into Jim's permanent file.

∽ *Stage 3: termination.* Since Jim has broken not only the rules but also the agreement, there is a clear reason for the termination.

This punishment-free formula for disciplinary action is known as **positive discipline.** Figure 10.4 compares it stage by stage with the negative discipline method. Positive discipline works. Many people who use it report that about 75 percent of the time employees decide to come back and follow the rules. They may not maintain their turnaround indefinitely, but three months or even three weeks of productive behavior is preferable to finding someone new—and it is infinitely better than the hostile employee you are likely to end up with after an unpaid layoff.

---

[2]This system was first described in John Huberman, "Discipline without punishment," *Harvard Business Review,* July–August 1964.

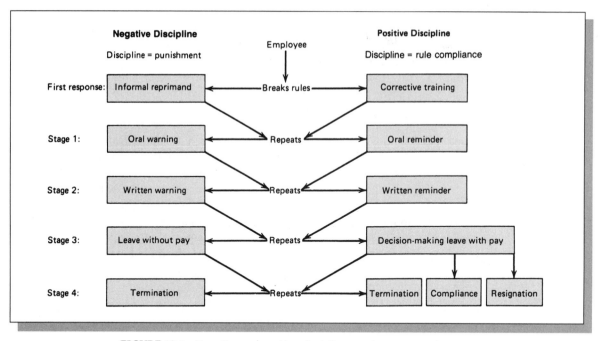

FIGURE 10.4   Negative and positive disciplinary action compared.

Check Your Knowledge

1. What is *discipline?* Whose responsibility is it?
2. List the three essential steps of successful discipline.
3. What is *negative discipline?*
4. What is the positive approach to discipline?

Advantages of the Positive Approach

Using a positive approach from the outset has distinct advantages over the negative system. Honest mistakes, infringements of rules, and violations of policies and procedures are educated out of people's work habits early, before they have time to become issues demanding confrontation. Many discipline problems simply do not happen. The negative consequences of punishment do not fester their way through the work climate. The worker feels no need to get even. The boss and the worker do not become adversaries.

Under a negative system the worker is likely to see the supervisor as someone to avoid and fear. With a positive approach the boss becomes the good guy in the white hat, the coach and counselor who facilitates the employee's work. There is an opportunity for a good relationship to develop. Even if a problem reaches the point of taking leave, the worker is not likely to come back hostile because the employee has no need to save face.

It is better to avoid confrontational situations by adapting a positive proactive approach to policy and procedure violations.

With a positive discipline system the supervisor is more likely to deal with problems early and to be consistent in discipline. A reminder is quick and easy. A reprimand takes time and is unpleasant; you are busy so you look the other way, and pretty soon everybody is taking advantage of you.

Positive discipline lowers costs by reducing the number of disciplinary incidents, reducing turnover, reducing mistakes and poor workmanship, and providing an orderly work environment and a positive work climate favorable to productivity and good morale. Such savings are hard to measure. Punitive discipline raises costs by increasing turnover, reducing motivation, and causing hostility and disruptive behavior. Such costs are also hard to measure.

The cost of the paid leave is one that many managers boggle at: Why should you pay a rule-breaker to stay home and think about it, on top of paying someone to replace the rule-breaker at work? However, that is *all* you pay for the opportunity to end the rule breaking once and for all. Overall, considering the savings of the positive system and the hidden costs of the punitive system, you come out way ahead.

One of the most important contributions of a positive discipline system is that the **decision-making leave with pay** does turn some people around permanently. It brings them face-to-face with themselves and puts their future in their own hands. This can become a new starting point for them. The supervisor can then play a key

∾ profile

ADRIANA VILLAGRANA

Courtesy of Adriana Villagrana

There are some great tips for being a good leader and supervisor. As an operations coordinator at the Hotel del Coronado not only do I have the chance to use my tips, but everyday I learn a new one. Using my personal experience I can explain what I consider helpful to be a successful supervisor.

The first tip is always to remember that to be a supervisor you must always remember to be a great leader first. All the skills that a job requires can be learned with time, but we must also remember that we must be great leaders so that your team can follow your ideas and regulations. Being a leader is to be a great example that employees will be proud to follow.

My second and very important tip is that we need to remember that every person has a different perspective and nobody sees the same thing or works in the same way. In my experience as a supervisor I have learned how to read people and under-

role by supporting all attempts to improve and by giving encouragement, positive reinforcement, and recognition for success. This is one of the few ways of transforming a hostile employee into a responsible and productive worker. It is a very rewarding kind of supervisory success.

Shifting from Negative to Positive Discipline

The biggest problem of using the positive approach is in shifting from one approach to the other. As a person starting out in your first supervisory position, you might not have this problem. But supervisors who are used to administering penalties and punishments often have trouble shifting gears. To begin with, they may have difficulty accepting the idea of paying an employee to stay home and think things over. It seems like a reward for bad behavior, and it seems unfair to the people who follow the rules and are working hard for their day's pay.

The second problem is shaking loose the habit of thinking in terms of punishment and substituting the attitude of educating and helping people to avoid breaking rules. Supervisors may *believe* in punishment. They may have been brought up with this type of discipline both at home and at school. It is hard to begin to teach, to help, to develop a rule-breaker when you have always reprimanded, warned, threatened, and punished. It requires an entirely new set of attitudes as well as a new tone of voice. It takes at least a day of intensive training and practice for supervisors to learn how to carry out positive discipline. But companies that use it report significant reductions in turnover, absenteeism, and disciplinary problems.[3]

[3]David N. Campbell, R. L. Fleming, and Richard C. Grote, "Discipline without punishment—at last," *Harvard Business Review,* July–August 1985.

stand the way they think. I consider this to be a very helpful ability. I have learned to ask for the same thing in 20 different ways. To have the same task completed by different people, I have learned that some people first need to really understand the reason behind the task, whereas others don't really care as long as they feel part of the team.

Finally, I would recommend always going back to what we call the "line of fire." Not only does it show one's support but also helps one to continue being a great leader. By going out and working side by side with your team, you can realize first-hand what your team is lacking and also their needs. If you spend enough time working on the front line, you never forget where you started and the reason for all your hard work. This is a win–win situation because you show that you care, learn the needs of your team, and get the gratification of knowing that things run smoothly thanks to all the hard work of you and your team.

I enjoy being a supervisor, but I like to consider myself as a leader who has willing followers. By seeing myself as a leader, I remember that I must be a great example and trustworthy in order to maintain happy and productive employees.

Administering Discipline

We talked in Chapter 1 about management in the hospitality industry being reactive rather than planned—that is, reacting to events as they happen, dealing with problems as they come up. Certainly, enforcing the rules is one of the most reactive aspects of the supervisor's job. Even when the general outlines and the essentials are clear in your mind, each instance of enforcing the rules and procedures makes its own special demands, and positive and negative approaches seem less clear-cut and obvious.

Adapting Discipline to the Situation

Many companies have a **uniform discipline system** that prescribes the specific disciplinary action for each rule violation each time a given employee breaks that rule. Figure 10.1 gives you an example. A system such as this provides a companywide set of directives that tells the supervisor exactly what to do. It takes the subjectivity out of disciplinary action and gives support to the supervisor, especially when drastic action is needed.

Yet even with a company system there is a good deal of room for your own method of administering it. Seldom are discipline situations black and white. You have to investigate the facts and exercise your own judgment in the light of all the relevant factors. Human skills and conceptual skills are involved.

Usually, disciplinary action should be adjusted to circumstances. One of the things that you should consider is the intent of the rule-breaker. Was it an accident? Was the person aware of the rule or requirement? Was it a case of misinformation or misunderstanding? Could it have been your fault? Another consideration is extenuating circumstances such as severe personal problems or a crisis on the job. Still another consideration is the number of times that a person has done this type of thing before. Another is the seriousness of the offense. What are its consequences for the product, the customer, your department, the company? What will be the impact of your response as a deterrent to others?

You may handle different people differently for the same violation: You may take a hard-line approach with a hostile troublemaker but treat an anxiety-ridden first-time offender gently. This does not mean that you are being inconsistent; you are enforcing the rules in each case; you are not permitting either of them to go against regulations. As with everything else in this profession, you must be able to adapt your discipline to your own leadership style, to your workers and their needs and actions, and to the situation at any given time and all the time.

Some Mistakes to Avoid

One of the biggest mistakes that new supervisors make is to start off being too easy about enforcing the rules. They want people to like them, and they let people get away with small things that are against the rules, and perhaps even a few big things, just because they think people will like them for it. For example, you see one of your people lighting up a cigarette 5 minutes before closing and you just look the other way. If you were promoted from an hourly position, you may still have the worker's view of the rules and you can empathize with that person's feeling about that cigarette and that rule against smoking on the job. You may even disapprove of some of the rules you are supposed to enforce. It is very easy to let many things slip by.

This is just about the most difficult way you can start off your supervisory career. By saying nothing when a violation occurs, you are actually saying, "It's okay to do that." Right off, some people will begin to test you, to see how far they can go before you take any action, and pretty soon you will have a real problem on your hands getting people to follow rules and meet standards.

It is always easier to start out by strictly enforcing every rule and regulation than it is to try to tighten up later. People feel betrayed when you switch from leniency to enforcement, and they suddenly decide that you are bad, mean, and tough to work for. Besides, it is your obligation as a manager to enforce the rules. Even when you think rules are unfair, you do not take it upon yourself to change them by not enforcing them. Rules can be changed, but the way to do it is to go through channels and get the changes approved. Often, supervisors look the other way because they are simply too busy to cope with discipline. You just don't have time for this today, you don't want the hassle, and you've got to get the work out, so you let things slide.

Sometimes, correcting people's behavior just doesn't seem to do any good. You go over and over and over a procedure with a certain worker but nothing seems to change, and you reach a point where you start taking those little white pills your doctor gave you for indigestion, and finally, you stop wrestling with the problem and do nothing. Still another reason for doing nothing is that if you fire this person, you might get a new employee who is even worse. Another reason is that you don't think your supervisor will back up your action, so you just don't take any.

All these reasons for letting people get by with rule-breaking or substandard performance add up to the same problem: It gets harder and harder to maintain discipline. And it gets harder and harder to manage your people in other ways as well, because you lose their respect. In effect, *they* gradually take charge of the way they do things. The work suffers, quality of product and service suffers, customers complain, costs go up, and you are failing at your job as a manager.

Another mistake in disciplining is to act in anger. Anger will make the worker defensive and hostile, and you will seldom use good judgment in what you say and do. You won't stop to get the facts straight, you may be harsh and vindictive, you may make a threat you can't carry out, or do some other thing you will regret later. If you overreact, if you are wrong, you lose face and you lose some of your control over your people.

Threatening to take any action that you do not carry out is very common, and it is always a mistake. It is like looking the other way: It invites testing and rule-breaking. You have to stick to whatever you say you will do: You have no alternative.

Putting somebody down in front of other people is another way to ask for an uncooperative employee. It is one thing to correct someone quietly in the presence of others: "I just want to remind you that we always use the guard on the slicer." This approach informs and teaches on the spot, and although it is a form of public discipline it does not belittle, embarrass, or humiliate. But yelling, threatening, or making a fool of someone in front of others will certainly have the familiar consequences of resentment and hostility.

A different kind of mistake is to exceed your authority in taking disciplinary action. You must know exactly what your job empowers you to do as well as everything there is to know about company policy and practice. If there is a company system of procedures and penalties, you must follow it. If you are thinking of terminating someone, make certain that you have the authority to do so and find out the termination procedures your company requires. It could be quite embarrassing if you threatened to fire someone and then found out you couldn't. And it would be a disaster all the way around if you fired somebody and then had to take that person back.

Another critical error is to try to evade the responsibility for taking disciplinary action by shifting it to your boss or the personnel department or by delegating it to someone under you. If you do this, you simply become a straw boss and your people will have no respect for you. Discipline is an obligation of supervision, and your success as a manager depends on it.

Unexpected discipline will always meet with resistance and protest. This often happens when a rule has not been enforced for some time and the supervisor suddenly decides to tighten up. It is important to give warning about either a new rule or a new policy of enforcing an old rule, with a clear statement of the consequences of breaking it.

Some other things to avoid are:

∾ *Criticizing the person rather than the behavior.* Keep personalities out of discipline.

∾ *Waiting too long to take action.* The longer the gap between incident and action, the more likely the action is to be interpreted as a personal attack.

- ∾ *Touching someone when you are disciplining.* It can be interpreted as intent to do physical harm or as sexual harassment.
- ∾ *Being inconsistent.* You must avoid partiality, and your actions must be fair in your workers' eyes.

Taking the Essential Steps

The set of procedures that follows is one you should use when you are confronted with a serious infringement of regulations or a less serious but chronic failure to observe the rules of the operation or the requirements of a job. There are six formal steps to enforce compliance. These steps apply no matter what approaches to disciplinary action—negative or positive—you intend to follow. They apply to each stage of the disciplinary sequence (Figure 10.4) and they amplify what should take place at each stage.

1. *Collect all the facts.* Interview any employees involved and any witnesses, especially other supervisors or managers. Write it all down. Make every effort to sort out fact from opinion, both in what others say and in your own mind. Avoid drawing conclusions until you have the full picture. Use these questions as a guide:
   a. Was the employee's action intentional? Was it an accident? Was it the result of misinformation or misunderstanding? Could it have been your fault?
   b. Was the employee aware of the rule or requirement?
   c. Were there extenuating circumstances, such as severe personal problems or a crisis on the job?
   d. How serious is the offense? What are its consequences for the product, the guest, your department, the company?
   e. What is the employee's past record? Is this the first time something like this happened, or has it happened before? How long has the employee worked here?
   f. Did you witness the violation? If not, what kind of evidence do you have? Are your sources other management personnel? Do you have enough evidence to justify action?

2. *Discuss the incident with the employee.* Do this as soon as possible after the incident; after all, justice delayed is justice denied. Plan to sit down with the employee in a quiet setting where you will not be interrupted. Also, line up a witness to sit in on the interview. Here are the steps to follow:
   a. Tell the employee that you are concerned about the incident that took place and that you would like to hear his or her side after you describe the facts as you see them.
   b. Stay calm and without assigning blame, go over what you know. Also explain the consequences of the action. For example, if a server failed to clean up her station at the end of the shift, explain how this affects the other servers and the guests.
   c. Now ask the employee to tell you his or her side. Listen actively, encourage, stay calm, and do not get into an argument. Ask questions as needed. This step is crucial because it gives the employee **due process.** Due process is the opportunity to defend yourself against charges.

3. *Decide on the appropriate action if any is to be taken.* To do this, you must consider what both yourself and others have done in similar cases. Your action should be consistent with that of others throughout the company or you may inadvertently set a precedent. You want to make sure that any action you take is not discriminatory. Before deciding on any action, be sure to consult your boss, and you may also be required to discuss this with a representative from the human resources department.

4. *Take the appropriate actions, such as a written warning, and develop an improvement plan with the employee using these steps:*

   a. Explain to the employee the action you are taking, in a serious but matter-of-fact tone of voice, avoiding any trace of vengefulness or anger. Also state clearly the consequences that will follow if the behavior recurs.

   b. Ask the employee to identify some actions that he or she can take so that this does not happen again. Develop mutually an improvement plan and a date by which it is expected that the improvement will be made. Make it clear that you are willing to work with the employee but that it remains the employee's responsibility to make the changes.

   c. If your policy requires it, ask the employee to sign a disciplinary report (Figure 10.5). This is normally done so that you have written proof that the employee was informed of the contents of the report. From time to time you will have an employee who refuses to sign the report because he thinks that his signature will signify that he agrees with the contents of the report, or in other words, he is guilty as charged. When this happens, explain that the signature signifies understanding of, not agreement with, what is stated. If the employee continues to refuse to sign, you should write "Refused to Sign" on the report.

   d. Close on a positive note by stating your confidence in the employee to improve and resolve the issue. Also express your genuine desire to see improvement.

5. *Make sure that you have everything written down.* Why is it important to have everything written? There are several reasons. First, in the event that the employee ever takes you to court or an unemployment compensation hearing, you will need written documentation to help build your case. Second, the process of writing down helps you see the situation more objectively and focus on job-related issues. Third, because your documentation includes the employee's improvement plan, it helps the employee to improve.

When documenting, be specific about what the employee did and the circumstances surrounding the situation. Focus on observable, verifiable facts; be nonjudgmental. Document facts, not opinions or hearsay—they have no place in documentation. Include who, what, where, when, and how. Document accurately and thoroughly, including information obtained during your investigation and during the disciplinary meeting. Always document as quickly as possible; otherwise, you will forget many of the details. Also include objectives for future performance and the consequences for not meeting the objectives.

6. *Follow up.* You do everything you can do to help the worker meet your expectations while staying on the lookout for further troublemaking of any kind. If the behavior does not meet your stated expectations, you must take the next step as promised.

DISCIPLINE REPORT

Employee: _____ Date: _____ Time: _____ Place: _____

Incident as you saw it:

Employee's account:

Witness name: _____ Position: _____
Witness's account of incident: (Must be a manager)

Extenuating circumstances:

Past record:

Details of disciplinary interview:

Action taken:

Date: _____ Supervisor: _____

FIGURE 10.5 Report form for developing a written record of a disciplinary incident.

Check Your Knowledge

1. Positive discipline can result in a reduction in what three areas?
2. What is the *uniform discipline system?*

Termination

Salvage or Terminate?[4]

If you had performance standards, you trained people carefully, and have evaluated and coached and corrected them on a more-or-less daily basis, you would pretty quickly spot people who are never going to make it in their jobs. They aren't exactly rule-breakers, they just don't perform well, are absent a lot, or do some dumb thing over and over and over and you just can't get them straightened out.

If you hired them, your best bet is to terminate them before their probationary period runs out, as suggested in Chapter 7. But you may think that you can turn them around, and you work and work and work with them, and finally, you have to admit that they are hopeless and you are stuck with them. You may also have inherited some of these people.

What are you going to do? Should you fire Jerry for going right on overpouring drinks although you have showed him every blessed day the right amount to pour? How can you get rid of Kimberly when you can't even figure out what to pin her trouble on, because it's something different every day? Can you terminate Alfred for being an alcoholic when he has been here five times as long as you have and is twice your age? Should you terminate any of them, no matter how bad their work is?

Sometimes managers will try to **dehire** people by making them want to leave the job or look for something else. In this approach, a manager gives other people all the work and leaves this person with nothing to do or in other ways hints that it would be wise to look for another job. It is a destructive way of handling a person, and it does not work very well for the manager either. Legally, it is a practice that is open to all kinds of discrimination lawsuits and should be avoided. You have no control and you have to wait for this person to take the step of leaving while you go on paying wages for little or no work done. It is both kinder and better either to terminate outright or to keep on trying to salvage this worker.

From the productivity point of view and your own frustration level, it would probably be far better if you simply terminated all these very poor performers. But there are other considerations. Length of service is one. The longer people have been working for a company, the harder it is to fire them. Company policy and if there is a union, union rules, come into play here; you may not have a choice. Seniority is one of the most sacred traditions in U.S. industry.

A person's past record is another consideration. You may have people who are chronically late to work, and if they always have been, they probably always will be.

---

[4]This section is adapted from Lawrence Steinmetz, "The unsatisfactory performer: salvage or discharge?" *Personnel*, Vol. 45, No. 3, 1968; and from Richard Martin, "Costly liability can result from botched dismissals, faulty paperwork," *Nation's Restaurant News*, September 25, 2000.

On the other hand, if a person has had a good performance record and there is a sudden change, whether it is coming in late or some other drop in performance, that person is probably salvageable. Another consideration is how badly you need a person's skill or experience. In a tight labor market, even somebody who does not meet standards is better than nobody.

It is very difficult to fire someone who desperately needs the job even if the person is terrible at it. You might bring yourself to do it if you had to look forward to 30 years of coping with this substandard worker. But if the person in question is a senior, you cannot terminate him or her on the basis of age, but you can terminate the person for inability to do the job to the standard required, once you have given the employee ample chance to improve and have been through the steps of verbal warning, written warning, and so on.

It is also difficult to fire someone who you are pretty sure will make trouble about it. In this case it is wise to consult with your boss or the human resources department or both. (Some companies have a policy that only the director of human resources and the general manager or department head may terminate an employee. In any event, there should always be a warning of the termination, in case of later legal action.)

Perhaps the most difficult question to figure out is the effect on your other workers of terminating someone. They may have resented that person's poor work and be glad to see you hire someone who they do not have to fill in for all the time. On the other hand, they may have been imitating this person and slowing down the whole operation—a bad example is always easier to follow than a good one. Or they may be fond of this character and will be angry if he or she is terminated. Some of them will be worried and upset about whether the same thing will happen to them. A termination is always something of an upheaval, and you may have to cope with some repercussions.

> When determining whether or not it is best to terminate an employee, first weigh the risks involved. As the employer, keep the legal aspects in view. What are the costly pitfalls of wrongful termination suits? Termination suits can help to alert litigation brought from workers over on-the-job discrimination issues. A common mistake of managers is not to treat all employees equally: for example, to reassign a tip-earning server who becomes pregnant to a less-compensated hostess position out of a sense of protecting her health and guarding against liability. It is not appropriate to discriminate against employees by giving only certain people one type of job.

You have to consider the cost and trauma of hiring a replacement against the cost and trauma of retaining this person. You also have to consider whether your authority entitles you to terminate. In fact, you should consider this first.

If you decide to salvage, you have a few options open. You can try people in different jobs. You can look for special talents and interests and try to motivate them with some form of job enrichment. You can counsel the alcoholic to go to a clinic for rehabilitation. You can investigate the case of the sudden performance drop and try coaching this person back to the old level. Or you can grin and bear it.

Just-Cause Terminations

If you think that it may be an appropriate time to terminate an employee, first make sure that it isn't something for which you can't fire the employee, such as discrimination (Table 10.1). You can fire employees for *just cause,* meaning that the offense

TABLE 10.1 ∾ When It Is Inappropriate to Terminate an Employee

- Discharging an employee based on race, color, gender, or national origin (Title VII of the Civil Rights Act of 1964)
- Discharging in retaliation for filing discrimination charges (Title VII of the Civil Rights Act of 1964)
- Discharging an employee for testifying against a company at Equal Employment Opportunity Commission hearings (Title VII of the Civil Rights Act of 1964)
- Discharging an employee for helping other employees who have been discriminated against by a company to exercise their legal rights (Title VII of the Civil Rights Act of 1964)
- Discharging an older employee, 40 years of age or more, because of age (Age Discrimination in Employment Act of 1967, as amended)
- Forcing retirement or permanent layoff of an older employee (Age Discrimination in Employment Act of 1967, as amended)
- Discharging an older employee in a permanent layoff using standards that are not applied universally to all affected employees (Age Discrimination in Employment Act of 1967, as amended)
- Discharging an employee because she is pregnant (Pregnancy Discrimination Act of 1978)
- Discharging an employee in retaliation for filing an OSHA complaint (Occupational Safety and Health Act of 1970)
- Discharging an employee in retaliation for requesting a state or federal inspection of unsafe working conditions (Occupational Safety and Health Act of 1970)
- Discharging an employee in retaliation for testifying against a company in an OSHA-related court action (Occupational Safety and Health Act of 1970)
- Discharging a handicapped employee because of the handicap (Americans with Disabilities Act of 1990)
- Discharging a Vietnam-era veteran during his or her first year of reemployment without "good cause" (Vietnam-Era Veterans' Readjustment Assistance Act of 1974)
- Discharging an employee to avoid paying a pension or benefit plan, such as a group health insurance plan (Employee Retirement Income Security Act of 1974)
- Discharging an employee because of his or her obligation to perform jury service
- Discharging for performing duties as a member of the National Guard
- Discharging in retaliation for refusal to perform an illegal act on behalf of an employer
- Discharging in retaliation for whistle-blowing concerning the illegal acts of an employer such as making false statements
- Discharging an employee who is exercising a legal right, such as filing for workers compensation
- Discharging for participation in union activities or union-organizing efforts
- Discharging in retaliation for helping the government prepare or prosecute a case against an employer

Source: Adapted from Axel R. Granholm, *Handbook of Employee Termination.* New York: Wiley, 1991.

must affect the specific work the employee does or the operation as a whole in a detrimental way. Before terminating anyone, ask yourself the following questions:

1. Did the employee know the rule, and was he or she warned about the consequences of violating the rule? Are these understandings confirmed and acknowledged in writing?

2. Were management's expectations of the employee reasonable? Was the rule reasonable?

3. Did management make a reasonable effort to help the employee resolve the problem before termination, and is there written proof of this?

4. Was a final written warning given to the employee explaining that discharge would result from another conduct violation or unsatisfactory performance?

5. In the case of misconduct, did the employee act in willful and deliberate disregard of reasonable employer expectations? Was the situation within his or her control? If the situation was out of the employee's personal control, he or she cannot be charged with misconduct.

6. Was management's investigation of the final offense done in a fair and objective manner, and did it involve someone other than the employee's direct supervisor? It is best that the employee's supervisor not function alone and fill the roles of accuser, judge, and jury. Is there substantial proof that the employee was guilty?

7. Is dismissal of the employee in line with the employee's prior work record and length of service? When an employee has many years of service that are documented as satisfactory or better, he or she is generally entitled to more time to improve before being dismissed.

8. Did the employee have an opportunity to hear the facts and respond to them in a nonthreatening environment? Was the employee able to bring someone into the disciplinary interview if requested?

9. Has this employee been treated as others in similar circumstances? Has this rule been enforced consistently in the past? If the rule has not been enforced consistently, you may have to forgo terminating the employee and instead, go back a step, such as to suspension. In the case where a rule that hasn't been enforced starts to be enforced again, you have to inform employees beforehand of the change.

10. Is the action nondiscriminatory? Has equal treatment been given to members of protected groups (minorities, women, employees over 40 years of age) and nonprotected groups?

These questions are only guidelines for determining **just-cause termination.** Even if you can answer yes to every question presented here, there is still no guarantee that you won't wind up in court. If you decide to terminate, all the basic procedural steps spelled out for disciplinary action apply to this final decision. You state the problem in writing, collect the facts, make your decision, and take the action.

The Termination Interview[5]

Few people like telling an employee that he or she is terminated, fired, dismissed. The best way to reduce your nervousness and make it less stressful for the employee is to prepare for the termination interview by using something like the termination interview checklist shown in Figure 10.6. The checklist can help you to:

1. Select a good time and place to conduct the interview.

2. Determine who will be present at the meeting (you should have at least one person as a witness), as well as whether the employee needs to be escorted out of the building.

[5]This section is adapted from Martin, "Costly liability."

TERMINATION INTERVIEW CHECKLIST

Employee Name: _____

Employee Position: _____ Department: _____

Employment Date: _____ Termination Date: _____

1. Decide on where the interview will take place and when.

(Avoid firing at end of workweek or near the time of major events such as birthdays and holidays. Choose a time when the employee can clear out his or her belongings without other employees present. Select a quiet place where you will not be interrupted and the employee will not disturb others upon leaving.)

_____

_____

_____

_____

2. Determine who will be present at the meeting and whether the employee needs an escort out of the building.

(There should be at least one person as a witness, and probably a representative from human resources as well. If the employee is a member of a bargaining unit, use the contract as your guide.)

_____

_____

_____

3. Develop an opening statement and practice it.

(Write out exactly what you are going to tell the employee. Make sure you state clearly that the employee is being terminated and include a brief summary of the reason(s). Make it clear to the employee that there are no options.)

_____

_____

_____

_____

4. Determine how best to respond to possible employee reactions.

(Think about how you expect the employee to respond and how you can handle each type of response. Your goal during the interview is to let the employee respond to the termination, within limits, and then proceed with getting the necessary information across.)

Possible Reactions: _____

_____

FIGURE 10.6 Sample termination interview checklist.

Your Responses: _____

_____

Record below any threats the employee makes about legal action during the interview.

_____

_____

_____

5. Determine the final pay, severance pay, and benefits to which the employee is entitled, and communicate them.

Pay:

_____ Pay in lieu of notice   _____ Workdays
(only in the case of unsatisfactory
work performance)

_____ Accrued vacation   _____ Workdays

Payment by: _____ Lump sum _____ Payroll checks

Benefits:

Entitled to: Explained:

_____   _____ Group health insurance continuation

_____   _____ Vested rights in pension plan

OTHER: _____

6. Clearance procedures.

Make sure employee hands in the following:

_____ Locker keys

_____ Uniforms

_____ Name tag

_____ ID card

Completed by: Date:

_____   _____

FIGURE 10.6 *(Continued).*

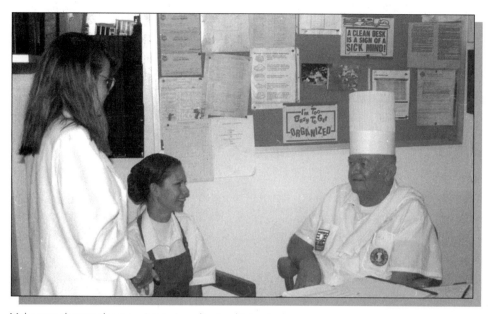

Make sure that you have a witness in a dismissal interview.

3. Develop your opening statement and practice it.

4. Determine how best to respond to possible employee reactions.

5. Determine the final pay, severance pay, and benefits to which the employee is entitled.

6. Develop a list of clearance procedures to be performed at the end of the interview. The timing and place for the interview are important. Although conventional wisdom says to fire an employee at the end of a workweek, that is not necessarily the best line. By firing the employee at the beginning of the workweek, you give him or her a chance to start immediately looking for a new job, instead of complaining and becoming upset at home. Nor is it wise to terminate employees near major events such as holidays, birthdays, or dates of their anniversary of beginning work with the company. Try to arrange a time when the employee can clean out his or her locker without other employees present.

The meeting should take place in a private room so that should the employee become unruly, guests and co-workers will not be disturbed. A room in the human resources department is ideal. Having prepared for the interview, it is time to speak with the employee. Although you may be nervous, it is probable that the employee is nervous as well. The employee probably knows what's going on and is anxious to get it over with, too. Employees who are fired are often relieved and go on to find new jobs that are much more satisfying. In some cases you might even feel that you did the employee a favor. Following are steps for a termination interview.

1. Do not beat around the bush. Avoid small talk and tell the employee that he or she is being dismissed, and why. Do so in a firm, calm manner. Avoid a discussion of all

TABLE 10.2   ∾   **How to React to Employees' Emotional Responses**

Type of Emotional Response	What You Can Do
1. Crying	■ Let the employee cry it out. ■ Do not apologize for your actions. ■ Show concern by offering a tissue, something to drink, or a moment of privacy if appropriate. ■ Staying calm and businesslike, think about the next step in the interview.
2. Shouting and cursing	■ Keep your own emotions under control and maintain a calm and cool demeanor. ■ Make it perfectly clear to the employee that you will continue the conversation only when the shouting stops. Use your normal tone of voice; do not show irritation. ■ Tell the employee that you would like him or her to know the arrangement for termination pay and benefits.
3. Unresponsive	■ Be empathic, but also continue the interview. ■ Do not ask the employee questions such as "How could you be shocked at this news?" Do not play counselor when the employee withdraws. ■ Confirm all details in a letter.
4. Employee leaves after your opening statement	■ Tell the employee that you really do not want him or her to miss hearing the arrangements made for termination pay and benefits.

the details leading up to this decision. This is not the time for that; there have surely been plenty of previous counselings. Instead, state the category under which the discipline problem falls, such as excessive absenteeism, and mention the last step taken and how it was made clear that the employee faced termination for one more offense. Clearly communicate that the decision has been made and there is no possibility for negotiation. Explain that the decision is a joint decision in which others, such as the general manager and human resources director, have been involved. Reinforced in this manner, your authority will not be questioned as readily.

2. At this point, listen to and accept the responses of the employee. Be prepared for any type of response, such as anger, tears, amazement, or hostility. Table 10.2 describes how to react to four different types of responses.

3. Now is the time to say something positive to the employee to maintain his or her self-esteem, which at this point is probably sagging. Make a statement about something that you, and others, really like about the employee. Perhaps the employee has a good sense of humor or was thoughtful of co-workers.

4. Move on to a discussion of final pay, severance pay, and benefits to which the employee is entitled.

5. Finally, explain your clearance procedures and give the employee clear instructions about what to do after your discussion. Do you want the employee to go straight to his or her locker, clean it out, and leave quietly? Is there someone who will escort the employee out of the building?

6. End the interview by standing up and moving toward the door. Avoid making any physical gesture, such as shaking hands or putting your hand on the employee's shoulder, which could be taken the wrong way by someone who is upset and angry. Try to close on a positive, friendly note.

Keep the pace moving during the termination interview. The entire interview should be over in about 10 to 20 minutes.

After the interview, be sure to document important details, including the employee's reaction, any threats that may have been made, and any comments made about the fairness of the decision. Routine terminations lacking clear resolutions can come back to haunt a business. Be sure to keep everything confidential; inform only those employees who must know. If you tell the employee's former co-workers about the dismissal, you are leaving yourself open to be sued for slander.

Special Disciplinary Concerns

Sexual Harassment[6]

As a supervisor you need to be able to recognize and confront **sexual harassment.** The Equal Employment Opportunity Commission (EEOC) issued guidelines on sexual harassment in 1980, indicating that it is a form of gender discrimination under Title VII of the 1964 Civil Rights Act. The EEOC states that sexual harassment consists of "unwelcome advances, requests for sexual favors, and other verbal or physical conduct of a sexual nature when: (1) submission to such conduct is made either explicitly or implicitly a term or condition of an individual's employment, or (2) submission to or rejection of such conduct by an individual is used as the basis for employment decisions affecting the person." This definition of sexual harassment is known as the **quid pro quo** definition. *Quid pro quo* means that something is given in exchange for something else. In this type of sexual harassment, submission to or rejection of a sexual favor is used as the basis for employment decisions regarding that employee. The employment decision may be an increase in pay, a promotion, or keeping your job. Only supervisors or other members of management can engage in quid pro quo harassment.

Another type of sexual harassment is **environmental sexual harassment.** In this case, comments or innuendoes of a sexual nature, or physical contact, are considered a violation when they interfere with an employee's work performance or create an "intimidating, hostile, or offensive working environment." In this situation, the harassment must be persistent and so severe that it affects the employee's well-being.

---

[6]This section is adapted from Amy Zuber, "EEOC suits put harassment on operator's front burner," *Nation's Restaurant News*, Vol. 33, No. 5, February 1, 1999.

A final type of sexual harassment is **third-party sexual harassment.** Third-party sexual harassment involves a customer or client and an employee. The customer or client may harass an employee, or the other way around. For example, a male customer may harass a female bartender.

The following examples of sexual harassment include an example of quid pro quo, environmental, and third-party sexual harassment. See if you can determine which is which.

> Complaints of sexual harassment in the workplace have risen dramatically in the last several years. The number of discrimination charges alleging sexual harassment has grown from 6883 in 1991 to 15,618 in 2000. Corresponding to the increase in sexual-harassment charges, the amount of money employers paid as part of related settlements before litigation jumped from $7.1 million in 1991 to $34.3 million in 2000. To cut down on these high numbers, it is important for companies to have sexual training programs as well as written policies that detail the steps that employees should follow in the event of a problem. Workers should be encouraged to come forward when an incident makes them uncomfortable or when they feel that a supervisor has acted inappropriately.

1. Beth is a new employee who works as a cook's assistant in a crowded kitchen. The men in the kitchen are constantly making crude, sexually oriented comments and jokes, and leave their X-rated magazines in full view of anyone walking by. Beth feels very intimidated and ill at ease. Unfortunately, the situation doesn't improve over the first two months, and Beth feels too stressed to continue working.

2. For the past few nights, after the dining room has closed, Susan's boss has asked her to go to his place for a drink. Although Susan has gone out with him and some friends once before, she is not interested in pursuing a relationship with him. When she tells him she is not interested, he tells her that a dining room supervisor job is coming open soon and that he could make sure she gets it if she takes him up on his invitation.

3. Barbara is a regular customer at a popular after-work bar where Bob works as a bartender. Barbara finds Bob to be a very good-looking fellow, so much so that she can't keep her eyes, or hands, off him. Bob doesn't like the attention Barbara gives him, but he feels he can't do much about it since she is the customer.

Such instances of sexual harassment can cost a company lost productive time, low morale, harm to its reputation, court costs, and punitive damages to harassment victims. In each of the situations above, there is an element of sexual harassment. While the second situation represents the typical exchange of sexual favors for employment opportunities, the first situation is an example of environmental sexual harassment in which the working environment was intimidating, hostile, or offensive due to physical, verbal, or visual (such as pornographic pictures) sexual harassment. The third situation represents third-party sexual harassment.

As a supervisor you are responsible for *recognizing, confronting, and preventing the sexual harassment of both female and male employees by other employees or by nonemployees* such as guests or people making deliveries. "An employer can be liable for customers who harass employees when the employer knew or should have known of the harassment and failed to prevent it."[7] Both you and your employer will be considered guilty of sexual harassment if you knew about, or should have

[7]Susan E. Long, "When customers harass, employers can be liable," *HR Focus,* Vol. 76, No. 3, March 1999.

known about, such misconduct and failed to correct it. If you genuinely did not know that sexual harassment took place, liability can be averted if there is an adequate sexual harassment policy *and* the situation is corrected immediately.

Following are some specific actions that you can take to deal effectively with the issue of sexual harassment:

- ∽ Be familiar with your company's sexual harassment policy. Figure 10.7 is a sample policy. This policy should include disciplinary guidelines for people who are guilty of sexual harassment and guidelines for harassers who retaliate against those who turn them in. This policy may also include a formal complaint procedure for employees to use if they think they have been victims of sexual harassment, with provisions for immediate investigations and prompt disciplinary actions when appropriate.

- ∽ Educate your employees on how to recognize sexual harassment, how to report it when it occurs, and the steps that will be taken if an employee is guilty of sexual harassment.

- ∽ When an employee informs you of a possible case of sexual harassment, investigate the situation promptly according to your company policy. Your investigation is much the same as that done for any possible case of misconduct as just described. Don't assume that anyone is guilty or innocent.

- ∽ When you witness an example of sexual harassment, follow your policy and take appropriate and timely disciplinary action.

- ∽ Provide follow-up after instances of sexual harassment. Check with victims and witnesses that harassment has indeed stopped and that no retaliation is taking place.

- ∽ Prevent sexual harassment by being visible in your work areas, being a good role model, and taking all reported incidents seriously.

Check Your Knowledge

1. What is meant by *dehire?*
2. What is a *third-party sexual harassment?*

Other Forms of Harassment

Harassment in the workplace is not limited to sexual harassment. All forms of harassment based on national origin, race, color, religion, gender, disability, or age are illegal. *Harassment* is defined as intimidating, hostile, or offensive behavior toward someone, or the creation of an intimidating, hostile, or offensive environment for someone, based on that person's national origin, race, color, religion, gender, disability, or age.

Intimidating behavior may involve threatening someone with harm of some type. Hostile behavior could include asking an employee to do something that is completely unrealistic, such as asking a potwasher to be in charge of washing all

I. Policy

The policy of XYZ Hotels is that all of our employees should be able to enjoy a work environment free from all forms of discrimination, including sexual harassment. Sexual harassment is a form of misconduct that undermines the integrity of the employment relationship, debilitates morale, and therefore interferes with the work effectiveness of its victims and their co-workers. Sexual harassment is a violation of the law and will not be tolerated or condoned.

II. Definition of Sexual Harassment

Sexual harassment consists of unwelcome advances, requests for sexual favors, and other verbal or physical conduct of a sexual nature when:

1. submission to such conduct is made either explicitly or implicitly a term or condition of an employee's employment, or
2. submission to or rejection of such conduct by an employee is used as the basis for employment decisions, or
3. the conduct interferes substantially with an employee's work performance or creates an intimidating, hostile, or offensive work environment.

Sexual harassment is not limited to actions of hotel employees. Customers and clients may also be victims, or perpetrators, of sexual harassment.

Following are examples of sexual harassment.

- Unwelcome intentional touching or other unwelcome physical contact (such as pinching or patting).
- Unwelcome staring or whistling.
- Unwelcome sexually suggestive or flirtatious notes, gifts, electronic or voice mail.
- Offering an employment-related reward in exchange for sexual favors.
- Verbal abuse of a sexual nature.
- Unwelcome display of sexually suggestive objects or pictures such as pinups.
- Conduct or remarks that demean or are hostile to a person's gender.

III. Coverage: XYZ Hotels

XYZ Hotels prohibits sexual harassment during work hours or while on company property by all employees and by all nonemployees, such as customers and suppliers.

IV. Responsibilities

XYZ Hotels managers are responsible for preventing sexual harassment and educating employees about this subject. They are also responsible for setting a good example, taking every complaint seriously, investigating complaints fairly, and maintaining confidentiality.

XYZ Hotels requests that any employee with a complaint regarding sexual harassment make every effort to promptly present the complaint to their immediate supervisor or the human resources director. If the complaint involves the employee's immediate supervisor, or if the employee feels uncomfortable discussing the complaint with the immediate supervisor, the employee may speak to another supervisor.

V. Investigation Procedures and Disciplinary Action

Once a supervisor has received a complaint, he or she is to immediately contact the Human Resources Department. After notification of the employee's complaint, a fair and confidential investigation will be initiated. The results of the investigation will be reviewed by the Human Resources Director for possible disciplinary action.

If warranted, disciplinary action up to and including termination will be imposed. Retaliation against employees who file complaints or assist in investigating complaints may also result in discipline up to and including termination.

FIGURE 10.7 Sample sexual harassment policy.

dishes as well. Offensive behavior is generally ridiculing or taunting someone because of his or her color, for example. As a supervisor, you should be constantly on the lookout for intimidating, hostile, or offensive behavior, because it has no place in the workplace.

Substance Abuse

The problem of substance abuse in the workplace is pervasive. Although it is not always seen, its effects can be devastating. Substance abuse is usually defined as working under the influence of, using, or being impaired by alcohol or any drug, where job performance or safety of employees and/or guests is adversely affected. Drugs include both illegal and some legal drugs, such as prescription or over-the-counter medications that, when abused, adversely affect job performance. Although drug abuse probably gets more publicity, the extent of alcohol abuse in the workplace is actually greater than that of all the illegal drugs combined.

It is estimated that as many as one in five American workers has a drug and alcohol problem.[8] A survey by the U.S. Department of Health and Human Services, released in 1997, showed that the foodservice industry had the highest percentage of drug users among all industries. About 4 percent of foodservice workers, or more than 400,000 employees, use illegal drugs such as marijuana and cocaine.

Employees with substance abuse problems present certain concerns to you as the supervisor. Drug abuse may lead to robbery and violence. Although there is no sure way to spot a restaurant employee who is prone to violence, there are some definite signals to look for. For example, people who talk a lot about guns and violence have a fixation; also be aware of people who feel troubled or feel they are outcasts.[9] These employees tend to be late for work more often, to take more days off for sickness, to be involved in accidents more often, and to be more likely to file for workers' compensation claims. The U.S. Department of Labor estimates that employee drug abuse alone costs U.S. businesses between $75 billion and $100 billion in lost time, accidents, breakage, healthcare, and workers' compensation costs. Frequently, these employees have difficulties meeting performance standards and getting along with their peers. Employee involvement with alcohol and drugs also affects employee morale and can affect your company's image adversely.

Based on the fact that substance abuse in the workplace has become a tremendous concern and that it can be dealt with effectively, there have been numerous government initiatives to deal with it. Of particular interest is the **Drug Free Workplace Act of 1988,** which requires that most federal contractors and anyone who receives federal grants provide a drug-free workplace by doing the following:

❧ Inform employees that they are prohibited from doing any of the following in the workplace: unlawful manufacture, distribution, dispensation, possession, or

---

[8]Robert Thompson, Jr., *Substance Abuse and Employee Rehabilitation.* Washington, DC: Bureau of National Affairs, 1990.

[9]Ron Friedman, "Troubled souls," *Restaurant Business,* Vol. 99, No. 22, November 15, 2000.

use of a controlled substance. Inform employees what actions they can expect if they do (this policy must be in writing).

❧ Give employees a copy of the policy and ask them to abide by it as a condition of continued employment.

❧ Inform employees of the dangers of drug abuse at work and available counseling, rehabilitation, and employee assistance programs.

❧ Make a good-faith effort to maintain a drug-free workplace.

These represent some of the major requirements. As a supervisor, you have several responsibilities for dealing with substance abuse in your workplace.

1. *Any disciplinary action that you take should be based on observable, job-related factors, such as substandard job performance or inappropriate workplace behavior rather than on the existence or suspicion of a substance abuse problem.* Substance abuse is generally regarded as a health problem, a disease, and as such it is very difficult to justify legally and defend disciplinary action based on an employee's substance abuse problem. Focus instead on the employee's inability to meet job and conduct requirements.

2. *You need to be familiar with your company's policy on substance abuse.* More and more companies are developing substance abuse policies, such as the one shown in Figure 10.8. In a substance abuse policy, the following topics are usually addressed:

❧ Rules regarding alcohol and drug possession and use

❧ Penalties for rule violations

❧ When employees may be subject to drug testing

❧ Programs available for counseling, education, and rehabilitation, such as **employee assistance programs**

Drug testing is probably the best way to reduce drug abuse in the workplace. More and more employers are doing drug testing of applicants, with applicants being denied employment if the results come back positive. Of companies that do drug testing, *for-cause testing* of employees is common. With for-cause testing, an employee is asked to take a drug test if the person's supervisor has a reasonable suspicion that the employee may be impaired due to substance abuse. Random testing is also used by some companies to monitor their employees for drug use.

3. *You need to be able to identify and confront constructively employees who are substance abusers to urge them to accept professional help.* Figure 10.9 lists behavioral indicators of an impaired employee. Obviously, no intervention can take place unless you identify that there is a problem needing your intervention. Early intervention is important, as the longer a problem exists, the more difficult it will be to resolve it. In addition, confronting the problem is most effective in producing a positive outcome when it occurs before the situation has deteriorated to the point where you have to take disciplinary action.

SUBJECT: SUBSTANCE ABUSE POLICY   EFFECTIVE DATE: 3/1/XX

I. *GENERAL POLICY*

We are committed to programs that promote safety in the workplace, employee health and well-being, and which promote a positive image of the institution in the community. Consistent with the spirit and intent of this commitment, we developed this policy statement regarding the sale, use, possession or distribution of drugs and alcohol by all employees.

Employee involvement with drugs and alcohol can adversely affect job performance and employee morale, jeopardize employee and patient safety and undermine the public's confidence. Such involvement is particularly unacceptable in an industry like ours in light of the nature of our role in society and the potentially disastrous consequences to patients which may result from an employee's impaired condition. Our goal, and the purpose of this policy, therefore, is to establish and maintain a safe workplace and a healthy and efficient workforce free from the effects of drug and alcohol abuse, and to extend to employees having an addictive disease an opportunity for effective treatment and rehabilitation.

II. *EMPLOYEE ASSISTANCE PROGRAM*

We encourage any employee with a drug or alcohol problem to contact the EAP, the Occupational Health Department, or any recognized external evaluation, referral, or treatment agency for assistance. We subscribe to the premise that addictive diseases are entitled to the same consideration and offer of treatment which is extended to any other disease. All communications and records will be maintained on a confidential basis. Employees will not be subject to discipline for voluntarily acknowledging their drug/alcohol problems; nor will job security or promotional opportunities be jeopardized as a consequence only of having an addictive disease except to the extent that the manifestations of the disease interfere with the employee's performance of his or her job. However, this will *not* excuse violations of the Substance Abuse Policy for which the employee is subject to discipline. Employees who utilized the Employee Assistance Program or any other treatment resource will be expected to meet existing job performance standards and established work rules within the framework of established administrative practices. A request for assistance does not exempt the employee from routine performance expectations, nor does it confer any immunity, legal or disciplinary, from the consequences of misconduct.

1. There may be limited exceptions to this guarantee in (1) instances where there may be a clear and present danger presented to the welfare of the employee or another person; (2) where records or testimony might be subject to subpoena or other legal process; or (3) where the employee consents to disclosure.

III. *RULES REGARDING DRUGS AND ALCOHOL*

Whenever the capacity of an employee to function on the job has been diminished to the point where he is unable to perform his job duties and/or is acting in an unsafe manner, supervisory personnel will have the responsibility for taking immediate action to: (a) remove the impaired employee from the work area; (b) initiate procedures; and (c) refer the individual to the Employee Assistance Program. The justification for taking such actions shall be observable unsatisfactory job performance or behavior.

A. *Use, Possession, Transportation, Sale, Distribution*

The use, possession, sale, or distribution of drugs or alcohol while on Medical Center property or Medical Center business shall be cause for immediate discharge. Illegal substances will be confiscated and the appropriate law enforcement agencies may be notified.

B. *Drugs/Alcohol in System*

1. *Alcohol*

An employee found to have a blood-alcohol concentration of .05% or more (or its equivalent as determined by a different diagnostic test such as a Breathalyzer) while on company property shall receive a 5-day suspension on the first offense and shall be required to participate in the Employee Assistance Program. In addition, the employee shall be subject to random drug and alcohol testing. If the employee refuses to participate in the EAP and the terms of a chemical dependency treatment agreement and/or violates any rules set forth in this policy at any time thereafter, he/she shall be subject to immediate discharge.

FIGURE 10.8   Substance abuse policy and procedure.

2. Marijuana/Hashish

An employee found to have detectable concentrations of marijuana (or its metabolites) in his or her system shall receive a 5-day suspension on the first offense and shall be required to participate in the Employee Assistance Program. In addition, the employee shall be subject to random drug and alcohol testing. If the employee refuses to participate in the EAP and the terms of a chemical dependency treatment agreement and/or violates any rules set forth in this policy at any time thereafter, he/she shall be subject to immediate discharge.

3. Drugs Other Than Marijuana or Alcohol

An employee found to have detectable concentrations of any drug other than marijuana or alcohol in his or her system, including, but not limited to, heroin, cocaine, morphine, phencyclidine (PCP), amphetamines, barbiturates, or hallucinogens (or metabolites of any such drugs), shall receive a 5-day suspension on the first offense and shall be required to participate in the Employee Assistance Program. In addition, the employee shall be subject to random drug and alcohol testing. If the employee refuses to participate in the EAP and the terms of a chemical dependency treatment agreement and/or violates any rules set forth in this policy at any time thereafter, he/she shall be subject to immediate discharge.

4. Testing for Drug/Alcohol in System

An employee may be required to submit to blood, urine, or other diagnostic tests to detect alcohol and/or drugs (or drug metabolites) in his or her system whenever the employee is involved in an on-the-job accident or the employee's observed behavior raises a reasonable suspicion of drug or alcohol use. See Fitness for Duty guidelines for criteria for what constitutes reasonable suspicion. (A bargaining unit employee is entitled to have a union representative present, if immediately available, during the initial collecting of a specimen.) If an initial screening test indicates positive findings, a confirmatory test will be conducted.

Employees with a prior violation of the Drug and Alcohol Policy will be subject to random testing.

Any employee who refuses to submit to testing shall be subject to disciplinary action up to and including discharge.

C. Other Rules and Provisions

1. Searches

The company reserves the right to carry out reasonable searches of employees and their property, including, but not limited to, lockers, lunch boxes and private vehicles, if parked on company property. (A bargaining unit employee whose person or property is to be searched is entitled to have a union representative present, if immediately available, while the search is being conducted.) An employee who refuses to submit immediately to such a search shall be subject to disciplinary action up to and including discharge.

2. Drug Paraphernalia

Employees are prohibited from bringing drug paraphernalia onto company property at any time. An employee who possesses or distributes such paraphernalia while on company property shall be subject to disciplinary action, up to and including discharge.

3. Off-Duty Arrests/Convictions

An employee who is arrested for, or convicted of, a drug offense which involves the off-duty sale, distribution, or possession of illegal drugs must promptly inform his supervisor of the arrest, the nature of the charges, and the ultimate disposition of the charges. Failure to do so is grounds for discipline, up to and including discharge. Such arrest/conviction may subject the employee to discipline, up to and including discharge, depending upon the circumstances involved.

4. Over-the-Counter or Prescribed Medications

Over-the-counter or prescription medications may have pharmacological effects which can impair job functioning and performance. Additionally, many such medications may be abused even if obtained through legal means by exceeding the customary dosage. Employees taking such medications are responsible for using such drugs in an appropriate manner, becoming aware of the potential side effects of any such drug, and informing their supervisor of their use of medications which might potentially impair their

FIGURE 10.8 *(Continued).*

job performance. Employees who intentionally abuse medications such as (but not limited to) tranquilizers, sedative-hypnotics, analgesics, anti-depressants, or diet pills shall be subjected to the same disciplinary sanctions prescribed for illicit drugs in this policy (i.e., a 5-day suspension, random testing and referral to the EAP). Employees whose impairment can be demonstrated to be the result of an inadvertent unpredictable, or a typical reaction to an over-the-counter or prescription medication shall be absolved of any responsibility for such an incident.

5. *Reporting Violations of the Drug and Alcohol Policy*

It is each employee's responsibility to immediately report unsafe working conditions or hazardous activities that may jeopardize his or her safety or the safety of fellow employees or guests. This responsibility includes the responsibility to immediately report any violation of the Substance Abuse Policy. An employee who fails to report such a violation may be subject to disciplinary action, up to and including discharge.

6. *Job Applicants*

Applicants for employment may be given blood, urine or other diagnostic tests to detect alcohol and/or drugs (or drug metabolites) in their system. Successful completion of the test is a condition of employment.

7. *Re-employment*

Any individual who leaves the company through layoff, resignation or termination for a period exceeding 90 days will be required to submit to blood, urine or other diagnostic tests to detect alcohol and/or drugs (or drug metabolites) in their system prior to re-entry into the workforce. Positive test results for alcohol or drugs will be considered in deciding whether the employee shall be permitted to return to work.

8. *Progressive Discipline Not Applicable*

The disciplinary steps set forth in the Employee Handbook providing for progressive discipline (e.g., 1st written warning, 2nd written warning, probation, discharge) or the 3 step process for Level II Infractions *do not apply* to violations of the Substance Abuse Policy. The discipline to be imposed for violations of the Substance Abuse Policy shall be governed solely by the provisions set forth herein.

FIGURE 10.8 *(Continued)*.

No one relishes confronting an employee with his job deficiencies, or informing him that his continued employment is in jeopardy. However, for an employee with a substance abuse problem that is causing impaired job performance, this intervention can be not only job-saving, but, in some cases, literally life-saving as well.

When confronting constructively an employee whom you suspect to be a substance abuser, you are basically saying two things to the employee about his or her poor performance. On the one hand, you are asking for accountability and change relative to the issue of job performance, while on the other hand, you are expressing sincere interest and concern coupled with an offer of help in the form of a referral to an EAP or other program. You need to strike a balance between these complementary facets of the process: being firm and being empathic. The employee has to experience both of these facets so that the probability of acceptance of the need for help is maximized. The use of confrontive messages is most effective in breaking through denial, which is so characteristic of substance abuse, while the constructive messages have the intent of motivating the troubled employee to comply with a referral.

4. *Don't try to diagnose or give employees advice on their substance abuse problems.* To do so complicates the entire situation, often leaves you open to manipulation, and

The following list of indicators ranges from those which are very clear and compelling to others which may be ambiguous. The supervisor is in the position of having to make a judgment based upon the facts at hand (i.e., the employee's immediately observable behavior as it relates to job performance). Supervisors should be particularly alert to behaviors which are abnormal, uncharacteristic, or inappropriate to the context of the work environment.

Physical Appearance:

Impaired coordination, unsteady gait, staggering, poor balance
Tremors, shakiness, dizziness, seizures
Impaired muscular control, poor performance of gross or complex motor tasks
Bloodshot eyes, dilated or constricted pupils, watery eyes
Excessive sweating, chills, nausea
Abnormal drowsiness, "nodding off," excessive fatigue, stupor
Blank expression, unresponsive
Inappropriate or bizarre dress, neglect of personal hygiene or appearance

Unusual/Abnormal Behavior:

Markedly poor judgment, impulsivity
Carelessness, risk-taking behavior, neglect of safety procedures
Marked irresponsibility, indifference, or rigidity
Marked anxiety, agitation, panic
Mood swings, erratic behavior
Apathy, lethargy, depression, despondency, suicidal thinking
Euphoria, elation, "high," excessively talkative, overactive (restless)
Over-reactiveness (verbal or physical) — boisterousness, irritability, argumentativeness, quarrelsomeness, belligerency, explosiveness, threats, assaultiveness, combativeness
Slurred speech

Cognitive (Mental) Factors:

Inability to concentrate or comprehend, distractibility
Memory deficits, lapses, forgetfulness
Preoccupation, brooding, excessive daydreaming
Confusion, disorientation, incoherence, irrelevancy
Diminished level of consciousness, "out of touch"
Impairment of communication — expressive or receptive
Hallucinations (perceptions which are false/unreal)
Marked suspiciousness, feelings of persecution, homicidal thoughts

FIGURE 10.9   Behavioral indicators of possible impairment/unfitness for duty.

may anger the employee, who may feel that the intrusion into his or her personal life is not warranted. Instead, focus on observable workplace behavior and leave the issue of possible substance abuse to professionals who are properly trained in this area. Things are not always as they seem, and for the manager, a consistent focus on job-related behaviors is the most secure footing.

Counseling programs called *employee assistance programs* (EAPs) are an expansion of traditional occupational alcoholism programs, which began appearing 40 years ago. Larger companies are more likely than smaller companies to have EAPs. Companies such as Marriott, KFC, and Lettuce Entertain You offer counseling and referral services to some or all of their employees.

The general purpose of an EAP is to provide a confidential and professional counseling and referral service to employees with problems such as addictions and dependencies, family problems, stress, and financial problems. An EAP can provide a comprehensive range of services:

- ᙐ *Assessment:* identification of the nature of the problem
- ᙐ *Intervention:* in the form of focused counseling by a counselor or referral to an appropriate community resource
- ᙐ *Follow-up:* including monitoring of employee progress and assisting with reentry of the employee into the workplace when the employee has left rehabilitation
- ᙐ *Managerial assistance:* providing technical assistance and emotional support to supervisors handling troubled employees

If your employer has an EAP program available to employees, be sure that you know how to refer an employee to it. When referring an employee to a program, also follow this list of do's and don'ts[10]:

- ᙐ Do emphasize confidentiality.
- ᙐ Do explain that going for help does not exclude the employee from disciplinary procedures, nor does it include special privileges.
- ᙐ Do stick to discussing job performance and explain in very specific terms what the employee needs to do to perform up to expectations.
- ᙐ Do give the employee the appropriate information in writing to contact an EAP counselor.
- ᙐ Don't try to diagnose an employee's problem and do not ask "why" the employee is performing in a certain way. This only leads to excuse making.
- ᙐ Don't go into depth with an employee about personal problems. Do not become the employee's counselor.
- ᙐ Don't take responsibility for solving an employee's problems.
- ᙐ Don't be swayed by emotional pleas, sympathy tactics, or hard-luck stories.

Check Your Knowledge

1. Employees with substance abuse problems present certain concerns to you as supervisor. What are these concerns?
2. As a supervisor you have several responsibilities for dealing with substance abuse in your workplace. What are your responsibilities?

[10]From Karen Eich Drummond, *Retaining Your Foodservice Employees.* New York: Wiley, 1991.

The Supervisor's Key Role

The orderly and obedient carrying out of the work of an enterprise depends almost entirely on the effectiveness of the first-line supervisor in establishing and maintaining discipline. It is the supervisor who transmits the rules and policies laid down by management. It is the supervisor who orients, trains, and provides continuous information to workers so that they know what to do, how to do it, to what standards, and what will happen if they don't. And if it comes to that, it is the supervisor who sees to it that what is supposed to happen does happen.

But the effective supervisor does not let it come to that. With prompt action, a teaching–helping approach to discipline, and sensitivity to people's motivations and feelings, supervisors can usually keep incidents from developing into disciplinary problems. Supervisors who are consistent and fair, who follow the rules themselves, who create and maintain a positive work climate with good communications and good person-to-person relations are usually able to maintain good discipline with a minimum of hassles, threats, and disciplinary actions.

On the other hand, the supervisor who attempts to maintain discipline through threat and punishment is usually plagued with ongoing disciplinary problems because of the resentment and anger that such methods provoke. Such supervisors often cop out by blaming workers for problems they have created themselves: "You just can't get good workers today." In this case, too, it is the supervisor who creates the prevailing condition of discipline.

Nobody ever claims that discipline is easy, and nobody has a foolproof prescription for success. It is supervisory leadership and example that set the climate and the direction, and it is the supervisor, acting one on one, who makes it all happen.

Check Your Knowledge

1. Explain the supervisor's key role.

ʕ key points

1. *Discipline* refers to a condition or state of orderly conduct and compliance with rules, and also refers to action to ensure orderly conduct and compliance with rules. Both aspects of discipline are the responsibility of the supervisor, and both are essential to supervisory success.

2. The four essentials of successful discipline are a complete set of rules that everyone knows and understands; a clear statement of the consequences of failing to observe the rules; prompt, consistent, and impersonal action to enforce the rules; and appropriate recognition and reinforcement of employees' positive actions.

3. Negative discipline uses a fear-and-punishment approach and a four-stage progressive formula for disciplinary action: oral warning, written warning, punishment (such as suspension), and termination.

4. The positive approach to discipline is continuous education and corrective training whenever the rules and procedures are not being observed. The four-stage formula for disciplinary action includes oral reminder, written reminder, decision-making leave with pay, and termination (see Figure 10.4).

5. With positive discipline, the negative consequences of punishment do not fester their way through the work climate, and the boss and worker do not become adversaries. Positive discipline can result in reduced turnover, absenteeism, and disciplinary problems.

6. Some mistakes to avoid include starting off too easy about enforcing the rules, acting in anger, threatening to take any action that you do not carry out, putting somebody down in front of others, exceeding your authority, evading responsibility for taking action by shifting it to someone else, or disciplining unexpectedly.

7. The set of procedures to use when confronted with a serious infringement of rules include collecting all the facts, discussing the incident with the employee, deciding on the appropriate action (if any is to be taken), documenting the process, and following up.

8. You can fire employees for just cause, meaning that the offense must affect the specific work the employee does or the operation as a whole in a detrimental way. In this chapter we outlined 10 questions that need to be asked, such as "Has the employee been treated as others have been in similar circumstances?" before deciding whether or not to terminate.

9. Figure 10.6 lists everything you need to think about before a termination interview. During the interview itself, you need to get right to the point, listen to the employee's response, state something positive about the employee, and then move on to severance arrangements and clearance procedures.

10. As a supervisor you need to be able to prevent, recognize, and confront the forms of sexual harassment (quid pro quo, environmental, and third-party) in the workplace.

11. Harassment in the workplace is not limited to sexual harassment. All forms of harassment based on national origin, race, color, religion, gender, disability, or age are illegal.

12. Employees with substance abuse problems present certain concerns to you as supervisor. These employees tend to be late for work more often, to take more days off for sickness, to be involved in accidents more often, and to be more likely to file for workers' compensation claims.

13. As a supervisor, you have several responsibilities for dealing with substance abuse in your workplace. First, any disciplinary action that you take should be based on observable, job-related factors, such as substandard job performance or inappropriate workplace behavior rather than upon the existence or suspicion of a substance abuse problem. Second, you need to be familiar with your company's policy on substance abuse. Third, you need to be able to identify and confront constructively employees who are substance abusers to urge them to accept professional help.

14. An employee assistance program provides confidential and professional counseling and referral service to employees with problems such as addiction and dependencies, family problems, stress, and financial problems.

❦ key terms

decision-making leave with pay
dehire
discipline
Drug Free Workplace Act of 1988
due process
Employee Assistance Programs
environmental sexual harassment
harassment
just-cause termination

negative discipline
positive discipline
progressive discipline
quid pro quo
sexual harassment
third-party sexual harassment
uniform discipline system
work rules

❦ review questions

Answer each question in complete sentences. Read each question carefully and make sure that you answer all parts of the question. Organize your answer using more than one paragraph when appropriate.

1. Define *discipline.* Why is it necessary in a hospitality operation?
2. In determining disciplinary action, to what extent should you as a supervisor consider circumstances, intent, past history, seriousness of the offense, and consequences of the disciplinary action? If you vary the penalty according to such factors, how can you avoid making subjective and inconsistent judgments?
3. Describe the four essentials of successful discipline.
4. Compare and contrast positive and negative approaches to discipline.
5. Describe five mistakes commonly made by supervisors regarding discipline. Why is each one a mistake?
6. For the third day in a row, you have heard complaints about foods prepared by Jimmy, the grill cook. You had a similar problem just last month and the month before. Describe the steps you will go through.
7. Explain what a just-cause termination is.
8. Before you terminate an employee, what questions should you ask yourself?
9. Describe the three forms of sexual harassment. What do sexual harassment and harassment have in common?
10. What should a supervisor do about sexual harassment and substance abuse in the workplace?
11. Describe the kind of person a supervisor might refer to an EAP counselor.

∾activities and applications

1. **Discussion Questions**
   - What does discipline have to do with discrimination? To avoid discriminating against them, must you be more lenient with a woman, an older person, a minority person, or some other person protected by law?
   - What relationships do you see between discipline and communication? Between discipline and performance standards? Between discipline and motivation? Between discipline and leadership?
   - Which style of discipline do you support: positive or negative? Why?
   - Discuss the state of discipline in a place where you work or have worked in the past. Was there a set of rules and consequences that most employees were familiar with? Was discipline prompt, consistent, and impersonal? Were employees recognized when they did things right?
   - Have you ever witnessed actions in the workplace that might be considered harassment or sexual harassment? If so, describe them. What action did management take regarding harassment?

2. **Group Activity: D-O-C-U-M-E-N-T**

Using the letters in the word *document,* think of how you should document employee performance, such as "descriptive" for the letter "d."

3. **Group Activity: Do's and Don'ts of Discipline**

In groups, write up a list of 10 do's and 10 don'ts concerning discipline as discussed in this chapter.

4. **Case Study: "They Like It the Way It Is"**

Rita is head cocktail server at a high-volume singles bar that serves both food and drinks. She has responsibility for a large staff of part-timers, most of whom she worked with as a server before she was promoted. They are a lively and individualistic bunch who regard themselves more as independent entrepreneurs doing business at this particular place than as loyal employees. Most of them pay little attention to rules about being on time, observing break times, wearing flashy jewelry, and smoking and drinking on the job. They are all high-volume performers, and that, she figures, is what matters. She looks the other way and lets them get away with a lot.

Yesterday, her boss, Sam, who was recently hired to manage the entire operation, called Rita in for "a little talk." He offered her a cup of coffee, paused a moment, and then plunged in. "I want you to be aware that the discipline in your part of this operation does not measure up to standard and is causing a great deal of trouble," he said. "The servers and kitchen staff are required to follow rules and are disciplined when rules are broken. They resent it when they see a cocktail server carry a drink into the employee lounge, have a cigarette with a customer, wear flashy jewelry, come in late and leave early, and take it for granted that the servers will cover for them. I'm sure you can understand how they feel."

"I don't see that their feelings are my problem," says Rita.

"I think they are," says Sam, "and I am asking you to begin enforcing the hours of work and the smoking and drinking rules for starters. How you do it is pretty much up to you, although I will be glad to help you work things out. I suggest we meet again tomorrow to discuss your plan and set some improvement goals."

Rita is astonished. "Listen, Sam," she says, "any one of my people could get a job anywhere else in town in 5 minutes and I could, too. Improvement goals! They like it the way it is!"

"I know," says Sam. "But nobody else does. In fact, it has become a major problem that even customers have noticed, and its effect on the other employees could affect business. Think it over and we'll talk again tomorrow."

Rita's first reaction is defiance and anger, but she senses that it won't do her any good. She would rather stay here than change jobs, she is proud of being a supervisor, the money here is the best in town, and it's a fun place. Her next reaction is panic. How in the world can she make her people toe the line?

QUESTIONS

1. What common mistake has Rita been making? What effects has it had?
2. Do you agree that high-volume sales are more important than enforcing rules? Defend your answer.
3. Is it workable to have different standards of discipline in different departments? Why or why not?
4. What is your opinion of Sam's approach to the problem? How well did he handle the interview? What risks is he taking?
5. What should Rita do now? Consider the following possibilities, the pros and cons for each, the possible consequences, and the likelihood of success.
   a. Resign and get another job (she has been offered one at the place across the street).
   b. Lay down the law and threaten penalties for noncompliance.
   c. Plunge right in and start slapping on penalties to show that she means business.
   d. Ask her people to go along with the rules for a while because she is on the spot.
   e. Start enforcing just one rule at a time.
   f. Tell her people what Sam has told her, lay out the rules and penalties, and announce that enforcement will begin next week.
   g. Ask Sam for help on strategy, tactics, and dealing with waitress reactions.
   h. Ask Sam to lay it out to her people.
6. How do you think that Rita's people will react to her change of supervisory style? How will she keep them from quitting, and what preparations should she make for this possibility?

chapter 11

Planning, Organizing, and Controlling

As we mentioned briefly in Chapter 1, there are various management functions, such as planning, organizing, coordinating, staffing, directing, controlling, and evaluating. These management functions can be seen as a sequence of steps that you take to get your job done:

1. *Plan* what is to be done.
2. *Organize* how it is to be done (this includes coordinating and staffing).
3. *Direct* the work being done.
4. *Control* or evaluate what has been done.

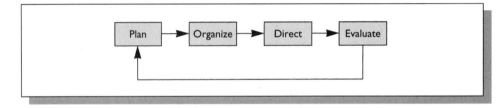

FIGURE 11.1   Management process.

During the final step, you evaluate whether the objectives of your original plan have been met, and you may end up revising your plan or leaving it intact. In this manner, you have gone full circle through the management process (Figure 11.1).

In this chapter we present planning, organizing, and controlling as a means of solving some problems, avoiding others, maintaining better control over events, and giving the supervisor more time to manage. It will help you to:

❧ Explain how planning at different levels provides the framework for other functions of supervision.

❧ Outline the steps of the planning process.

❧ Describe the features of an effective plan.

❧ List and describe different types of plans and their uses.

❧ Discuss the special problems of planning for change and explain techniques for overcoming resistance to change.

❧ Describe how hospitality supervisors can best plan their time on the job.

❧ Explain how effective organizing contributes to a department's maximum success.

❧ List ways hospitality supervisors control the work being done.

The Nature of Planning

Planning means looking ahead to chart the best courses of future action. It is one of the basic functions of management (see Chapter 1), and it typically heads the list in management textbooks, whether the list names four functions and activities or 40. The reason it comes first is that it provides the framework for other functions and activities, such as organizing, staffing, directing, coordinating, controlling, and so on. You have to have a plan in order to know where you are going and how to get there, how to organize, how to staff, what to direct and coordinate, how to control. Planning sets the goals and the direction and lays out the future course of action.

Levels of Planning

The future begins with the next few minutes and extends indefinitely. How far ahead does a manager plan? That depends.

Top-management planners in a large organization should be making long-range strategic plans. They should be looking at a three-, five-, or 10-year horizon and deciding where the organization should be heading over that time span and how it will get there. Such planning includes setting organizational goals, objectives, and policies and determining strategies, tactics, and programs for achieving the objectives. This level of planning is called **strategic planning.** It provides a common framework for the plans and decisions of all managers throughout an organization.

Middle managers in an organization with long-range plans typically make annual plans and sometimes plan for longer periods. These plans carry forward the strategies, tactics, and programs of the strategic plans within a manager's own function and area of responsibility.

As plans move down through channels to first-line supervisors at the operating level, management translates them into specific supervisory duties and responsibilities. Here the planning period is typically one week, one day, or one shift, and the plans deal with getting the daily work done. Yet whatever that work is, getting it done carries out some portion of the long-range plans made by planners at the top.

In the hospitality industry, and especially in foodservice, long-range planning has not been a conspicuous part of management philosophy. The traditional entrepreneurial style was a seat-of-the-pants approach—reactive, intuitive, pragmatic, and sometimes even antiplanning as a matter of principle. There is still a great deal of this philosophy in the industry, but the managerial style is changing. When enterprises that once were managed single-handedly by a successful entrepreneur on a day-by-day basis grow to a certain size, the seat of the pants is no longer big enough. To survive, the firm must develop professional management with a commitment to long-range planning.

Whether they work for an old-style enterprise or a large corporation with a commitment to planning, most supervisors look at a short time span and do not think of themselves as being part of a larger plan. To the degree that they plan ahead, they see planning as the most efficient way to get their work done. Many do very little planning and simply react to events as they happen. Often, it is impossible to plan very far ahead or to provide for everything that may happen. And even when we plan, things often do not turn out the way we thought they would.

A good plan deals with just this kind of uncertainty. Reasoning from the past and present to the future, it can establish probabilities, reduce risks, and chart a course of action that is likely to succeed. Let us see how this works.

The Planning Process

Planning is a special form of decision making: It makes decisions about future courses of action. Therefore, the steps in making a good plan resemble those in making a good decision:

1. Define the purpose or problem and set objectives.
2. Collect and evaluate data relevant to forecasting the future.
3. Develop alternative courses of action.
4. Decide on the best course of action.
5. Carry out the plan.
6. Control and evaluate results.

Much of a supervisor's planning is directed toward deciding, day by day, based on conditions that exist, the details of what is to be done. Since most of the work is a repetitive carrying out of standard duties in accordance with prescribed procedures, daily planning is often limited to adjusting the what, who, and how much to the probable number of customers.

Yet even for a limited problem such as this, planning is essential to efficiency. Careful planning will provide the best product and the best customer service at the lowest cost with the least waste and confusion. It will reduce the risk of emergency: running out of supplies, running late, not enough workers, poor communications, duplicate or overlapping assignments, poor customer service, and all the other hazards of attempting to manage the work as it is happening.

Defining the purpose or problem, setting objectives, and developing and carrying out the best course of action are done in much the same way as in decision making. The biggest difference between the two processes comes in the second step. In decision making, you focus on the present and gather mostly current facts. In planning, you gather data from the past and the predictable future as well as the present, and on the basis of these data, you forecast future conditions and needs.

Forecasting

Given a particular set of conditions, what has happened in the past and is happening in the present is likely to happen again in the future. To **forecast,** you find out what happened in the past and what is happening today. Then, *if none of the condi-*

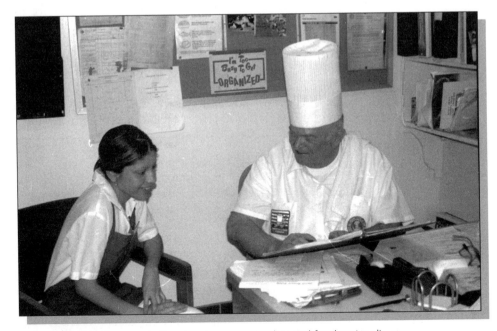

Forecasting is the first step in the planning process: a hospital foodservice director.

tions change, you can predict what can reasonably be expected to happen in the future. Forecasting business volume in the hospitality industry can be a tricky business and should be based on intelligent analysis. Forecasting is a very important function because it controls staffing, purchasing, and production decisions.

You may be involved in forecasting the number of covers for food for tomorrow night, the house count for next weekend in a hotel, the number of patients who will choose sliced roast beef tomorrow at lunch. For example, suppose that you want to plan the number of portions of each menu item to prepare for luncheon tomorrow, a Monday. You go to the sales records of the past 30 to 60 days to see how many of each item you have sold on Mondays. If conditions tomorrow will be the same as on Mondays in the past, you are safe in assuming that sales will follow pretty much the same pattern.

But suppose that conditions will not be the same: Suppose that tomorrow is Washington's birthday. If you are in a business district, you can expect fewer total sales because offices will be closed. If you are in a shopping or recreation area, sales will probably increase. To gather relevant data you will have to go back to previous holidays to see what happened then. If your menu or your prices have since changed, you have to consider that, too. Other things may also affect the expected sales: the weather forecast, an ad you are running in the paper, special outside circumstances such as conventions and civic events, a new restaurant holding a grand opening across the street. All these things must be evaluated when you make your forecast.

Sometimes you have reliable data on the future. You may have a party scheduled with a definite number of reservations and a preplanned menu. You may have other reservations, too, giving you specific data on numbers but uncertain data on items. These are welcome additions to your projections from the past and your calculations about tomorrow's conditions.

In the end your decision is the best estimate that you can make on the basis of available data. Often, this is simply a logical conclusion rather than the choice of alternatives specified in the standard planning procedures. The alternatives you have will be limited to various ways of handling the risks. Will you prepare more than "enough" and risk leftovers? Will you attempt to define an exact number with a runout time and plan to substitute a quickly prepared item? Will you plan to prepare additional portions of the original items if demand is high early in the serving period?

The Risk Factor

The future is always more-or-less uncertain. You reduce the degree of uncertainty, the **risk,** when you collect the relevant data and apply it to your forecast. If you have less than 1 percent of the relevant data, conditions are completely uncertain and the degree of risk is 99+ percent. You may have anything from no customers to a full house—you simply don't know. At the opposite extreme, if data and conditions are known, completely, there is complete certainty and no risk. The more relevant data you gather and apply to your forecast, the higher your percentage of certainty and the lower your risk.

In some foodservices the degree of certainty about tomorrow is high. In a nursing home, for example, the population is stable and the menu is prescribed or preordered. In a hospital the situation is similar, although occupancy is less predictable because patient turnover is higher. On a cruise ship, the number of guests is known, the guests' choices are predictable from the past, and the menu mix is fixed based on historical data.

Airline catering is preplanned according to the number of seats reserved and is updated for each plane as boarding passes are issued. Which of two choices customers will select is a forecast based on historical data, and it is usually slightly off—the last passengers served get the baked chicken. But seldom does anyone go without a meal, and seldom are meals left over. Planning in this case often goes right up to the cabin door.

Hotel occupancy is also fairly predictable, since most people make reservations ahead. There are also a predictable number of walk-ins based on past experience. Planning for the front desk, maid service, bell service, room service, restaurant and bar operations, and most other functions is based on the anticipated house count or occupancy rate. Usually, a weekly forecast session is held in which all the managers meet and are told the forecast for the week: "We're going to run at a 90 percent occupancy rate on Monday, we'll be up to 98 percent on Tuesday, we'll drop to 50 percent on Wednesday, then back up to 75 percent on Thursday, down to 27 percent on Friday," and so on.

This is the starting point of everyone's planning and scheduling for the week. Using the occupancy forecast, department managers can forecast their own needs. Restaurant counts are based on the occupancy forecast plus known group meal functions and historical data on walk-in customers. The housekeeping department can determine labor, laundry, and supply needs using the occupancy forecast. The front desk and the maintenance and security departments do the same. One forecast feeds all the others.

In planning repetitive work where most of the data are known or predictable and the risk factor is low, it is easy to decide on a final plan without generating and evaluating several alternatives. Usually, there is one obvious conclusion. But where many factors are unknown or questionable, it is wise to develop several alternatives and go through the entire decision-making process as time permits. You can also reduce the risk by having an alternative plan in reserve, known as a **contingency plan.** In deciding the number of portions to prepare on a holiday, for example, you make a contingency plan for running out of something. In scheduling, you plan to have extra people on call or have an alternative plan for dividing the work.

You can also reduce the risk factor for repetitive situations by keeping records that add to your data for projecting the future. If, for example, you keep records of portions served in relation to portions prepared, they can tell you how successful your planning was and give you additional data for future forecasting. Over a period of time, if you have a steady clientele, you can develop standard numbers of portions for specific days of the week, which you then vary for special conditions.

Another way of reducing risk is to consult people who have more experience or expertise than you do—your boss, or perhaps certain of your workers, or depending on the problem, an outside expert.

Check Your Knowledge

1. Define *planning* in your own words.
2. Why does planning come first?
3. State the four steps in making a good plan that resemble those in making a good decision.
4. How can you reduce the risk factors when planning?

Qualities of a Good Plan

The following are characteristics of a good plan. Not all of them apply in detail to every type of plan, but they all express general principles that apply to all plans and planning.

❧ A good plan provides a workable solution to the original problem and meets the stated objectives. (Will it solve the problem? Can you carry it out?)

This principle applies whether it is a small, specific plan for one person doing one 5-minute task or a long-range plan involving an entire enterprise. A good plan concentrates on the problem and does not attempt to deal with side issues. It is sometimes difficult to maintain this sharp focus. When you are up to your neck in alligators, it is easy to forget that your objective is to drain the swamp.

❧ A good plan is comprehensive; it raises all relevant questions and answers them. (Have you thought of everything?)

❧ A good plan minimizes the degree of risk necessary to meet the objectives. (Are these the best odds? What can go wrong?)

❧ A good plan is specific as to time, place, supplies, tools, and people (numbers, duties, responsibilities) needed to carry it out. (Can somebody else follow your plan?)

❧ A good plan is flexible. It can be adapted if the situation changes, or it is backstopped by a contingency plan. (What will you do if . . . ?)

Flexibility is especially important in the unpredictable restaurant or hotel setting, where anything can happen and often does. You will remember from Chapter 1 that a flex style of management is more suitable to hospitality operations than rigid, carefully structured plans and planning, simply because circumstances are in constant flux and problems often change before they can be solved. This does not do away with the need for planning, however. It simply requires flexible plans and managers who are able to adjust them according to the needs of the situation and the needs of the people involved. A flexible plan needs a flexible manager to make the most of it.

Types of Plans and Planning

Hospitality supervisors are likely to be so busy managing today's work that they seldom think of the future. But certain kinds of plans for the future can simplify daily management for all the days to come.

Standing Plans

One way to simplify future planning and managing is to develop plans that can be used over and over whenever the same situation occurs. Known as **standing plans,** these are established routines, formulas, blueprints, or a set of procedures that is designed to be used in a recurring or repetitive situation. A daily report is a standing

Standing plans help ensure that everyone knows what to
do in given situations. A foodservice director explains.

plan for reporting house count, income, meals served, rooms made up, and so on.
A procedures manual is a standing plan for performing particular duties and tasks.
A menu is a standing plan for the food to be prepared for a given meal. A recipe is
a standing plan for preparing a dish.

Any standing plan will greatly simplify a supervisor's task of planning and organizing the work. It does away with the need for a fresh plan each time the repeating
situation comes up. All that remains to be planned in each instance is to provide for
special circumstances. When such plans are put to use, they standardize the action so
that everyone does things in the same way. If the situation recurs every day and people are trained in the procedures, the supervisor's need to manage is reduced to seeing that the workers meet the standards set and to dealing with the unexpected event
that the plan does not cover. This is known as **management by exception.**

Most workers are happier with standing plans than they are being dependent on
the supervisor to tell them what to do. Knowing what to do gives them confidence
and makes them more independent. Gaps in communication are minimized. Work
can go forward if the supervisor is tied up dealing with a problem somewhere else.

Large companies usually have standing plans for all kinds of repeating situations, especially if these situations recur throughout the operation. But often, small
operations and individual departments of larger operations do not have predefined
ways to meet recurring needs for planned action. Then you have crisis planning and
firefighting and improvised solutions that may be different from day to day. You can
avoid this by developing standing plans of your own. Such daily planning as scheduling, figuring out production details, ordering supplies, assigning rooms, or plan-

ning special events can be reduced to a form to be filled out, as in Figure 11.2. You can set up a whole series of standing plans for each job that you supervise by developing a performance standard system.

You can also develop standing plans for training new personnel and for recruiting and hiring and evaluating performance. Although you do not use such plans daily, they are well worth the time and effort because they are ready when you need them. They take advantage of past experience, and they give you comprehensive solutions and consistent results.

Every hospitality operation must have standing plans and policies for dealing with matters affecting health and safety, such as sanitation, fires, and accidents. The law requires such plans. Usually, they consist of two parts: preventive routines and standard emergency procedures. It is a supervisor's responsibility to see that the department has plans that conform to company plans and to develop departmental plans if they do not exist. Part of all emergency planning is to train employees in all techniques and procedures and to hold periodic tests and drills to see that equipment is in order and people know what to do. Figure 11.3 is an example of an emergency standing plan.

> When planning, it is always best to assume the worst and plan backward. Therefore, if the worst situations occur, you will by now be prepared and know exactly how to handle them. There will be less stress for all those involved.

Company rules, procedures, and policies are another form of standing plan (see Figure 11.4). In this case the supervisor carries out plans rather than makes them.

You can also develop standing plans for special occasions such as customer birthdays, anniversaries, weddings, and Mother's Day. In fact, any repetitive situation is worth examining to see if a standing plan will reduce planning time and increase efficiency of the operation. Developing a standing plan often takes a great deal of time and thought. You have seen in earlier chapters the amount of work that goes into developing a performance standard system or a training plan. But in the long run the time spent on planning is time saved for other managerial activities.

Standing plans have certain potential drawbacks. One is rigidity: If plans are slavishly followed without adapting and updating them, they may result in a stagnant operation lacking in vitality. People come to resist change: "We've always done it this way" is a common expression of a common attitude. A standing plan should be flexible enough to adapt to daily realities, and supervisors should have the imagination and daily initiative to do the adapting.

Another drawback of such plans is that changes often evolve in practice but written plans are not kept up to date. Then a new worker or supervisor following a written plan will not be using current procedures and will be out of step with everybody else. This often happens when a new cook comes in and follows an old standardized recipe from the file.

It is a good idea to review and update standing plans on a regular basis. This kind of review offers an opportunity for the supervisor to involve workers in generating alternatives or modifications to current plans. The people who do the work often see it more clearly than the supervisor does and are likely to have ideas about ways to do it better. Also, if workers are involved in making changes, they are more willing to adapt to change in general and more committed to making new plans work. It is good motivation all around.

cc: Dining Room Supervisor _John Doe_
    Floor Supervisor _Jane Roe_
    Bulletin Board

Dining Room Order

Day _Friday_ **Date** _Nov. 30_ **Time:** Arrival _12 noon_ Service _12 noon_
Location _Gourmet Room_ **Guests:** Confirmed _36_ Set up _40_

Room setup diagram (please show waiter stations)

Mary 1-2-3-4-5

Frank 6-7-8-9-10

◇8 ◇5 ◇1
◇9 ◇6 ◇2
◇10 ◇7 ◇4

Servers Mary
           Frank

Uniform
           White shirts & black slacks

Setup and serving duties

Place setting diagram

Menu Minestrone Soup
          Vegetable Salad
          Banatha
          Italian Green Beans/Almonds
          Amaretto Cake

Equipment needed

Flatware		China		Glasses	
Knives	40	Plates		Water	40
Forks		Service		Other	
Dinner	40	Bread & butter	40	**Tablecloths**	10 , 54 × 54'
Salad	40	Dinner	40		
Dessert	40	Salad	40	**Napkins**	40
Spoons		Dessert	40	**Miscellaneous** (include rental	
Bouillon	40	Cups & saucers	40 & 40	equipment)	
Teaspoons	40	Soup cups	40 & 40 underplates		
Dessert		Fruit cups		Coffee pots — 5	
				Water pitchers — 5	
				Bud vases — 10	

Condiments

Salt & pepper _10 sets_
Sugar & creamers _10 sets_

Special arrangements

Head table:
Decorations:
Microphone:
Music:
Other

FIGURE 11.2 Standing plan for a dining room order, completed for a specific event.

340

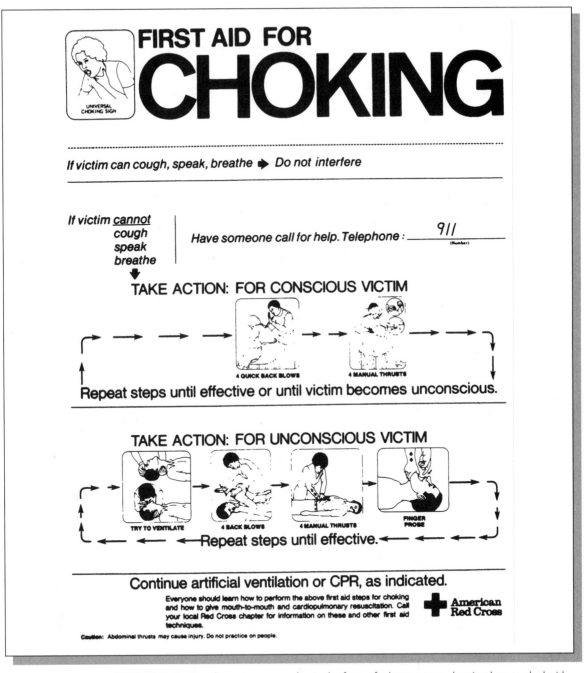

FIGURE 11.3 Standing emergency plan in the form of a large poster showing how to deal with a person choking on food. Training in carrying out the first aid is an essential part of the plan. *Source:* American Red Cross.

ABSENCES AND TARDINESS

POLICY: Regular attendance during all scheduled hours of work is expected of all employees. Unsatisfactory attendance is cause for disciplinary action.

PROCEDURE: Any employee who finds it impossible to report to work as scheduled must notify his or her immediate supervisor or unit manager prior to the scheduled time of reporting. State the cause of absence or tardiness and how long the absence will continue.

Unsatisfactory attendance is defined as being absent from scheduled work more than five times in a period of six months or tardy more than 10 minutes more than twice in one month. (See Disciplinary Procedure #2.)

FIGURE 11.4   Standing plan for dealing with absences and tardiness (page from a procedures manual).

Single-Use Plans

A **single-use plan** is a one-time plan developed for a single occasion or purpose. The nature and importance of the occasion or purpose will determine how much time you should spend on it. As in decision making, you have to keep your planning efforts in proportion to the consequences of carrying out the plan. If the occasion is an affair of no permanent significance and little risk, a plan can be made quickly, and if something goes wrong, there is little at stake. But some single-use plans may have effects that last for years or forever, or could produce consequences that are immediate and disastrous. In such cases, every step of the planning process must be given the full treatment.

Often, the purpose of a single-use plan is a major change of some sort. For such changes the planning must be very thorough: The risks must be carefully assessed and the effects of each alternative weighed carefully. Such a plan might involve a change in the way the work is done, such as introducing tableside service in your restaurant, installing new kitchen equipment, putting in an automatic liquor-dispensing system at the bar, or using computerized recipes in a hospital kitchen. You might plan a job enrichment program or a performance standard system. You might have to plan how to carry out a companywide plan in your department—for example, computerizing all the transactions of the enterprise.

Sometimes a supervisor is required to make a departmental budget—another kind of single-use plan. A **budget** (Figure 11.5) is an operational plan for the income and expenditure of money by the department for a given period: a year, six months, or a single accounting period. Upper-level management usually sets the goal or limitation, as the department's portion of the organizational budget, but sometimes the supervisor is included in the goal setting.

Preparing the budget requires forecasting costs of labor, food products, supplies, and so on. This, like other forecasting, is done on the basis of historical data plus current facts, such as current payroll and current prices of supplies and materials, plus estimated changes in conditions during the budget period—primarily, changes in needs and in costs. The completed budget is then used as a standard for measuring the financial performance of the department. Needless to say, this is one plan that you will make with great care.

Hamburgers Unlimited
Proposed Budget
2002-2003

Sales	
Food	$65,000
Beverage	20,000
	$85,000
Cost of Sales	
Food	$23,000
Beverage	5,000
	$28,000
Total Gross Profit	$57,000
Operating Expenses	
Salaries (includes FICA and benefits)	$24,000
Employees' meals	2,000
Equipment	4,000
Other operating expenses	11,000
Occupancy costs	6,000
Total Operating Expenses	$47,000
Net Profit	$10,000

FIGURE 11.5 Sample budget.

Day-by-Day Planning

Planning the day's work has top priority for the first-line supervisor. As noted earlier, this planning is concerned primarily with the details of what is to be done and who is to do it and adjusting various standing, plans to the needs of the day. Getting the day's work done also requires getting the necessary supplies, materials, and information to the people who need them in their work. Some of this must be planned daily, some must be planned a day or more in advance, and some is planned by the week. Purchasing may be planned daily, weekly, or monthly, depending on the department, type of enterprise, or location of suppliers. Scheduling may be planned by the week and updated daily as necessary. But things change daily, hourly, minute by minute in this industry, and whatever planning has been done in advance must be reviewed each day to see that everything needed is on hand—enough people to do the work, enough food, linens, liquor, cleaning supplies—whatever your responsibility is.

Plan before the day begins. Make it a regular routine. Many supervisors come in early or stay a few minutes late the day before to have some peace and quiet for this task.

Established routines simplify planning but do not take its place entirely. Ask yourself what is different about today. Stay alert and aware: Nothing is ever the same in this business.

Wherever possible, reduce risks by increasing predictability (more facts) and flexibility (more options). The more ways a plan can go into action, the more emergency situations you can meet.

Check Your Knowledge

1. A good plan has what four qualities?
2. Define *standing plan* and *budget.*

Planning for Change

Every organization goes through big and little changes all the time, to adapt to new circumstances, to enhance competitive position, to be more cost-effective, to improve product and service. If you stand still, you will soon be obsolete. Such changes are usually initiated at the top of the organization, but supervisors may be required to plan how to introduce these changes in their own departments. Sometimes, supervisors also initiate changes independent of what is going on in the rest of the company. Whether they can do this depends on the extent of their authority and responsibility.

As suggested briefly a few pages back, planning a change that affects the work must be done carefully and thoroughly. Although it is a single-use plan, it requires much time and thought because of the risks and consequences that a change involves. There are two sides to such planning. One is to plan the change itself, the other is to plan how to deal with the effects of the change on the workers. If you introduce a change without taking the workers into account, you may have real problems.

How Workers Respond to Change

Most workers resist change. Because any change upsets the environment, routines, habits, and relationships, it creates anxiety and insecurity in those affected. Even people who do not particularly like their jobs derive security from what is familiar. They know what to expect, life on the job is stable and predictable, and they have the comfort of belonging. Change upsets all this, exchanging the known for the unknown, the familiar for the new, the predictable for the uncertain. People worry and feel threatened. They will have to adjust to new circumstances, learn new ways of doing things, work with different people, readjust relationships. They don't know what to expect: Will they have to work harder? Will they be able to learn the new tasks? Can they get along with the new people? Will they lose their jobs?

People also resist change if it means a loss for them: less status, less desirable hours, separation from a friendly co-worker, fewer tips, more work. This builds resentment, which is probably more difficult to deal with than insecurity and anxiety. If even a whisper of change is detected by a worker, rumors begin to fly, and fears are magnified and spread rapidly through the employee grapevine. You cannot avoid dealing with them. It is best to do it sooner rather than later and to have a plan that will reduce resistance rather than to meet it head-on in battle or to steamroller the change through simply because you are the boss.

How to Deal with Resistance

The first essential for dealing with **resistance to change** is a climate of open communication and trust. You can reduce fears and stop rumors with facts: what the change will be, who will be affected and how, when it will take place, and why. Solid information will dispel much of the uncertainty, and it is always easier to adjust to something definite than to live with uncertainty and suspense, fearing the worst.

But the facts will not eliminate fear and uncertainty entirely. Workers must feel free to express their feelings, to ask questions knowing that they will get straight answers, to voice complaints. Venting one's feelings is the first step in adjusting to a new situation. Sometimes the change is advantageous to workers, and this should of course be emphasized. However, it is a mistake to oversell. If you try to persuade, or give advice, or become defensive about the change, or disapprove of people's reactions, or cut off complaints, or punish the complainers, you are shifting your ground from being helpful to being an adversary. Your people should feel that you want to make the change as easy for them as possible, that you understand their feelings, and want to help them adjust. You can reassure them that their jobs are not at stake (unless they are), that they will have any additional training they need, that they are still needed and valued, and that you are all in the new situation together. You should avoid promising anything that might not happen: That would diminish their trust in you.

Besides reducing fears with facts, open discussion, understanding, and support, you have another very good way to approach resistance: You can involve your workers in planning and carrying out the change. Some of them will certainly have ideas and useful information, even though some of it may be negative. At the very least they can give you another point of view that may help you in considering risks and consequences. Differing points of view are often more useful than agreement when you are trying to reach a sound decision.

Actually, most people will respond positively to being included in planning changes that concern them. It gives them a sense of having some say in their own destiny. They can be very useful in providing information for forecasting, in generating alternative solutions, and in evaluating risks and consequences. If you can gain their commitment through participative planning, resistance is likely to melt away. Participation in planning also makes it far easier to carry out the plan, since people already know all about it and have a stake in making it succeed.

Example of Planning for Change

Let us run through an example of planning for change to see how it resembles ordinary problem solving and how it differs, and how it affects the workers, and how you deal with that. Suppose that you are the owner of a 100-seat family-style restaurant. You have been in business six years and are well known for serving good food at affordable prices. But over the past year your sales have been dropping off slowly but steadily. You have missed some old familiar faces and new people are not coming in to take their place. You have to do something to bring in new people—but what?

After some thought and study you decide to freshen up your decor, change two-thirds of your menu items, and use some special promotions to reach patrons moving into the new apartments and condominiums nearby. The first part of your planning concerns the new menu items. They are central to your overall plan and its success.

1. *Define your problem and set your objectives.* Defining your problem is easy. Sales are dropping. Next, you try to formulate your objectives. You write down: *Introduce eight new entrées on the dinner menu, retaining the four most popular items (prime rib, chicken Maryland, sole meunière, sirloin burger), with the goal of attracting new customers and retaining old ones.* You start a worksheet on which you list all the factors involved in planning new menu items (Figure 11.6). After you have raised all the questions and answered several of them (columns 3 and 4), you write the following more detailed objectives:

   a. Select eight new dinner entrées that meet the following criteria:
   - ∾ Must appeal to present and prospective clientele in type of food, price, quality, taste, appearance, and variety and be compatible with each other and with items retained from the present menu.
   - ∾ Must be preparable with present staff, equipment, and kitchen space, with minor adjustments. New equipment may be considered if it becomes an obvious need.
   - ∾ Must require only minor variations in present serving procedures, or none.
   - ∾ Cost of each entrée must be compatible with cost/price guidelines; price must fall in present price range.

The first step in planning for change is to define your problem and set your objectives.

    b. Test all entrées considered. For final choices, standardize recipe and design plate layout.

    c. Complete selection in six weeks.

    d. Train all kitchen personnel in preparation and all dining room personnel in service and in explaining new entrées to customers.

    e. Coordinate introduction of new menu with decorating and promotional efforts.

    f. Include workers in planning as follows:

        ∾ Dining room supervisor and assistant manager in market research

        ∾ Head cook in developing new menu items, other kitchen staff on voluntary basis

        ∾ Servers to help in market research, search for new menu items, and evaluations on voluntary basis

        ∾ Rewards for participation to be given

    2. *Gather data from the past, present, and probable future in order to forecast what alternatives are most likely to succeed and to reduce the risks.* Here is where your market research comes in. Only after you have a good picture of your clientele and

Factors to Consider	Questions	Must Do	Objectives and Limitations
Market, customer appeal	Type of food? Price? Quality? Taste? Appearance? Variety?	Define market. Survey customers, competition, neighborhood potential.	Final choices must meet customer tastes in all categories.
Preparation	Prep time? Skills required? Holding problems? Prep space? Ingredient availability? Ingredient storage? Compatible with other menu items (equipment, timing)? Extra personnel? Training time?	Test recipes for taste, yield, proportions. Standardize recipes. Check suppliers. Train cooks.	Items must be feasible with present staff and space.
Equipment	Need new? Cost? Space for? Delivery time? Utility lines? Train for use? Special dishes, utensils?	Avoid conflicting use.	No new, at least for now.
Service	More work? New ways to serve? New plating, garnishing? Training required? Training time?	Train for serving. Train for describing (taste, how cooked, ingredients, goes with . . .).	No major changes in service.
Cost, price	Cost/price ratio? Costing? Who will cost? Budget? Equipment cost? Testing cost? Training cost? Cost of extra help?	Costing. Pricing. Budgeting.	Cost must meet cost/ price guidelines. Menu price must fit present range.
Employee resistance	Bring workers into planning? When? Voluntary or required? Rewards? Anxiety? Competition? Who needs what information?	Must handle positively.	Voluntary participation. Rewards.

FIGURE 11.6 Manager's worksheet for planning new menu items.

their needs and desires and a good idea of what other restaurants are doing to attract that clientele can you decide what kinds of entrées will please your customer group and how much they are willing to pay for them. Then you can begin your search for potential menu choices.

You will bring your workers into the picture as you begin your market research. You will begin with your supervisors: the assistant manager, the dining room manager, and the head cook. You will delegate responsibility to them for some of the market research, some of the search for menu items, and probably some of the training. You will also instruct them in handling worker resistance through information, listening, reassuring, and encouraging workers to contribute ideas.

Next you will tell everyone else about the overall project. You will present it with enthusiasm as a way of increasing business that will benefit everyone. You will explain the procedures and invite questions and ideas. You will invite them to take part in market research by talking to customers, to contribute menu ideas, and to taste-test and help evaluate items being considered. You will make clear how valuable they will be to developing a good menu. You will assure them that they will have the training and tryout time they need and that their questions will be welcomed at all times. You will watch for continuing resistance and have the supervisors deal with it on a one-to-one basis.

3. *Generate alternatives, evaluate the pros and cons of each, and assess their risks and benefits.* This step will be put in motion by having the cook prepare various new items for testing and asking everyone to contribute comments. You will continue to involve the workers by having them take part in the evaluation. Sampling the products will give them the experience of tasting and gain their cooperation in recommending items to customers. You might try out the most likely menu items one at a time as specials with your present menu and have your servers report on customer reactions. This would test the market and reduce the risk, and it would give both the kitchen and the servers a chance to experience the changes a little at a time.

You hope that by this time everyone will be involved and that a team spirit will develop. But you know that some workers will do better than others, that insecurities and jealousies may develop, and that ongoing routines may tend to be slighted. You hope to sustain enthusiasm for the new project while maintaining present product and service standards. You will do this through your own active leadership and through working closely with your supervisors. You will also introduce some sort of reward system.

You may have to hire extra help for testing and costing recipes. You will make this decision later after you see how the kitchen staff responds to the project. This is a contingency plan.

4. *Make the necessary decisions, after weighing each alternative in terms of the five critical decision-making questions: risk versus benefit, economy, feasibility, acceptability, and meeting the objectives.* You will ask for input on making these final evaluations from your supervisors. You want to make sure you have considered not only the desirability of each item but the possible consequences of using it, such as difficulties in production, extra work, service tie-ups, and so on. In the end you will make all the final decisions yourself. You will make this clear to your workers at the beginning of their involvement.

RICK NARGI

An amusing story about Rick is that when he was being considered for his present position as general manager for Sodexho, his area manager went to Rick's account and asked some of the employees, "Was Rick a good manager?" "The best we've ever had" was the response. Then the area manager remembered that he had also been a manager there!

When asked what makes him such a good supervisor/manager, Rick replies: "My philosophy is simple. If it's good for the guest, we'll do it." Rick's leadership style is to lead by example. He finds that employees respect the fact that he works hand in hand with employees—training as he goes by showing and then letting employees do the task, with objective feedback. In this way, his employees know that he knows how to do all their jobs.

Rick develops employees to think for themselves, based on standards that are set for the operation. He empowers employees to make guests happy. For example, if someone asks for a tortilla, and although they are not on the line, the employee goes and gets one instead of saying "I'll have to ask the manager." In an effort to make

Having planned your decision making, you now make out a detailed but flexible schedule and turn to planning your new decor and your promotion. You will call on outside consultants for help.

5. *Implement the plan.* If the plan has been made with care and in detail, this should go smoothly. The plan should meet all the criteria for a good plan cited earlier in the chapter.

Carrying out your menu plan will include training both servers and kitchen personnel. You will finalize your training plans—the who, what, when, where, and how of carrying out the plan—after you have decided on the final menu items. By that time you will know how much training is needed, how your supervisors have responded to their extra responsibilities, and how closely the workers are involved. You must also coordinate the changeover from one menu to another with the new purchasing requirements, the new menu card, and promotional plans. At this point you are satisfied that the plan for selecting and introducing the new menu items provides a flexible, workable program and that when the time comes you can make everything fall into place.

You can see that in broad outline, planning for change is very similar to making other kinds of plans. The main differences are in the extent of the forecasting, the degree of risk, and providing for the impact of the change on the people it affects. Perhaps this example will give you some understanding of how necessary the groundwork is: the forecasting, the market study, the testing, the careful defining of employees happy, Rick has open communications with his employees. He feels that if employees are happy, then guests will also be happy.

The qualities and characteristics that Rick feels make for a great supervisor/manager are:

- ❧ To be multitasked
- ❧ To have a high tolerance for stress and pressure
- ❧ To maintain a calm demeanor
- ❧ To be able to focus on detail
- ❧ To be friendly and outgoing
- ❧ To be a good listener and take an interest in employees' families during break times, but not becoming their personal friend or going out drinking with them
- ❧ To build up a diverse culture in your team
- ❧ To be caring and dedicated

In conclusion, Rick says that his biggest challenge is to recruit and retain good employees. But he is always optimistic and thinks about the "big picture" of keeping guests happy.

criteria, the detailed planning, and the need to consider the consequences of decisions before taking action.

Change involves risks that cannot be avoided, but doing nothing is sometimes riskier than anything else is. Careful planning can minimize the risks of change.

Planning Your Own Time

The most relentless reality about working as a supervisor in the hospitality industry is the lack of time. There is never enough private time for planning and reflective thinking. There are never enough long blocks of time in which to plan your time. Furthermore, how can you plan your time when most of your managing consists of reacting to things as they happen. How can you plan for that?

Planning your time is not going to give you any more of it; there are just so many hours in your working day. What it will do is enable you to make more effective use of those hours you work.

Your job requires that you spend the time in your day in several different ways:

- ❧ Planning, organizing, and communicating the day's work
- ❧ Responding to the immediate needs, demands, and inquiries of others (customers, workers, bosses, salespersons, suppliers, health inspectors, and so on)

∾ Managing your people: hiring, training, directing, coaching, evaluating, disciplining

∾ Dealing with crises, solving problems

∾ Making reports, keeping records, enforcing rules (maintenance activities)

∾ Doing some of the work yourself if you are a working supervisor

There are certain parts of the day when the job controls your time, when customer needs and demands are high: check-in and checkout times at the front desk, early mornings in housekeeping, food preparation for mealtimes in the kitchen, serving periods in the restaurant, and so on, depending on the function you supervise. At these times you must be at the disposal of anyone and everyone who needs you to answer questions, settle disputes, deal with crises, make decisions, and observe your people in action. It is important for you to be visible at such times, especially if your people serve customers directly. It is important to greet guests and to let them see that you take a personal interest in them and the way they are being treated. And it is important to your people to have you out there with them: They feel your support and they see your example. It is management visibility.

These are segments of your time that you cannot plan for other than to set them aside and let nothing else intervene. Certain other responsibilities may also be pegged to fixed points in the day: the housekeeper's report, end-of-shift sales figures, cash deposits, and so on. The rest of the time is yours to fill with all the other duties you are required to do.

What *do* you do? If you analyze the ways in which you spend your time now, you can probably find ways to spend it better. The first step is to keep a running log for at least one typical day, several days if possible. Put down everything, including interruptions, with a beginning and an end time for each activity. Figure 11.7 is a suggested format. To save making extensive notes, you can devise symbols such as those on the chart. But make your notes complete enough to make sense to you later when you analyze them. (If you can, get someone to help you with this activity; otherwise, making the notes may interfere with doing your job.)

The next step is to see what the record shows. Total the time you spent in each activity, and divide by the number of days to figure your daily average for each. Then ask yourself several questions:

∾ Is the amount of time spent per day appropriate to the activity? How can you reduce the time: Do it faster? Less often? Organize it better? Delegate it?

∾ How does the time spent on unimportant activities compare with time spent on highly important activities? Can you distinguish important from unimportant? How can you improve the ratio?

∾ Are you doing things that are not really necessary? Why are you doing unproductive work?

∾ Are you doing things that you could delegate to someone else?

∾ Can you group activities better as to time and place (for example, make all your phone calls for purchases at one time during the day)?

∾ Was time wasted that could have been avoided by better planning? Standing plans? Better training? Better communications? Less supervision, more trust?

Begin	End	Total (min.)	Activity	With Whom	Importance (Rate 1–5)
7:45	7:52	7	Plan for day	Self	1
7:52	7:52½	½	Q - sched change	Sam	3
7:52½	7:53	½	Plan	S	1
7:53	7:53½	½	Tel	Alice	1
7:53½	7:56	3½	Tel - replace Alice	4 people	1
7:56	8:00	4	Plan	S	1
8:00	8:13	13	Howdy rounds	0	1-2

C-E	Coaching-evaluating	Pl	Planning	1 = Most important
CR	Crisis	Pro	Production	5 = Least important
Cus	Customer	Q	Answering questions	
Dec	Decision			
Dir	Giving directions	R	Report	
Dis	Discipline	S	Self	
Int	Interviewing	Sol	Solving problems	
O	Other(s)	Tel	Telephone	
		Tr	Training	

FIGURE 11.7   Format for keeping track of how you spend your time.

Better records and better housekeeping? Saying no to unnecessary requests? Better decision making? An ounce of prevention?

∾ Does the log reveal that you do not spend any time at all on certain important but time-consuming activities you should be doing, such as making a list of sales prospects, developing holiday promotions, revising recipes, developing a procedures manual? Was it because you did not want to get started on a long project? When will you get started?

No doubt your log will raise other questions, and no doubt you will be able to work out some good answers to all the questions.

First, get rid of activities that waste time or are not worth the time they take. Major wastes of time for supervisors include the following.

> Remember that it's better to say "no" first because you can always change your mind to "yes"—but you can't say "yes," then change to "no"! To gain time to make the best choice, it is better to say, "I will make a decision and let you know the result."

∾ Too much socializing

∾ Accepting drop-in visitors

∾ Allowing interruptions and distractions

∾ Inability to say "no"

∾ Poor organization of papers

∾ Procrastination and indecision

∾ Reading junk mail

Stephen Covey, author of *The Seven Habits of Highly Effective People*,[1] writes about how crucial it is to spend your time on important matters and to control the amount of time spent on urgent matters, such as when the cook announces that the kitchen is running out of a popular entrée. Just because a matter is urgent doesn't mean that it is automatically important, although you will certainly have to deal with the cook's problem in a timely but not time-consuming manner.

1. To keep socializing to a minimum, ask friends and family to call at work only if there is an emergency. Also make sure that you don't spend too much time socializing with your peers and employees. To cut down on outside visitors dropping in, make it a policy that visitors must have an appointment. When you find that certain employees are forever running to you with every problem and question, help them to find their own answers, and if this doesn't help, ask them to save up several questions to go over at one time. To be a good supervisor, you also have to learn to say "no" to requests for time that are not reasonable or justified.

2. To organize your papers well, consider setting up your desk with these boxes or trays: in, out, action, pending, read, and file. All incoming papers go in the "in" box, and similarly, all outgoing papers such as memos you've written go in the "out" box. The "action" box contains papers and projects you are currently working on. The "pending" box has papers that need to be taken care of in the future. Some su-

---

[1]Steven R. Covey, The Seven Habits of Highly Effective People, New York: Simon and Schuster, 1989, pp. 146–182.

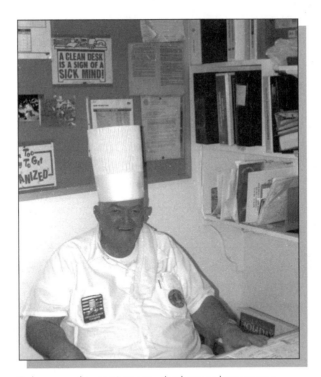

To be a good supervisor, you also have to learn to say "no" to requests for time that are not reasonable or justified.

pervisors set up 31 file folders numbered from 1 to 31 to represent the days of the month. Pending papers are then put into the proper date. This type of file system should be checked daily. The "read" box contains magazines and other material that can be read at your leisure. The "file" box contains papers that can simply be filed away. Each of these boxes is important, but the most important file in your office sits under your desk: the wastebasket. Don't think you have to hold on to everything!

3. Now that you have eliminated some of the time-wasters, *set priorities*. List *all* the things you want to get done today and divide them into *musts* and *shoulds* or number them 1 and 2. Do the must things (the 1's) first. It is said that 80 percent of your results can come from 20 percent of your efforts. Use a desk calendar (Figure 11.8) to plan and schedule the must items into the top 20 percent of your time. A weekly planning sheet is a useful supplement to your daily calendar. At the end of the day, transfer what you didn't get done to tomorrow's list, add today's accumulation of new musts and shoulds, reassess your priorities, and discard anything that no longer seems important. You will soon become adept at sorting out the time-wasters.

4. *Set aside regular periods of time without interruption* for interviews, problem solving, training, important decisions, and long-range projects. Every manager needs a quiet time each day for creativity and problem solving. Begin those

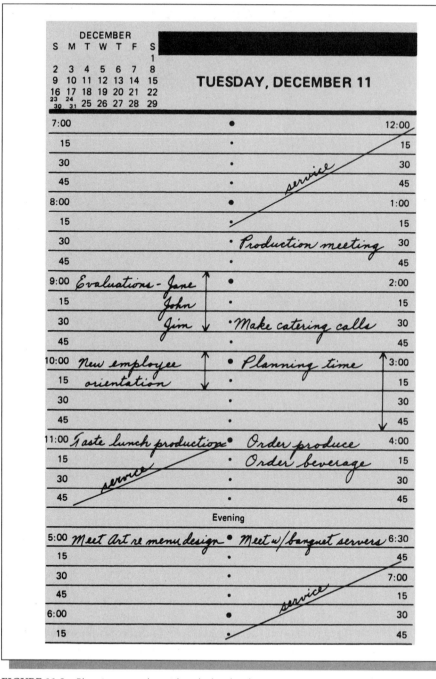

FIGURE 11.8 Planning your day with a desk calendar.

time-consuming projects; divide them into manageable segments and get started on them. Getting them under way, and getting one or two of them accomplished, will renew your energy and confidence. Sometimes a small success is a big boost for self-motivation.

5. *Initiate long-range solutions to your time problems*—standing plans, better training, more delegation, reduced turnover, better communications—things that will eliminate the need for you to be in the thick of everything all the time (although still remaining visible). You will have fewer crises, fewer fires, because everyone will know what to do and how to do it. You will have more people taking more responsibility. You will have time to develop your people, to motivate, to build trust, to exercise true leadership.

There will be many days when your plans are wiped out by unexpected events. When this happens, reschedule priority items for another day and go home and get a good night's sleep. Hanging on to feelings of frustration will eat you up. But don't give up planning just because your plans don't work out some of the time. Adjusting your plans continuously is part of the planning process in your kind of job. And you can't adjust your plans if you haven't made any.

Check Your Knowledge

1. How do workers respond to change?
2. List the five steps in planning for change.

Organizing for Success

The kind of long-range plans that will help you to solve your time problems have another, broader purpose: They will make your unit run more efficiently and effectively. One goal of this type of planning is effective organization. A well-organized and efficient unit is one in which:

- ∾ Lines of authority and responsibility are clearly drawn—and observed.
- ∾ Jobs, procedures, and standards are clearly defined—and followed.
- ∾ People know what to do and how to do it—and they do it.
- ∾ Standards of quality, quantity, and performance are clearly set—and met.

Setting everything up to run efficiently is **organizing.** Keeping it running efficiently and effectively is *managing.* Most hospitality supervisors move into a situation that has already been organized, whether well or badly, by someone else. If it has been organized well, their place in the company's organizational chart is clear, they know to whom they report, their authority and responsibility have been clearly defined, and they know the purpose (goal, function) of their department and their job. Each job classification is clearly defined, and there is a detailed procedures manual for each job. All necessary standards have been set, and people have been trained to meet them. Standing plans provide for repeating situations.

But many departments are not as well organized as this, and the lack of organization is a major contributor to crisis management. If you have inherited a badly organized unit, will you go on putting out fires, as your predecessor did, allowing yourself to be controlled by events instead of controlling them, developing the habit of nonplanning? It is an easy habit to develop and a seductive one: It gives you a sense of power, of being needed.

It is a short-run, shortsighted solution, and it will not contribute to your future in the industry. A better way to go is to set out to organize things better. How will you do it?

1. *Find out what you need to know about your own job.* Who is your boss—who directs you, and to whom are you accountable? What responsibilities and authority do you have, and what are you accountable for? How do your job and your department fit into the organization as a whole?

2. *Find out where poor organization is causing problems.* What you examine first depends on what is causing the most problems. Some areas to investigate follow.

   ∾ *Chain of command* (lines of authority and responsibility). Do all your workers know to whom they report—who has the right to tell them what to do and who holds them responsible for doing it? Does anyone take orders from more than one person? It is a primary principle of organization that each

Ensuring that you know who you report to, and what responsibilities and authority you have, is part of a good organization.

person should have only one boss (a principle known as **unity of command**). How many people do you supervise? Another principle of organization states that there is a limit to the number of employees one person can supervise effectively (known as **span of control**). One hundred people are too many; 50 are probably too many; generally, 20 to 30 are considered the maximum number that one person can supervise or lead effectively. If you are given responsibility for supervising too many people, you may be able to delegate certain supervisory duties to key people in your department: In other words, create another level below you in the chain of command.

❧ *Job content and procedures.* Are jobs clearly defined in terms of duties, tasks, procedures, and acceptable performance standards? Is there a procedures manual for each job? Are the written materials kept up to date? Are there things people do—or should do but don't—that are not assigned to any job? Do any jobs overlap: Are the same responsibilities assigned to more than one job? Are people carrying out their assigned responsibilities and following procedures correctly? Do some people have too much to do and others too little?

❧ *Training.* Do people know what to do and how to do it and what standard of performance is expected of them? Have they been well trained? Are they meeting the standards?

❧ *Evaluation and controls.* Have standards of quality, quantity, and performance been set, and are people meeting them? Are standards being used to evaluate and control products and services? Is there a system of performance review?

❧ *Standing plans.* Have standing plans been set up for repetitive tasks, routine reports, and emergency procedures? Are forms provided for reports, record keeping, information, and controls? Do people use them correctly?

Answers to such questions as these will give you a pretty good idea of the existing organization of your department and the degree to which it is functioning as it is supposed to.

3. *Plan what you will do to improve the organization and efficiency of your operation.* For this purpose many chapters of this book are at your disposal to help you along the way. Job descriptions will help you define jobs, set performance standards, develop procedures manuals, and provide the springboard for recruiting, training, and evaluation programs. The special chapters on these subjects will help you to develop and carry out such programs. Problem-solving and decision-making chapters will help you to define your problems, set your objectives, and choose the best courses of action.

Delegation, job enrichment, and employee participation offer you ways of reorganizing at least some of the work for better results. You can relieve yourself of detail, broaden job responsibilities for workers, and provide more time for managing. Standing plans can reduce the management of repeating tasks to dealing with exceptional conditions and events.

Controlling

Controlling is a process by which supervisors measure, evaluate, and compare results to goals and standards previously agreed upon, such as performance standards, and take corrective action when necessary to stay on course. There are visible controls throughout your workplace: door locks, time clocks, the bartender's measuring device, keys to the cash register.

A major area of control for hospitality supervisors is cost: food cost, beverage cost, labor cost, supply cost, energy cost. Cost control is a process by which supervisors try to regulate costs and guard against excessive costs in order to have a profitable business. It is an ongoing process and involves every step in the chain of purchasing, receiving, storing, issuing, and preparing food and beverages for sale, scheduling employees, and using supplies and energy. On a daily basis you will be involved in cost control techniques such as checking vendors' invoices and counting cash. The exact methods you use will vary from place to place, depending in part on the nature and scope of your business, but the principle of sparing your employer excessive costs remains the same.

In the hospitality industry, excessive costs are often due to inefficiency, theft, and waste, factors that you can influence. For instance, you may check production records against recorded sales to ensure that all quantities produced are accounted for. Table 11.1 displays additional examples of controls. As a supervisor you can use the following control techniques:

∾ Require records and reports (such as production reports).

∾ Develop and enforce performance standards.

∾ Develop and enforce productivity standards.

∾ Develop and enforce departmental policies and procedures.

∾ Observe and correct employee actions.

∾ Train and retrain employees.

∾ Discipline employees when appropriate.

∾ Be a good role model.

As discussed in Chapter 6, performance standards define how well a job is to be done (the quality aspect); **productivity standards** define the acceptable quantity of work an employee is expected to do (following performance standards, of course). For example, you may determine that it is a reasonable expectation for a housekeeping employee to complete cleaning a guestroom according to your performance standards in 30 minutes, for a server to be able to serve four tables at a time, or for a hospital tray line to produce three trays per minute.

Productivity has been defined as follows[2]: "A typed efficiency measure calculated by dividing a company's output by worker hours." In a restaurant, inputs such

---

[2]Paul A. Argenti, Editorial Director. *The Portable MBA Desk Reference,* New York: Wiley 1994, p. 321.

TABLE 11.1   ∾   **Examples of Controls**

Management controls	*Labor controls*
Preshift meetings	Weekly schedules
Weekly management meetings	Timecards
Management log	Labor forecasting forms
Management opening and closing checklists	*Accounting controls*
Guest comment cards	Weekly profit and loss statements
Mystery shopper reports	Daily reconciliation of cash receipts
Preventive maintenance schedules	End of shift report forms (X and Z outs)
Purchasing controls	Daily customer count
Purchase orders	Itemized sales reports
Food requisitions	*Employee controls*
Receiving procedures	Job descriptions
Food controls	Employee files
Monthly food inventory	Employee evaluation forms
Standardized recipes	Disciplinary action notices
Food cost worksheets	*Training controls*
Daily food production sheets	Orientation program
Beverage controls	Training manuals
Monthly beverage inventory	Training program
Standardized beverage menu recipes	
Beverage cost worksheet	
Daily perpetual beverage inventory	
worksheet	

Source: Adapted from Fred Del Marva, "Implementing controls: the secret to success," *Nation's Restaurant News,* November 13, 1989.

as food and labor are used to produce outputs such as meals. Productivity can generally be thought of as a ratio:

productivity

$$= \frac{\text{outputs (products or services: quantity and quality)}}{\text{inputs (resources to produce outputs such as food, labor, and supply costs)}}$$

Productivity measurements tell much about an operation's efficiency and performance and are the common denominator for comparing your operation with others. They also help when developing budgets and allocating resources. Productivity in the hospitality industry is as much a matter of quantity as it is quality. For example, a server may be able to handle six tables in 20 minutes, but the quality of the service is inferior to that of another server who takes care of fewer customers in the same period of time. Table 11.2 lists common foodservice productivity measures.

TABLE 11.2   ∾   Foodservice Productivity Measures

$$\text{Labor cost percentage} = \frac{\text{cost of labor}}{\text{sales}}$$

$$\text{Sales per labor hour} = \frac{\text{sales}}{\text{labor hours used}}$$

$$\text{Guests served per labor dollar} = \frac{\text{guests served}}{\text{cost of labor}}$$

$$\text{Guests served per labor hour} = \frac{\text{guests served}}{\text{labor hours used}}$$

Source: Jack E. Miller, David K. Hayes, and Lea Dopson, *Food and Beverage Cost Control,* 2nd ed. New York: Wiley, 2002.

∾ key points

1. As a supervisor, you need to plan what is to be done, organize how it is to be done (this includes coordinating and staffing), direct the work being done, and control or evaluate what has been done.

2. There are various levels of planning, from strategic planning (or long-range planning) to short-term planning.

3. The planning process involves the following steps: Define the purpose or problem and set objectives, collect and evaluate data relevant to forecasting the future, develop possible courses of action, decide on the best course of action, and carry out the plan.

4. You can reduce risk when planning repetitive work by having a contingency plan, consulting people who have more experience than you do, or by keeping records that add to your data for forecasting.

5. A good plan provides a workable solution and meets the stated objectives, is comprehensive, minimizes the degree of risk, and is specific and flexible.

6. A standing plan is an established routine or formula or set of procedures designed to be used in a recurring or repetitive situation. Examples include policies and procedures.

7. A single-use plan is a one-time plan developed for a single occasion or purpose, such as a budget.

8. Most workers resist change. You can reduce their fear and uncertainty with facts, open discussion, understanding, and support, as well as involving them in planning and carrying out the change.

9. The first step in planning for change is to define your problem and set your objectives. The second step is to gather data from the past, present, and probable future in order to forecast what alternatives are most likely to succeed and to reduce the risks. Next, generate alternatives, evaluate the pros and cons of each,

and assess their risks and benefits. The fourth step is to make the necessary decisions, after weighing each alternative in terms of the five critical decision-making questions: risk versus benefit, economy, feasibility, acceptability, and meeting the objectives. The last step is implementing the plan.

10. To make good use of your time, eliminate time-wasters, set priorities, use a planning calendar, set aside regular periods of time without interruption for interviews, and initiate long-range solutions to your time problems.

11. Setting everything up to run efficiently is organizing. The first step in organizing is to find out what you need to know about your job. The second step is to find out where poor organization is causing problems, such as chain of command, job content and procedures, training, evaluation and controls, or standing plans. The third step is to plan what you will do to improve the organization and efficiency of your operation.

12. Controlling is a process by which supervisors measure, evaluate, and compare results to goals and standards previously agreed upon, and take corrective action when necessary to stay on course. Table 11.1 gives examples of controls commonly found in the hospitality industry.

∾ key terms

budget	productivity standard
contingency plan	resistance to change
controlling	risk
forecast	single-use plan
management by exception	span of control
organizing	standing plan
planning	strategic planning
productivity	unity of command

∾ review questions

Answer each question in complete sentences. Read each question carefully and make sure that you answer all parts of the question. Organize your answer using more than one paragraph when appropriate.

1. Compare strategic planning to day-by-day planning.
2. Briefly describe the steps in planning. Why do they resemble the steps used in making a good decision?
3. How can you reduce your risk when planning repetitive work?
4. Discuss five qualities of a good plan, and explain why each is important.

5. Give five examples of a standing plan.

6. What is *management by exception?*

7. A budget is an example of what type of plan?

8. Why do employees resist change?

9. In the example of planning a new menu, what do you think of the manager's plan? What problems might there be? If you were the manager, would you have people participate even more, such as visiting competitors and reporting on their menus or contributing recipe suggestions? Why or why not? How would you reward the workers who take part?

10. List the five steps in planning for change.

11. What can you do to make more effective use of your time?

12. What areas of the operation might you investigate if poor organization is causing problems?

13. Give five examples of controls commonly found in hospitality operations.

∾ activities and applications

1. Discussion Questions

- Since planning involves forecasting the future, and since so much of the supervisor's job is dealing with things that are unpredictable, and since there is never enough time in the day anyway, do you think that planning is worth the time it takes? Defend your answer.

- Mary Lou says that standing plans free the supervisor for other management tasks; John says that standing plans are an excuse for laziness and a straitjacket on creative action. Which view do you agree with, and why? Can you somehow arrange to have the best of both views?

- How does planning relate to all the other aspects of a supervisor's job? Give specific examples of how lack of planning can complicate getting the job done, starting new personnel on the job, or other examples from your own experience.

- What responsibility does a supervisor have for departmental organization? If you were hired for a job in which organization was poor, how would you go about straightening things out? How would you deal with your own supervisor in reorganizing things?

- Planning your personal time can be as useful as planning your work time. How good a planner are you? What are your time-wasters? Do you set priorities? Do you use a calendar for planning?

2. Group Activity: Brainstorming Plans and Controls

In groups of four, brainstorm examples of plans and controls found in hospitality operations with which you are familiar. Have one person keep a list of plans and a separate list of controls. Share with the class.

3. Case Study: Preparing Employees for Change

Michael is beverage manager at the principal hotel in a middle-sized manufacturing town. The hotel has a steady business trade and is now reaching out to attract local customers for its restaurant and bar. The restaurant is to be enlarged and the bar off the lobby is to be remodeled and expanded into a cocktail lounge with table service. Michael is in charge of planning all aspects of the change.

All the bar equipment will be new, and Michael will work with the designer to determine what is needed. There will be a dozen tables served by waiters or waitresses whom Michael will hire and train. The bartenders will pour drinks for both the lounge and dining room servers in addition to customers at the bar, and Michael may have to add another couple of bartenders to the staff.

Michael knows the present bartenders will be worried about the change. They will be afraid they will work harder for fewer tips, since they will be competing with the table servers. They may also be concerned about the new layout and equipment. It is important for them to feel confident about working in the new setup and to be committed to the project and accepting of the new personnel.

QUESTIONS

1. When should Michael break the news, and how?
2. How should he deal with their fears about new personnel?
3. What can he do to increase their confidence?
4. How can he gain their commitment to the new project?
5. Make a detailed plan incorporating your answers for Michael to follow in dealing with his present bartenders.

✍ chapter 12

Decision Making and Problem Solving

overview

✍ Making decisions is a built-in requirement of a supervisory job. When workers run into problems, they bring them to you and you decide what they should do. When crises arise—equipment breakdowns, supplies that don't arrive, people calling in sick or hurting themselves or fighting or walking off the job—you decide what should be done. When workers can't or won't do their jobs, as they should, you decide whether to retrain them, motivate them, discipline them, or fire them. When things are not going well in your department, you are the one who decides what to do about it. Sometimes your entire day consists of one decision after another, and it seems to you that there is no time left to get any work done.

For a supervisor in this fast-paced, time-pressure industry, decision making is your work, like it or not. It is not you but the people you supervise who make the products or deliver the services. You plan their work, hire and fire them, solve their problems, settle their arguments, grant or deny requests, deal with the unexpected, troubleshoot, and by making countless small decisions you may not even think of as decisions, you see that the work gets done. How well the work gets done depends a great deal on how good your decisions are.

In this chapter we explore the kinds of down-to-earth decision making that supervisors in the hospitality industry are faced with day by day. It will help you to:

∾ Identify the three essential elements of a managerial decision, and explain how they help to clarify the decision-making process.

∾ Describe the steps in making good decisions and learn how to put them to work.

∾ List and describe common approaches to decision making.

∾ Describe the steps to make good decisions and describe how to apply them.

∾ Explain the relationship between problem solving and decision making, and apply decision-making techniques in solving problems.

∾ Discuss the pros and cons of participative problem solving and state an example of when it would be appropriate to use.

∾ List guidelines for approaching various kinds of people problems.

Decision Making

Human beings are constantly making decisions of one sort or another as they go about their daily lives. How do they do this, and what is special about a supervisor's decisions?

Elements in a Managerial Decision

Supervisory decisions derive from the role and responsibility of being a manager. A manager's **decision** should be a conscious choice among alternative courses of action directed toward a specific purpose. There are three key phrases in this definition that describe three essential elements in the decision-making process.

1. The first phrase is a *choice among alternatives.* If there is no alternative, if there is only one way to go, there is no decision to make: You do the only thing you can. Choice is the primary essential in decision making. Furthermore, the choice is *conscious:* You deliberately choose one course of action over others. You are not swept along by events or habit or the influence of others; you don't just go with the flow. You are making it happen, not just letting it happen.

2. The second essential of a managerial decision is a *specific purpose.* The decision has a goal or objective: to solve a specific problem, to accomplish a specific result. Like a performance-based objective, a decision has a *what* and a *how.* The specific purpose is the what.

3. The third essential is a *course of action.* The decision is to do something or have something done in a particular way. This is the *how.* Making a decision requires seeing that the decision is carried out.

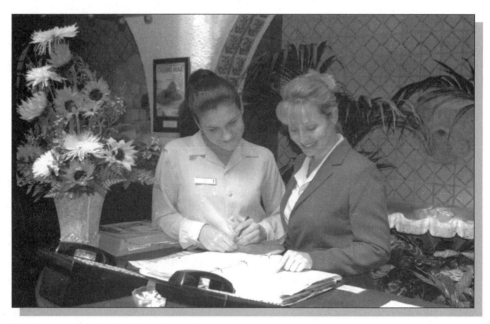

Manager considering decision alternatives.

Rational versus Emotional Decision Making

On occasions, all decision makers use too much emotion in making a decision. For example, consider a couple who spend a fortune in fancy decor when opening up a new restaurant. The rational part of decision making would question the amount being spent because it does not make sense if the restaurant cannot pay back the amount spent preopening. As managers it is important to weigh out the consequences of our actions before we react purely on emotion. In the hospitality field, managers need to learn how to approach decision making using both emotion and rationality.

A good decision is one in which the course of action chosen meets the objective in the best possible way—usually, the one with the least risk and the most benefit to the enterprise.

Approaches to Decision Making

Different people approach decision making in different ways. One way is to go deliberately through a series of logical steps based on the scientific method. You formulate your objectives and rank them, gather all the relevant facts, examine and weigh all the alternative courses of action and their consequences, and choose the one that best meets the objectives. This **logical approach** is recommended (with variations) by management scientists. It takes time, something busy hospitality supervisors do not have, and it is probably foreign to their habits: Most people in operations tend to be doers rather than deliberators. It is better suited to weighty top-management problems than to the day-in, day-out decisions of hotel and foodservice supervisors. Nevertheless, it can be adapted for solving their important problems, as we shall see.

At the opposite extreme is the **intuitive approach:** the hunch, the gut reaction, the decision that *feels* right. People who take this approach to decisions tend to be creative, intelligent people with strong egos and high aspirations. Some entrepreneurs are like this: They may be driving around and suddenly they will say, "There's a perfect location for a restaurant," and they buy it, build a restaurant, and make it a big success.

But this approach does not work for everybody; much of the time it does not work for the people who practice it. When it does, there is bound to be a lot of knowledge, experience, and subconscious reasoning behind the hunches and the gut reactions. Most people would do about as well flipping a coin: You have a 50 percent chance of being right. Your biases, habits, preconceptions, preferences, and self-interest are all at work right along with your knowledge, experience, and subconscious reasoning. It is almost impossible to see things clearly in a flash, even with extensive background and experience.

Many people have no particular approach to decision making. Some are **indecisive** and afraid of it: They worry a lot, procrastinate, ask other people's advice, and never quite come to the point of making up their minds. Others make **impulsive** off-the-cuff decisions based on whim or the mood of the moment rather than on facts or even intuition. Both types of people have trouble distinguishing important from unimportant decisions, and they confuse and frustrate their superiors and the people they supervise. Both types have a poor batting average in making good decisions and tend to be plagued with problems and frustrations.

Kinds of Decisions

The decisions a hospitality supervisor is called upon to make may range from deciding how many gallons of cleaning compound to buy, up to solving problems that are affecting production, people, and profit. Some decisions are easy to make: what supplies to order and whether to take advantage of special prices, number of portions to prepare, weekly schedule assignments, assigning rooms to be made up, granting or denying employee requests for time off or schedule change, what time to schedule an interview, whether to confirm a reservation in writing or by telephone, number of banquet waiters to bring in for a special event. All these decisions are simple to make because you have the historical data or the knowhow on which to base your decision.

Sometimes you have a set routine or formula for finding answers to recurring decisions, and if there is nothing new to affect today's decision, you just follow the routine of what has been done before and you don't have anything to decide. This is really a standard operating procedure that may have been established by usage or may be spelled out in your policy and procedures manual.

Many decisions are less clear-cut and more complicated. They may affect many people. There may be many factors to consider. The wrong decision may have serious consequences. Among such decisions are hiring and firing, delegating, and making changes in the work environment or in the work itself, such as introducing a new menu, redecorating a dining room, and changing work procedures. Such decisions require time and thought.

Complicated time-pressure decisions arise when emergencies occur: from equipment breakdowns to accidents, fights, people not showing up, and food that does not meet your quality standards. Even if you have established routines for meeting emergencies, you must still make critical decisions, and one decision may require a whole string of other decisions to adjust to new circumstances. If, for example, you pull a busperson off the floor to substitute for an injured kitchen worker, you have to provide for the busing, and when you ask servers to bus their own tables, you know that customer service will be affected and you have to handle that situation. A single incident thus demands one split-second decision after another.

This kind of decision-making requires a clear grasp of what is going on plus quick thinking and quick action: **decisiveness.** These are qualities that you develop on the job. You develop them by knowing your operation and your people well, by watching your superiors handle emergencies and analyzing what they did, and by building your own self-confidence and skill as you make decisions on everyday problems.

Perhaps the most difficult decisions are those necessary to resolve problem situations. In a sense, all decision making is problem solving. But in some situations you cannot choose an appropriate course of action because you do not know what is causing the problem. For example, you discover that customer complaints about room service have increased during the last few weeks, but you do not know why. The problem you are aware of (customer complaints) is really a symptom of a deeper problem, and you cannot choose a course of action until you know what that problem is and what is causing it. You need a quick study to isolate the problem: Is it in order taking, preparation, or delivery where the system or procedure has failed? This is a far more complicated decision than, for example, deciding what to do about a stopped-up drain.

Some of the decisions that come up in your job are not yours to make. Sometimes the decision is made for you by company policy, such as prescribed penalties for absenteeism or improper food portioning or smoking on the job. In such instances, the only thing you decide is whether the incident fits the policy specifications—was this the second or third time it happened, and does it deserve the penalty if the clock was fast and she thought it was closing time when she lit her cigarette?

You may have other problems that you do not have the authority to do anything about. If you supervise the dining room and your servers complain about one of the cooks, you do not have authority to discipline that cook. You can work with the head cook, who is on the same level you are, to resolve the problem. If this fails, you can send the problem up through channels to the food and beverage director. But you cannot give orders anywhere but in your own department. It is important never to make decisions or take action where you do not have authority and responsibility.

Since time is probably your biggest problem, *it is essential to recognize which decisions are important and which are unimportant, which decisions you must make now and which can wait.* As a rule of thumb, unimportant decisions are those that have little effect on the work or on people: Nothing serious will happen if you make the wrong choice. Should you put tonight's specials on menu fliers or let the servers describe them when they take orders? What kind of centerpiece should you use on the chamber of commerce lunch table? What color paper should you have the new guest checks printed on? Such decisions are worth little more than a few seconds' thought: What is the problem? Who is involved? What are your choices? Is there a clear choice? If there is no clear choice, make one anyway and move on. Getting hung up on inconsequential decisions can be a disaster. It impedes the work, your boss and your people lose confidence in you, and you lose your own perspective, your conceptual grasp of your job.

The opposite mistake—giving too little time to an important decision—can also have serious consequences. An important decision is one that has a pronounced impact on the work or the workers, such as a change in policy or procedures, what to do about a drop in productivity, or how to deal with friction between workers. In such situations the most serious mistake is not taking the time needed to consider the decision carefully. The wrong decision is hard to undo. It may cause serious consequences or perpetuate the problem you are trying to solve.

How to Make Good Decisions[1]

When you try to consider a decision carefully, you often go back and forth, over and over, and around and around without making any progress, and you become frustrated and feel like avoiding making any decision at all. Experts have developed a series of steps that can take you out of this maze.

The following six steps are a simple version of the logical approach. The procedure is elastic and can be expanded or shortened to fit circumstances.

Although all people have their way of approaching decision making, there are things that we must all consider when faced with a decision. A successful manager must include others in the decision-making process—this builds a valuable team for everyone. For example, menu changes are not most likely to start right away, but why not ask for input of employees? Poll the staff for their thoughts on the existing menu to determine which items are first on the hit list and which one can wait. Servers are catalogers of customer input, and the (good) cooks know best what the people want. When working with the staff you are able to learn what they want as well as what they feel the customers want. People don't want to be dictated to—they want to feel a part of the team.

1. Define the problem and set objectives. (What do you want to happen?)
2. Analyze the problem: get the facts: the relevant who, what, when, where, how, why.
3. Develop alternative solutions.
4. Decide on the best solution.
5. Convert the decision into action.
6. Follow up.

Figure 12.1 shows you how the pattern proceeds.

When you are out there on the job coping with an emergency, think about taking these steps. But chances are that you actually will without thinking, and this is as it should be. Suppose that the dishmachine breaks down suddenly at noon on one of the busiest days in the year. You don't think about defining the problem and the objective; they define themselves: you need enough plates, silverware, and glasses to get the food out to customers until you can get the machine fixed. You may ask how many clean dishes there are—or you may not even stop for this—you *know* you are going to run out. You generate alternatives at lightning speed: Wash by hand in the bar sinks? Use the bar glasses? Ask the restaurant next door (a friendly competitor) for help (borrow dishes or share their dishmachine)? Use paper and plastic? You don't have time to figure out the pros and cons of each choice: you make a judgment on which is best, and you may use all of

---

[1]This section is adapted from Michael Tsonton, "New Line Order," *Restaurants and Institutions,* Vol. 110, No. 12, May 1, 2000.

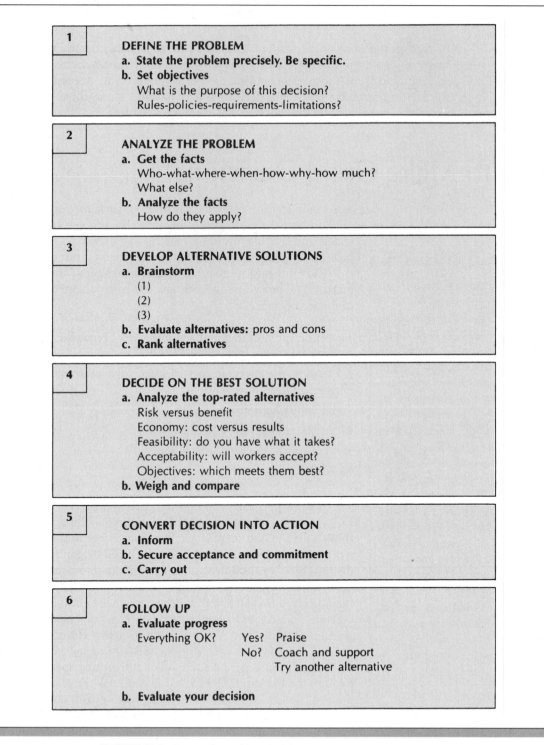

1	**DEFINE THE PROBLEM**
	a. **State the problem precisely. Be specific.**
	b. **Set objectives**
	What is the purpose of this decision?
	Rules-policies-requirements-limitations?

2	**ANALYZE THE PROBLEM**
	a. **Get the facts**
	Who-what-where-when-how-why-how much?
	What else?
	b. **Analyze the facts**
	How do they apply?

3	**DEVELOP ALTERNATIVE SOLUTIONS**
	a. **Brainstorm**
	(1)
	(2)
	(3)
	b. **Evaluate alternatives:** pros and cons
	c. **Rank alternatives**

4	**DECIDE ON THE BEST SOLUTION**
	a. **Analyze the top-rated alternatives**
	Risk versus benefit
	Economy: cost versus results
	Feasibility: do you have what it takes?
	Acceptability: will workers accept?
	Objectives: which meets them best?
	b. **Weigh and compare**

5	**CONVERT DECISION INTO ACTION**
	a. **Inform**
	b. **Secure acceptance and commitment**
	c. **Carry out**

6	**FOLLOW UP**
	a. **Evaluate progress**
	Everything OK? Yes? Praise
	No? Coach and support
	Try another alternative
	b. **Evaluate your decision**

FIGURE 12.1 Pattern for making decisions.

Making good decisions can sometimes take a team effort.

them. You take action immediately by directing your people and doing some of the work yourself. This requires more split-second decisions, a few of which may not work out, but you can work with what you have. In fact, what you did was to move logically through, but you also utilized one of the most critical success factors in decision making: **timing.** In many on-the-spot decisions of a supervisor's job, timing may be the overriding factor: A decision is necessary *now.*

The need to make hundreds of quick decisions every day may make you forget that there is any other way to make a decision. Quick decision making becomes a habit. Yet a quick decision is *bad* timing if it is something you need to think through. In the dishmachine breakdown you knew the necessary facts and the available alternatives, and you recognized the problem at once. But in other circumstances you may not know all the facts. You may not recognize the real problem. You may jump in with the first solution that comes to mind. You may not realize the consequences it could have. If your decision affects your people and their work, it is worth taking the time to ensure the best possible outcome.

Let us take an example and run through the decision-making process using our six-step method. You have just hired a new server, Cindy, to replace Gary. She will work a split shift, 11 to 3 and 7 to 11 Tuesday through Saturday, which is Gary's last day. Cindy must be trained well enough to start work on Tuesday. She is an experienced waitress, having worked in a restaurant similar to yours. In the next five sections we follow this decision through to its solution.

Defining the Problem

The first step has two parts: to *state the problem precisely* and to formulate your *objectives:* what you want to happen as a result of your decision. You start out by writing down *Who will train Cindy?* Then you realize that there is more to the problem than *who*; there are *when* and *what:* How much training does Cindy need? You restate your problem: *Give Cindy enough training to start on the noon shift Tuesday.* This statement broadens your approach: You begin to include the training itself in your thinking. Figure 12.2 shows your worksheet as you develop your decisions.

Your objectives should restate your problem in terms of the results you expect. They should also include any rules or policies that apply, any requirements as to where, when, how, and so on, and any limiting factors such as time and money. These things are sometimes referred to collectively as **conditions and limitations.**

For your objective, then, you write down: *Cindy is to meet minimum performance standards by noon shift Tuesday. JIT method, on site. Training expenses $50 maximum.*

Problem: ~~Who will train Cindy?~~
         Cindy trained to start noon Tue.
Objectives: Min PBO standards noon Tue.
         JIT - On site - $50 max.

Gary	11-3 & 7-11	Tue-Sat
Eloise	11-3	Mon-Sat
Robert	11-1:30 & 7-11	Mon-Sat
Karen	11-3	Fri-Sat
Rose	5-9	Thu-Sat
Charlie	5-11	Mon-Sat
Michael	5-11	Thu-Sat

Who: Eloise lunch   P + G + C + W + ?
       Karen lunch   P + G + C + W ?
       Charlie dinner   P + G + C + W +
       Michael dinner   P + G - C - W + wine + + +
       Self - lunch - dinner   4 +
What: Wine, guest check, Pretest results
When: Sat. - Fri.? - Here - JIT
How much $: trainers - Cindy
What else? Sat. luncheon

Choices	Alternatives	Pro	Con
	1. E + Ch. Sat.	2 best people	Sat. busy, Ch wine?
(M wine)'	2. E Fri, Ch Sat.	", less busy, C work Sat noon	$ 4 hours extra
	3. Karen either Fri or Sat.	3 + (W?)	Less experience - willing?
	4. Michael either Fri or Sat.	2 +, wine + + +	2 - (G + C)
2 (M wine)	5. Fri - Cindy 1-2 tables Sat.	Avoid Sat, C to start slow	$$ less tips for somebody
	6. Fri Self	4 +, no $, Cindy here	I am too busy, interruptions
3	7. Mon E + Ch.	Slow, Gary gone, Tues slow too	{ Cindy willing? Overtime
	~~8. Cindy, Sat coaching~~	Cheapest	($$, I'm off
			Bad policy, busy, customers, etc.

Risk - Sat ??
Economy - Mon $$$ but best results
Feasibility } O.K.
Acceptability }
Objectives: <u>No. 3 best</u>

FIGURE 12.2   Decision making: manager's worksheet on training for Cindy.

Analyzing the Problem

The next step is to assemble the relevant data, but don't overdo it: Keep the goal clear. It is easy to tell people more than they need to know, yourself included, so don't confuse yourself with too many facts. You can get more as you need them—and you probably will.

The easiest way to organize the **fact finding** is to go through the who–what–when–where–how–why routine. The first question is *who.* After studying the weekly schedule, you put down: *Eloise or Karen (lunch), Charlie or Michael (dinner).* Some of these servers would make better trainers than others, but you do not eliminate anyone at this point. You want to keep your mind open and your thinking positive. Besides, you need all the possibilities you can get because you may have to settle for a less than perfect solution. Then, reluctantly, you add *Self.* You really don't have the time.

The next question is *what.* You start to write *Server procedures,* and then you think, "Wait a minute, Cindy has been a waitress before; we don't need to train her from scratch." Then you think, "Just what does she know?", and right away you pick up the phone and call her to come in on Friday at 9:00 A.M. for a pretest. You know that she doesn't know wine service; they serve wine only by the glass where she worked before. She won't know your guest check system either. But a lot of things will be the same. She's bright, and it shouldn't take long to train her. You make a few notes: *wine, guest check, pretest results.*

The next question is *when.* You put down *Saturday* and then you think, Well, maybe part of Friday, too, since she's coming for the pretest anyway. And Saturday is so busy—you have that bridal luncheon for the mayor's daughter. You put down *Friday?*

The next question is *where,* and the answer is *Here,* with your equipment and your setup, just as though she were working.

The next question is *how.* You write *JIT, show and tell.* You will have to coach your trainers on this, but since they were trained this way themselves and you have performance standards to go by, it shouldn't take long, maybe an hour on Thursday.

The last question is *why,* and you have answered that in your objective.

Next you analyze the data you have gathered. Which server would make the best trainer? You rate them plus or minus on performance, guest relationships, communication, and willingness. What about costs? A few extra hours for the trainers and maybe an extra half day for Cindy. It shouldn't go over your $50 limit.

Anything else? *That luncheon on Saturday.*

Developing Alternative Solutions

Now that you have all the facts, your next step is to develop as many alternatives as you can. The first stage should be uninhibited **brainstorming:** You give free rein to your imagination and put down every possibility that you can think of without regard to its drawbacks or limitations. You do not want any negative thoughts to inhibit your creativity. Sometimes a totally impractical idea will suggest a really good solution or a way of adapting another solution for a better result. Sometimes an entirely new idea will suddenly emerge. Ideas spark other ideas, so keep them coming.

You jot down the following:

1. *Eloise and Charlie on Saturday.*
2. *Eloise Friday and Charlie Saturday.*
3. *Substitute Karen for Eloise either day.*
4. *Substitute Michael for Charlie either day.*

After a moment's thought, you add:

5. *Train Friday (Eloise or Karen and Charlie or Michael).*
6. *Yourself Friday.*

And then, since the idea of training on busy days is beginning to really bother you, you add:

7. *Train Monday (Eloise and Charlie—Michael and Karen off).*

Finally, in case all else fails, you add:

8. *Let Cindy start working Saturday and assign someone to coach her.*

At this point you run dry. You think you have some good possibilities.

You now move to the second stage of developing alternatives: You weigh the pros and cons of each. You consider the good and bad points, keeping in mind how these would help or hinder the outcome and whether there would be side effects or bad consequences. It is very easy, in concentrating on achieving your objectives, to overlook other results that a course of action might have (the operation is a success but the patient dies).

The larger the problem, the more important this step is. In a major problem affecting production and people, thinking through the consequences is one of the most important steps of all. In our example, some alternatives might produce poor training quality, which could result in problems of service and cost. Or a personality clash might start a good server off on the wrong foot.

You start by listing the pros and cons. As you do this you discover some things you hadn't thought of before. Here are your thoughts:

1. *Eloise and Charlie on Saturday.*
   Pro: Eloise probably 4+ (willing?). Charlie definitely 4+ except on wine.
   Con: Very busy day, Charlie wine?
2. *Eloise Friday, Charlie Saturday.*
   Pro: Best trainers. Friday not as busy, Cindy coming in Friday anyway. Cindy can work bridal luncheon Saturday.
   Con: Extra cost (Cindy 4 hours Friday).

3. *Substitute Karen for Eloise.*
    Pro: 3+ trainer (willing?).
    Con: Less experienced than Eloise, probably less interested.

4. *Substitute Michael for Charlie.*
    Pro: 2+ (excellent performer, willing), superb on wine.
    Con: 2− (goes too fast, condescending).

5. *Train Friday, Cindy work 1 or 2 tables both shifts Saturday.*
    Pro: Avoid training on Saturday. Break Cindy in on job gradually.
    Con: Extra cost, 1 or 2 fewer tables and tips for someone Saturday dinner—resentment??

6. *Yourself Friday.*
    Pro: 4+ as trainer. No training cost. Cindy coming in anyway.
    Con: Important morning appointments. Off 2 to 5. Interruptions.

7. *Train Monday, Eloise and Charlie.*
    Pro: Slow day. Best trainers. Gary gone. Tuesday good for first workday (slow dinner).
    Con: Will Cindy trade Saturday for Monday? Six-day week for Cindy. Your day off. Slightly over budget (overtime for Cindy).

8. *Cindy to work Saturday with someone coaching.*
    Pro: Cheapest.
    Con: Bad policy. Poor training, bad start, hidden costs. Too busy on Saturday. Customer confusion.

The final step of this stage is to weigh the pros and cons and rank your alternatives. When you are making a very important decision with momentous consequences and you have plenty of time, you will rank all alternatives carefully. But if you have several feasible alternatives and limited decision time, you should pick out the top three or four alternatives and rank them. But don't throw the others out; you may have to come back to them.

Moving on, then, here is what you end up with:

❧ *First choice:* No. 2. Eloise train for lunch Friday, Charlie for dinner Saturday. Use Michael for wine training Saturday.

❧ *Second choice:* No. 5. Cindy to pretest and train Friday with Eloise and Charlie and work her regular hours Saturday. Michael to teach wine Saturday. Cindy to work bridal luncheon and 1 or 2 Gary's dinner tables.

❧ *Third choice:* Train Monday, Eloise and Charlie. (Must shave cost a bit further.)

You now have three alternatives that will meet your objectives reasonably well. Of the five remaining, you cross off No. 8: After weighing the pros and cons, you find it unacceptable. The rest are feasible alternatives, but you should not bother with them at this point. At least one of your three choices is bound to work.

Deciding on the Best Solution

Before making any decision of consequence, the decision maker should test the top-rated alternatives by asking five questions:

1. *Risk.* Which course of action provides the most benefit with the least risk?
2. *Economy.* Which course of action will give the best results with the least expenditure of time, money, and effort?
3. *Feasibility.* Is each course of action feasible? Do you have the people and resources to carry it out?
4. *Acceptability.* Will each course of action be acceptable to the people it will affect?
5. *Objectives.* Which course of action meets your objectives best?

These questions require you to do some more analysis. You must analyze benefits and risks and weigh one against the other. You must figure time, money, and effort and weigh cost against results. You must determine whether you have the people and resources needed in each case and whether it will be acceptable to the people concerned. Finally, you must weigh one course of action against another and decide which meets your objectives best.

You can run through this pretty quickly.

1. *Risk.* There isn't much risk anywhere. The biggest risk is probably in your first choice—Saturday being such a hectic day and leaving the dinner training until Saturday night. Charlie might come in late or things might get busy early. And there really isn't time for Michael to teach wine. So there *is* some risk on training quality that might make trouble later. Now, how about Monday? Monday is your day off; is there a risk there? You could stop in to see how things are going, and with your best trainers, little could go wrong and there's time to deal with it.

2. *Economy.* Monday is definitely the most expensive, but it would probably give the best results, and it's not *that* much more; you could shave it down to budget some way.

3. *Feasibility and acceptability.* Those are definitely the big questions; they may decide the whole thing. You pick up the phone and call Cindy. You find that Monday is okay with her; in fact, she'd like the overtime. She could also meet the other two schedules, but they sound a little confusing. You check with Eloise and Charlie. They can both meet all three arrangements and would like to do the training. They both think Monday sounds best.

4. *Objectives.* Which solution meets them best? You decide on Monday, largely on the basis of risk and, in the end, economy. Although it costs a bit more, you think the training quality will be much the best, and Cindy will have a good start. It is a decision you are not likely to regret, and it will pay for itself in the long run.

Action and Follow-Up

The next step in decision making is to hand the decision over to the people who will carry it out. At this point good communication is the key to success. The people who will carry out the decision must fully understand it, and everyone affected must be informed. Every effort must be made to gain acceptance and commitment. If the people who must carry out a decision are involved in developing the alternatives, it usually pays off, but in our industry this often isn't practical.

You have already involved Cindy and Eloise and Charlie; you had to involve them before you could come to a decision. You know that they are committed. You pick up the phone again and tell the three of them that the plan for Monday is on. You give them the details of the Monday schedule and set a time on Thursday for training the trainers. You will give Cindy the pretest on Friday and pass along the necessary information to Eloise and Charlie. You inform the assistant manager, who will be in charge on Monday. The decision is complete.

Altogether this decision took you 15 minutes or less from beginning to end. Was it worth the time? You think so, definitely. You will start Cindy off on the right foot. She will know what to do and how to do it, she will be confident instead of confused and anxious, and she will feel good about the trouble you have taken to provide her training. She will probably stay beyond the critical first seven days and turn into a good, productive worker. You have probably saved yourself a lot of grief by not making a snap decision for Saturday training.

You also have a lot of new insights on making decisions and on training. You might decide later to delegate training on a regular basis to Eloise and Charlie and give them more training than the quickie things that you can give them in an hour. The last step in decision making is to follow up—keep tabs on how things are going. It is an important step for several reasons. If problems develop, you can catch

As a supervisor, it is important to have follow-up training for employees to see how they are progressing.

them early or even fall back on another alternative. If questions arise, you can answer them. Follow-up supports the people carrying out your decision: It reassures them and gives them confidence.

It also gives you a chance to evaluate your decision making. Is everything working out? Did you think of everything? Could you have done a better job in the time you had? Should you have given it more time? What have you learned from this decision? Such a review will help you develop skills and confidence.

Check Your Knowledge

1. How should a supervisor make his or her own decisions?
2. Describe three essential elements in the decision-making process.

Problem Solving

Problem solving is a special kind of decision making that involves more than a choice between courses of action: It involves identifying the cause of a problem and developing ways to correct or remove the cause. Usually you become aware of the problem through a symptom such as customer complaints, below-standard performance, or substandard food product or room cleanliness—some sort of gap between what is and what should be.

Pattern for Solving Problems

The chief difference between solving this kind of problem and simple decision making is that there are extra steps you must take before you can begin to generate alternative courses of action. The pattern goes like this:

1. Describe the problem.
2. Search out the cause (get the facts).
3. Define the real problem and set objectives.
4. Develop alternative solutions.
5. Decide on the best solution.
6. Implement the decision.
7. Follow up.

As you can see, the last four steps are the same as in any decision-making process. The difference is in the first three steps. You do your digging for data *before* you attempt to define the problem and set objectives for solving it. If you try to develop decisions on the basis of your first impression of the problem, you may take the wrong action and the problem will recur. You will have mistaken a symptom for the real cause.

Problem-Solving Example

To illustrate the problem-solving method, let us run quickly through an example. You are the manager of an independent restaurant and you have recently hired a new cook, a young graduate of a fine culinary school. This is her first full-time job. Your problem is that she is too slow. You think you will have to fire her; she is just too inexperienced. But the food has never been better, especially the daily "cook's specials" you asked her to develop. The customers are raving about the food but complaining about the service. What a dilemma! Where do you start?

The first step is to describe the problem as you see it now. This description should include not only what you see at this point as the primary problem but any other problem it is causing. You write down the following: *The cook is too slow, the food isn't ready at pickup time. Servers are angry because customers are blaming them for poor service. Customers are angry, too.*

The second step is to search out the cause of the problem. This involves getting all the relevant facts: the who, what, when, where, how, and why, the ongoing story of what is and is not happening, and any other relevant data.

It is obvious that you must get the cook's side of the story. When you first talk to her, she is very defensive. She says that the servers are harassing her and it makes her nervous and she can't work efficiently. You are sure there is more to it than that. That night you spend half an hour in the kitchen observing. Naturally, the servers do not heckle while you are there, but the cook still has problems. You are surprised at how quickly she works. But she cooks the special at the last minute and she can't do that and plate and garnish everything at the same time. She gets farther and farther behind, so you step in and help her plate the orders.

You make a date to talk to her tomorrow. She is almost in tears and obviously thinks you are going to fire her. You reassure her of your desire to help and you compliment her on the food.

The food is fantastically good. You talk to the customers and they rave about it, not only the special but also the regular menu items. It occurs to you that if you can solve this problem and keep this cook, the word will get around about the good food and your business will grow.

One of the ways to get at the basic problem is to ask a lot of comparison questions. What is being done that was not done before? What is different now, and what is the same? Let's see:

∾ The cook is different.
∾ The food is better, all of it.
∾ The menu is the same except for the specials.
∾ You also noticed that she is doing some special garnishes.
∾ The old cook cooked everything ahead except hamburgers and steaks. The new cook cooks the specials to order as well as the hamburgers and steaks.

The next day you talk to the new cook about the problem. You tell her how pleased you are with the food and you make it very clear that you want to solve this situation, which affects both of you. Can she help you analyze it? Finally, she says

∾ profile

TOBIE CANCINO

*Courtesy of
Tobie Cancino*

My typical Saturday night involves heart-pounding bass and synchronized lights, cocktails of all colors of the rainbow, and about 1000 of my closest friends . . . just like yours does. I am on the other side of it, however. I pour drinks in the VIP Room of the Zanzabar, the most posh nightclub in Waikiki. Glamorous? Maybe. Does it involve *supervision*? Yes and no. Officially, my job description does not entail this. But achieving a moneymaking, happy medium between cocktail servers, customers, management, owners, bar backs, and security certainly requires *super vision*. At least in my world, super vision is the ability to see and prevent possible disasters before they happen. In this atmosphere of alcoholic uncertainty, bionic power is definitely an advantageous trait.

Saturdays have become a concert, and I am the maestro. When I walk in at 8 o'clock, my bar is already set up. The ice well is full, mixers are topped off, garnishes are cut, and the water and solutions in the three-compartment sink are at the right temperatures. My bar back, Jack, asks for my liquor pull list, and returns promptly with a stacked hand truck in tow. I tell him simply, "You are the best," and he smiles. The "early" cocktail server arrives one half hour before me, and the room is immaculate. We share a little "girl talk," then I ask her to please push the Chilean Bordeaux blend. She sells three bottles. Our largest shareholder strolls in, and I immediately pour his regular drink, a glass of iced water and two cherries. The cocktail server and I tempt him to tie the cherry stems into knots with his tongue, and then joke with him about his oral abilities. He laughs and buys us dinner. As the night begins to pick up, the general manager storms in mumbling something about "mutts and morons wearing baggy pants in line downstairs." I hand him his black coffee and tell him that three bottles of the Chilean Bordeaux were sold. His frown disappears and he greets a few guests. As one of the bouncers comes in from the fire exit, I can tell that he just had to kick out a belligerent drunkard. All he needs is a "Hey there, Big Boy," a sexy smile, and a fruit punch. Life at Zanzabar did not always harmonize so well. Understanding people and coordinating their responsibilities to make music took a bit of rehearsal. The second movement of the concerto begins.

Customers march to different tunes, however. For the most part, 90 percent of our customers are regulars in the VIP Room. The staff and I have come to know most members by name, their drinks, their supplementary habits, and how far they can go without disrupting the music. There have been cases, though, when the bionic powers weakened and disaster was imminent.

that she has been afraid to mention it, but the cook's special is a lot of extra work. She is really doing more work than your last cook. You acknowledge that this is true. (Is this a piece of the problem?)

Besides, she says, more specials are being ordered than any other item on the menu, so that makes still more work, especially at dishup time. You ask her if she

- A table of six ordered a bottle of Cristal champagne ($300). They were in a festive mood, and decided to have another. The cocktail server was obviously elated, and I proceeded to serve it thinking that two glasses of champagne per person is acceptable. Suddenly, they started dropping like flies. One by one, they slouched in their chairs and fell asleep. Since overserving customers is a serious violation of liquor laws, I began to worry about unpleasant consequences. It is later discovered that these party animals had decided to wash down a few ecstasy tablets with their champagne.

- An appreciative boss buys a shot of MacCallan 18 ($15.00) for his strawberry daiquiri–drinking employee. It is a nice gesture, and I served it. In no time, I noticed chunks of red on the ivory tablecloth before her. I helped her to the rest room, washed my own hands, and then ran them under a sanitizer with full faith in quaternary ammonium.

Supervising is only for a certain type of person. You must be a public relations professional in dealing with customers, especially irate ones. You have to be a mentor by setting good, if not perfect, examples, thereby commanding respect. You have to be a cheerleader even in times of distress, by continuing to lead with positive energy and empowering words. You have to be a mother and sometimes remind your employees to tidy up after themselves and keep their mouths clean (in more ways than one). It is being a secretary since paperwork is unavoidable, in terms of forecasting, scheduling, controlling labor reports, and so on; the list can go on and on. You have to be a boss who strictly enforces rules and regulations. And above all, you should be a friend. It is said if an employee feels that he or she can turn to a manager with problems, even ones of a personal nature, a stronger work relationship will be built. After all, no employee will want to work hard for a boss who is not liked.

I am confident in saying that this is the career for me. Supervision is the first step to executive management and ownership. Forecasting and planning are extended to longer terms as one rises to higher levels. For now, though, short-term planning, both in my life and in the workplace, is gratifying.

Once upon a time, though, I was a bar manager at a restaurant that seated 600. A young owner noticed my drive, organization, and affinity for knowledge. Sure, I had the integrity, ability to communicate well, hard-working ethic, and positive personality that all supervisors should have. I quickly found out, though, that supervision necessitates management of *people*, whether your internal or external customer, above all else; and needless to say, the maturity to understand varied and complex human beings was not there.

It is the classic: "If I knew then what I know now. . . ." Great supervisors are all of the above. However, exceptional ones have the *super vision* to see what motivates employees and pleases guests.

could cook the specials ahead and hold them, and she says "No, it's the sauce made in the pan at the last minute that makes the difference." (Aha! Another clue!)

And the garnishes? She prepares them ahead, but it's true that you can't just plunk them onto the plate; you have to handle them carefully. You found this out last night. (Still another clue.)

You talk with various servers, and they verify that it seems to be the last-minute cooking that slows things up, and maybe the garnishes. Two waitresses confirm that some waiters are loud and nasty in their complaints while they wait for their orders and that the atmosphere gets very unpleasant.

As a stopgap solution to this aspect of your basic problem, you speak to the offenders, pointing out that they are only making their own problem worse. You believe that you have identified the real problem, and if you can resolve it, this side issue will disappear.

The third step in problem solving is to define the real problem precisely and set objectives. This corresponds to step 1 of the decision-making formula.

You have decided that you definitely want to keep this cook. But that does not solve any part of the problem. You write down what you now see as the real problem and state your objectives as follows:

Problem: Time between order and pickup is too long. Can't afford to lose this cook.

Objectives: To reduce the time between order and pickup to the standards specified in the cook performance standards, retaining the present cook. Present menu must be retained for the next four months. (You have just had it printed.) Cook's specials concept is to be retained if possible. Extra help may be hired if cost-effective. The cook must agree to the final decision (but not make it).

You start to add: *Long-range objective: to expand business.* Then you come to your senses. Building a business around the skills of a particular cook is an entirely different ball game. You have to solve your present problem within its own frame of reference.

You are now in a position to generate and evaluate alternatives, decide on the best solution, and put it to work, as in the basic decision-making formula.

Participative Problem Solving

In the case we have been following, it is logical for the manager at this point to consider bringing the cook into the next three steps of the problem-solving process. Is this a good idea in general? What are the pros and cons? In management theory there is a school of thought with a strong following that believes in **group decision making.** They argue that many heads are better than one because:

1. You get more information and expertise relevant to the decision.
2. You get more good ideas and can generate more and better alternatives.
3. People thinking together can arrive at better decisions because of the stimulation and interplay of different points of view.

They also argue that in practice:

4. People who have participated in making the decision are generally committed to carrying it out.
5. The coordination and communication necessary to carrying out the decision are simpler and better because everyone already understands what is happening.

This school of thought is associated with Theory Y management style (see Chapter 2). The experience of many managers who practice group decision making bears out that the theory can and does work.

Other people take a dim view of group decision making and find the following problems with it:

1. It takes longer for a group to decide something than it does for one person to make the decision. Furthermore, it takes everybody away from his or her other work. (The decision may be better, but is it worth the total work hours required to make it?)

2. Groups are often dominated by one person—usually the boss—because people want to please or are afraid to speak up or disagree, so there really is no advantage. (Here there is really no group decision.)

3. Group participants often get involved in winning arguments or showing off rather than in getting the best decision. (Groups often don't work the way they are supposed to.)

4. If **consensus** (general agreement of all participants) is required, people may go along with a decision they don't like just to get the meeting over with. (Not a true consensus.)

5. Consensus leads to mediocre decisions that will appease everyone rather than the best decision. It can also lead to "groupthink" or conformity rather than to the creativity that is supposed to happen. (Groups may produce worse decisions.)

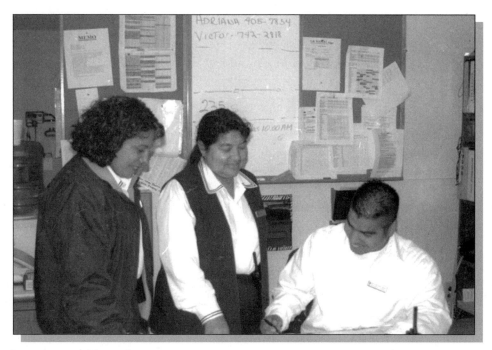

Participative problem solving.

6. Self-seeking managers can use groups for their own purposes to shift blame in case of mistakes or to manipulate people into agreeing to a decision they do not want to carry out. (Here, again, there is no group decision.)

Clearly, group decision making is not a panacea. It works better in some types of organizations than it does in others, and it is more suitable to some problems, some leaders, and some groups than it is to others. Generally, groups work best when:

∾ Members are accustomed to working together as a team and have differing expertise and points of view but common goals.
∾ The leader is skillful at keeping meetings on target without dominating or manipulating (or allowing others to do so).
∾ The group is rewarded for making good decisions.

This combination of conditions is found more often at high corporate levels, but teams of hourly employees are becoming more involved in group decision making. There are times when including workers at some stages of problem solving makes a lot of sense. This is especially true when the problem or decision involves specialized skills or experience that the supervisor does not have or when participation will motivate workers to accept the decision and carry it out. In our example, both conditions are present: the cook knows more than you do about cooking and about the particular problem, and you need her commitment to the decision.

The degree of participation in problem solving and decision making may also vary. This is similar to variations in leadership style running from autocratic to democratic (Chapter 2). Figure 12.3 illustrates such variations of participative prob-

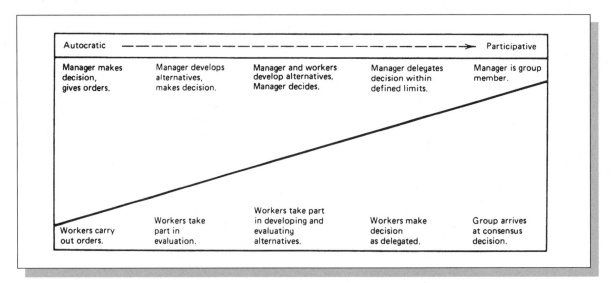

FIGURE 12.3   Range of participation in problem solving and decision making.

lem solving. At one end of the scale the autocratic manager will make the decision alone and tell the workers how to carry it out. For example, a manager will decide on a menu item for tomorrow and order the cook to make it. There is no participation whatever. Toward the middle of the scale the manager will originate an idea and put it out for comment: "As a server, as a cook, what do you think of this menu item—will it sell?" The workers participate in the evaluation, but they do not take part in generating alternatives. Farther along the scale the manager says, "Give me some ideas for menu items and let's discuss them." Here the cook takes part in everything but the decision. Still farther to the right is the manager who says to the cook, "I want you to come up with a couple of new menu items by next Monday, anything you choose within reason is okay with me." Here the manager delegates the decision with merely a precautionary restriction. At the extreme right is the group decision—clearly inappropriate to this simple problem.

Continuing our example, you as the manager invite the cook to help generate alternatives for solving the time-lag problem. The two of you come up with the following alternatives:

> Every guest is different, and "you have to push the right buttons at the right time to make a sale or to get the guest to open up. You have to be able to get around a guest's [negative] emotions to make his stay positive" states Rachael Vanderhorst, a hotel reservationist for Adams Mark Hotel & Resorts. Many interesting people call when thinking of making reservations. Without reservations there is no business. The most important thing to learn when working in the hotel business is listening to guest wants, and needs, and giving them your undivided attention. Each customer wants to be treated as if they are the only guest in the hotel.

- ❧ Develop specials that can be prepared ahead and simplify the garnishes.
- ❧ Keep the present cooked-to-order specials the customers like so well and hire a part-timer to cook hamburgers and to plate and garnish each order.
- ❧ Keep the present specials, simplify the garnishes, and have the servers plate and garnish the orders.

The cook thinks that she can handle any of the three. Although she will still be doing more work than your former cook, she likes the challenge of developing specials. She wants to work with you on the details of carrying out the decision.

Since your budget and the servers are involved, you will not include the cook in making the decision. You decide to have the servers participate in evaluating the third alternative. You hope they will see that the popularity of the current specials probably means increased business and higher tips in the future. But if they do not agree willingly to the extra work for them, this course of action would cause nothing but trouble. You need their commitment.

Solving People Problems[2]

Usually, your most difficult problems have to do with people. Problems about the work focus on products, procedures, schedules, time, costs, and other tangible things. Problems centered on people involve emotions, expectations, needs,

[2]This section is adapted from John Walsh, "Reservations manager maintains steady business stream," *Hotel and Management*, Vol. 215, No. 19, November 6, 2000.

motivation, and all the other intangibles associated with being human. The problem-solving steps are the same, but people problems require the sensitive practice of human skills.

People problems flag you with symptoms—a drop in output, substandard quality, absenteeism, customer complaints—any gap between standards and performance. The first thing to do is get the facts and dig for the real problem. Don't make a hasty decision.

Suppose that a cook comes in very late for the second time in a week and you slap a penalty on him as your company procedure requires. He messes up everything all morning: scorches the soup, leaves the herbs and garlic out of the stew, drops an entire crate of eggs, and walks off the job. Two days later you learn that his wife had walked out on him that day, leaving him with two little children to care for. You didn't get the facts. You didn't find the real problem. You made the wrong decision. You lost the worker.

Personal problems are not yours to resolve, of course, but listening when people need to talk can help them to solve their own problems or at least relieve their tensions enough to get on with their work. Advice is appropriate only if it helps to steer someone toward professional help. (You might have been able to help your distraught cook find a day care center.)

It is important to keep your own emotions out of your workers' problems and to maintain your supervisory role. Dependent people often try to manipulate the boss into telling them how to live their lives. Active but neutral listening, as described in Chapter 4, is the best approach to such problems. The time this takes is appropriate only if the problem is interfering with the work.

Problems involving conflicts between people who work together usually surface quickly because most people don't hesitate to complain about each other. The usual problem-solving pattern is very appropriate here. But getting to the real problem may take time because of the number of people involved, their emotions, and probably their disagreement about the facts.

Yet identifying the real problem and solving it is more important than ever. The more people are affected, the more it affects the work. And if people's emotions are running high, they will carry them to the front desk, the lobby, the dining room, the kitchen, or the hospital bed. Customers and patients will not get the treatment they expect and deserve.

A festering problem in many operations is the continuous antagonism between servers and cooks. Perhaps the underlying problem is unsolvable, since it probably has to do with self-image and professional jealousy. Often, each side looks down on the other. Cooks are proud of their skills and their salaries, and they think of themselves as artists. They look down on waiting tables, and they resent it when servers try to order them around. Servers, on the other hand, look down on cooks for very similar reasons. In some instances male–female rivalries are also involved. These are psychological conflicts that no manager has the skills to resolve.

There are, however, ways to eliminate the friction. Sometimes the best decision is to choose not to solve the real problem but to bypass it. Some managers have made the decision to use a food expediter to receive the orders from the servers and transmit them to the cooks, so the rivals have no contact at all.

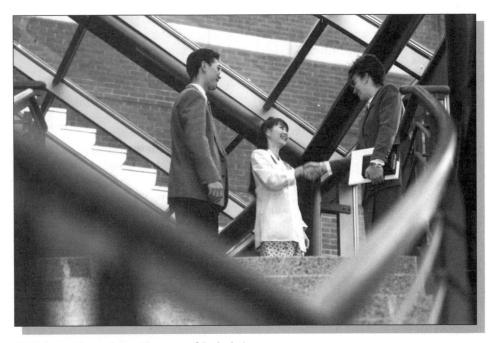

Win–win problem solving. (Courtesy of Sodexho)

Win–Win Problem Solving[3]

For dealing with problems involving one person, an interesting participative approach includes the worker from the beginning to the end of the problem-solving process. It is known as **win–win problem solving** because everybody wins. People who have used it say that it solves the problem 75 percent of the time.

The win–win concept is difficult for many supervisors to accept. When a supervisor is dealing with a worker who is causing a problem, it is very natural to think of the situation as a contest that the supevisor must win. Win–lose is a concept that pervades our culture: ball game, tennis match, arm wrestling, election, war—whatever the contest, there is a winner and a loser; that's what it's all about.

In win-or-lose terms, you as a supervisor have four possible ways of approaching the problem solving. The first is a *win–lose* stance: You say to the worker, "You've gotta shape up or else; if you don't shape up, you're fired." You win, the worker loses. Of course, you win the battle, but you lose the war: You either have to hire a new worker or, with a different penalty, put up with a continuation of the conflict on the guerrilla level.

The second approach is a *lose–win* posture: retreat and appeasement. You don't take a stand, you let the worker get away with things, and you back away from any decision. You lose and the worker wins. And soon you lose not only the battle but also your job.

---

[3]This section is adapted from Barbara Young, "Profitable partnership," *National Provisioner,* Vol. 214, No. 10, October 2000.

The third approach is *lose–lose:* compromise. You give up something in exchange for the worker's giving up something, and each of you has less than before. You both lose. Neither of you is satisfied and the problem is likely to reappear, perhaps in another form.

The fourth approach is *win–win:* You find a solution that satisfies both of you. You include the worker from the beginning of the problem-solving process, and you go through the following steps:

1. Together, you establish the facts and identify and define the problem. As the supervisor you make it clear that both you and the worker will benefit from getting the problem solved. You pull out all your interviewing skills; you listen, encourage, and let the worker vent feelings and complaints. Finally, you agree on the definition of the problem.

2. Together, you generate all possible alternative solutions—no vetos at this point. You keep going until neither of you can think of any more.

3. Together, you evaluate the alternatives and pick the one that is best for both of you.

4. Together, you carry out the agreement. You follow up at intervals to see how the solution is working.

> A good approach for a manager to handle situations is by **problem solving.** It is important for managers to get involved on the manufacturing floor and work with people on problems. Aim at learning the workers' roles and understand their daily challenges and the decision-making process. As supervisor it is important that you be able to do your employees' job, as well as your own. This makes it easier to be able to solve employee problems if you already know the situation. Take interest in how problems have been eliminated in the past, because this will help to solve unique situations in the future and move forward as a team.

Suppose, for example, that you have a desk clerk who does not get to work on time. After considerable discussion you agree that the problem is that her starting hour of 7:00 A.M. is incompatible with her home situation. She has two young children to get ready for school.

You generate alternatives: Let her husband deal with the children. Have her pay someone to come. Put her on a different shift. Have her work 9 to 5 instead of 7 to 3. Terminate her. Put her in a different job: typist, payroll clerk. And so on.

You go over the alternatives and finally agree that she will work the evening shift starting an hour late. She is happy that she can handle both ends of the schoolday and still make almost as much money. You are happy that you will not have to hire and train a new desk clerk. You already have someone on the evening shift who would like to trade shifts. You both win. For many supervisors the win–win approach represents a major shift in attitude. It denies the traditional assumption that problem employees are adversaries in a contest, replacing it with the far healthier assumption that both parties to the problem are in together. It goes right along with the Theory Y idea that jobs can be structured to fulfill personal goals and company goals at the same time. And it fits perfectly with the humanistic approach to management that seeks to build a positive work climate and an atmosphere of cooperation and trust. For supervisors who can make that shift in attitude, it is certainly another string to one's bow.

Check Your Knowledge

1. What does problem solving involve?
2. What is the difference between problem solving and simple decision making?

Building Decision-Making Skills

The ability to make good, sound, timely decisions is one of the most important qualities on which a manager is judged. It is essential to running a tight ship and to being a good manager of people. You can learn a great deal about making decisions from books and from observing people who are good decision makers. But the only way to build a skill is to practice it. Here are some guidelines to help you along the way:

∾ Make sure that the decision is yours to make, that you have both the authority and the responsibility. Make each decision in the best interest of your employer, not your own.

∾ Accept your responsibility fully: Face decisions promptly. Be ready to take unpopular stands when they are necessary.

∾ Sort out the important decisions from the inconsequential ones. Make minor decisions quickly. Make major decisions deliberately, seeking out the basic problem and considering consequences before you take action.

∾ Calculate the risks, and do not be afraid to take them if they are worth the benefits.

∾ Timing is important; often, it is everything. Adapt your decision making to this overriding requirement.

∾ Be alert to signs of problems. If you let a situation become a crisis, it may be too late for a good decision.

∾ Keep an open mind when investigating a problem. Avoid jumping to conclusions, and stay away from your own biases, prejudices, and self-interest. Remember, too, that the easiest solution is not necessarily the best.

∾ Do consult your supervisor when a problem is truly beyond your ability or experience.

∾ Make sure that you are not part of the problem yourself.

∾ You will make some bad decisions along the way–everyone does. Don't brood over them; learn from them.

∾ Follow up on your important decisions to see how they are working out. Were they good decisions? What would you do differently next time?

∾ Look at each situation from its own unique perspective. When presented with a situation similar to an earlier one, some supervisors will make the same decision as that used earlier. Although this may work sometimes, it's best to examine each situation individually.

❧ key points

1. A manager's decision should be a conscious choice among alternative courses of action directed toward a specific purpose.

2. Different people approach decision making in different ways. Examples include logical, intuitive, indecisive, and impulsive approaches.

3. The decisions that a hospitality supervisor is called upon to make range from those that are easy to make to complicated time-pressure decisions to problem solving.

4. It is essential to recognize which decisions are important and which are unimportant, which decisions you must make now and which can wait.

5. The following six steps are a simple version of the logical approach to decision making: Define the problem and set objectives; get the facts (who–what–when–where–how–why); develop and rank alternative solutions; decide on the best solution by examining risk, economy, feasibility, acceptability, and objectives; convert the decision into action; and follow up.

6. When making decisions, your timing can be very important.

7. Problem solving is a special kind of decision making that involves more than a choice between courses of action. It involves identifying the cause of a problem and developing ways to correct or remove the cause.

8. The chief difference between problem solving and simple decision making is that there are extra steps that you must take before you can begin to generate alternative courses of action. The pattern goes like this: Describe the problem, search out the cause, define the real problem and set objectives, develop alternative solutions, decide on the best solution, implement the decision, and follow up.

9. Group decision making is advantageous because you get more information relevant to the decision as well as more good ideas. People thinking together can arrive at better decisions, and people who have participated in making the decisions are generally committed to carrying it out. Critics of group decision making say that the process takes too much time and tends to be dominated by one person (usually, the boss). If consensus is required, critics say that it leads to mediocre decisions that will appease everyone rather than the best decision.

10. Group decision making is not a panacea. It works best when members are accustomed to working together as a team and have differing expertise and points of view but common goals, when the leader is skillful at keeping meetings on target without dominating or manipulating, and when the group is rewarded for making good decisions.

11. The degree of participation in problem solving and decision making may also vary.

12. For dealing with problems involving one person, an interesting participative approach, win–win problem solving, means that you find a solution that satis-

fies both of you. You include the worker from the beginning of the problem-solving process, from defining the problem, through to carrying out the agreement.

13. Some important decision-making skills include: Make sure the decision is yours to make, face decisions promptly, sort out the important decisions from the inconsequential ones, calculate the risks, think about timing, be alert to signs of problems, keep an open mind when investigating a problem, consult your supervisor when necessary, make sure that you are not part of the problem, learn from your decisions, and follow up on your decisions.

∾ key terms

approaches to decision making:
  impulsive, indecisive, intuitive, logical
brainstorming
conditions and limitations
consensus
decision

decisiveness
fact finding
group decision making
timing
win–win problem solving

∾ review questions

Answer each question in complete sentences. Read each question carefully and make sure that you answer all parts of the question. Organize your answer using more than one paragraph when appropriate.

1. What are the three essential elements in a managerial decision?
2. Describe four different approaches to decision making.
3. What is *decisiveness?*
4. Describe the six steps in decision making.
5. What is *brainstorming,* and what are its pros and cons?
6. How can you test which alternative is best?
7. Explain the relationship between decision making and problem solving. Why would you group them together? Why would you consider them separately?
8. Describe the pattern for solving patterns.
9. What are the pros and cons of group decision making?
10. What are the steps involved in win–win problem solving?
11. List 10 tips for making good decisions.

❧ activities and applications

1. Discussion Questions

- What is the difference between decisiveness and decision making? What is their relationship?
- What kind of decision maker are you: logical, intuitive, impulsive, indecisive? Do your decisions usually turn out well? How can you improve them?
- What relationships do you see between decision making and responsibility, authority, and accountability? What supervisory responsibilities discussed earlier in this book involve decision making? Give examples of the kinds of decisions required.
- What situations do you see in the hospitality industry where participative decision making would be useful? Explain. Where would it be detrimental or impossible? Explain. If possible, give instances from your own experience where workers participated in some phase of decision making, and comment on the process and outcome.

2. Group Activity: Decision Making

In a group of two, each person presents a work or school problem to work through in the group. Using the pattern in Figure 12.1, go through the steps for each problem. The person who brought up the problem should write down the results of the discussion on his or her problem.

3. Brainstorming

Brainstorming is a technique that can be useful in a variety of training and other supervisory situations. It requires a few ground rules to promote participation: All ideas must be accepted, the pace needs to be fast, ideas need to be recorded, and some of the ideas must be used. To learn more about brainstorming, take part in a brainstorming session in which you need ideas on (1) the advantages of participative problem solving, and (2) the disadvantages of participative problem solving. Were the ground rules met?

4. Case Study: Who's Managing This Place?

Leon has been head chef at the Elite Cafe since it opened 25 years ago. This little restaurant has been a landmark in a small seaside resort town and up to a year or so ago has always been crowded with customers who came back to enjoy the same fresh seafood dishes they remembered from years before. In the past year, however, there has been a noticeable drop in its business, owing to competition from several new restaurants that feature nouvelle cuisine, health food, and ethnic cuisines.

Leon's boss, Dennis, the restaurant manager, is an eager young man fresh out of a college hospitality program. He sees what is happening and wants Leon to change the menu, but Leon flatly refuses. He says that the food is as good as it ever was—the best food in town—and that Dennis simply isn't promoting it properly and is probably making a lot of other mistakes, too. Leon makes it clear that he has no respect for college graduates who haven't paid their dues and gotten their hands

dirty—a figure of speech that is all too appropriate for Leon, whose sanitation practices are old-fashioned, too.

The other personnel are aware of this ongoing situation between Leon and
Dennis and are beginning to take sides. Dennis is aware that he must do something
quickly. But what? Dennis sees his main problem as regaining the cafe's share of the
market and putting it out front where it has always been. He can see only the following alternatives:

1. Fire Leon for insubordination. This is what he would like to do. But Leon is an
   excellent cook and no one on his staff can duplicate his chowder, his lobster
   bisque, and some of the other classics, and there are no recipes to follow. Also, it
   would be difficult to hire someone who could develop a new menu quickly.
   There is also the problem that it is mainly a summer market; how do you hire a
   chef for six months of the year?

2. Try it Leon's way—a marketing program emphasizing an old-timey image and
   ambience—the good old days, tradition. Dennis's heart is not in this approach—
   he can't believe that Leon is right. He also thinks that giving in to Leon will put
   Leon in charge—which he very nearly is now—and will make it impossible for
   Dennis to maintain his authority with his other employees.

3. Discuss the problem with his boss, the owner of the cafe. She is an older woman
   who really doesn't understand the restaurant business, and besides, Dennis doesn't
   want to admit to her that he has this problem.

4. Get some expert advice on market trends and how to make a market study: Hire
   a consultant or pay a visit to his favorite professor at the Hospitality Institute.

Dennis has made a preliminary decision. He visits his former teacher and
comes back with a new perspective. He still has not made his decision, but he is
making headway.

QUESTIONS

1. What do you think of Dennis's four alternatives? What are the pros and cons
   of each? What are the consequences?
2. What do you think is the real problem? How would you define it?
3. What should Dennis's objectives be?
4. Is Dennis himself part of the problem? If so, does this make it harder or easier to solve?
5. Are there other alternatives besides those Dennis has listed? Suggest as many
   as you can, and give pros and cons for each.
6. Who do you think is right about the menu: Dennis or Leon?
7. Is it possible for Dennis to change Leon's opinion of him? If so, how?
8. Do you think Dennis and Leon might ever get together using the win–win
   problem-solving method? Would it be appropriate in this situation?

～ chapter 13

Delegating

～ You often hear managers in the hospitality industry, especially restaurant managers, talk about the 60, 70, even 80 hours a week they put in just to keep on top of their jobs. They tell you about the constant pressures of the job and how you can't get good people today, nobody takes responsibility, they have to do everything themselves, there just aren't enough hours in the day. . . .

There is no doubt that a manager is in a high-pressure position and that the industry is plagued with people problems. But does it have to be a constant, never-ending race between the work to be done and the time there is to do it? In this chapter we discuss one management tool for alleviating the problem—delegation.

Management experts always recommend delegation, yet the harassed management people in our industry seldom delegate. It is the management tool that is implemented least. Managers will drive themselves to the point of exhaustion, ulcers, and those little white pills the doctor prescribes rather than entrust their employees with any of their own responsibilities. Why won't they share them? And why won't the people who work for them take on such responsibilities?

Delegation is always recommended by management experts, yet the harassed management people in our industry seldom delegate. It is the least used of all management tools. Supervisors and managers will drive themselves to the point of exhaustion, ulcers, and those little white pills the doctor prescribes rather than entrust their employees with any of their own responsibilities. Why won't they share them? And why won't the people who work for them take on such responsibilities if, indeed, they will not?

In this chapter we examine the delegation process and suggest how to put it to work successfully in a hospitality enterprise. It will help you to:

∾ Define the concepts of responsibility, authority, and accountability, and explain their relationship to delegation.

∾ Explain how delegation benefits the supervisor, the workers, and the entire operation.

∾ Enumerate and discuss common reasons why both managers and workers avoid delegation.

∾ Discuss the conditions essential for successful delegation.

∾ List the essential steps in successful delegation and discuss the importance of each.

∾ List common delegation mistakes and explain techniques for avoiding them.

What Delegation Means

In a nutshell, **delegation** is a skill of which we have all heard but which few understand. It can be used either as an excuse for dumping failure onto the shoulders of subordinates, or as a dynamic tool for motivating and training your team to realize their full potential.[1] Since you are responsible for the entire output of your unit or department, you delegate responsibility for certain parts of the work to people you hire to do certain jobs—you delegate cooking to the cooks, front desk work to the front desk clerks, and so on. Certain responsibilities you keep for yourself: hiring, keeping track of labor and material costs, making key reports, and so on.

Usually, we do not think of giving people jobs to do as delegating responsibility for the work, but it is—or it should be. Supervisors who are on people's backs all the time—telling them what to do, telling them what they are doing wrong, directing them at every turn—have delegated little or nothing. Supervisors who train their people and then trust them to carry out the job have delegated the responsibility for doing the work. Which supervisor has more time and fewer hassles?

In nearly every job there are variations in the degrees of responsibility attached to that job. If the dishwasher discovers that the gauges are registering in the red zone, whose responsibility is it to correct the water temperature? If the manager has delegated this responsibility to the dishwater and has given the proper training, it is the dishwasher's responsibility. If not, the dishwasher must report the reading to the manager, and the manager must fix it. Who orders the supplies for the kitchen, the cook or the manager? Who receives the supplies? Who stocks the bar? Who closes the cash register? The manager who feels it necessary to attend to every last one of these things personally is the one who works 80 hours a week. In addition, things probably don't run very well and there are constant crises because the manager can-

[1]Gerard M. Blair, "The art of delegation," www.ee.ed.ac.uk/~gerard/Management /art5.html, February 8, 2001.

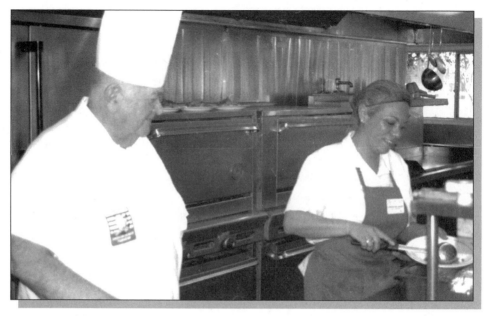

A supervisor delegating.

not be everywhere at once. In short, that manager is not delegating; that manager is trying to do all the work. That manager is not managing.

Essentials of Delegation

There are three aspects of delegation:

1. Responsibility
2. Authority
3. Accountability

As a supervisor, you have been given **responsibility** for certain activities and the results they are expected to produce. That is your job, your ultimate responsibility. Your boss delegated this responsibility to you when you took over the job. When you delegate, you give a portion of this responsibility to one or another of your workers—you pass along responsibility for certain activities and the results you expect them to produce. However, you maintain ultimate responsibility.

When you took over the job of supervisor, you were given the **authority** you need to carry out your responsibilities, the rights and powers to make the necessary decisions and take the necessary actions to get the job done. When you delegate a portion of your responsibilities, you in turn must give the person assuming these responsibilities the authority to carry them out, carefully defining its terms.

If you delegate responsibility without such authority, you make it impossible to fulfill the responsibility. Suppose, for example, that you give Tom responsibility for stocking the bar but you do not give him the authority to sign requisition slips. The storeroom is not going to release the liquor because Tom's signature has not been authorized, so Tom cannot fulfill his responsibility, and there is not going to be enough gin for the martinis when customers come in.

As a supervisor you are accountable to your boss for the results expected of you. **Accountability** means that you are under obligation to your boss to produce these results. People to whom you delegate are accountable to you for the results you expect. Accountability goes automatically with the responsibility delegated; it is the other side of the coin. Delegating responsibility does not relieve you of either responsibility or accountability. If your worker does not come through for you, you must find another way to achieve the results. You cannot shift the blame even though your worker is at fault. The ultimate responsibility is always yours.

The lines of responsibility and authority in an organization provide the anatomy of its organization chart, its **chain of command.** They are the lines along which responsibility is delegated from the top down to the least member of the organization. The chief executive officer delegates responsibility and authority to senior vice-presidents, who delegate to the managers who work for them, who in turn delegate to the people who report to them, and so on, right down to the night cleaner or the person who does nothing but spread mayonnaise on bread. At each level the person delegating has responsibility for the results expected from all those on down the line at whatever level, and the chief executive officer has responsibility for the entire operation.

Accountability moves right beside responsibility but in the opposite direction (see Figure 13.1). All employees are accountable to whoever delegated responsibility to them, so the accountability moves right up to the top along the same lines on which authority and responsibility move downward, and ultimately everyone is accountable to the chief executive officer, who is accountable to the owners or a board of directors.

This organizational anatomy tells who has responsibility at each level for everything that happens or fails to happen. It determines whose head will roll when someone fails to deliver the results expected. If the failure has dire consequences, it may not only be the head of the worker who failed to deliver but the head of the worker's supervisor who let it happen.

The lines of responsibility and authority are also the **channels of communication** from level to level up and down the organizational ladder. *Going through channels* means that when you send information or requests or instructions to people on levels above or below you, you go one level up or down your own channel. You do not ask the chief executive officer for authority to spend company money even if the CEO is your own father; you ask your immediate superior. You do not give the head cook's second assistant instructions about the dinner; you pass them through the head cook.

This keeps everyone informed of what is going on and keeps the lines of responsibility and authority straight. If you violate the chain of command, there is bound to be somebody who doesn't know about the delegation and that person's immediate reaction to someone new giving orders is: "Hey, you're not my boss, you're not supposed to do that!"

It is especially bad to cross channels. You do not give orders to someone on another channel because you do not have responsibility for their work and they are

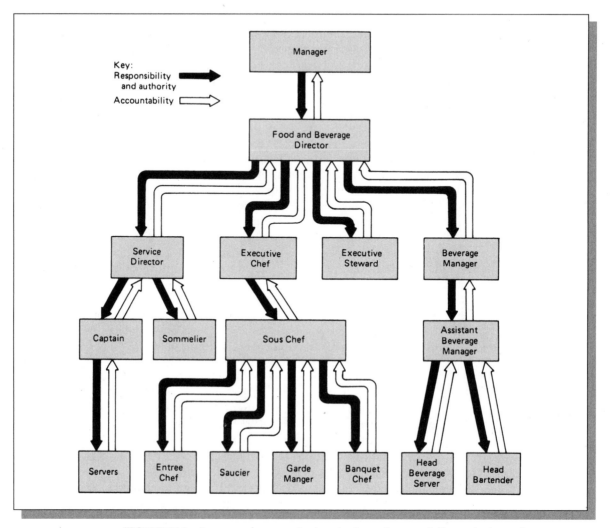

FIGURE 13.1 Anatomy of an organization: the lines of responsibility, authority, and accountability; the chain of command; the channels of communication.

not accountable to you. The dining room supervisor cannot give anyone in the kitchen something to do; it has to go up through channels to the manager of the restaurant or the food and beverage directory of the hotel and then down through the head cook or the executive chef to the right person. That way everybody knows what is going on. When you delegate responsibility and authority, you keep your own supervisor informed, because your boss too has responsibility for what you delegate and is accountable for its results.

Delegation, then, is a managerial tool by which responsibility for the work is divided among people, level by level, throughout the organization. Supervisors are concerned with getting the work done that has been delegated to them and achieving the results for which they are accountable. They have the authority to delegate portions of their responsibility to people who work for them. The question is: what responsibilities to delegate, to whom, and how to do it in a way that will secure the desired results.

To enable someone else to do the job for you, you must ensure that:

✿ They know what you want.

✿ They have the authority to achieve it.

✿ They know how to do it.

Source: Gerard M. Blair, "The art of delegation," www.ee.ed.ac.uk/ ~gerard/Management /art5.html, February 8, 2001.

Benefits of Delegation

When someone has been hired for a certain job, the supervisor expects that person to do the work assigned to that job classification. What often seems to be missing is the sense of responsibility for carrying out that work. This sense of responsibility does not just happen spontaneously, as the old-style Theory X manager thinks it should ("People these days don't take any responsibility"). It comes about when the supervisor specifically delegates responsibility to the worker.

In this delegation process the work is spelled out: what is to be done, how it is to be done, and what results are expected—and the worker is trained to do it. Then the worker can indeed be given responsibility for doing the work and the supervisor need not follow everyone around all the time. Responsibility for their own jobs is delegated to the workers, and they are accountable for results. Wherever specific procedures are not required, workers are given authority to do the work in whatever way achieves the best results. They are given the right to make decisions, a certain freedom of action, and the self-respect that comes from taking responsibility for what they do on the job.

The first benefit is that *once workers are trained, once they are given responsibility for results, the supervisor no longer has to keep close track and can fall back into a coaching and supportive role.* Supervisors who delegate responsibility for the work spend fewer hours watching and correcting worker performance. They can either spend fewer hours on the job, or devote more time to other aspects of supervision, or both.

A second benefit is one that may surprise an old-style Theory X manager: *People who are given responsibility generally work better and get more done because the boss is not on their backs all the time.* They are happier in their jobs, they are more involved, they take pride in their work, and they tend to stay around longer, so the supervisor does not have to hire and train new people all the time. More and better work is getting done, perhaps even with fewer people.

So far, we have been talking about delegating responsibility to people for carrying out their own jobs. But often, these jobs are narrowly defined to exclude everything with even a whisper of a risk. Many jobs could be broadened to include related responsibilities. The dishwasher job could include responsibility for correcting the water temperature. The bartender job should include stocking the bar. The cashier should close down the register. These things make more sense. Job descriptions and performance standards can be broadened to include these duties so that all workers in this job classification will be trained and given responsibility for them. The added responsibilities will make the employees in these jobs feel more important and at the same time free the supervisor of still more detail and interruption.

The supervisor may then see the possibility of giving the more promising people still more responsibility by delegating some of the routine management duties or even some duties that are not totally routine. It would mean careful planning, more training, more follow-up, but it would ultimately relieve the supervisor of still more time-consuming detail, and it would develop a promising employee in a new direction: more responsibility, new skills, a new interest, a new way of thinking that might produce fresh ideas, and better ways to do the task delegated. This is a third benefit of delegation: *developing your people and multiplying their contribution.*

Developing people is part of a supervisor's job. It is a way of putting people's capacities and potential to work for the benefit of the operation. Many people in our industry are underemployed, and these workers constitute a valuable untapped resource of ability and intelligence. To such high-potential workers you can delegate small units of your own job (a daily routine, a weekly report, a troubleshooting task). By training them to take over such tasks, you are increasing their skills and opening up their future while giving yourself more time to manage. People given new responsibilities and the opportunity to learn new skills become more motivated, more committed to their work, and they usually do it well, often with imagination and creativity.

In this way you can gradually expand such people's experience and prepare them for promotion. What if you lose them through promotion? You may be promoted yourself precisely because you are doing this kind of thing.

Delegation is a conceptual skill. It requires you to see your own job as a whole and find what parts of it can be delegated. Far from lessening your control over the work of your department, it actually tightens up the operation, leading to greater efficiency. Herein lies a fourth benefit: *Greater efficiency means less waste and confusion, lower costs, less conflict, higher morale, less turnover in personnel. Greater efficiency makes everybody happier, including the customers.*

Finally, delegation will *sharpen your leadership skills,* both conceptual and human. The essence of supervision is getting things done through people. Learning to delegate is not easy, but it will make you grow, both in your job and as a person. Success in delegating will increase your own confidence and your satisfaction in your job, and it will prepare you for advancement.

Delegation not only benefits the supervisor, but also the people to whom one delegates. Studies indicate that most people want more responsibility, and they want the opportunity to grow and develop. The ways that people to whom you delegate can benefit are:

Some of the benefits you can receive by delegating effectively are:

∞ Saves your time and energy for other responsibilities.

∞ Brings more hands and minds to bear on the problems, which results in making more effective decisions.

∞ Improves the skills of individuals as well as team productivity.

∞ Allows others to make contributions that give them self-satisfaction.

∞ Adds to the overall organization's success by providing more productive people, higher productivity, improved morale, better communication and teamwork, and greater profitability.

Source: Suzanne Laurent, "Carolina communiquè: delegating for results," www.stc-carolina.org/pubs/communique/feature/delegate.shtml, 1999.

∾ They become more productive and valuable to the organization and team.

∾ By learning new things, they improve their self-esteem.

∾ They become resources for people who need help and function as backups when needed.

They become more knowledgeable and skilled at handling the details and problems of running a team.[2]

Check Your Knowledge

1. What is *delegation?*
2. State the three aspects of delegation.
3. List the benefits of delegation.

Why People Resist Delegation

If delegation has so many benefits, why is it so rarely practiced in the hospitality industry? There are two sides to the answer. On the one hand, it is very difficult for many supervisors to delegate, or even to believe that it will work. On the other hand, many workers do not want to assume responsibilities. Sometimes the supervisor's reasons and the worker's reasons feed on one another and make it even more difficult to initiate the process.

Why Managers Have Trouble Delegating

The Theory X manager —and there are still many of them in the hospitality industry— simply does not believe in delegation. Since this type of manager believes that people are by nature lazy and avoid responsibility and must be coerced, controlled, and threatened with punishment to get anything done, the matter ends right there. *They will not believe that delegation, properly carried out, can work and that at least certain kinds of people will take responsibility.* They will not even try it. If they were to try it, they would not do it right, they would not trust their people, they would expect it to fail, and it would.

Many supervisors are afraid that if they let go of the work—if they delegate—the work will not be done right. They, too, do not trust their people. This is why they are on their people's backs all the time, overseeing, correcting, looking for mistakes. This may be their idea of on-the-job training, but it breeds resentment and causes people to leave. It is true that work delegated may not always be done right; you have to train people carefully, trust them, and expect some mistakes at first. If you don't, delegation will not work for you either.

[2]Suzanne Laurent, "Carolina communiquè: delegating for results," www.stccarolina.org/pubs/communique/feature/delegate.shtml, 1999.

∾ profile

RYAN ADAMS

*Courtesy of
Ryan Adams*

There are many examples of good supervision that I could cite. However, there is a distinctive difference between what is taught and what is realistic. The first three words that I think of in terms of good supervision are *legal, ethical,* and *moral*. Books tend to give black-and-white examples with black-and-white results. This is not reality in the hospitality industry.

A good supervisor must be respectful of everyone on every level. You are in the middle of the line-level employees, the middle managers, and the top management. You have to be able to juggle the concerns of your direct manager, with the challenges of your staff and still try to impress the top-level managers when they are around. This can be a difficult balancing act.

You have to draw a line—often the most difficult decision for a supervisor. Most supervisors have climbed their way up the ladder and are often viewed as one of the crew. You must distinguish yourself as a manager or else your staff will try to take advantage of you. Everything you do is being watched on every level. Now more than ever it is essential to put your foot down and establish your mark. It is often said that "being a manager is not a popularity contest"—this could not be more true. Being a supervisor can often be a lonely position.

When an employee comes to you, stop what you are doing and give the person your undivided attention. Look the employee in the eye and really hear what he or she is saying. When the person has finished talking, paraphrase what has been said so that you understand and can empathize with the feelings expressed so that he or she is validated, and then offer counseling to help resolve the concern. This is easier said than done.

As a supervisor, you always have to be on top of your game. This means knowing policy and procedures, knowing the union contract if your business is unionized. You have to be an expert in the human resources field. If you do not know, you always

Some managers believe that their constant presence and their personal control of every last detail are indispensable to the success of the operation. This is an ego problem: They have to feel that without them everything will fall apart, that something terrible will happen if they are not there. Perhaps secretly, even unconsciously, some are afraid that *nothing* will happen and that things will move right along without them, and they do not want to find this out. For some, this may be the most compelling reason of all for not delegating anything. For such people, power, authority, and tight control are essential to their own security.

Supervisors who are not confident in their own jobs may be afraid to delegate because workers may turn out to do the work better than they did themselves. This is a very threatening idea. How could they handle this, how could they save face? Would have your manager to fall back on or the human resources department. If you are not sure, ask; it is better to find out than to make a error that can cost big money.

If you do not know the answer to a particular question, tell the employee that you will get back to him or her with the answer. Make sure that you follow up or the person will feel that you are incompetent and untrustworthy. If this occurs, you will have to make huge strides to improve that relationship.

Trust and empower your people. If you really want to shine and make your staff feel good about their jobs, trust them. Delegate side duties and additional responsibilities. Make sure that you give them the proper praise for their work; they will not forget that you did not praise them for their help and may be reluctant to offer in the future. Let your staff make decisions. Give them the guidelines to make decisions and train them. Role-playing is a great way to prepare them for the chaos they will experience. This will enable you to take on more responsibility from your managers, and your staff will be confident to respond to smaller problems that would otherwise tie up your day.

In discipline situations, never have the paperwork already filled out. Make notes, but do not just present the write-up without talking to your employee first. They will feel like you did not even give them a chance to explain. You assumed they were guilty right off the bat and they will feel like they never had a chance.

Always check on your staff and make sure that you take time out of your day at some point to make small talk. Often, when an employee makes the transition to supervisor, he or she forgets how he or she wanted to be treated when an employee. It is easy to adopt negative or undesirable traits of managers of the past. Always be objective and never lose the person you are—that is what got you there in the first place.

Always be on time to meetings or at least call in advance to notify someone that you cannot attend. Make your managers concerns your priority, your staff's needs mandatory, and the vision and values of your company your guiding principles. If you do not believe in what the company stands for, it is difficult to share that vision with others. Remember, you are not just a manager, you are a leader. This means taking your staff to a place they would not have gone otherwise. As a manager, what gets done gets measured. Not that this is right—it is a fact and thus a big part of your evaluation.

the workers want more money, or even take over their job? Would they lose these good workers through promotion? Such fears are powerful inhibitors.

Many supervisors do not want to take responsibility for the mistakes of others. They may be afraid to be dependent on others. They may worry about what will happen to their own job if they delegate responsibilities and their people do not come through with the results. They may be afraid of what their boss will do, and in some cases this may be a very legitimate fear.

While fear of one sort or another is a major reason for not delegating, in other cases the reason may be habit or momentum. Some people simply cannot delegate. They have always done things themselves. They have gotten where they are by doing, not by letting others do, and they cannot let go. You see this sometimes in family corporations or companies where the president is 97 years old and is still running the business. These people cannot let go of the reins and they are still trying to do it all. They do not know how to do it any other way.

Many supervisors who are newly promoted from hourly jobs also have trouble shifting from doing to managing. We have talked about this boomerang type of management before: Supervisors slip back into doing the work themselves because it is easier and more comfortable than getting others to do it. This may very well be the most common reason for failure to delegate. When you are not at home with your new responsibilities, delegating them can be a scary and painful prospect.

Sometimes, the momentum of the operation takes over common sense. *Many supervisors say that it is quicker to do something yourself than to train someone else to do it.* A manager will tell you, "I can make coffee in a 5-gallon urn in 5 minutes, but it will take me half an hour to train a worker to do it." The manager never has half an hour to spare, so the manager makes the coffee and it becomes part of the manager's job. But training a worker, a one-time expenditure of 30 minutes, would save some 60 hours a year of the manager's time. Hundreds of such decisions are made in hospitality enterprises because short-term pressures override the long-term gains of delegation, or because the supervisor cannot see beyond the next 5 minutes, or has the habit of *doing* rather than delegating.

> You create barriers that prevent you from delegating when you:
>
> ∾ Prefer to do the work yourself or think no one else can do it as well.
> ∾ Feel a strong need to work at tasks with which you are familiar.
> ∾ Feel threatened by the possibility that someone else might not complete a task for which you are responsible.
> ∾ Fear the loss of power.
> ∾ Delegate without planning. It is very important to set deadlines, explain the task's objectives, and transfer authority.

Sometimes, tasks that could easily be delegated to a promising worker might involve important people in the organization, or perhaps information the manager might not want to share with any of the workers. Or they might be detailed tasks that the manager really enjoys doing. In such cases a manager may decide that the personal gains in hanging onto these tasks outweigh the time saved or other benefit to the organization. This is a decision of questionable wisdom but not an uncommon one.

Sometimes, for both good and bad reasons, supervisors resist delegation simply because they do not want to lose touch with what is going on.

Sometimes, there are reasons more substantial than fears or habits or self-interest that keep supervisors from delegating. *There may be no workers who are qualified and willing to take on work the supervisor would really like to delegate.* The ability and willingness of the workers are of critical importance to the success of delegation, so let us see why workers do not want the responsibilities delegation entails.

Why Some Workers Won't Accept Responsibility

Some workers in the hospitality industry are barely able to do their jobs at the minimum level of acceptability. Others are very dependent people who want to be told what to do all the time and are afraid to make decisions. A few are hostile types who are just waiting for a chance to get hold of the ball and run with it in the opposite direction; they don't trust you and you don't trust them. None of these are good candidates for delegation beyond the specific bare-bones tasks of their jobs. Even if they were willing, they are not able to assume additional responsibilities.

In delegation, fear plays a part for many workers just as it does for managers. *Fear of failure* is common among people who lack self-confidence; they doubt their own capabilities to carry out new tasks. They do not trust themselves.

Others fear the consequences of the mistakes they may make in a new assignment. They may be afraid of the boss's criticism or anger. Their relationship with the boss may not be good enough to make them willing to risk the mistakes.

Sometimes a worker who is offered an extra responsibility may be afraid of rejection by other workers. If others are jealous, or see the new assignment as a defection to the management side, or think it is unfair to themselves, they may give the worker in question a hard time—or at least the worker may think they will. Getting along with one's peers, being part of a group—that feeling of belonging—may be more important than having responsibilities and rewards.

Many workers will refuse added responsibilities if they see them simply as meaningless extra work that they have to do. If there is nothing in it for them—no interest, no reward, no extra pay, no recognition or independence or challenge or opportunity for growth, just more drudgery—they will perceive the added work as an imposition and they will resent it. They will refuse it outright or find ways not to do it, and the attempt to delegate will backfire. Adding more work without adding interest, challenge, or reward, known as **job loading,** is to be avoided at all costs.

Finally, there are highly capable workers who are satisfied with what they are doing and *simply do not want to be given more responsibility or to be developed and pushed up the corporate ladder.* Not every cook aspires to be a food and beverage director; some people just love to cook. Most people who are "only working until" are not interested in taking more responsibility; they are only marking time. Some people want a routine job that makes no demands on the mind because they are writing the great American novel. The professional dishwasher we mentioned several chapters back was utterly happy as a dishwasher and refused all offers of advancement. The dishroom was his empire, he was in charge, he was proud of it, nobody bothered him, it was where he belonged, and it filled all his needs.

Delegation, then, may be a relationship between two fearful and reluctant parties. How can one avoid its fears and follies and reap its benefits and rewards?

How to Delegate Successfully

Certain conditions are essential to successful delegation. You have met them in earlier chapters.

Conditions for Success

One condition is *advance planning.* This should include an overall review of who is responsible for what in your department at this time, what further responsibilities could be delegated, who is qualified to assume greater responsibilities, what training would be necessary, how various shifts in responsibilities would affect others, and when these shifts would appropriately take place. Delegation involves rearranging things, and it brings your conceptual skills into play. You have to look beyond the daily operational detail to the larger picture and get it all into focus. In addition to general overall planning, delegation requires a specific plan for each instance of delegation so that everything is clear to everyone concerned and the groundwork is prepared properly. We will say more about this in the next section.

A second condition for successful delegation is a *positive attitude toward your people.* You cannot have Theory X beliefs about your people and expect delegation to work. You don't have to be an all-out Theory Y manager, but you must have good relationships with your people, know their interests and their capabilities, and be sensitive to their needs and their potential. You must respect them as individuals and be interested in developing them, for both your sake and theirs. You need to develop the kind of leadership skill that gives people belief in themselves and makes them want to come through for you.

A third condition is *trust.* There has to be trust between you and the people to whom you delegate: You trust them enough to share your responsibility with them, and they trust you not to put something over on them or get them in over their heads. Only if you both have this trust can you get the commitment necessary to make delegation work.

A fourth condition of successful delegation is the *ability to let go and take risks,* to let your workers make some mistakes and to give yourself the same privilege. Each time you delegate a responsibility it is going to be new for you and new for the other person,

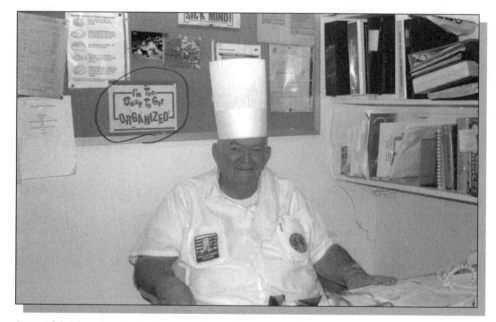

Successful delegation. One of the conditions of successful delegation is to have a *positive attitude towards your people.*

and some mistakes are bound to be made; it is not going to be perfect from day 1. But when a mistake happens, you don't panic and you don't jump on the other person. You take a coaching approach. The worker learns under your leadership, and you improve your leadership skills, and that is what true on-the-job training is all about. You can both learn something from every mistake, and that is how you both grow.

A fifth condition of successful delegation is *good communications.* You must keep the channels open and use them freely, send clear messages, and keep everyone informed who is affected by the delegation: the person to whom you delegate, the workers in that area, and your boss. Make sure that the people to whom you delegate know the terms of their authority and the extent of their responsibility. The more you delegate—the more people there are who share your responsibility—the more important good communications become.

The sixth condition is *commitment.* If you can involve your people in the planning and goal setting for their new tasks, they will become committed to achieving the results. You, in turn, must be committed to train, coach, and support as needed. You don't just dump the job on somebody else and abdicate.

Steps in Delegation

The first step in delegation is to *plan.* You need to identify tasks that can be assigned to someone else, and you need to figure out which of your people are able and willing to take them on. You begin by listing all the things you do. You might find it useful to keep a chart for several days on which you note absolutely everything you do in each quarter-hour. Then you sort out your activities and responsibilities into groups, as shown in Figure 13.2. After you have done this, you can arrange things that should and could be delegated in some kind of order: order of importance, or ease of delegating, or time saved, and choose which one or two you will tackle first.

Next you must look at your people. Choosing the right person for the responsibility is a key ingredient in successful delegation. Figure 13.3 can be useful to you here. Motivation and ability are both essential to success. Who among your people is both able and willing? If there is no one with both qualities, is there someone you can train, or someone who would be willing if you could overcome their fears or make the content of the task more attractive or offer appropriate recognition and reward?

Once you have identified the task and the person you want to have perform it, the second step is to *develop the task in detail* as a responsibility to be delegated. You define the area of responsibility, the activities that must be carried out, the results you expect, and the authority necessary to fulfill the responsibility. This is all very similar to the procedure you use in developing performance standards. In fact, a system of performance standards is an excellent tool for use in delegating responsibility. You can turn people loose in their jobs because you have told them exactly what you want, have set the achievement goals, and have trained them in the skills needed. They can take the responsibility from there and leave you free to manage.

In any delegation you do the same thing. You spell out the essential content and detailed requirements of the task, you define the limitations, and you specify the results expected. Within these limits people will be free to do the job in their own fashion. You will also spell out the specific authority that goes with the responsibility delegated: what kinds of decisions can be made without checking with the boss,

Things you must do yourself (e.g., hiring, evaluation, rewards, discipline, termination)

Things you should do yourself that someone could help you with and could do when you cannot be there (e.g., scheduling, data for cost percentages)

Things you now do yourself that someone else could be trained to do (e.g., training new personnel, requisitioning, ordering, receiving)

Things you should have others do with help and guidance from you (e.g., customer counts, time sheets, guestroom counts, occupancy rates)

Things others must do (e.g., their own jobs)

Things no one is doing that others could do (e.g., new menu items, specialty drinks, promotion ideas)

FIGURE 13.2 A way of organizing tasks that can be delegated.

Able and willing (great candidate)	Unable but willing (needs training)
Able but unwilling (needs motivation)	Unable and unwilling (poor candidate)

FIGURE 13.3   A way of planning the assignment of tasks to be delegated.

what money can be spent, what actions they are authorized to take on behalf of the boss or the enterprise, and so on. You figure all this out ahead of time, and then you take the third step—you delegate.

The third step has three parts: you *delegate responsibility* for the task and the results expected, you *delegate the authority* necessary to carry it out, and you establish accountability. As we have seen, these are the three interlocking parts of delegation, and they must be spelled out clearly.

When you delegate, you meet with the chosen employee—John and Susan or whoever—in a private interview in which you describe the task, the results you expect, and the responsibility and authority it entails. It should be an informal person-to-person discussion. You should present the new assignment in a way that will stimulate interest and involvement: ask for ideas, make it a challenge, mention its present and future benefits, offer rewards if appropriate, and express confidence. Take a "we" approach, indicating your availability for support and your continuing interest in John's or Susan's success. Promise training if it is needed. However, do not put pressure on by ordering, threatening, or making it impossible to refuse. *There must be agreement on the employee's part to accept the delegation.*

Delegation is a **contract.** You cannot just give responsibility to people; they must *accept* the responsibility. They must also accept the accountability that goes with the responsibility. Unless you have fully given responsibility and authority and the other person has fully accepted responsibility and accountability, true delegation has not taken place.

It is important for your employees to know that you are sharing your responsibility with them; you are not dumping it on them and abandoning them. You, too, are accountable for the results. Give them plenty of chance for questions and plenty of reassurance for lingering doubts.

If you have matched the right person with the right assignment and have communicated it in the right way, John and Susan will be interested, pleased, motivated, challenged, and glad to have more responsibility. If you include them in setting goals for the project, you will gain their commitment to achieving them.

Set checkpoints along the way for following progress. They give you the means of keeping the employee and the assignment on target. You can modify or adjust the assignment, correct mistakes, and give advice at critical points without taking back the entire job. Checkpoints are your controls. If you can't set up controls, either don't delegate the job or redesign it so that you have some other means of tracking performance.

The fourth step in delegation is to *follow up.* Train your people as needed. This is something they have never done before, so you go through the whole story: what you want done, how you want it done, to what standard. If you don't, they will take the easiest way to do it. When they are ready to go, communicate the new status to everyone concerned, following channels, and make good on immediate rewards promised, such as relieving them from other duties to make time for the new ones. Then slip into the coaching role. Stay off their backs: Don't oversupervise and overcontrol; let them work out their own problems if they can. If they have trouble making decisions and keep asking you what to do, turn the questions back to them—ask them what *they* think. Encourage them to go it on their own. Don't let the responsibility you have given them dribble back to you.

When employees try to dump their assignment back to you, it is called **reverse delegation.** It may occur because the employee lacks confidence, doesn't really know enough to do the job, is afraid of making a mistake, or simply does not want the added responsibility. You need to listen to the employee and discuss the impasse, but make it perfectly clear that the task is still the employee's responsibility to complete. If you take back incomplete work, you will support the employee's dependence on you. The best way to handle reverse delegation can be stated as follows: "Don't bring me problems, bring me solutions."

Observe the checkpoints, assess progress, give feedback, and help Susan and John reach independence in their new assignments. Then congratulate yourself on two things: You are learning how to delegate successfully, and you are developing your promising employees. This is genuine on-the-job training (not the magic apron type), and you are developing genuine management skills.

Check Your Knowledge

1. Certain conditions are essential to successful delegation. What are these conditions?

Common Mistakes in Delegation

When you have had no experience in delegating, it is easy to make mistakes. Perhaps one of the most common is *not communicating clearly.* Susan and John must understand what you want done, how you want it done, what results they are accountable for, and what the goals and standards are. They must understand the area, extent, and limits of their responsibility. They must know what authority they have and its limitations—what they are empowered to do, what decisions they can make on their own, and what decisions they must refer to you.

If you have done your homework carefully before you meet with them, you can communicate to John and Susan clearly. You can make sure they have understood by asking them to summarize for you the essentials of the agreement. In many cases it may be wise to put things in writing.

But often in this time-pressure industry it is easy to skip the planning stage, and it is easy to crowd the delegation of a responsibility into one of those 48-second interchanges of which your day is made. This is taking a big risk. You cannot communicate the details of the assignment itself and the implications of responsibility, authority, and accountability in that length of time. After you have delegated for a while to people who have become experienced in sharing your responsibilities, 48 seconds may be enough. But the first time you delegate to first-time delegates, make it a big deal. Communicate everything clearly, and check to see that everything is understood between you.

Another mistake it is easy for a first-timer to make is to *oversupervise,* simply because you are nervous about the whole thing. In this case you soon revert to being the boss and taking back the responsibility you have delegated. You have to remember that it won't all go perfectly, that you have picked someone you trust, that you do have checkpoints and controls, and that the only way to learn to delegate is to stop being bossy. If you jump in and correct small mistakes all the time, John and Susan are not going to come to you for help when they have a real problem.

It is also easy to make the opposite mistake—*not taking time enough to train* John and Susan in their new responsibilities and *not giving them enough support.* In this case they may become discouraged and lose their enthusiasm. The may do a poor or mediocre job, or they may leave because things are not going well for them and they are discouraged about themselves. You must take time to give them the training they need, and they must always have the feeling that you are supporting them and that they can come to you to discuss problems. Furthermore, they must experience success and build confidence if the delegation is to prove fruitful.

Delegating without setting up controls—built-in ways to monitor performance—is another common mistake. If you have not had much experience with delegation, you may overlook this essential. You need checkpoints—periodic reports, reviews, conferences—so that you can keep track of things without being involved in the work but can intervene if necessary to keep things from getting out of hand.

Still another common mistake is *job loading,* mentioned earlier—increasing the workload without adding any new responsibility, interest, or challenge. Suppose that you raise the number of rooms that must be cleaned in a given time period. This is not delegation. It is bound to cause resentment and will complicate rather than simplify your life. It demotivates the worker. In contrast, a task that includes new responsibilities can be a motivator even when extra work is involved, as long as the worker welcomes the responsibility and as long as the work can be done in the time there is to do it.

A similar mistake is to *assign dead-end, meaningless, boring, unchallenging tasks without offering any kind of incentive or reward.* In this case an increase in responsibility is not enough—it is just an extra burden, and there is nothing in it for them. You have to make it worth their while: extra money, more status, shorter hours, a promise of something better at a specific time, whatever will cause a worker to accept the responsibility willingly.

Delegating to the wrong person is another common mistake. If you know your people well and plan the delegation carefully, this will not happen to you.

A few supervisors make the mistake of *delegating unpleasant parts of their job that involve the boss–subordinate relationship, such as discipline or termination.* This simply amounts to abdicating the role of boss. The employee cannot handle it and everyone loses respect for the boss who passes the buck. As President Truman said, "The buck stops here."

Setting up overlapping responsibilities is another mistake that people sometimes make. You may carelessly give the same task to two different people, or give someone an assignment that involves someone else's department without clearing it with that department head. If your own boss is a disorganized person and the lines of authority and responsibility are not too clear, you may even find yourself delegating a responsibility that does not belong to you. Be sure that you know where you stand in the organization and what you are doing, and be careful to keep everyone informed.

You can avoid these mistakes if you plan carefully, know your people and your own responsibilities, keep in touch with what is going on, and keep your overall goals in sight—to manage your people to produce a smooth-running operation with everyone contributing the best of which each is capable.

Adapting Delegation to Your Situation

There are few universal rules about what tasks you should delegate and what you should keep for yourself. Generally, you should not delegate responsibility that involves your relationship with subordinates, such as hiring, evaluating, disciplining,

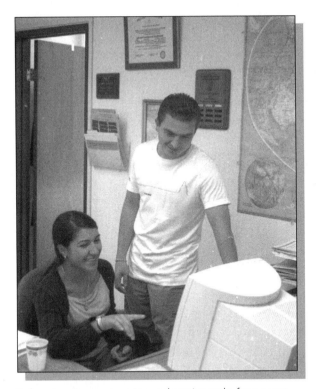

Delegating time-consuming and routine tasks frees your
time and attention for managing.

terminating. You should not delegate tasks that require technical expertise that only
you have, or tasks that involve confidential information, and you should not dump
unpleasant tasks on people who don't want them by passing them off as "delegating
responsibility." Other than these, there are few tasks that you should avoid delegating if the delegation makes sense.

It makes sense to delegate time-consuming and routine detail that other people
can and will take care of. It frees your time and attention for managing.

It makes sense to train others to take over tasks and responsibilities that must
continue when you are not there. You must provide for emergencies and for your
off-hours and vacations. You must have people who can assume your day-to-day responsibilities when necessary. If your unit or department cannot run without you
for a while, you are not doing your job.

It makes sense to delegate tasks and responsibilities that motivate and develop
your people. If you know your people and their interests, talents, and shortcomings,
you can match the responsibility to the person. You can give them work that interests them, challenges them, makes them feel important and valued, gives them the
satisfaction of achievement, and helps them grow.

It makes sense to plan such growth for people of high potential, to add further
responsibilities over a period of time, to groom them to take your place someday or

climb your company's career ladder or move to a better position somewhere else. Although you may lose them in the end, they will more than repay you in what they contribute to you and your operation as they grow.

You are the only person who can decide what makes sense in your area of supervision. You are the only one who knows the tasks and the people. Taking the first steps of delegating can be scary and even painful, but once you have done it, you are on your way to being a manager in every sense of the word. You do not have to do it all at once; there are degrees and stages of delegation. Take it one task at a time, one step at a time, and start with a task and a person you are pretty sure are made for each other.

Delegating responsibilities, making jobs more interesting and challenging, and helping people grow multiplies your own effectiveness many times over—far, far beyond anything you could do by keeping all your responsibilities to yourself.

∾ key points

1. Delegation is a managerial tool by which responsibility for the work is divided among people, level by level, throughout the organization.

2. There are three aspects of delegation: responsibility, authority, and accountability. As a supervisor you have been given the responsibility for certain activities and the results they are expected to produce, the authority (or rights and powers) to carry out your responsibilities, and the accountability (or obligation to your boss) to produce these results.

3. The lines of responsibility and authority in an organization provide the chain of command. Accountability moves right beside responsibility but in the opposite direction. All employees are accountable to their boss, so the accountability moves right up to the top along the same lines on which authority and responsibility move downward.

4. The lines of responsibility and authority are also the channels of communication.

5. The benefits of delegation include the fact that the supervisor can spend more time coaching and performing other duties instead of watching and correcting performance; the employees can usually work better; the supervisor can develop employees; and greater efficiency results, which means less waste and confusion, lower costs, less conflict, higher morale, less turnover, and happier customers.

6. The Theory X manager does not believe in delegation because he or she believes that employees will not take responsibility and/or the job will not be done right. Some managers believe that their constant presence and personal control of every last detail are indispensable. Other managers don't delegate because they are afraid the workers may do the work better than they did it themselves, or simply out of habit. Sometimes, supervisors resist delegation simply because they do not want to lose touch with what is going on.

7. Employees at times may not accept new responsibilities because of fear of failure or fear of being rejected by co-workers, dislike of meaningless extra work, or simply a lack of desire to be pushed up the career ladder.

8. Conditions for delegating successfully include advance planning, a positive attitude toward your people, trust, the ability to let go and take risks, good communications, and commitment.

9. The steps in delegation include planning, developing the task in detail, delegating responsibility for the task and results expected, delegating the authority and establishing accountability, setting checkpoints along the way for following progress, and follow-up.

10. Reverse delegation is when employees try to dump their assignment back to you.

11. Common mistakes in delegating include not communicating clearly, oversupervising, not taking time enough to train and give support, not setting up controls, job loading, assigning dead-end work without any reward, delegating to the wrong person, delegating unpleasant parts of the job that involve the boss–subordinate relationship, and setting up overlapping responsibilities.

❧ key terms

accountability
authority
chain of command
channels of communication
contract

delegation
job loading
responsibility
reverse delegation

❧ review questions

Answer each question in complete sentences. Read each question carefully and make sure that you answer all parts of the question. Organize your answer using more than one paragraph when appropriate.

1. The ability to delegate has been called one of the hallmarks of a good manager. Explain its importance to management.

2. Discuss in detail the three aspects of delegation.

3. Why do some supervisors resist delegation? Why do some employees resist delegation?

4. What conditions are necessary for delegation?

5. Describe the steps in delegating tasks.

6. What is *reverse delegation?*

7. Discuss common mistakes in delegating.

↬ activities and applications

1. Discussion Questions

- How can a supervisor delegate responsibility, yet retain it at the same time? How does this principle work out in practice? Give examples.
- In what ways do the concepts of a performance standard system apply to the delegation process? How does delegation draw on communication and training skills?
- With what management styles is delegation compatible? Why doesn't delegation work for a Theory X manager?
- Why does delegation so often involve fear; and why does it require courage?
- Have you ever been delegated a task while working? How did your supervisor handle it? How did you feel about it?

2. Group Activity: Delegation Role-Play

In a group of four, think of a situation in which a hospitality supervisor delegates a job to an employee. While two students role-play the supervisor telling the employee about the delegated task, the other two students can be observers. When the role-play is done, the observers can take a turn being supervisor and employee.

3. Case Study: Too Much Too Fast?

Joanne is manager of an in-plant self-service cafeteria for an insurance company headquarters with 1000 employees, most of whom eat breakfast and lunch there. In addition to managing the cafeteria, she is responsible for stocking sandwich and dessert vending machines. She has been supervising all her workers directly but has decided that it would be better if she delegated the major food-preparation responsibilities to her three best workers in order to devote more time to customer relations.

After lunch on Wednesday she calls the three workers together and explains her plan.

"I am going to delegate to each of you responsibility for preparing the food in your department and keeping the counters and steam table stocked during the serving period. Ellen, you will be in charge of salad and sandwich preparation. Michelle, you will do the desserts and baked goods. You two will also prepare the food for vending. Robert, you will be responsible for all the hot food: soups, entrées, vegetables, and so on.

"Your present co-workers—you each have two—will become your assistants, and you will direct their work. I will be on hand at all times, but I will be talking with customers and supervising the rest of the staff: the breakfast cooks, cashiers, cleanup crew, dishwashers, and so on. I will also continue to do the ordering, receiving, staffing, and so forth.

"Now, you all have seen me in action in your departments, and you know what my methods and standards are. Make the usual menu in the usual quantities. just do everything as I would do it, and come to me with questions. We will start tomorrow."

The first day of the new regime is a near-disaster. No one makes the beverages, and no one stocks the vending machines, although the food is prepared for them as usual. Both Michelle and Ellen prepare the cantaloupe and the fruit/cheese plates.

One of Robert's assistants does not show up, and instead of asking Joanne to get a substitute cook, he and his other assistant try to keep up with the demand. The result is a large and growing crowd of complaining customers waiting for the hot food. Ellen's two assistants refuse to take orders from her and go to Joanne saying, "Hey, she's not our boss, who does she think she is, telling us what to do?" One of Michelle's assistants resigns in a huff in the middle of lunch because she thinks she should have had the job instead of Michelle, and Michelle is snapping at her. The other complains to Joanne about Michelle after the serving period is over.

Joanne spends the entire day putting out fires (some of them are still burning), dealing with complaining customers, and trying to find a replacement for the worker who resigned. She ends the day harassed and embarrassed. She is pretty sure that all her workers except those who are mad are laughing at her, and she will probably have trouble with everyone for several days, including the customers. She hopes that her boss at the catering company she works for does not hear about this.

QUESTIONS

1. What basic mistakes did Joanne make?
2. Why do you think she did not foresee what happened?
3. How could she have avoided the reaction of Ellen's and Michelle's assistants? How could she have avoided the reaction of Robert, who tried to work short-handed?
4. What should she do now? Should she withdraw the delegation or try to make it work? If the latter make a detailed plan for her to carry out.
5. How will she handle all her other workers tomorrow to keep their respect?
6. What should she do about pacifying customers?
7. Should her boss at the catering company headquarters be involved in any way? Does her boss share the responsibility for what happened?

❧ chapter 14

Additional Supervisory Topics

overview

Safety and Security Management

AIDS and the Hospitality Worker

Guide to the Family and Medical Leave Act of 1993

Unions

Ethics

The Supervisor as Mentor

❧ It is a universal human need to want to be safe and secure. As a supervisor, one of your top priorities is making sure that the workplace is safe and secure for both workers and guests. Safety hazards abound in a hospitality operation: There are cleaning chemicals that can burn your skin, slicers that can cut more than bologna when you're not watching, heavy boxes to lift that can wrench your back, computer keyboards that can cause numbness in your hands, wet floors that you can go sliding across, and poorly lit stairs that you can fly down (with an order of hot soup in your hands).

After negotiating the numerous safety hazards, keep your eyes open because the back door has been left wide open. Before a thief sees this wonderful opportunity, slam that door shut, and lock it, then find out who left the door open in the first place.

In this final chapter we look at a number of important topics that every supervisor needs to be aware of: safety and security issues, AIDS and the hospitality worker, the Family and Medical Leave Act of 1993, unions, ethics, and mentoring. In this chapter we help you to:

∾ Explain the importance of providing a safe work environment for workers.

∾ Describe what is included in a comprehensive safety program.

∾ Explain how a supervisor implements the Hazard Communication Standard.

∾ Identify steps to take to ensure guest safety and security.

∾ State guidelines for handling an employee who is HIV-positive.

∾ Outline the provisions of the Family and Medical Leave Act of 1993.

∾ Describe the role of unions, and list guidelines for working effectively with them.

∾ Define the term *ethics,* and state five questions you can use to determine if a decision is ethical.

Safety and Security Management

Let's first look at safety for workers and then safety for guests.

A Safe Workplace

The foodservice sector of the hospitality industry has fortunately become a safer place to work. According to the Bureau of Labor Statistics, the number of nonfatal on-the-job injuries to employees of eating and drinking establishments has been steadily decreasing since 1992. In 1992 it averaged 8.9 employee injuries per 100 foodservice workers, compared to 8.3 for all private-sector workplaces. In 1996 it averaged 6.1 employee injuries per 100 foodservice workers (compared to 6.9 for all workplaces). By 1999 that figure had dropped to 5.5.

Besides causing pain and suffering to the injured employee and incurring the cost of lost work time, there are other direct and indirect costs to consider when an accident occurs.

∾ Lost time and productivity of uninjured workers who stop work to help the injured employee or simply watch and talk about the incident (Productivity normally decreases for a number of hours, but if morale is negatively affected, it could be much longer.)

∾ Lost business during the time that the operation is not fully functioning

∾ Lost business due to damaged reputation

∾ Overtime costs to get the operation fully functioning again

∾ The costs to clean, repair, and/or replace any equipment, food, or supplies damaged in the accident

∾ Cost to retrain the injured employee upon return to work

∾ Increased premiums for workers' compensation

∾ In the case of a lawsuit, legal fees and possible award to the injured employee

Of course, not only employees become involved in accidents; guests do also.

In 1971, the **Occupational Safety and Health Administration** (OSHA) was created as an agency within the U.S. Department of Labor. Its purpose is to "assure so far as possible every working man and woman in the Nation safe and healthful working conditions and to preserve our human resources." OSHA sets mandatory job safety and health standards, encourages both employers and employees to decrease hazards in the workplace, conducts compliance inspections, issues citations in cases of noncompliance, and asks for record keeping of injuries. OSHA also requires you, as the supervisor, to train your employees as to any known hazards in their work area.

Safety programs are common in hospitality operations as a way to increase safety awareness and to prevent accidents. Safety programs usually include the following components.

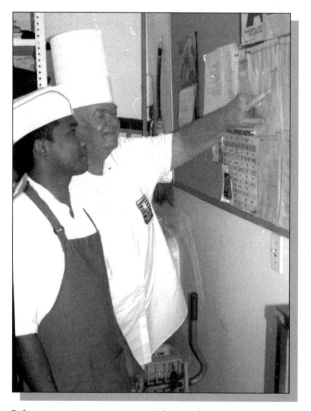

Safety programs are common in hospitality operations as a way to increase safety awareness and to prevent accidents.

1. Safety policies and procedures
2. Employee training
3. Safety committee
4. Safety inspections
5. Accident reporting and investigation
6. Constant supervision

Supervisors themselves are very involved in the safety program. After all, you oversee the day-to-day monitoring and enforcement of safety rules, report and correct unsafe conditions, train and retrain employees, maintain safety records, check that the first-aid kit is well stocked, and act as a role model. If you are safety-minded, you are more likely to create an environment where safety is practiced and respected.

Safety policies and procedures state what behaviors are expected from employees in order to prevent accidents, what safety training employees receive, how often safety inspections occur, and what to do when accidents happen. Figure 14.1 is a sample safety policy and procedure regarding safety inspections.

Policies and procedures form the basis for your employee training program. Safety training should start at orientation and this information should be put into the employee handbook. The accident rate for employees is higher during their first

Policy: In order to maintain adequate safety to meet or exceed the standards for all regulatory agencies, the General Manager will perform monthly safety audits of the restaurant.

Procedures:

1. At the beginning of each month, the General Manager asks two supervisors and two employees to set a time to do a safety inspection of the entire facility.

2. The Safety Inspection Team uses the "Restaurant Safety Survey" form to inspect the facility, noting problems as appropriate.

3. Copies of the survey are given to the supervisors, who are given two weeks to resolve any problems noted and to document this on the survey form.

4. The General Manager reviews the returned surveys and takes any additional appropriate action. The results of the survey are discussed with the Owner.

5. Reports are saved for three years.

FIGURE 14.1 Policy and procedures for safety inspections.

month of employment than for any subsequent month. Safety training should be repeated and updated at least once a year for all employees. At the end of training, employees need to be evaluated on what they know, and rewarded or recognized for working safely. Figure 14.2 is a page from a training plan on kitchen safety rules.

Safety committees are often formed within hospitality operations. They meet periodically to discuss safety matters. The safety committee is often involved in reviewing data on the number and types of accidents to date, inspecting the facility, suggesting new and revised policies and procedures, and overseeing safety training.

As a supervisor, you may periodically be in charge of a safety inspection to check for and correct any unsafe conditions, such as a slicer's frayed electric cord. Figure 14.3 is a page from a safety inspection form for a kitchen. In addition to managers and supervisors, employees can take part in the inspection process to encourage them to take a more active role in preventing accidents.

When accidents do happen, regardless of how minor the injury appears to be at the time, it is the supervisor's responsibility to report them. Early reporting of all the facts works to the advantage of all concerned. The supervisor can move quickly to correct the unsafe condition that caused an accident, the injured person can re-

---

Kitchen Safety Checklist
Preventing Cuts

1. Know how to operate equipment.

2. Pay attention when using sharp equipment.

3. Use guards when provided on equipment.

4. Use tampers to push food into equipment, not your hands!

5. Turn equipment off before adjusting.

6. No loose sleeves, ties or dangling jewelry should be by equipment.

7. Use knives carefully.

8. Carry dishes and glassware carefully.

9. Sweep up broken glass.

10. Use a special container to dispose of broken glass, dishes, and other sharp objects.

11. Remove nails and staples in shipping cartons and crates, and wear gloves.

12. Remove can lids entirely from cans and put back into empty cans for disposal.

FIGURE 14.2 Page from a training plan on kitchen safety rules.

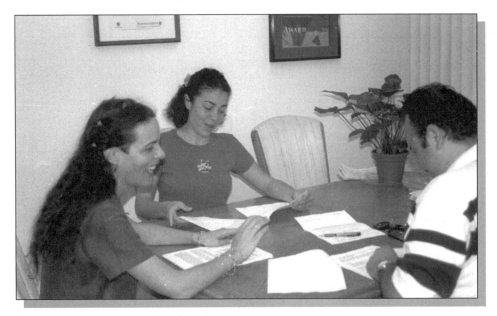

A safety committee reviews the safety plan.

John Pinkerton, who is responsible for overseeing risk management for Hard Rock Café, says, "Perhaps the easiest definition of what we do is the protection of people, property and profits. "An injured employee is going to impact your bottom line and cost you money," Pinkerton acknowledges. "It's a disruption to both you and the employee. You need to protect your operation just as you would your home. You're not going to be in a business long if you don't provide a safe environment. Your job is to get that employee back to work as soon as possible."

Source: Bill Carlino, *Weekly Newspaper of the Food Service Industry,* Vol. 34, No. 39, September 25, 2000.

ceive prompt and effective medical care if needed, and in the case of an employee who can't return to work immediately, he or she can receive workers' compensation benefits without unnecessary delay. Also, the company can make preparations in the event of pending legal action such as a lawsuit.

Figure 14.4 is an example of an accident reporting form that supervisors complete when there has been an accident. The fact that all accidents should be properly reported cannot be overemphasized. In many cases, incidents that appear trivial develop into major hazards at a later time. If accurate and complete facts are not recorded at the time of the accident, it could be difficult to compile information should the incident develop into a claim against the company.

Implementing the Hazard Communication Standard

Most U.S. businesses must comply with the **Hazard Communication Standard** issued by OSHA. The purpose of this standard is to give employees the right to know what chemicals they are working with, what the risks or hazards are, and what they can do to limit the risks. You probably know of a number of hazardous materials in your workplace, such as all-purpose cleaners, detergents, oven cleaners, degreasers, and pesticides. These products often present physical hazards, such as exploding or burning, and/or health hazards, such as irritating or burning skin.

AREA: Receiving and Dry Storage **INSPECTED BY:** **DATE:**

QUESTION	YES	NO	PROBLEM NOTED	CORRECTIONS	WHEN DONE
1. Are floors and walls in safe condition: dry, clean, no tiles missing or broken, no worn areas?					
2. Are "Wet Floor" signs available and used when needed?					
3. Is all lighting in working order and adequate?					
4. Are any tables, counters, and equipment free from sharp corners or dangerous projections?					
5. Is ventilation sufficient?					
6. Are doors and aisles kept clear of supplies?					
7. Are there sufficient waste receptacles of leakproof nonabsorbent material?					
8. Are waste receptacles covered?					
9. Is the receiving dock in good repair?					
10. Are incoming supplies being inspected for damage?					

FIGURE 14.3 Page from a safety inspection form.

Accident Reporting Form

Date of Accident _____ Time of Accident _____

Today's Date _____

- -

Location of Accident:_____

Description of Accident (Include who was involved and what each person was doing at the time):

_____

_____

_____

_____

_____

_____

_____

List who was involved in the accident:

Name	Employee or Guest?	Describe any injuries & treatment given

List witnesses to the accident:

Name	Employee or Guest	Phone Number

Supervisor's Signature _____ Date _____

General Manager's Signature _____ Date _____

FORWARD ONE COPY TO SAFETY COMMITTEE

FIGURE 14.4 Accident reporting form.

The Hazard Communication Standard requires employers to do the following:

1. Post a list of hazardous substances found in your operation.
2. Post **Material Safety Data Sheets** (MSDSs). For each hazardous product you have, the manufacturer has a MSDS that explains what the product is, why it is hazardous, and how you can use it safely.
3. Explain to employees how to read and use the MSDS and also the labels on hazardous products.
4. Train employees how to use hazardous chemicals properly and what to do in case of an emergency.

Basic tips on safely handling hazardous chemicals are given in Table 14.1.

Guest Safety

You may think that guests face far fewer hazards than workers do, but even though they are far away from deep-fat fryers and slicers, guests still fracture bones slipping on your stairs, get serious burns from spilled hot coffee, die from allergic reactions to certain foods, and get foodborne illnesses. Not paying attention to guest safety can cost your operation hundreds of thousands and even millions of dollars in lawsuits.

As a supervisor you don't want to see guests get hurt any more than you want employees to get hurt. So what can you do about it? You are already involved in the operation's safety program as just described, so you know your safety policies and procedures, train employees, take part in safety committee meetings and/or safety inspections, report accidents, and supervise with safety uppermost in your mind. Many guest safety concerns revolve around the following.

TABLE 14.1   ∞   **Do's and Don'ts of Safe Chemical Handling**

1. *Do* know where the Material Safety Data Sheets are posted and read them.
2. *Do* read the labels of all products before you use them.
3. *Do* follow the directions for proper storage, handling, and use for all chemicals you use. Measure chemicals carefully.
4. *Do* ask your supervisor any question or express any concern you may have about a certain product.
5. *Do* know how to call for medical help in case of an emergency.
6. *Do not* ever mix chemicals together.
7. *Do not* store chemicals in unmarked containers. If chemicals are transferred to different containers, each new container must be labeled with the contents and hazards.
8. *Do not* store chemicals in or close to food storage, preparation, or serving areas.
9. *Do not* leave aerosol spray containers near heat or spray close to an open flame or your eyes.
10. *Do not* dispose of any empty chemical container until you have checked the label for the proper procedure.

- ∾ *Slips, trips, and falls.* Steps are most often the culprit behind slips, trips, and falls. Stairs and steps, both inside and outside, should be well lit, covered with a non-skid surface, and have handrails. Wet floors cause their share of problems as well. Try to mop during off-hours and be sure to use "Wet Floor" signs and possibly even rope off the area. Guest parking areas should be clear of trash and free of ice in the winter.

- ∾ *Burns.* Hot beverages, such as coffee, can be a danger when not handled carefully. Your operation may have special hot beverage temperatures and rules to prevent burns. Guests should always be warned about hot plates.

- ∾ *Food allergies.* Some people experience a severe response when they eat certain foods to which they are allergic. Their throat swells up to the point where air can't get down to the lungs. This type of reaction, called **anaphylactic shock,** can kill. Two things can be done to prevent this problem: have a policy and procedure that tells servers how to handle a guest's question about a dish containing an allergic ingredient, and stock the first-aid kit with "Epi Pens," a medication that suppresses anaphylactic shock symptoms (managers must be trained to use it).

- ∾ *Foodborne illness.* Foodborne illnesses make millions of Americans sick each year and kill almost 10,000 people. High-quality sanitation standards and well-supervised procedures are needed to prevent outbreaks.

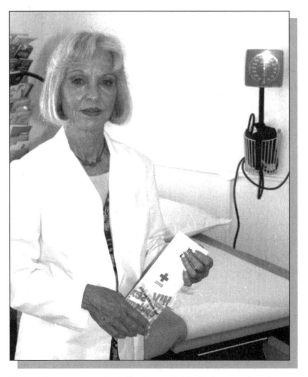

First-aid emergency training is available from your local Red Cross center.

᧬ profile

ALEXIA GREENBERG

*Courtesy of
Alexia Greenberg*

There are many key qualities that a supervisor must have not only to get the job done but also to satisfy clients and the staff that serves them. A great supervisor must have technical expertise in the department they supervise. It is essential that a supervisor demonstrate a depth of knowledge in his or her technical or specialized areas in order for the department to run smoothly and have mistakes corrected before they occur. For example, when one is supervising in the convention floor department, focusing on the customer is crucial. By being knowledgeable about the department, focusing exactly on what the meeting planner wants in regards to meeting room setups is simplified. My knowledge enables me to prepare the staff and myself mentally to deliver what is asked for, with even some time to spare for last-minute changes. If a supervisor is able to develop and maintain effective relationships with both internal and external customers and at the same time promote a customer-service orientation within an organization, customers will continue to return based on the specialized one-on-one service they are given when patronizing the organization.

When supervising my staff I think of myself not only as a leader but also as an "organizational leader." When working with staff I show the example I want others to follow and make clear what is expected of them on a daily basis. By pursuing self-development and learning new information pertaining to my area of expertise, I am able to improve my personal, professional, and most important of all, unit growth. These actions pay off by allowing me to enhance the shared learning that occurs in my department. I am also very big on developing others. A supervisor who provides a staff member with the opportunity to grow and develop his or her skills in turn benefits from a more knowledgeable worker who is able to handle a more difficult task level than expected. Such trained workers will become more confident when per-

First aid is emergency treatment given before regular medical services can be provided. To protect both guests and employees who fall ill and are hurt, it is important to have at least one person per shift trained in first aid and in **cardiopulmonary resuscitation** (CPR), a procedure used in case of cardiac arrest (the heart stops beating).

Security Concerns

According to the Educational Foundation of the National Restaurant Association, the purpose of a **security program** is to protect the belongings or assets of your facility (including the building, grounds, equipment, furnishings, food, beverages, supplies, cash, employees, and guests) from incidents such as employee theft, vioforming tasks and have a better chance of meeting any challenges with which they are faced. This will improve overall customer satisfaction and distinguish the department from others.

Fostering teamwork and relationships is essential in the hospitality environment. By fostering relationships and a positive climate to build effective teams that are committed to organizational goals and initiatives, I am able to supervise a staff that consists of team players that are willing to rally and work together to accomplish any task with which they are faced. Even though my staff and I are faced with difficult times, we are able to work successfully under pressure as a team because we constantly motivate each other to get the job done and in turn are rewarded with positive comments on our guest satisfaction scores.

As a supervisor, I concentrate on managing work execution in order to ensure that all work is completed effectively in the convention floor department. Monitoring the progress of work completed against schedules and budgets can easily help a supervisor accomplish this goal. To be effective when overseeing staff functions, a supervisor must obtain leadership. By providing steps forward to access difficulty issues and guiding others toward the accomplishment of identified meaningful goals, I feel I am able to exemplify the leadership skills I have acquired while working in the industry. Also, communication is an important asset of being a successful supervisor. Communicating openly with others creates an atmosphere in which timely and high-quality information flows smoothly both upward and downward through the organization. This open form of communication allows all associates to be on the same page and facilitates the decision-making process.

A supervisor who demonstrates such top qualities along with dedication, detail orientation, and patience will be able to provide exceptional service when performing on the job. However, a supervisor can never say that he or she has mastered the art of overseeing a staff because in the hospitality industry one learns something new every day. This ongoing learning process is what allows supervisors continually to incorporate new practices into everyday tasks and improve their ability to manage responsibilities.

lent crime, and burglary. Much of your work as a supervisor involves security, from doing reference checks on applicants to following cash-handling procedures, restricting access to keys, and handling a security emergency such as theft. To protect yourself, your employees and guests, and your company from damage, familiarize yourself with all security policies and procedures, and more important, enforce them without hesitation.

Check Your Knowledge

1. Safety programs are common in hospitality operations as a way to increase safety awareness and to prevent accidents. What do these safety programs include?

2. What is the purpose of the Hazard Communication Standard?

AIDS and the Hospitality Worker

AIDS, or **acquired immunodeficiency syndrome,** is a serious illness that harms the body's ability to fight infection. A virus called **HIV (human immunodeficiency virus)** causes AIDS. The HIV virus is spread by unprotected sex or sharing needles with someone who is HIV positive, body piercing, and tattoos. **There is no evidence that the HIV virus can be spread through food handling or casual contact.** Persons with HIV initially show no signs or symptoms. As time goes on, and it may be years, they display symptoms of HIV infection, such as fatigue, diarrhea, weight loss, and wounds that don't heal. An infected person is diagnosed with AIDS when he or she develops serious infections or cancers.

Employees with HIV/AIDS are now protected by the Americans with Disabilities Act (see Chapter 7), so it is illegal to fire an HIV-positive employee or otherwise discriminate in employment matters. They can continue to work as long as they are able to perform the essential functions of their position. Reasonable accommodations, such as flexible work assignments and hours, may be necessary.

Now that you know you can't get AIDS from working with an HIV-infected employee, and you can't discriminate against these employees, what do you do when one of your employees tells you that he is HIV-positive? As usual, there is plenty you can do as a supervisor, but first see if your employer has a written AIDS policy that you should follow.

❧ Show support. Many HIV-infected employees fear for their jobs and their benefits. Explain that he or she will continue to be treated according to existing policies and will continue to receive the same medical benefits. Review the employee's sick time, vacation time, and insurance coverage. Offer other support that may be available in the workplace, such as employee counseling services or employee-financed emergency funds.

❧ If the employee is starting to show symptoms, discuss any reasonable accommodations that you can make, such as more frequent breaks or fewer work hours.

❧ Review the basics of the Family and Medical Leave Act (to be discussed in a moment).

❧ Keep the employee's medical information confidential.

❧ If you haven't done so already, train your employees about AIDS to reduce any fears. Such a person could involve a guest speaker from the local American Red Cross, a videotape about AIDS, and printed materials.

Of course, if you have one or more employees who are HIV-positive, you want to make sure that your employee sanitation and safety training is up to par to make sure that the employee's condition does not present any health concerns.

Guide to the Family and Medical Leave Act of 1993

The **Family and Medical Leave Act of 1993** (FMLA) entitles eligible employees to take up to 12 weeks of unpaid, job-protected leave in a 12-month period for specified family and medical reasons. To be eligible for FMLA benefits, an employee must work for an employer who employs 50 or more employees, have worked for the employer for a total of 12 months, and have worked at least 1250 hours over the previous 12 months. If the employee meets these conditions, he or she can ask for a total of 12 workweeks of unpaid leave during any 12-month period for one or more of the following reasons.

∾ Birth, adoption, or foster care of a child
∾ To care for an immediate family member (spouse, child, or parent) with a serious health condition

The Family and Medical Leave Act allows eligible employees the opportunity of taking unpaid leave for up to 12 weeks.

❧ To take medical leave when the employee is unable to work because of a serious medical condition

Employees who want to use FMLA leave are required to provide 30 days' advance notice. You may require an employee to provide medical certifications supporting the need for leave due to a serious health condition (affecting the employee or an immediate family member) as well as periodic recertifications or reports during leave regarding the employee's status and intent to return to work.

During FMLA leave, an employee is entitled to continue receiving whatever health insurance coverage was provided before the leave was taken. As the employer, you are required to hold open the employee's position or place the employee in an equivalent position upon return to work, except in one case. Key employees, who are among the highest-paid 10 percent of all employees employed within 75 miles, may not have their job restored if taking the leave creates "substantial and grievous injury" to the business operation.

As a supervisor, when an employee asks for time off, you need to ask enough questions about the nature of the leave to determine if it might qualify as FMLA leave. If it does, you need to communicate to the employee what his or her rights and responsibilities are under FMLA. You also need to act within two business days to let the employee know that the time off will count as FMLA leave.

Unions

As a supervisor, you may find yourself at one time or another working with employees who belong to a **union.** This is particularly true if you work for a larger hotel, restaurant, or hospital in a metropolitan area such as New York, Chicago, Las Vegas, or Atlantic City, where the unions have been successful in organizing hospitality employees. According to the Bureau of Labor Statistics, about 14 percent of all U.S. workers were in unions in 1996. The percent of hospitality workers who are unionized is less than the national average.

So what exactly is a union? A union is an organization that employees have designated to deal with their employer concerning conditions of employment such as wages, benefits, and hours of work. The conditions of employment negotiated between management and the union are written into a **labor contract.** Table 14.2 lists typical topics covered in a labor contract. **Collective bargaining** is the process by which the labor contract between the union and management is negotiated. A labor contract is typically in place for two to three, or more, years. In addition to collective bargaining, unions also administer the labor contract, represent bargaining unit members in **grievance procedures,** conduct **strikes** (employee work stoppage) or other work actions, look for new members, and collect dues from current members.

A grievance is a complaint about a section of the labor contract that an employee, or the union, feels has been violated. For example, an employee may feel that a disciplinary action against him or her was unfair. Grievance procedures are gen-

TABLE 14.2   ∾   **Content of a Labor Contract**

Recognition of the union as the employees'
   representative
Management rights
Wages and benefits
Hours of work, break times, and overtime
Holidays and vacations
Sick days, personal days, and leaves of absence
Meals, uniforms, and locker rooms
Safety and health
Determination of seniority and seniority rights
Probationary periods for new employees
Training
Discipline
Prohibition of discrimination
Grievances
Job posting, evaluation, promotion, and transfers
Local union representatives and stewards
Union dues
Strikes and lockouts
Reduction or increase in workforce
Duration of agreement
Modification and termination of agreement

erally outlined in the labor contract and, although a little different in each contract, follow a procedure such as the following:

1. The employee meets with the supervisor and the union steward to discuss the grievance. Most grievances can be resolved, and are resolved, at this step.
2. If the grievance is not settled, there is a conference between the union steward, the employee, and the supervisor's boss or another manager, such as a human resources manager.
3. If the grievance continues to be unsettled, representatives from top management and top union officials try to settle it.
4. If still unsettled, the grievance is given to a neutral third party such as an arbitrator or mediator. A mediator listens to both sides and suggests ways to revolve the grievance but has no authority to force either side to accept anything. In arbitration, both parties must agree in advance that the decision given by the arbitrator will be final and binding.

Now that you understand a little bit about what a union does, let's take a look at why employees want unions. Often, employees are dissatisfied with working conditions and feel that management is not being responsive to their needs. Working conditions may include employee satisfaction with wages, benefits, job security, treatment by supervisors (whether it is fair and consistent or smacks of favoritism), the physical environment, and chances for promotion. Employees may believe in collective bargaining and feel that they are better off being represented by the union than not. Finally, some employees join unions due to social or peer pressure—in other words, because everyone else is doing it. Table 14.3 explains the steps that a union goes through to try to organize a group of employees into a union.

The existence of a union and a labor contract changes the way you can interact with your employees and therefore your efforts to build a positive work climate. Because unions most often use seniority to determine matters such as who gets promoted and who gets overtime, you have less leeway to reward and recognize employees based on merit and abilities. Additionally, instead of dealing directly with your employees, you will have to deal with the **union steward,** or **shop steward,** on all matters covered by the labor contract. The union steward is an employee designated by the union to represent and advise employees of their rights, as well as to check on contract compliance. You may feel at times that dealing with the union steward is not as quick or as personal as dealing directly with your own employees. You may also feel at times that it is difficult to win your employees' loyalty to the company when the union is competing for the same sense of loyalty.

As a supervisor of unionized employees, there are many actions that you may take to work effectively with the union and at the same time create and maintain a positive work climate. *First, know every detail of the labor contract.* Make it your responsibility to know the labor contract even better than the union steward does. In this manner, you can enforce the contract while protecting management rights. Also be sure to follow all provisions of the contract, whether or not you agree with them.

Next, endeavor to have a good working relationship with the union steward. If you take a moment and look at the roles of supervisor and union steward, you will see a number of similarities. Both of you are in the middle, working between groups of employees and higher-level management or union officials. You represent management to the employees and the employees to management. The union steward represents the union officials to the employees and the employees to the union officials. Rather than establishing an adversarial relationship with the union steward (which will only make your job harder and more frustrating), try to see this person as someone who is in much the same position as you are and work together.

Take every grievance seriously. When you are presented with an employee grievance, gather all the information needed and weigh all the facts before deciding how to handle it. Work with the union steward and the employee to try to resolve the grievance at the first step, where everyone involved is most likely to be familiar with the circumstances and the most concerned about its outcome. Unfortunately, as the steps proceed, you, as the first-line supervisor, are bypassed and the grievance often becomes a win–lose situation instead of one that is mutually worked out.

How you handle an attempt at organization will affect relations with your employees for years to come, no matter whether you win or lose the unionization battle. "If you get in a bloodbath and try to win at all costs, you'll lose either way," says Paul E. Clark, associate professor of labor studies at Penn State University. "You'll lose the election and have a union as mad as hornets when they come to the bargaining table. Or you'll win the election and have a workforce that's mad as hell and disillusioned."

Source: Gillian Flynn, "When the unions come calling," *Workforce,* Vol. 79, No. 11, November 2000.

TABLE 14.3   ∾   Steps in Union Organizing

1. Present employees contact union or union organizers contact employees
2. Employees work with the union organizers to get authorization cards (the card authorizes the union to represent that employee during negotiations) signed
3. When 30% of employees have signed authorization cards, the union can file a petition with the National Labor Relations Board
4. The National Labor Relations Board has a hearing on the petition to determine the bargaining unit (a group of employees with common employment conditions that can reasonably be grouped together for collective bargaining) and other issues
5. If the questions from the hearing have been answered to the satisfaction of the NLRB, a date is set for the union election
6. Election campaign starts
7. Representation election
8. If the majority of ballots cast are for the union, it becomes the bargaining agent and bargaining begins

Never discriminate against an employee because he or she belongs to the union. For example, you cannot discriminate against an applicant simply because he or she is prounion. You cannot discipline, fire, transfer, or demote an employee because of his or her union activities. You also cannot interfere with an employee's right to join in union activities. Similarly, you cannot give special treatment to employees who do not join in union activities.

Check Your Knowledge

1. Employees with HIV/AIDS are protected by which act?
2. What does FMLA stand for? To what does it refer?
3. What is a union?

Ethics

Although there are many definitions of **ethics,** ethics can generally be thought of as a set of moral principles or rules of conduct that provide guidelines for morally right behavior. To give you an idea of how ethics are involved in your job as a hospitality supervisor, let's look at three scenarios.

1. You've completed interviewing a number of candidates for a security position. One of the top three candidates is a relative of a supervisor in another department with whom you are close friends. You've been getting pressure from your friend to hire this candidate, and you don't want to alienate him, so you hire his relative even though one of the other candidates is more suited for the job.

2. Business at the hotel could be better on weekends, so you advertise 25 percent discounts on rooms. To keep profitability high, you inflate the room rate before taking the discount.

3. As purchasing manager, you know that the policy is not to accept free gifts from vendors. But one day when you are out to lunch with a vendor, he offers you free tickets to a major league baseball game and you accept them. You can't wait to take your son to the game.

As you can see from these examples, moral principles and standards of conduct are just as necessary in the workplace as they are in your personal life. There are ethical considerations in many of the decisions that you will make, from personnel management issues to money issues to purchasing and receiving practices. Unfortunately, the hospitality industry as a whole has not written its own code of ethics, but you will find that some operations have written their own.

Why is a code of ethics needed for hospitality operations? Just look at the temptations: stockrooms full of supplies that can be used at home and are often loosely inventoried, any kind of alcoholic beverage you want, empty hotel rooms, gambling, high-stress jobs, irregular hours, pressures to meet guests' needs. It can be easy to lose a sense of right and wrong in this field.

Hall suggests five questions that you can use to help decide how ethical a certain decision is[1]:

1. Is the decision legal?
2. Is the decision fair?
3. Does the decision hurt anyone?
4. Have I been honest with those affected?
5. Can I live with my decision?

These questions can provide much guidance.

The Supervisor as Mentor

This topic is a wonderful way to finish this book on supervision. As you become more experienced and proficient at being a hospitality supervisor, it is more likely that you will be a mentor to those who are less experienced and less skilled. A **men-**

[1]S. S. J. Hall, "The emergence of ethics in quality," in *Ethics in Hospitality Management: A Book of Readings.* East Lansing, MI: AH & MA Educational Foundation, 1992.

Superior mentoring an employee. Mentoring helps employee retention development.

tor is a leader, an excellent role model, and a teacher. A supervisor often functions as a mentor to a worker by providing guidance and knowledge on learning the operation and moving up the career ladder. The relationship often resembles that between a teacher and a student. At other times, the mentor simply provides an example of professional behavior with minimal or no interaction with the worker. Being a mentor can provide feelings of pride and satisfaction because you have contributed to someone else's career development.

∿ key points

1. Besides causing pain and suffering to the injured employee and the cost of lost work time, there are other direct and indirect costs to consider when an accident occurs, such as lost business and possibly a lawsuit.

2. OSHA sets mandatory job safety and health standards, encourages both employers and employees to decrease hazards in the workplace, conducts compliance inspections, issues citations in cases of noncompliance, and asks for record keeping of injuries.

3. Safety programs are common in hospitality operations as a way to increase safety awareness and to prevent accidents. They usually include the following components: safety policies and procedures, employee training, safety committee, safety

inspections, accident reporting and investigation, and constant supervision. Supervisors are very involved in the safety program.

4. The purpose of the Hazard Communication Standard issued by OSHA is to give employees the right to know what chemicals they are working with, what the risk or hazards are, and what they can do to limit the risks. Supervisors must post Material Safety Data Sheets and train employees how to use MSDS and labels so that hazardous chemicals can be used safely.

5. Some of the concerns for guest safety revolve around slips and falls, burns, food allergies, and foodborne illness. Appropriate policies and procedures, employee training, and constant supervision are essential to ensure guest safety.

6. To protect both guests and employees who fall ill or become hurt, it is important to have at least one person per shift trained in first aid and in cardiopulmonary resuscitation.

7. Security programs are involved with preventing theft and other unlawful acts within a company.

8. Employees with HIV/AIDS are protected by the Americans with Disabilities Act. They can continue to work as long as they are able to perform the essential functions of their position. Reasonable accommodations may be necessary.

9. There is no evidence that the HIV virus can be spread through food handling or casual contact.

10. If an employee tells you that he or she is HIV-infected, you should follow your company's AIDS policy (if available), show support, discuss reasonable accommodations if appropriate at the time, review the Family and Medical Leave Act, and keep the employee's medical information confidential.

11. In view of the fact that one or more of your employees may be HIV-infected, it's important to train all employees about AIDS in order to reduce any fear and to make sure that your employee sanitation and safety training are up to par.

12. The Family and Medical Leave Act of 1993 (FMLA) entitles eligible employees to take up to 12 weeks of unpaid, job-protected leave in a 12-month period for specified family and medical reasons.

13. The existence of a union and a labor contract changes the way you interact with your employees and therefore your efforts to build a positive work climate.

14. To work effectively with unionized employees, know every detail of the labor contract, endeavor to have a good working relationship with the union steward, take every grievance seriously, and never discriminate against an employee because he or she belongs to the union.

15. Ethics can be thought of as a set of moral principles or rules of conduct that provide guidelines for morally correct behavior. The five questions presented in the chapter provide guidance for making ethical decisions.

16. A supervisor often functions as a mentor to a worker by providing guidance and knowledge on learning the operation and moving up the career ladder. The relationship resembles that between a teacher and a student.

∾ key terms

acquired immunodeficiency syndrome (AIDS)	labor contract
	Material Safety Data Sheet
anaphylactic shock	mentor
cardiopulmonary resuscitation	Occupational Safety and Health
collective bargaining	Administration
ethics	safety committee
Family and Medical Leave Act of 1993	safety program
first aid	security program
grievance procedures	strike
Hazard Communication Standard	union
human immunodeficiency virus (HIV)	union steward (shop steward)

∾ review questions

Answer each question in complete sentences. Read each question carefully and make sure that you answer all parts of the question. Organize your answer using more than one paragraph when appropriate.

1. Name the potential direct and indirect costs of an accident in a hospitality operation that causes injury.

2. What are the functions of OSHA?

3. Describe the six components of a hospitality safety program.

4. As a supervisor, what are your responsibilities for implementing the Hazard Communication Standard?

5. In what ways can guests get hurt in a hotel or restaurant, and how can each situation be prevented?

6. Describe two components of a security program.

7. How is the HIV virus spread?

8. What do you do if an employee tells you that he is HIV-positive and is starting to feel tired?

9. Under what conditions is an employee eligible to take FMLA leave? How long can a FMLA leave be? For what reasons is FMLA allowed? Does an employee get pay or benefits during the leave?

10. What is a *grievance*? What are typical steps in a grievance procedure?

11. Why do employees join unions?

12. What can you do as a supervisor to work effectively with a union?

13. Describe *mentoring*.

❧ activities and applications

1. Discussion Questions

- Was safety emphasized in one of your past or present jobs? Describe your experiences. What actions or inactions made you feel that safety was important or unimportant? Was guest safety more important to management than employee safety?
- How do you feel about working with an employee who is HIV-positive? What support could you provide?
- Would you use the FMLA if you qualified? Why or why not?
- As a hospitality worker, what might attract you to join a union? As a supervisor, how might you view having unionized versus having nonunionized employees? Which would you prefer, and for what reasons?
- Have you ever had someone who was a mentor to you? Describe how the relationship benefited you and the mentor.

2. Group Activity: Ethical Decisions

Using the three situations depicted in the section "Ethics," use the five questions from Hall that are listed in that section to examine how ethical each decision was. Discuss each question as a group and have one person record your ideas.

3. Group Activity: Material Safety Data Sheets

Using a MSDS supplied by your instructor, extract from it the following information: (a) is the product a fire hazard; (b) is any kind of special protection necessary; (c) how do you store it; (d) how do you handle it; (e) how do you dispose of it; and (f) what do you do in case of an emergency?

4. Case Study: Slips and Trips

Charlie is the manager of a 100-seat restaurant in a resort area in Pennsylvania. As the dinner crowd starts to thin out one night, he hears a sound outside the side door of his restaurant. When he opens the door, he sees that the wife of one of his customers is sitting on the steps holding her ankle. The light beside this door isn't very bright, but he thinks he sees her husband rushing to the car. Charlie asks if there's anything he can do to help and the woman tells him that her husband is taking her right to the emergency room to get her ankle checked out. She tells Charlie that he'll be sure to get the hospital bill and more. Her husband pulls up alongside her, gets his wife in the car, and tells Charlie, "You'll hear from me!" As promised, the next day her husband drops off the hospital bill to Charlie and threatens a lawsuit. Charlie tells him that he doesn't understand; after all, he did ask if he could help, and he explained that the door they used was not the proper exit for guests. It was an employee entrance and exit. At this point, the man tells Charlie, "You'll hear from my lawyer."

QUESTIONS

1. What could Charlie have said and done when he saw the woman holding her ankle that would have been much more helpful and possibly prevented the probable lawsuit?

2. If the employee door was not to be used by guests, what should Charlie have done to make sure that guests did not use it?
3. What wasn't safe about the employees' door?
4. What could Charlie have said and done when the man returned with the hospital bill to possibly prevent a lawsuit?
5. What can Charlie do to be more proactive about situations like this?

glossary

Accountability. A worker's obligation to a supervisor to carry out the responsibilities delegated and to produce the results expected.

Acquired immunodeficiency syndrome (AIDS). A serious illness that harms the body's ability to fight infection.

Active listening. Encouraging a speaker to continue talking by giving interested but neutral responses which show that you understand the speaker's meaning and feelings.

Adult learning theory. A field of research that examines how adults learn.

Age Discrimination in Employment Act of 1967 (ADEA). An act that makes it unlawful to discriminate in compensation, terms, or conditions of employment based on a person's age. The ADEA applies to everyone 40 years of age or older.

Agenda. A written statement of topics to be discussed at a meeting.

Americans with Disabilities Act (ADA). An act that makes it unlawful to discriminate in employment matters against the estimated 43 million Americans who have a disability.

Anaphylactic shock. An allergic reaction in which the throat swells up to the point that the victim cannot get air into the lungs. Without proper treatment, it can be fatal.

Appraisal. See **Performance evaluation.**

Appraisal interview, appraisal review, evaluation interview. An interview in which a supervisor and an employee discuss the supervisor's evaluation of the employee's performance.

Approaches to decision making: impulsive (making an off-the-cuff decision), **indecisive** (never quite making up one's mind), **intuitive** (making decisions that feel right), **logical** (making a deliberate stepwise process to make decisions).

Authority. Possessing the rights and powers needed to make the decisions and take the requisite actions to get a job done.

Authority, formal. The authority granted by virtue of a person's position within an organization.

Authority, real or conferred. The authority that employees grant a supervisor to make the necessary decisions and carry them out.

Autocratic. Behaving in an authoritarian or domineering manner.

Behavior modification. Effecting behavioral change by providing positive reinforcement (reward, praise) for the behavior desired.

Big Brother/Big Sister training method. See **Buddy system.**

Body language. Expression of attitudes and feelings through body movements, positions, and gestures.

Boomerang management. Reverting from management's point of view to the worker's point of view.

445

Brainstorming. Generating ideas without considering their drawbacks, limitations, or consequences (typically, a group activity).

Buddy system. Training method in which an old hand shows a new worker the ropes; also known as the **Big Brother/Big Sister system.**

Budget. An operational plan for the income and expenditure of money for a given period.

"Can do" factors. An applicant's or employee's job knowledge, skills, and abilities.

Cardiopulmonary resuscitation (CPR). A procedure employed after cardiac arrest (when the heart stops beating) in which massage, drugs, and mouth-to-mouth resuscitation are used to restore breathing.

Carrot-and-stick motivation. The use of promised rewards plus punishment to motivate performance.

Chain of command. Lines along which responsibility and authority are delegated from top to bottom of an organization.

Channels of communication. The organizational lines (corresponding to the chain of command) along which messages are passed from one level to another.

Civil Rights Act of 1964, Title VII. An act that makes it unlawful to discriminate against applicants or employees with respect to recruiting, hiring, firing, promotions, or other employment-related activities, on the basis of race, color, religion, gender, or national origin.

Coaching. Individual, corrective, on-the-job training that is focused on improving performance.

Coaching style. Within the managerial grid, a supervisory style that uses lots of directive and supportive behaviors with an employee.

Collective bargaining. Process by which a labor contract is negotiated.

Communication zones. See **Personal space; Public distance; Social distance.**

Communications. The sending and receiving of messages.

Conceptual skill. The ability to see the whole picture and the relationship of each part of the whole.

Conditions and limitations. Factors such as rules, policies, specific requirements, and limiting factors (e.g., time) that may apply when a problem is being defined.

Consensus. General agreement within a group.

Contingency plan. An alternative plan for use in case the original plan does not work out.

Contract. An agreement between two parties that is fully understood and accepted by both.

Control. Built-in method for measuring performance or product against standards.

Controlling. Measuring and evaluating results to goals and standards previously agreed upon, such as performance and quality standards, and taking corrective action when necessary to stay on course.

Coordinating. Meshing the work of individuals, work groups, and departments to produce a smoothly running operation.

Counseling. Counseling occurs when a counselor meets with a client in a private and confidential setting to explore a difficulty the client is having, distress he may be experiencing, or perhaps his dissatisfaction or loss of a sense of direction or purpose.

Culture. The socially transmitted behavior patterns, art, beliefs, institutions, and all other products of human work or thought characteristic of a community or population.

Culture bound. Believing that your culture and value system are better than all others.

Decision. A conscious choice among alternative courses of action directed toward a specific purpose.

Decision making. Using a logical process to identify causes and solutions to problems or to make decisions.

Decision-making leave with pay. The final step in a positive discipline system in which the employee is given a day off with pay to decide if he or she really wants to do the job well or would prefer to resign the position.

Decisiveness. The ability to reach a firm conclusion.

Dehiring. Avoiding termination by making an employee want to leave, often by withdrawing work or suggesting that the person look elsewhere for a job.

Delegating style. Within the managerial grid, a supervisory style that is low on directive and supportive behaviors because responsibility is being turned over to an employee.

Delegation. Giving a portion of one's responsibility and authority to a subordinate.

Demographics. Characteristics of a given area in terms of data about the people who live there.

Demotivator. An emotion, environmental factor, or incident that reduces a person's motivation to perform well.

Directing. Assigning tasks, giving instructions, training, and guiding and controlling performance.

Directing style. Within the managerial grid, a supervisory style that uses lots of directive and few supportive behaviors with an employee.

Direct recruiting. On-the-scene recruiting where job seekers are, such as at schools and colleges.

Discipline. (1) A condition or state of orderly conduct and obedience to rules, regulations, and procedures. (2) Action to enforce orderly conduct and obedience to rules, regulations, and procedures.

Dissatisfier. A factor in a job environment that produces dissatisfaction, usually reducing motivation.

Diversity. Physical and cultural dimensions that separate and distinguish individuals and groups: age, gender, physical abilities and qualities, ethnicity, race, sexual preference.

Doing the right things right. To be both a leader and a manager; to be both effective and efficient.

Drug Free Workplace Act of 1988. A federal law that requires most federal contractors and anyone who receives federal grants to provide a drug-free workplace.

Due process. An employee's right of self-defense in a disciplinary process.

Economic man theory, economic person theory. The belief that people work for money alone.

Employee assistance program (EAP). A counseling program available to employees to provide confidential and professional counseling and referral.

Employee handbook. A written document given to employees which tells them what they need to know about company policies and procedures.

Employee Polygraph Protection Act of 1988. A federal law that prohibits the use of lie detectors in the screening of job applicants.

Employee referral program. A program under which employees suggests to others that they apply for a job in their company. If a person referred gets a job, the employee often receives recompense.

Employee self-appraisal. A procedure by which employees evaluate their own performance, usually as part of a performance appraisal process.

Employment agencies. Organizations that try to place persons into jobs. **Private agencies:** privately owned agencies that normally charge a fee when an applicant is placed. **Temporary agencies:** agencies that place temporary employees into businesses and charge by the hour. **Government agencies:** employment agencies run by the government.

Employment requisition form. A standard form used by departments to obtain approval to fill positions and to notify the recruiter that a position needs, or will need, to be filled.

Empowering. To give employees additional responsibility and authority to do their jobs.

Environmental sexual harassment. A type of sexual harassment in which comments or innuendos of a sexual nature, or physical contact, are considered a violation when they interfere with an employee's work performance or create an intimidating, hostile, or offensive working environment.

Equal employment opportunity (EEO). The legal requirement that all people be treated equally in all aspects of employment, regardless of race, creed, color, national origin, age, gender, or disability unrelated to the job.

Equal Employment Opportunity Commission (EEOC). A federal office responsible for enforcing the employment-related provisions of the Civil Rights Act of 1964 as well as other EEO laws.

Equal Pay Act of 1963. A law that requires equal pay and benefits for men and women working in jobs requiring substantially equal skills, effort, and responsibilities under similar working conditions.

Evaluating. See **Controlling.**

Evaluation form. A form on which employee performance during a given period is rated.

Exempt employees. Employees, typically managerial personnel, who are not covered by the wage and hour laws and therefore do not earn overtime pay. To be considered an exempt employee, the following conditions must be met: The employee spends 50 percent or more of his time managing, supervises two or more employees, and is paid $250 or more per week.

External recruiting. Looking for job applicants outside the operation.

Fact-finding. The process of collecting all the facts about a certain situation.

Family and Medical Leave Act of 1993. An act that allows employees to take an unpaid leave of absence from work for up to 12 weeks per year for the birth or adoption of a child or a serious health condition of the employee or his or her spouse, child, or parent.

First aid. Emergency treatment given before regular medical services can be provided.

First-line supervisor. A supervisor who manages hourly employees.

Forecasting. Predicting what will happen in the future on the basis of data from the past and present.

Formal authority. See **Authority, formal.**

Formal leader. The person in charge based on the organization chart.

Formative evaluation. An ongoing form of evaluation that uses observation, interviews, and surveys to monitor training.

Generation X. The group of Americans from age 18 through 34.

Grievance procedures. A formal company procedure that employees can follow when they feel they have been treated unfairly by management.

Group decision making. A process in which a group of people work together to come to a decision.

Halo effect. The tendency to extend the perception of a single outstanding personality trait to a perception of the entire personality.

Harassment. Intimidating, hostile, or offensive behavior toward someone, or the creation of an intimidating, hostile, or offensive environment for someone based on the person's national origin, race, color, religion, gender, disability, or age.

Hazard communication standard. A regulation issued by the Occupational Safety and Health Administration that gives employees the right to know what hazardous chemicals they are working with, the risks or hazards, and what they can do to limit the risk.

Hierarchy of needs. A theory proposed by Maslow that places human needs in a hierarchy or pyramid. As one's needs at the bottom of the pyramid are met, higher-level needs are encountered on several levels up through the top of the pyramid.

Hourly workers. Employees paid on an hourly basis who are covered by federal and state wage and hour laws and therefore guaranteed a minimum wage.

Human immunodeficiency virus (HIV). The virus that causes AIDS (acquired immunodeficiency syndrome).

Human relations theory. A theory which states that satisfying the needs of workers is *the* key to productivity.

Human skill. The ability to manage people through respect for them as individuals, sensitivity to their needs and feelings, self-awareness, and good person-to-person relationships.

Humanistic management. A blend of scientific, human relations, and participative management practices adapted to the needs of the situation, the workers, and the supervisor's leadership style.

Hygiene factors. Factors in the job environment that produce job satisfaction or dissatisfaction but do not motivate performance.

Immigration Reform and Control Act (IRCA). A federal law that requires employers to verify the identity and employment eligibility of all applicants and prohibits discrimination in hiring or firing due to a person's national origin or citizenship status.

Informal leader. The person who, by virtue of having the support of the employees, is in charge.

Internal recruiting. Searching for job applicants from within an operation.

Interpersonal communication. The sending and receiving of messages between people.

Interviewing. Conversation with the purpose of obtaining information, often used in screening job applicants.

JIT. Job instruction training.

Job. A specific group of tasks prescribed as a unit of work.

Job analysis. Determination of the content of a given job by breaking it down into units (work sequences) and identifying the tasks that make up each unit.

Job description. A written statement of the duties performed and responsibilities for a given position, and used to provide opportunity for achievement, recognition, learning, and growth.

Job evaluation. The process of examining the responsibilities and difficulties of a series of jobs to determine which are worth the most and should therefore be paid more.

Job instruction. For every detail of a given job in a given enterprise, instruction in what to do and how to do it.

Job instruction training (JIT). A four-step method of training people in what to do and how to do it on a given job in a given operation.

Job loading. Adding more work to a job without increasing interest, challenge, or reward.

Job posting. A policy of making employees aware of available positions within a company.

Job Service Center. An office of the U.S. Employment Service.

Job setting. The conditions under which a job is to be done, such as physical conditions and contact with others.

Job specification. A list of the qualifications needed to perform a given job.

Job title. The name of a job, such as cook or housekeeper.

Just cause termination. Employee termination based on the commission of an offense that affected detrimentally the specific work done or an operation as a whole.

Labor contract. The written conditions of employment that are negotiated between management and a union.

Labor market. In a given area, the workers who are looking for jobs (the labor supply) and the jobs that are available (the demand for labor).

Leader. A person in command who people follow voluntarily.

Leadership. Direction and control of the work of others through the ability to elicit voluntary compliance.

Leadership style. The pattern of interaction that a manager uses in directing subordinates.

Leading. Guiding and interacting with employees regarding getting certain goals and plans accomplished; involves many skills, such as communicating, motivating, delegating, and instructing.

Learning. The acquisition of knowledge or skill.

Level of performance. Employee performance measured against a performance standard. **Optimistic level:** superior performance, near-perfection. **Realistic level:** competent performance. **Minimum level:** marginal performance, below which a worker should be terminated.

Line functions. The personnel directly involved in producing goods and services.

Listening. Paying complete attention to what people have to say, hearing them out, staying interested but neutral. See also **Active listening.**

Maintenance factors. See **Hygiene factors.**

Management by example. Managing people at work by setting a good example—by giving 100 percent of your time, effort, and enthusiasm to your own job.

Manager. One who directs and controls an assigned segment of the work in an enterprise.

Managerial skills. The three types of skills that a manager needs: technical, human, and conceptual. See the individual skills.

Mass communication. Messages sent out to many people through such media as newspapers, magazines, books, radio, and television.

Material safety data sheet (MSDS). An information sheet put out by the manufacturer of a hazardous product that explains what a product is, why it is hazardous, and how it can be used safely.

MBWA. Management by wandering around: spending a significant part of your day talking to your employees, your guests, your peers while listening, coaching, and trouble-shooting.

Mentor. An experienced and proficient person who acts as a leader, role model, and teacher to those less experienced and less skilled.

Merit raise. A raise given to an employee based upon how well the employee has done his or her job.

Morale. Group spirit with respect to getting a job done.

Motivation. The why of behavior; the energizer that makes people behave as they do.

Motivator. Anything that triggers a person's inner motivation to perform. In Herzberg's theory, motivators are factors within a job that provide satisfaction and that motivate a person to superior effort and performance.

Negative discipline. Maintaining discipline through fear and punishment, with progressively severe penalties for rule violations.

Negligent hiring. The failure of an employer to take reasonable and appropriate safeguards when hiring employees to make sure that they are not the type to harm guests or other workers.

Nonexempt employees. Employees who are paid by the hour and are not exempt from federal and state wage and hour laws. Also called hourly employees.

Nonverbal communication. Communication without words, as with signs, gestures, facial expressions, or body language.

Obstacle thinkers. Those who focus on why a situation is impossible and retreat from it.

Occupational Safety and Health Administration (OSHA). A federal agency created to assure safe and healthful working conditions and to preserve the nation's human resources.

Open (or two-way) communication. The free movement of messages back and forth between supervisor and worker and up the channels of communication as well as down.

Opportunity thinkers. Those who concentrate on constructive ways to deal with a challenging situation.

Organization chart. A diagram of a company's organization showing levels of management and lines by which authority and responsibility are transmitted.

Organizational communication. The sending of messages from the top of an organization down—usually the same message to everyone.

Organizing. Putting together the money, personnel, equipment, materials, and methods for maximum efficiency to meet an enterprise's goals.

Orientation. A new worker's introduction to a job.

Overgeneralization. In interviewing and evaluation, translation of a single trait or piece of information about a person into an overall impression of that person.

Participative management. A system that includes workers in making decisions that concern them.

Patterned interview. A highly structured interview in which the interviewer uses a predetermined list of questions to ask each applicant.

Performance dimensions or categories. The dimensions of job performance chosen to be evaluated, such as attendance and guest relations.

Performance evaluation, performance appraisal, performance review. Periodic review and assessment of an employee's performance during a given period.

Performance standard. Describes the what and how of a job, and explains what an employee is to do, how it is to be done, and to what extent.

Performance standard system. A system of managing people using performance standards to describe job content, train personnel, and evaluate performance.

Personal space. The area within close proximity of a person which "belongs" to the person and should not be invaded (the space varies according to culture).

Planning. Looking ahead to chart the best course of future action. See also **Strategic planning.**

Position. Duties and responsibilities performed by an employee.

Positive discipline. A punishment-free formula for disciplinary action that replaces penalties with reminders and features a decision-making leave with pay.

Positive reinforcement. Providing positive consequences (praise, rewards) for desired behavior.

Power. The capacity to influence the behavior of others.

Pregnancy Discrimination Act of 1978. An act that makes it unlawful to discriminate against a woman on the basis of pregnancy, childbirth, or related medical conditions.

Pretest. Testing an experienced worker's job performance before training.

Primary dimensions of diversity. Cultural and physical dimensions of individuals or groups that cannot be changed, such as age, gender, and race.

Problem solving. Using a logical process to identify causes and solutions to problems or to make decisions.

Productivity. How efficiently an operation converts an input (e.g., food) into an output (e.g., a meal).

Productivity standards. A definition of the acceptable quantity of work that an employee is expected to do (e.g., the number of rooms that can be cleaned in 60 minutes).

Progressive discipline. A multistage formula for disciplinary action.

Projection. Investing another person with one's own qualities.

Promoting from within. A policy in which it is preferable to promote existing employees rather than filling the position with an outsider.

Public distance. Often defined as from 7 to 25 feet away from a person—too far for giving directions or conversing.

"Quid pro quo" sexual harassment. A type of sexual harassment: submission to or rejection of a sexual favor used as the basis for employment decisions regarding an employee.

Rating system. A system, usually a scale, for evaluating actual performance in relation to expected performance or the performance of others.

Real authority. See **Authority, real.**

Reasonable accommodation. Any change or adjustment to a job or work environment that will enable someone with a disability to perform essential job functions.

Recruiting. Actively looking for people to fill jobs. **Direct recruiting:** going where the job seekers are, such as colleges, to recruit. **Internal recruiting:** looking for people within a company to fill jobs. **External recruiting:** looking for people outside a company to fill jobs.

Representing. Representing an organization to customers and other people outside an enterprise.

Resistance to change. A reaction by workers to changes in their work environment that may be accompanied by feelings of anxiety, insecurity, or loss.

Responsibility. The duties and activities assigned to a given job or person, along with an obligation to carry them out.

Retraining. Additional training given to trained workers for improving performance or dealing with something new.

Reverse delegation. A situation in which you delegate a job to an employee and he or she tries to give it back to you.

Reward and punishment. A method of motivating performance by giving rewards for good performance and punishing for poor performance.

Risk. A degree of uncertainty about what will happen in the future.

Role model. A person who serves as an example for the behavior of others.

Safety committee. A committee that meets periodically to discuss safety matters and to perform other functions related to workplace safety, such as inspecting a facility and overseeing safety training.

Safety program. A plan, consisting of elements such as safety rules and employee training, that attempts to keep a workplace safe.

Scheduling. Determining how many people are needed when, and assigning days and hours of work accordingly.

Scientific management. Standardization of work procedures, tools, and conditions of work.

Secondary dimensions of diversity. Cultural and physical dimensions of individuals or groups that can be changed, such as occupation, education, and income.

Security program. A plan to protect company assets and people by preventing theft and other unlawful acts.

Self-actualization. According to the motivational theorist Maslow, the desire to fulfill one's own potential.

Sexual harassment. Unwelcome advances, requests for sexual favors, and other verbal or physical conduct of a sexual nature when compliance with any of these acts is a condition of employment, or when comments or physical contact create an intimidating, hostile, or offensive working environment.

Single-use plan. A plan developed for a single occasion or purpose.

Situational leadership. Adaptation of leadership style to the needs of a situation.

Small-group communication. Communication that takes place when two or more group members attempt to influence one another, as in a meeting.

Social distance. Often defined as from 4 to 7 feet away from a person—suitable for communication between boss and subordinate.

Social man (person) theory. The idea that fulfillment of social needs is more important than money in motivating people. See **Human relations theory.**

Span of control. The number of employees that a manager supervises directly.

Staff functions. Personnel who are not directly involved in producing goods and services but advise those who do, such as human resource and training directors.

Staffing. Determining personnel needs and recruiting, evaluating, selecting, hiring, orienting, training, and scheduling employees.

Standing plan. An established routine, formula, or set of procedures used in a recurring situation.

Stereotype. A belief that a person will have characteristics generally attributed to members of a particular racial or social group simply because he or she is a member of that group.

Strategic planning. Long-range planning to set organizational goals, objectives, and policies and to determine strategies, tactics, and programs for achieving them.

Strike. A work stoppage due to a labor dispute.

Summative evaluation. A form of evaluation that measures the results of training after a program has been completed.

Supervisor. A person who manages employees who are making products or performing services.

Supporting style. Within the managerial grid, a supervisory style marked by highly supportive behaviors with an employee.

Symbols. Words, images, or gestures used to communicate messages.

Task. In job analysis, a procedural step in a unit of work.

Teaching methods. Ways in which teachers and trainers convey information to learners.

Technical skill. The ability to perform the tasks of the people supervised.

Theory X. The managerial assumption that people dislike and avoid work, prefer to be led, avoid responsibility, lack ambition, want security, and must be coerced, controlled, directed, and threatened with punishment to get them to do their work. A **Theory X manager** is one whose direction of people is based on these assumptions.

Theory Y. The hypothesis that (1) work is as natural as play or rest; (2) people will work of their own accord toward objectives to which they feel committed, especially those that fulfill personal needs of self-respect, independence, achievement, recognition, status, and growth; and (3) arranging work to meet such needs will do away with the need for coercion and threat. A **Theory Y manager** is one who holds and practices this view of employee motivation.

Third-party sexual harassment. A type of sexual harassment that involves a customer or client and an employee.

Timing. Selecting that time when taking action will be most effective; making a decision at the moment it is most needed.

Total quality management (TQM). A process of total organizational involvement in improving all aspects of the quality of a product or service.

Training. Teaching people how to do their jobs; job instruction.

Training objective. A trainer's goal: a statement, in performance standard terms, of the behavior that shows when training is complete.

Training plan. A detailed plan for carrying out employee training for a unit of work.

Transactional leadership. Leadership that motivates workers by appealing to their self-interest.

Transformational leadership. Leadership that motivates workers by appealing to their higher-order needs, such as providing workers with meaningful, interesting, and challenging jobs, and acting as a coach and mentor.

Truth in hiring. Telling an applicant the entire story about a job, including the drawbacks.

Two-way communication. In communication, when messages move freely back and forth from one person to another.

Uniform discipline system. A system of specific penalties for each violation of each company rule, to be applied uniformly throughout a company.

Union. An organization that employees have designated to deal with their employer concerning conditions of employment, such as wages, benefits, and hours of work.

Union steward. An employee designated by a union to represent and advise employees of their rights as well as to check on contract compliance. Also called a shop steward.

Unit of work. Any one of several work sequences that together comprise the content of a given job.

Unity of command. The organizational principle that each person should have only one boss.

"Will do" factors. An applicant's or employee's willingness, desire, and attitude toward performing a job.

Win–win problem solving. A method of solving problems in which supervisor and worker discuss a problem together and arrive at a mutually acceptable solution.

Work climate. The level of morale within a workplace.

Work rules. Rules for employees that govern their behavior when working.

Work simplification. The reduction of repetitive tasks to the fewest possible motions, requiring the least expenditure of time and energy.

Work supervisor. A supervisor who takes part in the work task itself in addition to supervising.

≈ index